Security and Game Theory

Global threats of terrorism, drug-smuggling, and other crimes have led to a significant increase in the need to deploy limited security resources to maximize their effectiveness. Game theory provides a sound mathematical approach for such effective deployment of limited security resources. A typical resulting approach is to randomize security schedules to avoid predictability, taking into account the importance of different targets and potential adversary reactions.

This book distills the forefront of this research on game theory for security to provide the first and only study of long-term deployed applications of game theory in the security of key organizations such as the Los Angeles International Airport police and the U.S. Federal Air Marshals Service. The author and his research group draw on their extensive experience working with security officials to intelligently allocate limited security resources to protect targets, outlining the applications of their algorithms in research and the real world.

The book also includes professional perspectives from security experts Erroll G. Southers; Lieutenant Commander Joe DiRenzo III, U.S. Coast Guard; Lieutenant Commander Ben Maule, U.S. Coast Guard; Commander Erik Jensen, U.S. Coast Guard; and Lieutenant Fred S. Bertsch IV, U.S. Coast Guard.

MILIND TAMBE is a Professor of Computer Science and Industrial and Systems Engineering at the University of Southern California (USC). His research is in the area of Artificial Intelligence, specifically agent-based and multi-agent systems. He is a Fellow of the Association for Advancement of Artificial Intelligence and recipient of the Association for Computing Machinery's Autonomous Agents Research Award. He is also the recipient of the Christopher Columbus Fellowship Foundation Homeland Security Award, a special commendation given by the Los Angeles International Airport's police from the city of Los Angeles, Commander First Coast Guard District's Operational Excellence Award, the USC Viterbi School of Engineering's use-inspired research award, an Okawa Foundation faculty research award, the USC Steven B. Sample Teaching and Mentoring award, and the ACM recognition of service award.

T0331593

Security and Game Theory
Algorithms, Deployed Systems, Lessons Learned

MILIND TAMBE
University of Southern California

CAMBRIDGE
UNIVERSITY PRESS

CAMBRIDGE UNIVERSITY PRESS
Cambridge, New York, Melbourne, Madrid, Cape Town,
Singapore, São Paulo, Delhi, Mexico City

Cambridge University Press
32 Avenue of the Americas, New York, NY 10013-2473, USA

www.cambridge.org
Information on this title: www.cambridge.org/9781107096424

First published 2012
Reprinted 2013

A catalog record for this publication is available from the British Library.

Library of Congress Cataloging in Publication Data

Tambe, Milind, 1965–
Security and game theory : algorithms, deployed systems, lessons learned / Milind Tambe.
    p. cm.
Includes bibliographical references and index.
ISBN 978-1-107-09642-4 (hardback)
1. Computer security. 2. Game theory. 3. Security, International–Mathematical models.
I. Title.
QA76.9.M35T36 2011
005.8–dc23   2011038733

ISBN 978-1-107-09642-4 Hardback

To Sonali, Arjun, and Raam

Contents

PART IV: FUTURE RESEARCH

Acknowledgments

The research described in this book has only been possible due to the exceptional collaboration with the personnel at LAX (Los Angeles World Airports) police department and the Federal Air Marshals Service, the Transportation Security Administration, and the Coast Guard of the United States. While there have been significant contributions from many individuals at each of these organizations to ensure smooth transition of research from my research group to fielded applications, I would like to thank a few people in particular. At LAX, I wish to thank former Assistant Chief of Airport Police Erroll G. Southers, who is now my colleague at the University of Southern California and has continued to be a fantastic collaborator. I also wish to thank James B. Curren, Mark Kukulich, and Steven McHugh of the Federal Air Marshals Service; Erin Steigerwald of the Transportation Security Administration; and Craig Baldwin, Ben Maule, and Joe DiRenzo of the U.S. Coast Guard; all very wonderful collaborators. I and my students have gained tremendous new research insights from the many discussions with them. I also wish to thank Shane Cullen, from the Department of Homeland Security Science and Technology Directorate, who was the program manager for several of the research projects described in this book.

Furthermore, I wish to thank my current and former students and postdocs (Manish Jain, Christopher Kiekintveld, Janusz Marecki, Praveen Paruchuri, Jonathan P. Pearce, James Pita, Christopher Portway, Shyamsunder Rathi, Matthew E. Taylor, Jason Tsai, Craig Western, and Zhengyu Yin) and collaborators (Vincent Conitzer, Erim Kardeş, Dmytro Korzhyk, Sarit Kraus, and Fernando Ordóñez), whose papers appear in this book, without whom this research effort would not have been possible. Finally, this research was supported by the United States Department of Homeland Security through the

Center for Risk and Economic Analysis of Terrorism Events (CREATE). I thank the former and current leadership at CREATE (Randy Hall, Detlof von Winterfeldt, Steve Hora, and Isaac Maya) and staff (Kelly Gribben and Sabrina Feeley) for their enthusiastic support of this research.

1

Introduction and Overview of Security Games

Milind Tambe and Manish Jain

1.1 Introduction

Game theory's popularity continues to increase in a whole variety of disciplines, including economics, biology, political science, computer science, electrical engineering, business, law, and public policy. In the arena of security, where game theory has always been popular, there now seems to be an exponential increase in interest. This increase is in part due to the new set of problems our societies face, from terrorism to drugs to crime. These problems are ubiquitous. Yet, limited security resources cannot be everywhere all the time, raising a crucial question of how to best utilize them.

Game theory provides a sound mathematical approach for deploying limited security resources to maximize their effectiveness. While the connection between game theory and security has been studied for the last several decades, there has been a fundamental shift in the relationship due to the emergence of computational game theory. More specifically, with the development of new computational approaches to game theory over the past two decades, very large-scale problems can be cast in game-theoretic contexts, thus providing us computational tools to address problems of security allocations.

My research group has been at the forefront of this effort to apply computational game theory techniques to security problems. We have led a wide range of actual deployed applications of game theory for security. Our first application, *Assistant for Randomized Monitoring Over Routes* (ARMOR), successfully deployed game-theoretic algorithms at the Los Angeles International Airport (LAX) in 2007 and has been in use there ever since. In particular, ARMOR uses game theory to randomize allocation of police checkpoints and canine units. Our second application, *Intelligent Randomization in Scheduling* (IRIS), has been used by the U.S. Federal Air Marshal Service since 2009 to deploy air marshals on U.S. air carriers. A third application, *Game-theoretic Unpredictable and*

Randomly Deployed Security (GUARDS), for the U.S. Transportation Security Administration is being evaluated for a national deployment across more than 400 U.S. airports. A fourth application, *Port Resilience Operational/Tactical Enforcement to Combat Terrorism* (PROTECT), for the United States Coast Guard, is under development and has been demonstrated at the Port of Boston for evaluation; and many other agencies around the globe are now looking to deploy these techniques.

This set of applications and associated algorithms has added to the already significant interest in game theory for security. Yet this research is not confined to computer science; there has always been a wide variety of interest in game theory for security in researchers involved in risk, operations research, psychology, and other disciplines. Our applications of game theory have now generated interest in this topic from analysts and practitioners – police, security officials – who wish to deploy these solutions.

This book addresses some of this interest. My aim here is to bring together my research group's work over the past several years comprehensively in one book, describing the applications we have developed, the underlying research, and security officials' perspective on the problems. The book is designed to be of interest to (i) researchers and graduate students in the area of game theory for security who wish to understand the topic in more depth; (ii) security analysts and practitioners interested in obtaining an overview of this research (even if they skip details of our algorithms); and (iii) other researchers, generally familiar with game theory, who wish to jump into this area of research.

The book is divided into four parts. Part I is based on contributions of security officials; it provides their perspective on the challenges and needs for a game-theoretic approach to security. The remaining three parts contain papers I have co-authored with my current and former students, post-doctoral researchers, and colleagues. Part II provides an overview of applications we have developed, using key papers describing our applications. Part III will discuss our algorithms in depth using selected papers and finally, Part IV will outline some key directions of future research. To those familiar with game theory, and particularly computer scientists, all four parts will be easily accessible. *Those unfamiliar with game theory can still follow the first two parts.*

The rest of this chapter provides a high-level and *informal* overview of the material presented in the rest of the book. We begin in Section 1.2 by briefly outlining the key motivation for applying game theory to security; of course, Part I of this book delves much more deeply into this motivation. More importantly, Section 1.2 will also provides relevant background in game theory and, in particular, the types of games used in our work. Next, Section 1.3 provides an overview of Part II of this book, that is, of the deployed applications. Section 1.4 similarly provides an overview of Part III; and Section 1.5, of Part IV.

1.2 Motivation: Security Games

Part I provides us with the motivation for the security work discussed in this book. A key motivating concern is infrastructure security: We have to protect our ports, airports, buses and trains, transportation, and other infrastructure. Yet we often have limited security resources to accomplish this goal, which means we cannot provide a security cover for everything twenty four hours a day. Security resources have to be deployed selectively. Unfortunately, our adversaries can monitor our defenses and exploit any patterns in these selective deployments. For example, if we check trains only on Tuesdays and Thursdays, an adversary will observe and exploit this pattern. Similarly, in patrolling an airport, if the patrols are at Terminal 1 at 9 AM, Terminal 2 at 10 AM, Terminal 3 at 11 AM, an adversary will learn this information. The key here is that an adversary conducts surveillance and then plans an attack exploiting any patterns in our security activities. Chapter 2 by Erroll Southers in Part I of the book provides a detailed outline of the terrorist planning cycle and the role of surveillance.

Game theory can provide us with a method to allocate limited security resources to protect infrastructure, taking into account the different weights of different targets and an adversary's response to any particular infrastructure protection strategy. Typically, the solution suggested by using a game-theoretic approach is a weighted randomization strategy. Security resources are allocated in a randomized fashion, but with higher weights on some targets than others, as specified by a game-theoretic solution concept. To accomplish this goal, we rely in particular on specific types of games called Bayesian Stackelberg games. For the benefit of those who are unfamiliar with these games, or perhaps even with game theory in general, we will provide a brief, informal introduction. Obviously, this is a very short introduction to a topic that has entire textbooks devoted to it (Fudenberg and Tirole, 1991); knowledgeable readers may skip one or both subsections as appropriate.

1.2.1 Game Theory

Game theory is an abstract mathematical theory for analyzing interactions among multiple intelligent actors, where the actors may be people, corporations, nations, intelligent software agents, or robots. In a security context, the intelligent actors may be security forces or police, on the one hand, and adversaries on the other. In providing a mathematical basis for understanding intelligent actors' interactions with each other, game-theoretic approaches assume that these intelligent actors will anticipate each other's moves, and act appropriately.

The origins of game theory are in the 1940s with the work of John von Neumann and Oskar Morgenstern (Neumann and Morgenstern, 1944), although some readers may be more familiar with John Nash's celebrated work in the 1950s (Nash, 1951). While it started out in the area of economics, game theory has now been used in analysis in many academic disciplines: political science, philosophy, biology, and others. Perhaps the latest entry into this arena of applying and making contributions in game theory is the discipline of computer science. This has led to computational approaches to game theory, thus providing us computational tools to analyze large-scale interactions of multiple intelligent actors. We have leveraged precisely these computational techniques in our work.

1.2.2 Bayesian Stackelberg Games

In our work, we appeal to a special class of games, called Bayesian Stackelberg games. Before we get into Bayesian Stackelberg games, I will attempt to explain the notion of Stackelberg games (so named due to their origins in the work of Heinrich von Stackelberg [Stackelberg, 1934]). I will explain this class of games starting with a simple example, but before doing so, I emphasize again our assumption that we have limited security resources, which must protect multiple potential infrastructure targets of varying importance.

Consider a simple airport with two terminals, Terminals 1 and 2. There is only one police unit to protect the terminals and one adversary. Terminal 1 happens to be more important than Terminal 2 in this example. The game in Figure 1.1 shows this situation; by a "game" we mean a mathematical description of the problem of interaction between the multiple actors. The result is the matrix shown below, with the police's choice of actions depicted along the rows and the adversary's choice of actions shown along the columns. In this case, the police can protect Terminal 1 or Terminal 2; the adversary can attack Terminal 1 or Terminal 2. The numbers in the matrix describe the payoffs to the police and the adversary, as described in Figure 1.1.

Knowing that Terminal 1 is more important than Terminal 2, the police may choose to always protect Terminal 1. However, an intelligent adversary will conduct surveillance and, after learning that the police always protect Terminal 1, will attack Terminal 2. That is, the police have played the strategy described by the Terminal 1 row in the game matrix; and the adversary has responded with

Adversary

		Terminal 1	Terminal 2
Defender	Terminal 1	5, −3	−1, 1
	Terminal 2	−5, 5	2, −1

Figure 1.1. Stackelberg game.

the strategy described by the Terminal 2 column. We assume here that since there are no police at Terminal 2, the adversary's attack succeeds. The entry (−1, 1) at the intersection of the intersection of the Terminal 1 row and the Terminal 2 column describe the payoffs to the police and the adversary. Specifically, the police will get a payoff of −1 since the adversary's attack succeeds, and the adversary gets a payoff of 1. In this case, we are assuming all payoffs are in the range of −5 to 5. The payoff is a way of quantitatively representing the loss or gain due to a successful attack. For example, it may specifically represent some measure of loss of life or economic loss or a combination of both and other factors.

This payoff is each actor's (police or adversary) view of his/her own utility. It is thus quite possible that the loss to the adversary may not be symmetric with the gain to the police and vice versa. For example, had the adversary attacked Terminal 1 when the police were stationed at Terminal 1, the police would have captured the adversary; then the adversary would be the one with a negative payoff of −3, and the police, having captured the adversary, will have a positive payoff of 5. The reason the adversary's payoff may not be −5 is that the adversary may view even a failed attack as not the worst outcome, possibly due to the publicity received for the attempt to attack an important terminal.

How can we arrive at a precise estimate of such a payoff in a game? Typically, these payoffs result via knowledge acquisition from domain experts. In our own applications, these payoffs arise from calculations based on a set of answers to a set of key questions (created by domain experts) about the impact of adversary success and failure quantified in terms of loss of lives, damage to property, and other measures; in some cases, these payoffs are generated by other researchers with expertise in risk analysis. Later, we will also discuss algorithms that handle uncertainty over such payoffs. For now, we assume that these payoffs are specified with precision. We will return to the payoffs after the discussion of Bayesian Stackelberg games.

Of course, an intelligent adversary will not attack Terminal 1 if the police always guard Terminal 1. Similarly, if the police were to switch their strategy and always protect Terminal 2, an adversary conducting surveillance will observe that, and subsequently will attack Terminal 1. In this case, the adversary again gets a positive reward of 5 and the police get a negative reward of –5. Thus, an adversary can easily defeat any deterministic police strategy of choosing to always protect either Terminal 1 or Terminal 2.

If, however, the police were to randomize their actions, for example, if they were to be at Terminal 1 60% of the days, and spend the remaining 40% of the days at Terminal 2, then that would lead to a better result. An adversary conducting surveillance will know that the police spend 60% of the days at Terminal 1, and 40% at Terminal 2, but precisely where they will be tomorrow remains unknown. This increases adversary uncertainty and improves the expected reward for the police.

These types of games are called Stackelberg games because the police commit first to a strategy, for example, the 60%/40% splitting of their resources between Terminal 1 and Terminal 2. An adversary acts after conducting surveillance. Notice that the police have committed to a randomized strategy, also called a "mixed strategy." The adversary responds with a single action – an attack – not a randomized response; the adversary's reaction here is a "pure strategy" reaction (in this simple game, we did not model the adversary's action of switching to another airport entirely; had we done so, that would be another pure strategy reaction modeling the adversary's being deterred from attacking this airport). Thus, the model matches the attack methodology provided in Part I of this book: Adversaries conduct surveillance over an extended period of time to get an understanding of police (security) strategy and then launch an attack on a target. The assumption here is that the adversary will only know the general resource allocation strategy (e.g., its 60%/40% distribution of resources) due to prior surveillance but will not know exactly how the security resources will be allocated on the day of the planned attack (because the schedule for the day is generated at random).

These Stackelberg games are also called "attacker-defender games," and we will sometimes use the terms "defender" and "attacker" playing this game. A key point to note here is that we assume that the attacker (adversary) has perfect knowledge of the defender's mixed strategy, and that the adversary will react rationally to this strategy, maximizing his/her own expected utility. (In the rest of this chapter, to disambiguate the defender and attacker in our descriptions, we will use "she" to denote the defender and "he" to denote the attacker.)

The key question of course is whether the 60%/40% splitting of resources is the optimal way to divide the defender's resources. Or should it be 65%/35%, or 50%/50%? We focus on this question of optimal division of resources. With two terminals and one police unit, we could easily solve this problem by hand. With

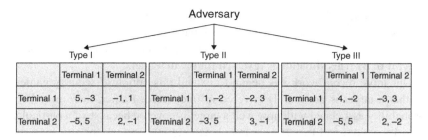

Figure 1.2. Bayesian Stackelberg game.

hundreds of targets and multiple police units, the problem requires efficient computational solution approaches.

Furthermore, the problem in reality is even more complex: From Stackelberg games, we now move into Bayesian Stackelberg games. In Bayesian Stackelberg games, we admit uncertainty over different adversary types. For example, one adversary type may consider Terminal 1 to be more important than Terminal 2. Another adversary type may consider Terminal 2 to be equal in importance to Terminal 1 for some symbolic reason. A third adversary type may not be able to attack Terminal 1 effectively, and so on. Thus, there is not only one payoff matrix, but many of them, each corresponding to a different adversary type, as shown in Figure 1.2.

1.2.3 Security Games

In our work, we often appeal to a further specialization of the Bayesian Stackelberg games called "security games." Security games have the characteristic that what is good for the attacker is bad for the defender and vice versa. However, we do not require that the sum of the payoffs be zero. If the sum was always zero, then we would have zero-sum games. However, in general, the games we address need not be zero-sum. There has been a significant discussion in the literature on why these games are not zero sum (Powell 2007), but some reasons could be that the adversary views some targets as particularly important for his/her audience for their symbolic value, whereas they may not be of equal importance to the police. Or as mentioned earlier, an adversary may not view even a failed attack as a negative outcome because of the publicity and fear it generates. Or the adversary may need to incur a significant cost in mounting a particular attack that may not be particularly important to the police.

In essence, in a security game, if an attacker attacks a target that was covered (protected) by the defender, then the attacker has a worse payoff than if the attacker had attacked the same target when it was not covered. For example, when the attacker in Figure 1 attacked Terminal 1, when the police were protecting Terminal 1, the attacker has a worse payoff (payoff of −3) than when the attacker attacked Terminal 1 when it was not covered/protected by the police (payoff of 5). This situation is reversed for the defender.

Our more recent work has begun to extend this notion of security games, so that a target is not merely covered or uncovered. Rather, there may be a probability associated with how well a target is covered because of a particular security action; and the attacker may have multiple options for attacking the target as well. Appropriate generalization of this concept remains an issue for active research.

Given such Bayesian Stackelberg games, whether in the form of security games or not, the key is to find the optimal allocation of security resources that will optimize the defender's expected reward. Technically, what we are interested in finding is a *strong Stackelberg equilibrium* (SSE). Formal technical definitions of SSE are provided in the papers in Part III of this book. However, the key to remember in SSE is that it assumes that the adversary has perfect knowledge of the defender's mixed strategy and reacts with perfect rationality to that strategy, choosing to react in a way that maximizes his expected utility. In a SSE, the defender has no incentive to change her strategy since it is the optimal strategy, and the attacker has no incentive to change his response because it is the optimal response to the defender's mixed strategy.

Deterrence from attacking the set of targets being protected can be modeled in such games by introducing a new action for the attacker: The *Not Attack Targets* action (which may actually involve attacking another target or performing another action that provides a certain positive rewards). In some cases, given the defender's SSE strategy, the attacker's best response is to not attack any of the targets that the defender is aiming to protect; that is, the targets have been hardened enough that the attacker is deterred from attacking this set of targets. The key point here is that deterrence emerges due to the adversary's choice of this new action; this action is chosen by the adversary only if it is the adversary's best response to the defender's mixed strategy. However, beyond this initial step, understanding and modeling deterrence in more depth remains a topic for future work.

As mentioned earlier, for a small 2 x 2 game as shown earlier, we might be able to compute the SSE by hand. When we have hundreds of targets and even just ten resources, the problem of computing SSE becomes extremely difficulty to solve by hand and requires a computational solution. Even this computational approach runs into difficulties as we scale up beyond that − because it is difficult to enumerate in memory all of the defender's possible choices. Our contributions are in finding an optimal solution quickly.

1.3 Overview of Part II: Applications of Security Games

Part II of this book discusses our applications in depth; key papers include discriptions of one ARMOR (Pita et al., 2008), IRIS (Tsai et al., 2009), and GUARDS (Pita et al., 2011). In addition to providing a brief overview of these applications, this section describes some on-going work not reported in Part II, and some opportunities for further applications.

1.3.1 ARMOR

Our first application of security games was ARMOR (Assistant for Randomized Monitoring Over Routes). As detailed in Part I, this application emerged in 2007 after police at LAX approached us with the question of how to randomize deployment of their limited security resources. For example, they have six inbound roads into LAX, and they wished to set up checkpoints. There are not enough police to have checkpoints on all roads at all times. So the question is where and when to set up these checkpoints. Similarly, they have eight terminals but not enough explosive-detecting canine units to patrol all terminals at all times of the day (a canine unit is limited by the number of hours a dog can work per day). Given that LAX may be under surveillance by adversaries, the question is where and when to have the canine units patrol the different terminals.

The police approached us in April 2007, after we had designed our first set of algorithms. Although the algorithms were ready, we needed to spend several months acquiring knowledge, learning how different police units performed their duties, what constraints there were in terms of shifts of operations, obtaining detailed data on passenger loads at different times of day at different terminals, and so on. The passenger data, for example, influences how payoffs are determined in our underlying game representation – our adversaries would want to cause maximum harm to civilians and the higher the passenger load, the higher the payoff to the adversaries.

By August 2007, after multiple iterations, the police started using ARMOR in setting up checkpoints and, later for canine patrols. The backbone of ARMOR is the algorithms for solving Bayesian Stackelberg games; they recommend a randomized pattern for setting up checkpoints and canine unit patrols. Police provide inputs like the number of available canine units; ARMOR then provides to the police an hour-by-hour schedule of where to set up canine patrols.

ARMOR continues to be used at LAX and has undergone periodic updates to its software. The ARMOR system has received numerous accolades. I discuss some criteria for evaluation of ARMOR a little later in this chapter, and Chapter 13 is dedicated to evaluation of all of our deployed systems.

1.3.2 IRIS

After our ARMOR experience, we were fortunate enough to be contacted by the Federal Air Marshals Service (FAMS). Their challenge is to randomize allocations of air marshals to flights to avoid predictability by adversaries conducting surveillance (e.g., these might be part of an insider threat), yet to provide adequate protection to more important flights. We are focused in particular on some sectors of international flights. Even within that domain, there are a very large number of flights over a month, and not enough air marshals to cover all of them.

To accomplish the goal of randomizing the allocation of air marshals to flights, we constructed a system called IRIS (Intelligent Randomization in Scheduling). We delivered the system to FAMS in the Spring of 2009. After extensive testing, they started using this system in October 2009. At its back-end, IRIS casts the problem it solves as a Stackelberg game and, in particular, as a security game. We focused on the special nature of the security game framework to build fast algorithms for IRIS. Initially, IRIS used the ERASER-C algorithm as described in (Tsai et al., 2009); more recently, IRIS switched to the ASPEN algorithm (Jain et al., 2010). Both ERASER-C and ASPEN are discussed in Part III of this book.

1.3.3 GUARDS

After IRIS, our next focus was GUARDS (Game-theoretic Unpredictable and Randomly Deployed Security). GUARDS was developed in collaboration with the United States Transportation Security Administration (TSA) to assist in resource allocation tasks for airport protection at more than 400 U.S. airports. Unlike ARMOR and IRIS, which focus on one installation/application and one security activity (e.g., canine patrol or checkpoints) per application, GUARDS reasons with multiple security activities, diverse potential threats, and also hundreds of end users. The goal for GUARDS is to allocate TSA personnel to security activities that protect the airport infrastructure; GUARDS does not check passengers.

GUARDS again utilizes a Stackelberg game but generalizes beyond security games and develops a novel solution algorithm for these games. GUARDS has been delivered to TSA and is currently undergoing evaluation and testing for scheduling practices at an undisclosed airport. If successful, TSA intends to incorporate the system into its unpredictable scheduling practices nationwide.

1.3.4 Beyond ARMOR/IRIS/GUARDS

Beyond ARMOR, IRIS, and GUARDS, we have recently started a pilot project with the United States Coast Guard to build a new system called PROTECT

(Port Resilience Operational/Tactical Enforcement to Combat Terrorism). The goal in PROTECT is to recommend randomized patrolling strategies for the coast guard while taking into account the weights of different targets protected in their area of operation and adversary reaction to any patrolling strategy. We have begun with a demonstration and evaluation in the port of Boston and, depending on our results there, will proceed to other ports.

There are many other security agencies in the United States and internationally that have expressed an interest in using the Stackelberg game model for improving their operations. One application might be protecting important locations in a city by setting up randomized citywide checkpoints. For example, following the devastating attacks in November 2008, police in Mumbai set up randomized checkpoints throughout the city's road networks. Furthermore, while counterterrorism has remained a key focus of the work so far, new projects are now extending the application arena to include crime suppression and other objectives. For example, one such application might be the improved randomized checking of ticketless travelers on trains; yet another one might be randomized checking to support the food-distribution networks of charity organizations.

1.4 Overview of Part III: Algorithmic Advances to Achieve Scale-up in Security Games

At the heart of our applications are the efficient algorithms created to solve the very large games to provide optimal defender strategies in the Stackelberg games that are deployed. Discovering fast Stackelberg game solvers is the primary research challenge we have addressed to this point, but it remains a daunting one. Part III of this book focuses on this challenge; the advances reported here were necessary for the deployed application. Key papers included in this section are Paruchuri et al., 2009, Kiekintveld et al., 2009, and Jain et al., 2010.

In this section, I present an overview of Part III of the book, which discusses the algorithms we have developed. Section 1.4.1 is a general overview, while Section 1.4.2 provides a more detailed description of our first set of algorithms.

1.4.1 Efficient Algorithms: Overview

We begin with the challenge of building efficient algorithms for solving very large-scale Stackelberg games. Scale-up challenges arise in these games for at least three reasons:

1. *Growth in the number of defender strategies:* There may be a very large number of ways in which limited defender resources may be allocated to targets. For example, in the IRIS system, with just 100 flights and 10 air marshals, we have C_{10}^{100}, that is, 1.73×10^{13} different ways of allocating air marshals to flights.

2. *Growth in the number of attacker strategies:* The attacker may have multiple different ways of evading defender actions and then attacking particular targets. This explosion of attacker strategies is seen to arise in the GUARDS system. Indeed, is also seen in applications where the defender's actions involve protecting targets embedded in a network, such as protecting important locations embedded in the city's road network as in the case of cities such as Mumbai. In such situations, the attacker can follow many different paths to get to the targets of interest.

3. *Growth in the number of attacker types:* When there is an increase in the number of attacker types (the Bayesian games introduced earlier), each attacker type adds an exponential complexity.

To address these complexities, we have created a range of different algorithms, described in the table in Figure 1.3. The first game-theoretic algorithms were designed in 2007, and newer algorithms continue to be designed to address ongoing challenges. Papers describing key algorithms are presented in Parts III and IV of this book. Further improvements are required, and we anticipate that newer algorithms providing additional speedup techniques will continue to emerge.

In the table shown in Figure 1.3, the first three columns show the type of scale-up such algorithms aim to achieve. I have used only "low," "medium," and "high" as informal indicators of the how large a scale-up that particular algorithm can handle in the particular dimension. For defender and attacker actions, "low" means 100s or 1000s, "medium" means billions or trillions, and "high" would increase the numbers of actions in the same proportion. For the adversary-types column, low means 5 or less, medium is of the order of 10s or 100s, and high would be of the order of 1000s.

The fourth column shows whether the algorithm exploited domain structure. While early algorithms did not do this, further scale-ups and speedups required exploiting domain structure, which introduces specialization in the algorithm for security games but provides benefits of increased speed.

The fifth column indicates whether the algorithm provides an exact or an approximate solution. An exact solution is one where the optimal answer is calculated. For example, if we are interested in the SSE of a game, we obtain the exact defender mixed strategy that yields the SSE. An approximate solution

Scale-up: Defender actions	Scale-up: Attacker actions	Scale-up: Attacker types	Domain Structure exploited	Exact or approx.	Type of equilibrium	Algorithm
Low	Low	Medium	None	Approx.	SSE	ASAP (2007)
Low	Low	Medium	None	Exact	SSE	DOBSS (2008)
Low	Low	Medium	None	Exact	Rationality/ observation	COBRA (2009)
Medium	Low	Low	High (Security game, 1 target)	Exact	SSE	ORIGAMI (2009)
Medium	Low	Low	High (Security game, 2 targets)	Approx.	SSE	ERASER–C (2009)
Medium	Low	Low	Med (Security game, N targets)	Exact	SSE	ASPEN (2010)
Medium	Medium	Low	High (Zero-sum game, graph)	Approx.	SSE	RANGER (2010)
Medium	Medium	Low	High (Zero-sum game, graph)	Exact	SSE	RUGGED (2010)
Low	Low	Medium	None	Exact	SSE	HBGS (2011)
Medium	Low	Medium	Med (Security game, N targets)	Exact	SSE	HBSA (2011)

Figure 1.3. Progression of algorithms designed to address the challenges in security games.

is one where we may not obtain an exact solution, the goal again being to trade off optimality for speed.

The sixth column indicates the solution concept used. While in most of the algorithms, we aimed at attaining the SSE, COBRA (Pita et al., 2009) is an exception. COBRA was explicitly designed to assume that the adversary may not necessarily act with full rationality and perfect knowledge of defender's mixed strategy. This is discussed in Part IV.

The final column shows the name of the actual algorithm developed and the year it was published. We began with the ASAP algorithm designed in 2007 (Paruchuri et al., 2007), which was an approximate algorithm; this was superseded by the DOBSS algorithm in 2008 (Paruchuri et al., 2009). Both ASAP and DOBSS were aimed at the ARMOR application. These algorithms focused on Bayesian Stackelberg games, which scale up the number of adversary types. These are general-purpose algorithms in that they do not assume any structure to the underlying game, such as in the payoff-structure restrictions of a security game. The general-purpose nature of DOBSS makes it useful in the GUARDS application, which is based on an enhancement to security games.

Even prior to the ASAP and DOBSS algorithms, a set of algorithms was proposed that focused on randomization of plans without necessarily focusing on an adversary's set of actions (Paruchuri et al., 2009). These algorithms, developed for the randomizing plans generated by Markov decision problems (MDPs) and distributed MDPs, assumed that we have no knowledge of the set of actions available to the adversary, and the only assumption made is that any deterministic actions in the defender's plans would necessarily lead to a negative outcome for the defender.

In contrast, ORIGAMI, ERASER-C (Kiekintveld et al., 2009), and ASPEN (Jain et al., 2010) are a series of algorithms designed for IRIS that exploit the special nature of the payoffs and structure of security games. These three algorithms scale up the number of defender strategies because, as mentioned earlier, there is a very large number of choices for assigning air marshals to flights. Of these three, ORIGAMI is the simplest. Unfortunately, it assumes that air marshals are scheduled to only one flight at a time, which is not appropriate – air marshals must take a tour of flights, so they fly to a destination abroad and can then return home. ORIGAMI may leave air marshals stranded abroad. However, ORIGAMI showed us that significant speedups are possible by exploiting the structure of security games. ERASER-C generalized ORIGAMI, air marshals allowing to take pairs of flights rather than individual flights, that is, a tour of just two flights. ASPEN generalized ERASER-C's capability even further by allowing air marshals to take tours with arbitrary numbers of flights. Additionally, ASPEN is seen to be significantly faster than ERASER-C. As a result, ASPEN is the algorithm of choice in IRIS.

COBRA (Pita et al., 2009) is currently not in use in any application. We have shown that when playing against human subjects in the lab, it outperformed DOBSS (which assumes full rationality). Whether to deploy COBRA or algorithms of a similar type that do not make assumptions of full rationality is a question currently under discussion.

The algorithm RANGER (Tsai et al., 2010) and its successor RUGGED (Jain et al., 2011a) are designed for setting up randomized checkpoints in a city. This work was motivated by the problem faced by police forces in cities such as Mumbai. As mentioned earlier, following the devastating terrorist attacks in Mumbai, police there set up checkpoints in a randomized fashion throughout the city. The key here is that a city is seen as a graph, and checkpoints are set up in a randomized fashion on the streets to protect key targets. In such graph-based domains, the number of defender strategies is very large because a large number of combinations of checkpoints can be set up in a graph, and the attacker can pursue many different paths – many different ways of traversing the graph – to attack city targets.

The final two algorithms, HBGS and HBSA (Jain et al., 2011b), use a hierarchical structure to extend non-Bayesian algorithms to Bayesian games. For example, HBSA uses ASPEN and extends it to solve a Bayesian Stackelberg game, where the defender can have many combinations of actions. This is currently an active area of research.

1.4.2 Efficient Algorithms: A More Detailed View

This section is intended for readers who are particularly interested in following the algorithms in the previous section in more detail. Others may skip this section. While Part III of the book provides the key set of papers on these algorithms, this section provides an overview and motivation. These algorithms are all formulated as mixed-integer linear programs (MILPs).

Previous work has shown that finding an optimal solution to a Bayesian Stackelberg game with multiple attacker types is NP-hard[1] (Conitzer and Sandholm, 2006). While an earlier approach led the way by providing one of the first algorithms for a non-Bayesian version of Stackelberg games (Conitzer and Sandholm, 2006), this approach is shown to be inefficient for the Bayesian case: It requires a Harsanyi transformation of the Bayesian game to an acceptable input, which leads to exponential blowup in the input size (Harsanyi and Selten, 1972).[2]

DOBSS was introduced to counter this inefficiency (Paruchuri et al., 2009). One key advantage of the DOBSS approach is that it operates directly on the Bayesian representation without requiring the Harsanyi transformation, avoiding the exponential increase in input size. We present DOBSS in its most intuitive form as a mixed-integer quadratic program (MIQP); this MIQP may be transformed into a linearized equivalent MILP. While a more detailed discussion of the MILP appears in Part III, the current section may at least serve to explain the concept at a high level.

In DOBSS, we explicitly represent the defender actions and the optimal actions for the attacker types. We denote by x the defender's policy (mixed strategy), which consists of a vector of probabilities distributed over the defender's pure strategies. Hence, the value x_i is the proportion of times a defender's pure strategy i is used in the policy. We denote by q^l the vector of strategies of attacker type l. We also index the payoff matrices of the defender and each of the attacker types l by the matrices R^l and C^l. Let M be a large positive number.

---

[1] NP-Hardness is a measure of the computational complexity of a problem. For more information, refer to (Garey and Johnson, 1979).

[2] We skip details of the Harsanyi transformation in the interest of space; the key is that it causes an exponential increase in the input size.

Given a priori probabilities p^l of facing each attacker type l, the defender solves the following:

$$\max_{x,q} \quad \sum_{i \in X} \sum_{l \in L} \sum_{j \in Q} p^l R_{ij}^l q_j^l$$

$$\text{s.t.} \quad \sum_{i \in X} x_i = 1$$

$$\sum_{j \in Q} q_j^l = 1$$

$$0 \le (a^l - \sum_{i \in X} C_{ij}^l) \le (1 - q_j^l) M$$

$$x \in [0,1]$$

$$q_j^l \in \{0,1\}$$

Figure 1.4. DOBSS mixed-integer quadratic program.

The key to this DOBSS model is that it works directly with multiple smaller matrices R^l and C^l as its input, thus exploiting decomposition in this Bayesian game instead of constructing a single, exponentially large, Harsanyi-transformed matrix as its input. As a result, DOBSS could be used for the ARMOR program, allowing it easily solve problems at LAX that were unsolvable in reasonable time by previous methods (Pita et al., 2008).

Unfortunately, DOBSS is extremely inefficient for solving even a limited version of the FAMS domain. The reason is that DOBSS explicitly represents all the defender's pure strategies. Thus, even in a very limited version of the FAMS domain, with just 10 air marshals to be allocated to just 100 flight tours, DOBSS requires us to explicitly represent all the different allocation combinations, that is, C_{10}^{100} actions. Even representing the input to DOBSS in this fashion is a major computational burden – it simply runs out of memory on regular laptops.

Studying the FAMS domain led us to identify security games as a class of games. A key feature of the problem structure is that payoffs depend only on whether or not the attacked flight is defended (covered) by a FAMS, that is, it does not matter whether or not an air marshal covers any unattacked flight. Thus, from a payoff perspective, many allocations of air marshals to flights are identical. This problem structure is not specific just to the FAMS domain but is found

Table 1.1. *Runtime comparison of DOBSS and
ERASER-C*

	Actions	DOBSS	ERASER-C
LAX (6 canines)	784	0.94 sec	0.23 sec
FAMS (Location-A)	6,048	4.74 sec	0.09 sec
FAMS (Location-B)[3]	85,275	—	1.57 sec

to generalize across many security domains, requiring allocation of defender resources to multiple targets. This feature of the FAMS domain allowed us to discover a more compact representation that explicitly avoids enumerating all possible combinations of allocating air marshals to flights. The resulting algorithm ERASER-C (Kiekintveld et al., 2009) thus allows us to solve much larger problem instances. For example, Table 1.1 below shows runtime comparisons between ERASER-C and the best previously known algorithm, DOBSS, for the LAX and the FAMS domains. It can be clearly seen that ERASER-C is orders of magnitude faster than DOBSS, which did not even complete the large Location-B problem instance, reaching a memory limit after an hour of runtime.

While providing orders of magnitude improvement over DOBSS, ERASER-C still fails to tackle the problem of allocating air marshals throughout the entire international sector, let alone the more complex problem in the domestic sector or the problem that results from combining the two sectors. ERASER-C is also confined to tours consisting of exactly two flights, one going abroad and one return flight.

ASPEN avoids this shortcoming by allowing multi-city tours for air marshals, providing further speedups over ERASER-C. However, even with ASPEN, we are still not able to solve the entire FAMS allocation challenge, and further efficiency improvements are necessary. Further enhancements to ASPEN are introduced in the HBSA algorithm discussed earlier.

1.5 Part IV: Toward the Future

These major deployments of security games have unleashed a number of fundamental research challenges in computational game theory. Some of the key ones include:

1. *Efficient algorithms for solving very large games to provide optimal strategies for the defender in the Stackelberg game:* As mentioned earlier,

the challenge of scale-up for Stackelberg game solvers is the primary research challenge we have addressed to this point and it remains a daunting one.

2. *Developing algorithms that can address human adversaries in terms of exploiting their biases and preferences and addressing their bounded rationality*: While game-theoretic solution concepts typically assume perfect rationality on part of the adversary, human adversaries may have cognitive limitations and biases requiring us to devise new algorithms that address these weaknesses.

3. *Addressing the uncertainty that may arise because of an adversary's inability to conduct detailed surveillance*: Our Stackelberg model has assumed an adversary capable of conducting detailed surveillance of all our activities over a prolonged period of time – our algorithms are built assuming that the adversary has perfect knowledge of the defender's mixed strategy. In reality, our adversaries may not have such capabilities, and we therefore may need to derive a new set of algorithms that handle the uncertainty about the adversary's surveillance capabilities.

4. *Addressing the defender's uncertainty about attacker's payoffs:* A defender may not have perfect knowledge of adversary's exact payoffs; it may have only an approximate understanding of adversary's preferences over multiple targets. Once again, our algorithms need to be able to address this uncertainty.

5. *Coordinated attack by multiple simultaneous attackers, attacker deception:* Attackers may conduct many simultaneous attacks on the same target. Attackers may also first conduct a diversionary attack and then a real one. Defenders may need to create strategies that are robust against such attacker strategies.

Part III focuses on the first challenge on this list; this advance was necessary for us for the deployed application. Part IV deals with the ongoing work that has begun to address the remaining challenges, and the papers by Pita et al., 2009, Yin et al., 2010 and Kiekintveld et al., 2011 focus on the second, third, and fourth challenges, respectively. Finally, beyond these research challenges in computational game theory, a major topic of research is the evaluation of the deployed applications. Evaluation of real-world deployed research, away from the laboratory, is difficult. The final paper included in this book focuses on the evaluation challenges.

There are many other research groups currently active in this area of research. We have not been able to include papers from all these groups, but readers interested in pursuing this topic can find some pointers in the work of Basilico et al. (2009), Dickerson et al. (2010), Korzhyk et al. (2010), Vanek et al.

(2010). In addition, Yin et al. (2010) bring up the challenge of multiple attackers conducting a coordinated attack on a single target.

Thus, it is important to note that this is not a closed area of research; rather it is a very open research area with practical and important implications. In other words, while the game-theoretic methods that have been deployed are indeed an advance over previous approaches, much work remains to be done. Indeed, these five challenges are not even a complete list of all of the research challenges we must address in the future.

In the rest of this chapter, we provide an overview of the research challenges in Section 1.5.1. Section 1.5.2 outlines the key issues in evaluation of deployed applications.

1.5.1 Overview of Research Challenges

Classical game-theoretic solution concepts (e.g., SSE) typically make strong assumptions about both the knowledge players (i.e., attackers and defenders) have and how they will choose strategies. First, players are assumed to have common knowledge of the game model; that is, all players know all relevant information about the players, actions, and payoffs, and they know that all players have this information. Secondly, players are assumed to act in a perfectly rational manner; they will always optimize their expected payoffs given correct beliefs. These assumptions are idealizations that have allowed us to develop our initial applications. However, our goal is to develop novel approaches for analyzing security games that are more robust to different types of uncertainties. These uncertainties include the following:

1. *Human biases and cognitive limitations*: The emerging field of behavioral game theory uses laboratory experiments to explore human decision making in games (Camerer, 2003). These studies have produced a growing body of evidence that human players often deviate from the predictions of the Nash equilibrium and other models based on perfect rationality. They have also identified alternative solution concepts that make more accurate predictions about human play. In our work, we focus on developing new algorithms that are robust against human decision making and capable of exploiting human limitations and biases. As such, our work has led to a new area of research combining behavioral or experimental game theory with computational game theory. Our initial effort, from Pita et al. (2009), outlines some new, efficient algorithms with a significant amount of empirical evaluation against human subjects.

2. *Uncertainty over attacker's observational capabilities:* A fundamental assumption in using Stackelberg games is that the defender first commits to a

randomized strategy; the adversaries or attackers act after surveillance of this randomized strategy. Yet, in some situations, the adversary may have only a limited surveillance capability. In these situations, the adversary may have an imprecise understanding of the defender's strategy. In general, there may be significant uncertainty over the adversary's precise surveillance capability: How should a defender's strategy be computed given such uncertainty? In Yin et al. (2010), we provide the first steps toward addressing this challenge, considering first a situation in which the attacker may not be able to conduct any surveillance at all.

3. *Model uncertainty:* Most game-theoretic analysis takes the game model as a given and assumes that it is known by all players. In practice, we rely on domain experts to provide a game model, possibly based on evidence from intelligence analysts or other sources. The resulting models are the best available estimate of the information needed to evaluate potential security strategies, but they still contain inherent uncertainty, especially with regard to the capabilities and priorities of adversaries. Taking this uncertainty into account in the game analysis can result in far superior strategy choices compared to applying standard game analysis techniques that assume perfect information. Our initial effort, from Kiekintveld et al. (2011), outlines new algorithms that address a defender's uncertainty over an adversary's priorities and payoffs.

In summary, these different types of uncertainties contribute to unpredictable choices by opponents. Accounting for these factors can lead to strategies that perform much better than the idealized models.

1.5.2 Challenges in Evaluation of Deployed Security Systems

Having provided an overview of our research, particularly of the algorithms we have developed, we turn to the evaluation of these algorithms and their deployments. Evaluating the research advances is somewhat straightforward: In a controlled simulation environment, we can perform hundreds of simulations (or lab experiments) comparing "before" and "after" results to establish that a particular algorithmic advance has made a significant difference along the dimension of interest. For example, we can compare the runtimes of a previous algorithm with a new algorithm over hundreds of problem instances to establish that the new algorithm is indeed significantly faster.

In performing an evaluation of our real-world deployments, we are interested in understanding the magnitude of the impact of our research on the application. In other words, our algorithm may be performing in the lab as expected, but we are interested in establishing that our models and assumptions when deploying the algorithm are reasonable.

Unfortunately, evaluation of the real-world deployments is difficult. The fundamental difficulty is that we cannot conduct hundreds of controlled experiments in the real world, as we do in the lab. Indeed, academic reviewers have often raised questions attempting to arrive at a real-world evaluation in different ways, and it is worth repeating some of these questions and our answers to clarify some of the fundamental difficulties:

- *Do the deployed algorithms work? Have they made the protected infrastructure safe?* In response to this question, we have learned from our collaborators in law enforcement that there is no such thing as a 100% security guarantee. The most we can aim to achieve is to increase the adversary's costs and uncertainties. So, the question we should be asking is whether our game-theoretic methods have increased adversary cost and uncertainty over previous methods. Part II discusses this.
- *Can we perform any type of controlled experiments to compare "before" (previous methods) and "after"(game-theoretic methods)?* In addition to the ethical challenges such an experiment presents (by possibly providing inadequate security), the fundamental difficulty here is that our adversaries, by definition, are not going to cooperate in any such experiments.
- *Can we get detailed real-world data from all security violations, arrests, and any other related data before and after deployment of the game-theoretic software to perform analysis ourselves?* Security sensitivities preclude any total release of such data, but some selective data has been made available.
- *Could we perform "Red Team" experiments with mock attackers to see if there any increase in difficulty from "before" to "after"?* This is a possibility, but it is very expensive and requires significant expertise to be assembled. It is certainly something that researchers themselves cannot easily undertake. Nonetheless, some security agencies are performing such tests with our software.

In summary, these are real-world deployed security systems, and their evaluation in practice is extremely difficult; they do not allow for easy, controlled experiments. So what can we do? Our solution is to do the best we can using many different methods including mathematical models, simulations, experiments against human subjects in the laboratory, any available before vs. after scheduling data and expert evaluations to compare previous methods with our newer game-theoretic approaches. The following previous methods are reasonable alternative strategies that are in use or have been suggested to us: (i) human schedulers; (ii) uniform random strategies that are equivalent to simply rolling dice to determine a schedule; (iii) weighted random strategies that try to weigh the distinct targets differently – in essence, it's a dice roll with weighted dice, but without paying attention to *both attacker and defender utilities* as in a game-theoretic approach. We have compared these different strategies using the following methods:

- *Running simulations*: We have run many simulations in the ARMOR and IRIS domains comparing our game-theoretic approach to previous approaches. These simulations assume an "artificial intelligence" attacker who applies machine learning to discover the defender's strategy and then choose an attack. These simulations consistently illustrate the benefit of a game-theoretic approach over competing approaches.
- *Experiments with human subjects in the lab*: Games in the lab simulate an attacker-defender game; human subjects are typically students who are paid money to launch an attack after surveillance. These experiments have also emphasized the benefits of a game-theoretic approach over simpler approaches.
- *Expert evaluations*: These evaluations refer to the evaluations done by security experts. For example, the mayor of Los Angeles recently appointed a blue-ribbon panel to study the LAX security challenge. Other experts have evaluated the impact of the ARMOR system at LAX.

In addition, some real-world scheduling data comparing human schedulers to our software's output, and some results from red teaming exercises have been made available to us. Based on all of these, in general, our evaluation so far reveals that our competing approaches suffer from the following shortcomings:

- *Human schedulers tend to fall into predictable patterns*: It is well established that humans are poor at randomizing (Wagenaar, 1972); thus, it is easier to spot patterns in human-generated schedules. Indeed, this point is made in the comments by Director Butts of LAX police (Murr, 2007) with regard to the scheduling of checkpoints and canines, and also in a GAO report (2009), regarding the scheduling of FAMS by human schedulers.
- *Uniform randomizers*: By not weighing different targets, this method squanders scarce security resources by deploying them in the service of unimportant targets. For example, a uniform random strategy would more frequently send police officers to protect very sparsely crowded terminals at LAX.
- *Weighted randomizers:* Weighted randomizers do better than uniform randomizers but still suffer from two difficulties. First, as mentioned earlier, just enumerating all defender actions is often problematic in our games. Unfortunately, to generate appropriate weights, we do need to enumerate

these actions – this would require us to invent new compact representation techniques. Second, if we do not pay attention to both attacker and defender utilities, they may still perform very poorly. Third, naïve weighted randomizers don't explicitly take into account that the attacker is conducting surveillance and responding to the defender's strategy.

Chapter 13 on evaluation is a further in-depth discussion of the challenges of evaluation. There is some evaluation of the individual deployed applications in the particular papers focused on those applications as well.

1.6 Summary

This book describes the marriage of the latest research in game theory with significant practical deployed applications. On the one hand, these applications have revealed fundamental challenges for game-theory research, leading the way to a new-generation game theory that requires us to address not only a scale up toward large-scale problems, but also uncertainty of players toward each other's payoffs, observation capabilities, and decision-making procedures. On the other hand, game-theoretic approaches have provided an improvement over previous approaches, such as scheduling by hand or by other simpler methods. However, much work remains to be done, and I excitedly look forward to further research and practical deployments over the next few years.

PART I

Security Experts' Perspectives

2

LAX – Terror Target: The History, the Reason, the Countermeasure

Erroll G. Southers

2.1 Introduction

The history of plots and attacks on LAX suggests that it has achieved a level of importance in the minds of a diverse collection of terrorist organizations. The counterterrorism community is challenged by an intelligent and adaptive adversary who is prone to return to targets and continues to demonstrate sustained intent and an evolving attack methodology. LAX seems to present itself as an elusive trophy, as homeland security forces struggle, along with the rest of the world, to achieve and maintain a level of resistance capable of thwarting a man-enabled catastrophe.

"Over 5,000 deaths have resulted from terrorist attacks on civil aviation since 1980; about 200 deaths occurred in attacks on airports themselves, as opposed to aircraft."[1] Although the aviation domain has become the hardest critical infrastructure since the terror attack on September 11, 2001, it remains the most desirable for the attacker. There are essentially three fundamental strategies for attacking the aviation system – hijackings, bombings, and airport assaults. Security countermeasures designed to reduce the threat of in-flight incidents suggest attacks on airport facilities are probable.

2.2 A Brief History of Significant Events

Terrorism has long been a serious threat to the air transportation system of the United States and other nations. In 1972, three members of the Japanese Red Army initiated what is now known as the Lod Airport Massacre. In an attack involving "active shooter" tactics (a strategy whereby assailants engage targets of opportunity while moving through a location) utilizing automatic weapons

---

[1] See the Memorial Institute for the Prevention of Terrorism (MIPT) Knowledge Base, online at http://www.tkb.org.

and grenades, the assailants killed twenty four people and injured seventy eight others at the Lod Airport, now known as the Ben Gurion International Airport in Tel Aviv, Israel.

The first in-flight terrorist attack resulting in the death of passengers occurred on Cubana flight 455 on October 6, 1976, which was en route from Barbados to Jamaica. Two bombs, detonated by timers, downed the flight, killing seventy three people in what was described as the deadliest terror airline attack in the western hemisphere. The vulnerabilities associated with airline security at the time were fairly obvious.

The earliest demonstrations of simultaneous attacks, or "simultaneity," involving the aviation domain occurred on June 23, 1985. The lack of appropriate training, technology, and understanding of the terrorist threat contributed to the single deadliest airline disaster. A bomb went undetected by airport security as it was placed onboard Air India flight 182, and the resulting explosion during the flight caused the aircraft to crash into the Atlantic Ocean, killing 329 people.

Approximately an hour earlier, a bomb had exploded at Tokyo's Narita International Airport, killing two baggage handlers. The bomb was in a bag intended to be loaded onto Air India flight 301, scheduled to depart for Bangkok International Airport with 177 passengers onboard. A miscalculation of the time zones when the bomb was placed onboard may have saved the flight. Subsequent investigations revealed that the incidents were related and connected to a Sikh separatist group operating in Canada, known as the Babbar Khalsa. The significance of simultaneity was not embraced at the time, though it would become the standard to which terrorist groups would aspire in future years.

In 1995, a bomb containing a liquid form of nitroglycerine was detonated on Philippine Airlines flight 434, killing one passenger but failing to make headlines. The bomber was Ramzi Yousef mastermind of the first World Trade Center bombing and architect of Operation Bojinka, a plan to detonate bombs onboard twelve aircraft over the Pacific Ocean. The plan never got off the ground because it was discovered and thwarted by the Manila police. However, the concept of operations evolved.

Six years later, Richard Reid was apprehended attempting to detonate his infamous shoe bomb, proving once again that an improvised explosive device could withstand the scrutiny of explosives technology and be placed onboard an aircraft (see Figure 2.1). The bomb contained TATP, the peroxide-based explosive of choice of suicide bombers in the Middle East, and PETN, a key ingredient of Semtex, the Czech-made military explosive used to down Pan Am flight 103 in Lockerbie, Scotland, in 1988.

It is interesting to note that Reid chose to board an aircraft in another country after assessing Israel's Ben Gurion International Airport and determining that

(a)

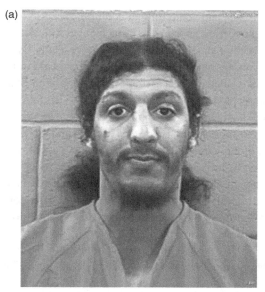

(b)

Figure 2.1. (a) Richard Reid; and (b) One of Reid's shoes.

it was too hard a target. No doubt, Reid based his assessment on the extensive questioning he was made to endure before departing Tel Aviv the summer before the attack. After the interview it was reported, "They didn't like the look of him, so they checked everything in his bags, and everything he was wearing, and then they put an armed sky marshal in the seat right next to him."[2]

[2] 60 Minutes, "The Safest Airline: A Secure Example Set by Israel's El Al." (August 21, 2002) http://www.cbsnews.com/stories/2002/01/15/60II/main324476.shtml.

In the United States and some foreign countries, security policies requiring passengers to remove their shoes were implemented following this incident to reduce the shoe-bomb risk. The threat would evolve again. By 2006 a plan was in the works, involving placing liquid explosives onboard at least ten airlines traveling between Canada, Great Britain, and the United States. Again, law enforcement intercepted and terminated the plot. In actuality, this conspiracy was nothing more than Operation Bojinka in reverse. The original plot evolved from shoebombs to sports-drink bottles, as carriers and targeted aircraft bound to the east coast of the United States, instead of the west coast.

Years of efforts to increase in-flight security resulted in hardened cockpit doors, the presence of federal air marshals, and airport terminal enhancements such as TSA behavioral detection officers; explosives detection canines facilitated another evolution of the threat. Another attack on an airport appeared to be inevitable and came to fruition in 2007.

On June 30, 2007, terrorists drove a car bomb into the entrance doors of the Glasgow International Airport terminal and set it ablaze. The driver of the vehicle was seriously burned in the ensuing fire and five others were injured. Strategically placed security bollards mitigated the intended result by preventing the vehicle from actually entering the terminal. Unfortunately, much like the Operation Bojinka–liquid bomb nexus, this attack methodology had been devised in a previous plot.

The attack at Glasgow Airport bore a striking similarity to Dhiren Barot's disrupted Gas Cylinders plot, devised in 2004 to destroy the New York Stock Exchange and Citigroup headquarters in New York, the International Monetary Fund and World Bank buildings in Washington, D.C., and Prudential Financial headquarters in Newark, N.J. The scheme, demonstrating the hallmarks of al-Qaeda simultaneity, involved limousines containing dirty bombs made with radioactive-laced explosives, to be driven beneath the three locations and detonated in concert with attacks on a London subway car as it passed beneath the Thames River and several landmark London hotels.[3]

Barot (Figure 2.2) is also credited with authoring a thirty-nine-page memo that advocated the use of simple explosives composed of materials available from local pharmacies and hardware stores. The memo was intended for al-Qaeda operatives and was discovered on the laptop detailing the Gas Cylinders plot.[4]

Despite the implementation in increased passenger-screening technology and additional layers of airport security, the aviation industry barely escaped disaster

---

[3] Tucker Reals, "British Terror Plotter Gets Life in Prison." CBS News World (Nov. 7, 2006) http://www.cbsnews.com/stories/2006/11/07/world/main2158113.shtml

[4] Craig Whitlock, "Homemade, Cheap and Dangerous: Terror Cells Favor Simple Ingredients in Building Bombs." Washington Post Foreign Service (July 5, 2007)

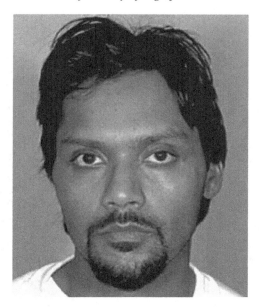

Figure 2.2. Dhiren Barot, mastermind of the Gas Cylinders plot.

when a PETN-based bomb was brought onboard Northwest flight 253 in an underwear garment in 2009. Umar Farouk Abdulmutallab, a Nigerian citizen, also known as the "underwear bomber," unsuccessfully attempted to detonate the device, which could have killed 289 people. Fortunately, operator failure prevented a catastrophe (Figure 2.3).

On October 29, 2010, intelligence sources from Saudi Arabia led to the discovery of two IEDs (improvised explosive devices) concealed in printer cartridges (Figure 2.4a) on separate cargo planes. The bombs, discovered at en route stopovers in England and in Dubai in the United Arab Emirates, were shipped from Yemen and bound for the United States.

One week later, al-Qaeda in the Arabian Peninsula (AQAP) took credit for the attack.[5] The details of the plot, identified as Operation Hemorrhage, were subsequently described in a special issue of al-Qaeda's magazine *Inspire* (Figure 2.4b). The plot was allegedly developed for $4,200, with the intent of initiating an aviation security response costing billions, with AQAP stating

---

[5] CNN Wire Staff, "Yemen-based al Qaeda group claims responsibility for parcel bomb plot." (November 6, 2010) http://edition.cnn.com/2010/WORLD/meast/11/05/yemen.security. concern/?hpt=T2

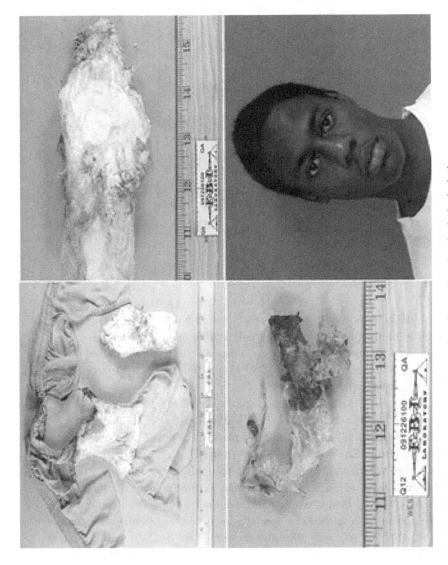

Figure 2.3. AbdulMutallab and the underwear he was allegedly wearing when the device ignited.

Figure 2.4.   (a) Cargo bomb printer cartridge; and (b) Al Qaeda's magazine *Inspire*, November 2010.

"our objective is not a maximum kill but to cause a hemorrhage in the aviation industry."[6]

2.3 Terrorism and the Economic Significance of the Aviation Domain

The sophistication and intelligence of al-Qaeda and its affiliates cannot be over-stated. Unlike most terrorist organizations, al-Qaeda understands the value and leverage of asymmetric combat and is attentive to the economic impact of its attacks. On October 21, 2001, in his first interview with Tayseer Allouni, the Kabul correspondent of al-Jazeera, Osama bin Laden provided his detailed economic analysis of the 9/11 attacks:

I say the events that happened on Tuesday, September 11, in New York and Washington, that is truly a great event in all measures, and its claims until this moment are not over and are still continuing ... According to their own admissions, the share of losses on the Wall Street market reached 16 percent. They said that this number is a record, which has never happened since the opening of the market more than 230 years ago. This large collapse has never happened. The gross amount that is traded in that market reaches $4 trillion. So if we multiply 16 percent by $4 trillion to find out the loss that affected the stocks, it reaches $640 billion of losses from stocks, by Allah's grace. So this amount, for example, is the budget of Sudan for 640 years. They have lost this due to an attack that happened with the success of Allah lasting one hour only. The daily income of the American nation is $20 billion. The first week they didn't work at all due to their psychological shock of the attack, and even until today some don't work due to the attack. So if you multiply $20 billion by one week, it comes out to $140 billion, and it is even bigger than this. If you add $640 billion, we've reached how much? Approximately $800 billion. The cost of the building losses and construction losses? Let us say more than $30 billion. Then they have fired and liquidated until today ... from the airline companies more than 170,000 employees. That includes cargo plane companies and commercial airlines, and the American studies and analysis have mentioned that 70 percent of the American people even until today still suffer from depression and psychological trauma after the incident of the two towers, and the attack on the Defense Ministry, the Pentagon – thanks to Allah's grace. Those claims cannot be calculated by anyone due to their very large scale, multitude and complexity – and it is increasing thanks to Allah's grace – so watch as the amount reaches no less than $1 trillion by the lowest estimate – thanks to Allah's grace – due to these successful and blessed attacks. We

[6] Ikrimah Al-Muhajir, Explosives Department, translated by al-Malahem Media, "Technical Details." Inspire Magazine (November 1431/2010) p. 7.

implore Allah to accept those brothers within the ranks of the martyrs, and to admit them to the highest levels of Paradise.[7]

2.3.1 National Perspective

The significant economic value of commercial aviation to the local and national economy makes civil aviation a highly attractive terrorist target. As early as 2002, the Airports Council International (ACI) reported that the United States maintains the world's most extensive airport system. The importance of aviation to society in commercial transportation, cargo movement, and national defense cannot be overstated. Accordingly, globalization continues to increase the relative importance of the airports and aviation. Thus, our national, regional, and local economic growth ultimately depends on the U.S. airport industry.

During the same reporting period, the ACI forecast that United States airports, during the period of 2002 to 2013, would create $507 billion in total annual economic activity. Currently, there are approximately 1.9 million jobs in United States airports, and an additional 4.8 million jobs are created in local municipalities, for a total of 6.7 million airport-related jobs. These employment opportunities translate into earnings of $190 billion. Airports generate $33.5 billion in local, state, and federal taxes and more than 1.9 million passengers daily rely on aviation as their mode of business or leisure travel. Additionally, more than 38,000 tons of cargo transits U.S. airports daily.

2.3.2 Los Angeles International Airport

LAX creates jobs. According to the 2007 Los Angeles Economic Development Corporation study, an estimated 59,000 jobs are attributable to LAX and located on or near the airport. The City of Los Angeles generates 158,000 jobs, and there are an additional 408, 000 jobs in the adjacent region. In short, 1 in 20 employment opportunities in the region is attributable to operations at LAX.

In 2009, LAX handled 58 million passengers, making it the third busiest airport in the United States and the sixth largest airport in the world. It remains the number one point-of-origin and point-of-destination airport in the world. During 2009, this meant that 75% of those passengers started or ended their flight at LAX, and the remaining 25% made connecting flights.

Apart from the costs of major changes in the nation's defense posture, we know that the economic impact of the 9/11 terrorist attacks were relatively short term. One of the first studies undertaken at the Department of Homeland Security National Center for Risk and Economic Analysis of Terrorism Events

---

[7] Tayseer Allouni, transcript of an interview with Osama bin Laden, October 21, 2001, translated from Arabic by the Institute for Islamic Studies and Research (www.alneda.com)

(CREATE) at the University of Southern California considered the short-term economic costs of an attack on the U.S. commercial air system. The basis of the analysis consisted of a model of a seven-day shutdown of the entire U.S. commercial air transportation system, followed by a two-year period of recovery, using the post-9/11 experience of the system. The resulting overall loss estimates for the seven-day period totalled $23.5 billion, and the two-year termination of air services yielded a projected loss of $248 to $394 billion.[8]

In real dollars, the 9/11 "attacks themselves caused approximately $40 billion in insurance losses, making it one of the largest insured events ever."[9] The cost of the 9/11 attacks in terms of the loss of pure physical assets plus initial cleanup and rescue efforts has been estimated at $28 billion. For a terror operation costing approximately $500,000, the return on investment, or "utility" of this attack was unprecedented. Unfortunately, based on current passenger figures ten years after the attack, LAX has yet to recover.

2.4 Aviation Security

In the 1960s, American airports maintained minimal security arrangements. Security strategy was focused on defeating aircraft hijackings, in response to the aforementioned incidents.

In the following decade, the industry introduced sky marshals, the predecessor to today's Federal Air Marshals Service (FAMS). Despite their deployment, insufficient staffing levels proved to be a detriment, as hijackings continued. Again, the Israelis were ahead of the curve when an onboard security officer prevented the February 18, 1969, attack of an EL AL plane by four terrorists. In the ensuing gun battle, two people, including one terrorist, were killed. These incidents prompted the Federal Aviation Administration (FAA) to respond, requiring the airlines to screen passengers and carry-on baggage by January 5, 1973.

The 9/11 attacks prompted even tougher security regulations, such as limiting the number of and types of items passengers could carry on board aircraft and requiring increased screening for passengers who fail to present government issued photo identification. Additionally, the Aviation and Transportation Security Act (ATSA) generally required that by November 19, 2002 all passenger screening was to be conducted by federal employees. As a result, passenger and

---

[8] Gordon, Peter. *The Economic Impacts of a Terrorist Attack on the U.S. Commercial Aviation System*. Center for Risk and Economic Analysis of Terrorism Events (CREATE) Report #05-026. (2005)

[9] Makinen, Gail (September 27, 2002). The Economic Effects of 9/11: A Retrospective Assessment. Congressional Research Service. pp. CRS–4. http://www.fas.org/irp/crs/RL31617.pdf

Layers of U.S. Aviation Security

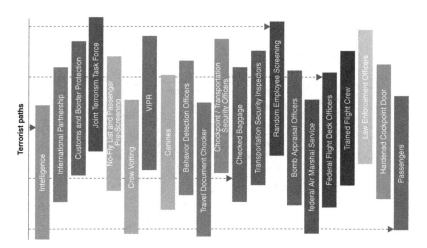

Figure 2.5. Transportation Security Administration, layers of U.S. aviation security in place today.

baggage screening is now provided by or in compliance with the Transportation Security Administration (TSA) Security Directives (SDs), as part of the Department of Homeland Security.

Prior to 9/11, private contractors provided security at category X airports, which are the largest and busiest in the United States as measured by volume of passenger traffic. As a result of that high volume level, category X airports, such as LAX, with potentially high kill-ratios onboard or on the ground, provide a high utility quotient for terrorists. The TSA, in accordance with successful "circles" of security models utilized in Israel, instituted its layers-of-security approach to American airport security (Figure 2.5). Some of these layers are invisible to the traveler and thus the attacker, and are designed to provide for the opportunity to detect, deter or defeat a terrorist attack.

2.5 LAX Terror History

LAX has been described by RAND as "a leader in implementing new security measures."[10] It was one of the first major airports to implement a 100%

---

[10] Stevens, Donald, Thomas Hamilton, Marvin Schaffer, Diana Dunham-Scott, Jamison Jo Medby, Edward W. Chan, John Gibson, Mel Eisman, Richard Mesic, Charles T. Kelley, Jr., Julie Kim, Tom LaTourrette, K. Jack Riley, *Implementing Security Improvement Options at Los Angeles International Airport,* Santa Monica, California: RAND Corporation, 2006.

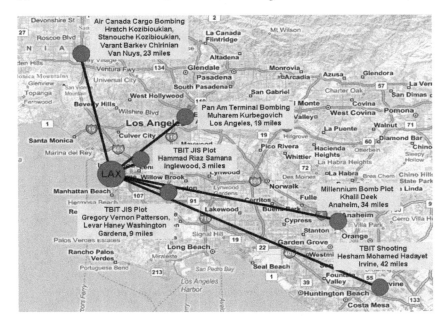

Figure 2.6. Residence locations of various attackers who have targeted LAX in relation to the airport.

baggage-screening program, to create a dedicated, and high-visibility police department, to use an on-site bomb squad and the largest number of explosives detection canine teams at any national airport, to employ and a dispersed central terminal design. Despite this level of protection, LAX is still viewed as an attractive target by some terrorist organizations, having been targeted six times – more than any other airport in the nation!

Since 1974, LAX has been the target of two bombings, two attempted bombings, one gun attack and one combination bombing/active shooter attack. All the attackers lived, worked or grew up within fifty miles of the airport (Figure 2.6).

In 1974, the "alphabet bomber" Muharem Kurbegovic, detonated a bomb in the LAX international terminal, killing three people, and injuring eight. At the time, it was described as the most destructive bomb ever detonated at an air terminal. In 1980, a bomb exploded in the China Airlines luggage processing facility, causing extensive damage but no injuries. In May 1982, three members of the Armenian Secret Army for the Liberation of Armenia were arrested after placing a bomb at the Air Canada cargo office. The bomb, defused by the Los Angeles Police Department Bomb Squad was the largest bomb they had neutralized to date.

In 1999, Ahmed Ressam was caught crossing into the United States with bomb-making equipment. His plan, later known as the Millennium Plot, was to detonate four timed luggage bombs inside and curbside the Tom Bradley International Terminal (TBIT). It was determined that "the millennium plotting in Canada in 1999 may have been part of Bin Laden's first serious attempt to implement a terrorist strike in the United States." Ressam told the FBI that he conceived the idea to attack LAX by himself, but that bin Laden lieutenant Abu Zubaydah encouraged him and helped facilitate the operation.[11]

On July 4, 2002, Hesham Hadayet approached the El Al counter at LAX carrying two handguns, and fired, killing two and injuring four. Hadayet, a limoshine driver, killed two people and injured four others, before being killed by an El Al security officer. In 2005, a radicalized al-Qaeda-based group called Jamiyyatt Ul Islam Saheeh (the Assembly of Authentic Islam) was formed in California's Folsom Prison by Kevin James. Once out of prison, James was joined by former Los Angeles gang member Levar Haney Washington, naturalized American and Pakistani national Hammad Riaz Samana and LAX employee Gregory Vernon Patterson. Their plot included another attack on the EL AL ticket counter. In addition to the LAX location, they targeted the Israeli consulate, two National Guard recruiting centers, and several synagogues in a plan consisting of simultaneous bombings and active shooter operations across Los Angeles. When the suspects were convicted, they admitted to being two weeks away from executing the attacks.

EL AL, the official airline of the State of Israel has been the target of half of the attacks at LAX. Historically, in addition to the Lod Airport Massacre, EL AL was victimized by simultaneous attacks at the Rome and Vienna airports on December 27, 1985. The attacks left 20 dead and 140 wounded when active shooters opened fire and threw grenades at travelers at El Al airline ticket counters.

2.6 RAND Study

In 2004, the RAND Corporation was commissioned by Los Angeles World Airports to conduct a series of studies on options for protecting the airport from terrorism. The resulting analysis identified 11 major classes (Figure 2.7) of attacks. These attacks were not the only possible attacks, but RAND determined them "to be the most likely and most difficult to prevent."[12] The classes of

---

[11] Bergen, Peter L., *The Osama bin Laden I Know*. Free Press, New York, N.Y. (2006) pp. 289–290.
[12] Stevens, Donald et al., Implementing Security Improvement Options at Los Angeles International Airport. RAND Corporation (2006) p.viii.

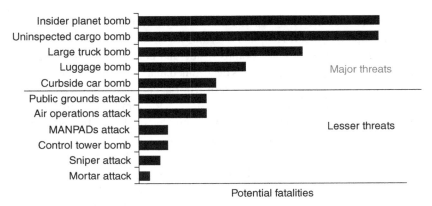

Figure 2.7. Band Corporation analysis (2004) of possible terror threats to LAX.

attacks in the following ascending order were: mortar attack, sniper attack, control tower bomb, MANPADS attack, air operations attack, public ground attack, curbside bomb attack, luggage bomb, large truck bomb, uninspected cargo bomb, and insider planted bomb. The top-5 scenarios involve explosive devices, vehicle, and/or employee access. The report served as the cornerstone for the reorganization of command, control, and operational aspect of the Los Angeles World Airport Police Division.

Closer examination of the major threats yielded an interesting collection of potential attack methodologies and the attacker. Regarding methodology, what became readily apparent was the repeated option to utilize an IED. The global terrorist attack lexicon consists of chemical, biological, radiological, nuclear, and explosive (CBRNE) options, with increasing concerns of the cyber threat. Because of its low cost, transportability, and lethality, the IED, conventional or dirty, was the weapon of most concern.

The second and most important concern is the attacker – the human element. The "insider planted bomb" and the "uninspected cargo bomb" scenarios were placed at the top of the Major Threats category, understanding the tactical advantage presented if an attacker could be employed at the airport, preferably in a position with access to the facility, critical airport information or both. LAX would understand the importance of RAND's assessment inasmuch as the JIS Plot disrupted the next year, involved an attacker who was an airport employee.

In addition to the RAND study, LAX is routinely evaluated as part of a joint vulnerability assessment (JVA) by the TSA and FBI. LAX was also the subject of a security study and a peer review summary conducted by personnel from Israel's Ben Gurion International Airport in 2006, 2008 and 2011, respectively.

2.7 Los Angeles World Airports Police

The Los Angeles World Airports (LAWA) Police Division, a division of the Los Angeles World Airports department of the City of Los Angeles, is the primary law enforcement agency at LAX. The organization maintains the largest airport law enforcement agency in the United States, with more than 1,000 sworn and civilian personnel. Staffing levels of 536 police officers, and 374 traffic and security officers, reflect increases of 49% and 57% respectively since the 9/11 attacks. The agency's uniformed presence has increased more than 52% over the same time period, supported by a budget of almost $100 million. The LAWA Police Division is further supported by Los Angeles Police Department officers located onsite, for an additional $19 million. As a result, approximately 23% of the LAX operating budget is dedicated to police resources.

The LAWA Police Division acted upon the RAND recommendations by reorganizing the homeland security operations and instituting the Office of Homeland Security and Intelligence. The reorganization facilitated an effective response to the five major terror scenarios by assigning the responsibilities for all terrorism and airport security credentialing activities under the auspices one organizational element. In addition to ensuring an efficient and effective counter-terrorism strategy, the design was intended to reduce bureaucracy, increase individual unit responsibility, and ensure management accountability. This Office consisted of the Critical Infrastructure Protection Unit, Vulnerability Assessment and Analysis Unit, Emergency Services Unit, Dignitary Protection Unit, Canine Unit, and the Security Credential Unit.

2.7.1 Critical Infrastructure Protection Unit (CIPU)

The CIPU is charged with identifying all structures on LAWA property that are essential to the operation of the airport and developing a criticality assessment based on the National Infrastructure Protection Plan model, per Homeland Security Presidential Directive-7 (HSPD-7). This directive mandates the identification, prioritization, and protection of the nation's critical infrastructure. Understanding that terrorist organizations conduct extensive assessments of the criticality of potential targets during their decision-making process, the identification of these facilities is a crucial element of any counterterrorism strategy. The CIPU also develops, plans, practices, facilitates, and continually updates the framework by which law enforcement and other public safety agencies respond to and operate within LAX during unusual occurrences and emergency situations. CIPU also coordinates and participates in ongoing interdisciplinary research and development efforts in collaboration with the DHS Science and Technology Directorate.

2.7.2 Vulnerability Assessment and Analysis Unit (VAAU)

The VAAU is the operational unit responsible for the coordination of the security activities of all persons and property at LAX. This unit is critical to the safe movement of passengers, cargo, and airport employees in compliance with appropriate federal security regulations. The CIPU and VAAU work in concert with local, state, and federal regulatory airport partners, managing the Cargo Security Task Force. Each month, the task force conducts unannounced inspections of cargo facilities to evaluate all personnel-, security-, and safety-related compliance issues. At its inception, the Cargo Security Task Force was believed to be the only interagency operation of its kind in the nation. With the growing concern regarding this specific terror threat, LAX has provided the national model.

2.7.3 Emergency Services Unit (ESU)

The ESU is a rapid-response unit for major incidents, emergency calls, unusual occurrences, and tactical situations with the intent to identify, neutralize and/or stabilize the incident or threat until follow-on resources with a greater capability and/or jurisdictional responsibility than currently deployed arrive. ESU augments other responding law enforcement and/or public safety resources to ensure an appropriate level of force is maintained following established protocols. This unit provides support to the patrol operations functions during heightened security alert levels and special-problem assignments. Most important, ESU provides primary support for high-risk or security-sensitive flights, particularly EL AL.

Inasmuch as EL AL has been targeted three times since the new millennium, the ESU provides special weapons and tactics security for EL AL passengers during ticketing/check-in, escorts their busses to the terminal and remains on the airfield until the aircraft departs. In addition to their already unique skillset, all members of ESU have completed the DHS Prevention and Response to Suicide Bombing Incidents Training Course. EL AL has stated LAX is the only airport outside of Israel that affords them this level of security.

2.7.4 Canine Unit

The Explosives Detection Canine Unit is responsible for deterring and detecting the introduction of explosive devices into the transportation system. This is accomplished using high visibility in public areas and by conducting random and directed searches of cargo facilities, terminals, U.S. mail, aircraft, and baggage areas. Their most important function is the response to investigate unattended bags and vehicles. LAWA Police also deploy "dual-trained" canine teams, assigned to criminal suspect searches, in addition to their explosives detection duties.

2.7.5 Dignitary Protection Unit (DPU)

The DPU provides appropriate training for 104 Los Angeles-based consulates. DPU is responsible for facilitating the safe and efficient movement of dignitaries, politicians and other high profile persons into and out of LAX. In addition to serving as a liaison to a variety of protective agencies from around the world, DPU also coordinates appropriate intelligence information to ensure current situational awareness for the protectee. DPU personnel undergo specialized training as provided by several federal law enforcement VIP protection agencies.

2.7.6 Intelligence Section

A DPU Investigator of the LAWA Police Division is assigned to the FBI Joint Terrorism Task Force (JTTF) and the Los Angeles Joint Regional Intelligence Center (LA-JRIC), respectively. The JTTF is a partnership of local, state, and federal law enforcement agencies, which was piloted in 1980 in New York City in a memorandum of understanding (MOU) between the New York Police Department and the FBI. There are now more than 100 JTTFs nationwide and at least one at each of the 57 FBI field offices, except Portland, Oregon. Due to the terror threat level and history of attacks on LAX, there is a JTTF housed onsite. Joint Terrorism Task Forces are charged with taking action against acts of terrorism. Their activities include investigation, surveillance, intelligence source development, electronic monitoring, and interviews.

The LA-JRIC is one of the first "fusion" centers initiated in the United States. Its mission is to collect information using an all-crimes approach, convert the information into operational intelligence, and disseminate the intelligence to prevent terrorist attacks and combat crime in the Central District of California. Inasmuch as a LAWA Police Investigator is assigned to the center, LAX is provided global situational awareness of raw and actionable intelligence.

2.7.7 Security Credential Section

The duties of the Security Credential Section are to effectively direct, control, monitor and coordinate access and movement in restricted areas. LAX maintains more than 45,000 active badge holders, with more than 850 companies enrolled in the badging system. Their section processes almost 500 transactions daily for applicants, current employees, and contractors.

2.7.8 Airport Security Advisory Committee

In addition to LAWA Police and LAPD, the airport is home to several law enforcement, fire, emergency management, and regulatory agencies. In 2004, LAWA Police Division took the lead in developing the Airport Security Advisory Committee (ASAC). The ASAC convenes top-level representatives from public safety, security and emergency response agencies, in addition to airport stakeholders to regularly assess, prioritize, and recommend appropriate policies, procedures, and technologies to myriad related issues facing the airport.

2.8 Terrorist Operational Planning Cycle

Al-Qaeda remains a transnational threat despite the lack of state sponsorship or a region it can call home. A terrorist organization could not survive for more than two decades without being adaptive, innovative, and flexible.

Terrorist groups, particularly al-Qaeda, conduct surveillance and reconnaissance to select potential targets and gain strong situational awareness of the target's activities, design, facility vulnerabilities, and security operations. Because part of the preoperational surveillance involves establishing patterns, terrorists conduct surveillance multiple times. However, the more often they conduct surveillance, the greater the chances that they will be observed. If this happens, the defender has an opportunity to disrupt the attack path by alerting security personnel that something is being planned.

Al-Qaeda training guidebooks, including the infamous "Military Studies in the Jihad against the Tyrants," and their online training magazines instruct operatives to perform surveillance and detail what types of information to gather. In July 2004, the arrest in Pakistan of an individual identified by U.S. officials as Mohammad Naeem Noor Khan revealed that his personal computer contained detailed information about potential economic targets in the United States, including the Gas Cylinders plot of Barot. The targets included the New York Stock Exchange and Citigroup headquarters in New York, the International Monetary Fund and World Bank buildings in Washington, D.C., Prudential Financial headquarters in Newark, New Jersey, and locations in the United Kingdom, including Heathrow Airport. From the information on the computer, it appeared that the targets had been under surveillance for an extended period.

In the case of the aforementioned pre-attack planning cycle, there was a high degree of detail and awareness of site vulnerabilities, security operations, law enforcement and emergency response at the time the reports were written. In addition to intelligence obtained from surveillance, each of the surveillance reports exhibited extensive use of open sources to obtain much of the background information on the target. It should be noted the report provided for

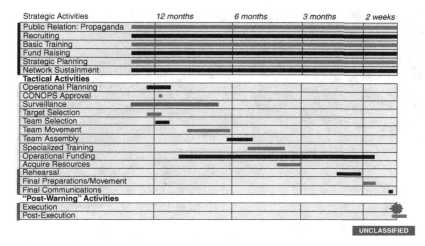

Strategic Activities	12 months	6 months	3 months	2 weeks
Public Relation: Propaganda				
Recruiting				
Basic Training				
Fund Raising				
Strategic Planning				
Network Sustainment				
Tactical Activities				
Operational Planning				
CONOPS Approval				
Surveillance				
Target Selection				
Team Selection				
Team Movement				
Team Assembly				
Specialized Training				
Operational Funding				
Acquire Resources				
Rehearsal				
Final Preparations/Movement				
Final Communications				
"Post-Warning" Activities				
Execution				
Post-Execution				

Figure 2.8. Generic al-Qaeda operational planning cycle.

alternative targets in the event attacking the primary site proved to be logistically unfeasible. The focus on collecting data on alternate, less protected locations indicates al Qaeda's interest in softer targets. This may be reflective of al Qaeda's evolution from a centrally directed organization to a more decentralized structure with individual units possessing greater control over target selection.

Surveillance can last as little as one week or take place over several years in advance of an attack, and can be used to support target selection, midoperation reconnaissance, and final, pre-attack reconnaissance. The surveillance activity is typically conducted in a covert manner and can involve any number of collectors (surveillants) either on foot or in vehicles. Figure 2.8 shows a generic operational planning cycle. Successful counter-surveillance can yield indications of an attack in the planning phase. The problem is separating "terrorism" from "tourism." Herein lies the importance of employing future counter-terrorism strategies that will facilitate "looking for the bombers and not the bombs."

2.9 CREATE Pilot Project

As identified previously, the National Center for Risk and Economic Analysis of Terrorism Events (CREATE) is an interdisciplinary national research center based at the University of Southern California and funded by the Department of Homeland Security (Figure 2.9). The Center is focused on risk and economic

Figure 2.9. The CREATE research center.

analysis of the U.S. infrastructure and comprises a team of experts from twenty universities from across the country and the nations of Australia, Israel, and the United Kingdom. It is the first of twelve existing Centers of Excellence in the nation.

As previously described, the al-Qaeda planning cycle depends on the comprehensive situational awareness acquired via pre-attack surveillance and reconnaissance of the intended target. It is most important for the attackers to determine the design and level of physical security, including protective policies, procedures, and technology. A team of researchers at CREATE led by Dr. Milind Tambe, working with our department, developed software that would offer assistance regarding the deployment of critical terrorism countermeasures. Dr. Tambe's expertise is in the area of security in multi-agent systems by policy randomization.

The RAND study identified vehicles that could access LAX through six unsecured access roadways. Inasmuch as there were no checkpoints at which to examine incoming vehicles for bombs, the subsequent recommendations in 2004 included infrastructure investments for permanent vehicle checkpoints. Our challenge became influencing the behavior of an adversary that would use a VBIED (Vehicle-borne improvised explosive device) based on our understanding of terror planning cycles requiring periods of surveillance and of attack rehearsals.

Dr. Tambe suggested that the solution required shaping the situation so that in any attack scenario the intended outcomes from the terrorists' point of view

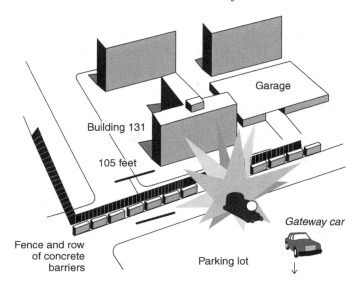

Figure 2.10. Drawing of the 1996 Khobar Towers bombing.

are unacceptable. Thus, he confirmed the RAND study with regard to recommending a "deterrence" strategy designed to present countermeasures which presented themselves as unpredictable. The goal of our project was to leverage Dr. Tambe's success by randomizing vehicle the checkpoints that would be deployed along airport access roads, rendering LAX as an unsatisfactory target, not worth a terrorist's effort or investment.

More than 50,000 vehicles and 165,000 people enter LAX daily. Actionable intelligence, accompanied by education, awareness, and technology are essential resources to be effective in these efforts. A debrief of the June 25, 1996, bombing on the Khobar Towers (Figures 2.10 and 2.11), determined the target was surveilled more than forty times over a seventeen-month period by the same three attackers. On at least ten of those reconnaissance missions, the attackers visited the site in the same vehicle. The need to detect the surveillance activity and determine the stage of the plot relative to the execution date exacerbates the challenge for security forces.

The resulting pilot program was named ARMOR – Assistant for Randomized Monitoring Over Routes. ARMOR was based on Bayesian Stackelberg game theory and developed to allow for the input of certain constraints regarding the checkpoint, the avoidance of certain days for deployment, and the necessity for the checkpoint to be in effect during specific times during the day. Based on these constraints, the program provided a randomized schedule, in conjunction

Figure 2.11. Khobar Towers.

with a mathematical measure of randomness. Additional features are added to the program to facilitate the input of the constraints and create a report at the end of a checkpoint in operation.

Such scheduling is based on several requirements:

a) Scheduling must be randomized to avoid predictability.
b) Scheduling must take into account constraints of officers at LAX.
c) Scheduling must take into account passenger load data.
d) Scheduling must also take into account other possible resource constraints, dynamic shifts, and so on.

The USC CREATE team focused on the scheduling problem in a multiphased approach. The first phase focused on scheduling checkpoints, in particular, on using criteria (a) and (b). The checkpoints (Figure 2.12) were staffed by LAWA police officers, explosives detection canine officers, and traffic and security personnel who were assigned the task of sweeping under vehicle chassis for IEDs and TSA behavioral detection officers who observed behaviors of the driver and other occupants in the vehicle.

The next step in the project incorporated the explosives-detection canine team deployment into the program development. Inasmuch as LAWA maintains thirty

Figure 2.12. ARMOR checkpoint: Century Boulevard entrance to LAX.

six explosives detection canine teams, LAX is the ideal environment for this research.

2.10 Summary

Counterterrorism is a risk-management proposition. Our goal is to contain the threat through deterrence, detection, and defense. Unfortunately, until a terrorist is taken into custody and admits that a specific security scheme influenced his planning, as some suggest Richard Reid did after his experience at Ben Gurion, we will never know how many times we have thwarted an attack. Quantifying prevention and protection is always a daunting endeavor. The lack of terrorists' testimony or other evidence regarding the LAX security enhancement provided by the ARMOR system renders the concept of operations vulnerable to scrutiny by academic disciplines seeking demonstrable, quantifiable, deterrence value. This is an age-old law enforcement challenge. How does one measure a nonevent?

Inasmuch as LAX is the nation's leading airport terrorist target, we were not seeking just "any research solution," but an intelligent countermeasure that considered terrorists' target priorities and their reaction to our actions. Appropriately, LAX maintains the most robust airport homeland security resources in the nation. The responsible management of those resources is always a priority. ARMOR facilitated the ability to deploy our personnel in an unpredictable design in response to an ongoing threat. As a result, we were able to support a diversity of security layers, some overt and some covert, in a manner that allowed us to be as agile as our opponent.

The fact is that an interdisciplinary countermeasure has been developed, implemented, and advertised without compromising the integrity of the system. It provides LAX protective schemes with the opportunity to become unpredictable, a significant hurdle for an adversary dependent upon definitive patterns and routines for the purpose of developing a successful attack path. The death of Osama bin Laden does alter the terrorist focus on the aviation domain. The utility of a successful attack could result in a high kill-ratio and major disruption in transportation infrastructure, and would undermine public confidence in our security strategies.

The results of this premier engagement in "Research Transition," that is, research that transitions directly from the laboratory to the field and the operator(s), could not have been anticipated. The LAWA Police Division's Office of Homeland Security and Intelligence responded to inquiries from a host of U.S. federal agencies and countries around the world. ARMOR has been briefed to DHS Secretaries Michael Chertoff and Janet Napolitano, numerous Members of Congress, at the Joint Chiefs of Staff Level-IV antiterrorism seminars, and in testimony before the full Congressional Committee on Homeland Security. ARMOR continues to be sought after by entities attempting to address similar complex problems associated with the threat of terrorism.

3

Maritime Transportation System Security and the Use of Game Theory: A Perfect Match to Address Operational and Tactical Concerns

Dr. Joe DiRenzo III,
Lieutenant Commander Ben Maule, Lieutenant
Commander Erik Jensen,
and Lieutenant Fred S. Bertsch IV

Since the days of Sparta and Athens the use of the world's Maritime Transportation System (MTS) to move goods and services has been a critical facet of a nation's economic well-being. The MTS served as a "center of gravity" with nations trading as far away as distant continents or as close as two ports located in the same country or region. Corbett and Winebrake (2008: 6) summarized that the MTS "is an integral, if sometimes less publicly visible, part of the global economy" and that the MTS consists of "a network of specialized vessels, the ports they visit, and transportation infrastructure from factories to terminals to distribution centers to market." The security of this system is imperative as goods move through the ports and waterways within national boundaries, into the littorals, and out into the world-wide Global Maritime Commons.

The issue of security within this global system is complicated because the number of attack vectors and methods an adversary can take are endless. The attackers also hold an advantage in their ability to select the time, place, and method of an attack ... and to abort an attack if counterdetection occurs. The introduction of suicide attackers has made the security challenge even more daunting as bombers are willing to give their own lives for their cause. Pape (2003: 344) noted that "suicide terrorism is strategic. The vast majority of suicide attacks are not isolated or random acts by individual fanatics." Pape (2003: 344) further adds that "the most promising way to contain suicide terrorism is to reduce terrorists' confidence in their ability to carry out such attacks on the target society." Pape's commentary goes beyond suicide attacks and can be

51

applied to security threats across the MTS. There remains a question of how best to apply efforts to afford security forces maximum opportunity to address aggressor movements. Using game theory may be effective in reducing risks in the MTS, which would have global implications.

To fully understand the complexity of MTS security and how game theory could be applied to it, one can take a closer look at the fundamental variables of risk using the widely accepted formula: risk = threat × vulnerability × consequence. MTS security is challenged by a wide range of threats that may exploit vulnerabilities anywhere within a vast MTS global infrastructure. The United States, for example, has over 95,000 miles of coastline and 361 ports, and it hosts thousands of visits by foreign flagged vessels a year. Of special concern are ports and waterways with limited maneuverability and natural international choke points, such as the Houston Ship Channel, the Straits of Gibraltar, the Bab El Mandeb Strait, and the Gulf of Aden. A successful attack in one of these points could have cascading consequences throughout the world.

In this chapter we concentrate on one category of threat to MTS security – specifically, how game theory may be useful in analysis of the small boat attack vector. History has underscored that this method has been extremely popular. The attacks against the Arleigh Burke-class destroyer USS *Cole* in October 2000 in Yemen and the super-tanker *M/V Limburg* in October 2002 illustrate how large vessels, whether warships or large oil tank vessels, are vulnerable to a ramming attack by small vessels carrying explosives. Small vessels as attack vectors have also been successfully used by pirates off the coast of Somalia against merchant vessels, such as the *Maersk Alabama*, on April 8, 2009.

Although the attacks off the coast of Somalia have taken place as many as 300 miles or more offshore, ships ultimately face the greatest vulnerability during slow port and restricted waterway transits. Attacks within ports can be realized through physical attacks against critical infrastructure, facilities, or actual vessels. Disruptions to the MTS can also be realized through secondary effects such as impeding vessel transits, for example, channel mining and blocking, which can interrupt commerce for prolonged periods of time. The potential of an asymmetric threat via subsurface means, such as swimmers and submersibles, also exists. These methods have been used by Sri Lanka's Tamil Tigers. These types of attacks create havoc in the MTS and have the potential to significantly disrupt national economies and even the global economy.

Ships may not be the only targets for a small boat attack – infrastructure along the MTS from chemical plants to water treatment plants should also be considered targets. Currently, security authorities led by the U.S. Coast Guard assess existing risk to identified maritime critical infrastructure and key resources

(MCIKR) in order to prioritize response capabilities, identify layered defenses through coordination with other agencies, and create deterrence.

There are many methods making a potential target for less attractive. Internationally, many countries have begun to require the owners and operators of ships and port facilities to develop comprehensive security plans. However, large commercial vessels are limited in their ability to prevent waterborne improvised explosive attacks, particularly in confined waterways. Other countries, such as the United States, have developed port security plans that augment the individual ship and port facility security plans. These port-level plans highlight the governments' responsibility to protect MCIKR from terrorist attacks, such as small vessel attacks against deep draft vessels. However, one can spend significant resources "hardening" a target to make it more resistant to attack by erecting physical barriers, which may also hinder the free flow of goods and services.

Another option available to security authorities is to leverage existing efforts by partnering with other agencies. If the partner agencies are already conducting patrols that are in the vicinity of MCIKR but that were not previously dedicated to actively patrolling the MCIKR, the efforts of the partner agencies may contribute to deterrence by their mere presence and visibility. Stressed budgets at all levels of government – federal, state, and local – make considerations of coordinated security efforts more difficult; however, it is critical that the effort to create this surgery be made. Surveillance and security systems, roving foot patrols aboard and surrounding facilities, active escorts of transiting vessels, and randomizing patrol efforts are all efforts that should be considered to help reduce the occurrence of maritime terrorism events. However, many of these are expensive to implement. We propose that the application of game theory may provide appropriate insights into how to best address these challenges.

Within the security field, game theory is often used to represent a decision-making process occurring between two competing entities. The attacker entity attempts to destroy a target that is protected by the defender entity. This framework, which is often used in homeland security, applies particularly well to the dilemmas between security forces and terrorists. In the maritime domain for instance, the U.S. Coast Guard conducts various security efforts, such as escorts, boardings, and patrols, to deter, prevent, and disrupt potential terrorist attacks. The Coast Guard, represented as defenders in the game theory model, must determine the best strategy for minimizing the risk or damage to the nation and its citizens. Conversely, the attackers, terrorists in this example, seek the opposite goals, attempting to maximize the damage they inflict. The damage from an attack, which varies depending on many factors, including the type of attack executed, the response by security forces, and the vulnerability of the target to attack, is represented in the game as the payoff (or expected utility). The terrorists receive larger positive numbers for the more damage they inflict; whereas, the Coast Guard receives larger negative numbers for higher damage, which is seen as a representation of the failure of its security plan. In perhaps the simplest application of game theory, both participants act simultaneously and without knowledge of the other's actions.

The simplified version of a game theory situation depicted in the following chart represents a zero-sum game in which the payoff represents the damage done in millions of dollars. Therefore, the damage from a successful attack is considered a negative result for the Coast Guard and a positive result for the terrorists when both organizations are attempting to maximize their expected utility. The negative number for the Coast Guard indicates that its security plan failed by that magnitude, which corresponds with the amount of damage accomplished by the terrorists. For the Coast Guard, the closer the number is to zero, to or being positive, the better the outcome; whereas the terrorists want the largest possible positive number. The Coast Guard can choose between two different security plans just as the terrorist can choose between two different attacks, as the following chart shows:

Attack on a vessel	Terrorist Attack Plan #1	Terrorist Attack s Plan #2
Coast Guard Security Plan #1	–4, 4	–8, 8
Coast Guard Security Plan #2	–2, 2	–4, 4

In this hypothetical situation, an equilibrium point based on dominated strategies is reached because no matter what option the opposing player chooses, the player acting rationally, meaning that it always makes the decision that best accomplishes their desired outcome, will always choose the same action. In this case the Security Plan #2 for the Coast Guard maximizes its expected utility because no matter what type of attack the terrorists choose, plan #2 minimizes the damage, that is, provides the maximum expected utility for the Coast Guard. For the terrorist Attack Plan #2 is for similar reasons also a dominant strategy, leading to this equilibrium point.

Despite the limitations and simplifications involved in this particular application of game theory, these types of models can still provide potentially useful information to security analysts. Based on the specifics in the previous example, the Coast Guard's security analysts may be attempting to assess the difference between conducting an escort of a vessel with one armed boat (Coast Guard Security Plan #1) or two armed boats (Coast Guard Security Plan #2). It could be hypothesized, based on the known resources and capabilities of the terrorist organization, that the terrorist has the alternative of conducting an attack against the vessel with either a rocket-propelled grenade (Terrorist Attack Plan #1) or a small boat (Terrorist Attack Plan #2). In this situation, the security analysts can clearly establish that providing an armed, two-boat escort for the vessel is always desirable, regardless of the attack mode of the terrorists. In this scenario, the terrorists also determine that they can maximize their intended outcome by attacking with a small boat regardless of the security plan implemented by the Coast Guard.

Although it is useful in analyzing specific examples like the one outlined, this simplified application of game theory limits the usefulness of the game-theory approach. At a minimum, the application of game theory can be expanded by including more choices for the two players involved, as shown with the previous example. Potential alternatives for the Coast Guard to consider could be providing no escort, utilizing three boats for the escort, combining small-boat escorts with a larger, more capable vessel, or even integrating a port security system consisting of cameras, barriers, and security zones. Similarly, the options for terrorists expand exponentially to include attack scenarios that incorporate divers, mines, aircraft, and many other possibilities. Such a scenario might result in the following expression of the expected payoffs:

Attack on a vessel	Terrorist RPG	Terrorist small boat	Terrorist diver	Terrorist multiple small boats
Coast Guard one-boat escort	–4, 4	–8, 8	–6, 6	–10, 10
Coast Guard two-boat escort	–2, 2	–4, 4	–4, 4	–6, 6
Coast Guard boat and cutter escort	–1, 1	–4, 4	–3, 3	–4, 4
Coast Guard boat escort and port security system	–2, 2	–2, 2	–6, 6	–4, 4

In this instance, no dominant strategy exists for either the terrorists or the Coast Guard since the optimal choice for each one of them depends on what the other chooses. Although this application is beneficial to determining the effects of security efforts in reducing risk, it still fails to account for numerous intricacies involved in real-life decisions, such as uncertainty and the value of targets.

The basic game theory approach demonstrated here assumes that the participants make simultaneous decisions and that no knowledge by either entity regarding the other's action is known ahead of time. In real life, this is unrealistic. For instance, security forces like the Coast Guard conduct active intelligence gathering and monitor terrorist capabilities. Meanwhile, terrorists, like individual citizens or tourists, are able to observe or study security efforts prior to initiating their decision to attack, gaining beneficial information that may allow them to improve their utility and decision making. Game theory can then be adapted to employ a sequential decision-making process that better reflects of reality. Applying a sequential decision-making process to the previous scenario, the security forces would adapt and implement a plan first, which the terrorists are then able to observe, gathering additional knowledge to use in determining the plan to employ for a terrorist attack.

For the port scenario, it is likely that terrorists would use divers if the Coast Guard's security effort were a combination of a boat escort and port security system as described previously; whereas, in response to other security efforts, the terrorists could use multiple small boats for an attack. Representing the scenario as a decision tree reflects the sequential nature of the game, that is, security forces are forced to implement a strategy and then the terrorists are able to adapt a plan in response. The last two branches for this example are displayed in Figure 3.1.

The foregoing examples, while applicable to numerous security elements besides the Coast Guard and terrorism, are limited in scope and fail to reap the entire benefit of more advanced game theory applications. In those examples, the game was structured as a zero-sum game. The utility between the two entities always added to zero; meaning that as one did better the other did worse, and vice versa. In reality, however, costs and benefits are hardly ever zero-sum situations. Instead, the results from an effort may have a net impact that may be greater or less than zero because the benefit to one player does not correspond to a comparable loss by the other. Such a situation could arise when the costs of security efforts are incorporated into the expected utility. For example, implementing security efforts within the MTS may hinder or cause

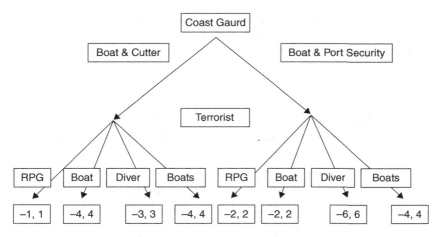

Figure 3.1. The last two branches of the port scenario decision tree.

commerce, the costs of delays which need to be incorporated into the final outcomes, along with the security benefits.

Depending on the game setup, these additional costs may only affect one player, for example, the shipping industry, decreasing its utility over what the associated utility increase is for the terrorists. Similarly, security efforts require resources and funding which could offset the benefits gained by efforts implemented by agencies such as Customs and Border Protection, the Coast Guard, and Immigration and Customs Enforcement. Revisiting our first example, these impacts are displayed in the following chart for the scenario that the Coast Guard Security Plan #1 cost $2 million to implement while Security Plan #2 cost $5 million to implement. As the chart demonstrates, there is no dominant strategy for the Coast Guard since the optimal strategy depends on the expected attack by the terrorist.

Attack on a vessel	Terrorist Attack Plan #1	Terrorist Attack Plan #2
Coast Guard Security Plan #1	−6, 4	−10, 8
Coast Guard Security Plan #2	−7, 2	−9, 4

Attackers are not immune to costs and impacts from lost opportunities either. Certain attacks require more resources which will influence their net results. This is particularly true when they can not stop the attack chain once it has started or if their resources are limited. For instance, if terrorists seeking to carry out a radiological attack have enough material to conduct one attack may opt for a plan, then with potentially less destruction but a higher probability of success. These influences of resources can be modeled for terrorists in game theory models just as they are modeled for defenders.

Besides the attacker-defender situation, game theory can also be used in the maritime environment to analyze efforts among or between security and shipping entities. These models do not necessarily involve an attacker and a defender but instead incorporate two players with similar interests. For instance, the prisoner's dilemma situation in classic game theory of a can be used to assess decisions facing countries, companies, and security forces. As in the typical prisoner's dilemma in which prisoners each act independently and separately from their accomplices, companies contemplating implementing security efforts may face similar situations. As demonstrated in the following chart, maritime shipping company A could implement security efforts, achieving $3 million in additional sales if company B also implements security efforts. However, company A receives no additional sales if company B does not also implement security. Company B however, would receive $5 million in additional sales if it does not implement the security while Company A did. The opposite is true if Company A and B reverse their decisions.

Additional sales in millions of $	Company B implements security	Company B does not implement security
Company A implements security	3, 3	0, 5
Company A does not implement security	5, 0	1, 1

In this dilemma, assuming the companies act independently and in their own self-interest, both would opt to not implement security in order to maximize their profits. In a slightly different twist, the companies may compare the number of attempted terrorist attacks when the companies implements security efforts against the decision to not implement the security efforts. In this scenario, described in the following chart, both companies would decide to implement security efforts in order to minimize the number of attempted terrorist attacks. This means that, irrespective of the other company's action, it is in each company's best interests to implement security efforts. Applying game theory to similar situations could demonstrate the dilemmas that countries face when countries deciding whether or not to implement security efforts in their ports as well as whether or not to arm vessels with security teams to protect against pirate attacks.

Attempted terrorist attacks per year	Company B implements security	Company B does not implement security
Company A implements security	2, 2	1, 8
Company A does not implement security	8, 1	4, 4

The foregoing dilemmas remain based on noncooperative games in which the participants work separately to achieve the best benefits according to their own self-interest. However, advanced game theory applications account for cooperation between entities. This is critical in modeling reality and the complexities facing decision makers. As shown in the first example between the two companies, if both companies would implement security together, then both would receive more sales than if both do not implement the security efforts. In a cooperative game, two players are able to work together and form binding agreements to assure each other's actions. Cooperation is often based on a legal or binding agreement.

Game theory can also be used to analyze the decisions made by countries and companies to participate in international security efforts, for example, the Customs Trade Partnership Against Terrorism (C-TPAT). C-TPAT is a voluntary security program launched by the U.S. Customs and Border Protection Agency that provides benefits to member companies in return for their participation and agreement to increased *security efforts on the members' behalves*. In return for agreeing to increased security levels, conducting self-audits, and participating in the program, companies are subject to fewer inspections, have improved cargo processing time, and face fewer examinations.

The incorporation of information into game theory analysis is an important step in modeling real-world situations as well. As previously discussed, players in a sequential game often have information regarding the state of the game following the first player's actions. Rarely is the information completely perfect, as is assumed in our previous Coast Guard example. It is far more likely that the second player only has partial information, often called "imperfect information," about the first player's actions or the state of the modeled game. Advanced game theory techniques can help model situations in which knowledge is only partially known. For example, a terrorist planning an attack on a piece of waterside MCIKR may only be able to observe a portion of the security efforts, such as maritime patrols or waterside barriers. The terrorist might not be able to account for hidden defense measures, such as response teams or intrusion detection devices, and instead must make decisions based on partial information. Similar situations arise for analysis by game theory with cooperative security efforts between countries. Countries may not always share all the details of their maritime security efforts and response capabilities with their allies, keeping some information secret in hidden. The incorporation of probability and uncertainty into game theory allows analysts to model such scenarios by reflecting how the players may respond based on limited information.

Modeling imperfect information in a game-theoretic framework can also be used to simulate deceptive actions. Security forces working with limited resources often try to present an image of stronger security than they actually have, hoping to deceive the attackers into believing an attack will be tougher to execute than it actually is, thereby deterring the attack. The reverse may also occur, with terrorists attempting to deceive defenders into planning for one type of attack or to invest in security at one location when the true intentions of the terrorists may be to attack elsewhere or in a different manner. These kinds of efforts are again modeled using probability in game theory applications because imperfect information also leads into variability and uncertainty.

Reality does not allow for every aspect of a game to be determined or known. Some uncontrollable factors may impact the decisions made and outcomes.This is accomplished by introducing probability into a game, known as a Bayesian game. These games can be used to model each player's beliefs about the other player's capabilities and account for randomness in events and outcomes. For maritime security, Bayesian games allow a system to be developed that reflects the defender's latest intelligence and knowledge about adversaries. Incorporating knowledge of the adversary's capabilities and desires allows weights based on probabilities or probability functions to be assigned to more likely or desirable attacks, better reflecting actual decision making by players in the real world. Whereas all these examples and brief descriptions are focused on two-player games and a small subset of decision making, game theory is expandable to incorporate multiple players and decisions. This is a critical component for the MTS and its numerous stakeholders.

Game theory has extensive application potential to the complex decision environment faced in the maritime domain. One of the most highly debated security efforts within the MTS involves the use of inspections. Inspections occur throughout the system in a variety of ways, ranging from document inspections to individuals' inspecting vessels, or even x-ray systems inspecting containers. Proposed and actual strategies range from conducting random inspections to inspecting of every container. Applying game theory to the inspection process allows analysts to model and analyze the decision-making process to determine the best strategy. The game developed can be set up and analyzed in a variety of ways, from determining which inspection strategy hinders terrorists the most to identifying the strategy that encourages the participation and cooperation of private industry. It would be beneficial for such decisions as determining whether ports should install radiological detection systems or establish an intrusive, physical-inspection strategy for government agencies like Customs and Border Protection.

Game theory can also be beneficial to security forces in determining their best use of assets. While many security efforts rely on randomizing efforts to avoid giving the adversaries an advantage in planning attacks, uniform randomization of these efforts often exposes more valuable targets or fails to optimally use the limited resources. Instead, game theory can accommodate the incorporation of weights and target value for various items into the decision-making process as well as account for the opponents' reactions to security efforts. Doing so within the maritime domain can promote more effective patrolling of MCIKR, efficient boarding of high-interest vessels, and can even help determine a strategy for conducting random escorts of vessels.

A Coast Guard station responsible for a large port may be required to randomly patrol and visually inspect numerous pieces of MCIKR. Treating them all equally may not be appropriate, depending on the goals of the terrorist or the risk associated with the target. Instead, randomizing the patrols based on weighted criteria could improve the overall expected outcome of the game and achieve better results by protecting higher value targets or areas more vulnerable to attack with the limited resource available. These same principles could be applied to randomizing customs agents' inspection schedules and locations throughout the United States, planning surge periods in security activities in various U.S. ports, and even establishing a schedule of random patrols by Navy vessels to counter piracy.

Protecting a port, its facilities, and the activities that occur in it requires significant resources and effort. Numerous stakeholders, ranging from local police and private industry to federal agencies within the Department of Homeland Security, play a role in providing security in America's maritime transportation system. Coordinating security efforts between these entities could promote efficiency as well as increase effectiveness. Many stakeholders, however, may be apprehensive about participating in coordinated security efforts for a multitude of reasons, which range from lack of trust to the desire to protect only their own interests.

The planning of cooperative security efforts between stakeholders is another area game theory that presents unique ways of assessing and determining outcomes. Since game theory is able to capture the various options and combinations of outcomes that influence decision makers, it can be used to represent, plan, and analyze negotiations or cooperative agreements. By demonstrating the benefits of cooperation and of permitting these types of arrangements, game theory can model the potential for improved results through coordinated security efforts. The application of cooperative strategies in game theory can be used to demonstrate the improvements possible for the stakeholders and to assist in the coordination of security efforts within a port. Similar arrangements between countries or within the shipping industry could also be facilitated by the application of game theory.

One of the primary applications of game theory is to support decision making between alternative security efforts. One challenge facing homeland security policy makers is deciding the proper security effort or efforts to implement. This is especially true in the MTS because stakeholders have limited resources and must continue to facilitate commerce while decreasing the risk from homeland security threats. Using a game theory approach to compare the potential outcomes of alternatives provides the analysts and decision makers with the justification they need to decide upon and implement a particular strategy. Additionally, including outside influences, imperfect information, and probability improves model accuracy and provides decision makers with better, more realistic information.

The comparison of alternative security efforts can also be extended to outline and determine impacts on interrelated systems using game theory. The MTS is an integral component of commerce and the global supply chain. Besides its role in determining security efforts used to protect ports, it is critical to assess the integral components of the port and the nation that allow the ports to continue to function. For instance, port facilities rely on roads, railways, and airports to continue the journey of goods to other parts of the country. These systems need to be factored into security decisions. Port facilities can use a game theory approach to aid in the assessment of the alternative security options in which they could invest to protect the various components of the port and supply chain.

Alternatively, ports are home to many of the nation's MCIKR that do not directly involve the transportation of goods. Examples include nuclear power facilities, naval bases, and highly concentrated population events like sports arenas. Security issues at these venues, too, should be factored into security decisions since attacks on them are possible and could have cascading impacts throughout other areas of society. The destruction of power facilities could shut down commerce and cause physical and economic damage within the port, beyond the immediate damage to the facility and workers. Using game theory to incorporate prior knowledge about the capabilities and desires of terrorists can help decision makers target their security efforts. Similarly, the outcomes presented in the game theory model can include the secondary consequences and cascading impacts that follow the immediate damage associated with terrorist attacks.

Game theory's flexibility gives it numerous potential applications that could benefit homeland security efforts within the maritime domain. Using game theory to model the decision environment and challenges faced by analysts allows such components of real-life situations to be incorporated as cooperation, influence, imperfect information, and the interconnectedness or relatedness of outcomes that other mathematical approaches may not facilitate or include. Employing game theory throughout the MTS could be beneficial to multiple stakeholders, from private industry to federal government agencies, as because it can be used to support security strategies, determine security investments, optimize randomized efforts, and facilitate cooperation between the stakeholders. Additionally, its application can help analysts understand the impact of decisions between interdependent systems, weigh alternatives for improved targeting, and account for intelligent adversaries that react to security efforts. Securing the maritime domain also involves providing recovery and response efforts in the wake of natural disasters, in addition to manmade attacks. Game theory can also be used to map out decision making in these situations. Similarly, game theory provides a way to analyze deceptive attacks and ensure that vulnerabilities are not created in response to diversions. Using game theory to support procedural development, resource allocation, and security plans strengthens the efforts and decision-making ability of maritime homeland security providers. The maritime environment, with its intricate challenges and situations, provides a unique opportunity for applying game theory.

PART II

Deployed Applications

4

Deployed ARMOR Protection: The Application of a Game-Theoretic Model for Security at the Los Angeles International Airport

James Pita, Manish Jain, Janusz Marecki, Fernando Ordóñez,
Christopher Portway, Milind Tambe, Craig Western,
Praveen Paruchuri, and Sarit Kraus

4.1 Introduction

Protecting the national infrastructure, such as airports, historical landmarks, or locations of political or economic importance, is a challenging task for police and security agencies around the world, one that is exacerbated by the threat of terrorism. The protection of important locations includes such tasks as monitoring all entrances or inbound roads and checking inbound traffic. However, limited resources mean that it is typically impossible to provide full security coverage at all times. Furthermore, adversaries can observe security arrangements over time and exploit any predictable patterns to their advantage. Randomizing schedules for patrolling, checking, or monitoring is thus an important tool in the police arsenal to avoid the vulnerability that comes with predictability. Even beyond protecting infrastructure, randomized patrolling is important in tasks varying from security on university campuses to normal police beats to border or maritime security (Billante 2003; Paruchuri et al. 2007; Ruan et al. 2005).

This paper focuses on a deployed software-assistant agent that can aid police or other security agencies in randomizing their security schedules. We face at least three key challenges in building such a software assistant. First, the assistant must provide quality guarantees in randomization by appropriately weighing the costs and benefits of the different options available. For example, if an attack on one part of an infrastructure would cause economic damage while an attack on another could potentially cost human lives, we must weigh the two options differently – giving higher weight (probability) to guarding the latter. Second, the assistant must address the uncertainty in the information that security forces have about the adversary. Third, the assistant must enable a

Previously published in *Proc. of 7th Int. Conf. on Autonomous Agents and Multiagent Systems (AAMAS 2008)- Industry and Applications Track*, Berger, Burg, Nishiyama (eds.), May 12–16., 2008, Estoril, Portugal. Copyright © 2008, International Foundation for Autonomous Agents and Multiagent Systems (www.ifaamas.org). All rights reserved.

67

mixed-initiative interaction with potential users, rather than dictate a schedule; the assistant may be unaware of users' real-world constraints, and hence users must be able to shape the schedule development.

We have addressed these challenges in a software-assistant agent called ARMOR (Assistant for Randomized Monitoring over Routes). Based on game-theoretic principles, ARMOR combines three key features to address each of the three challenges. Game theory is a well-established foundational principle within multi-agent systems used to reason about multiple agents who are each pursuing their own interests (Fudenberg & Tirole 1991). We build on these game-theoretic foundations to reason about two agents – the police force and its adversary – in providing a method of randomization. In particular, the main contribution of our paper is mapping the problem of security scheduling as a Bayesian Stackelberg game (Conitzer & Sandholm 2006) and solving it via the fastest optimal algorithm for such games, thus addressing the first two challenges. While a Bayesian game allows us to address uncertainty over adversary types by optimally solving such Bayesian Stackelberg games (we obtain optimal randomized strategies as solutions), ARMOR provides quality guarantees on the schedules generated. The algorithm used builds on several years of research reported in the AAMAS conference main track and AAMAS workshops (Paruchuri et al., 2005, 2006, 2007). ARMOR employs an algorithm that is a logical culmination of this line of research; in particular, ARMOR relies on the DOBSS algorithm (Decomposed Optimal Bayesian Stackelberg Solver), which was reported at AAMAS 2008 (Paruchuri et al., 2008). DOBSS is superior to its competitors, including ASAP, and it provides optimal solutions rather than approximations. The third challenge is addressed by ARMOR's use of a mixed-initiative-based interface, where users are allowed to graphically enter different constraints to shape the schedule generated. ARMOR is thus a collaborative assistant that iterates over generated schedules, rather than a rigid, one-shot scheduler. ARMOR also alerts users when overrides deteriorate the schedule quality below a given threshold. This can include repeatedly scheduling an action which has a low probability in the optimal mixed strategy, or repeatedly forbidding an action which has been assigned a high probability.

ARMOR thus represents a very promising transition of multi-agent research into a deployed application. ARMOR has been successfully deployed on a trial basis since August 2007 (Murr 2007) LAX to assist the Los Angeles World Airport (LAWA) police in randomized scheduling of checkpoints; and since November 2007 generate randomized patrolling schedules for canine units. In particular, it helps police to determine where to randomly set up checkpoints and to randomly allocate canines to terminals.

4.2 Related Work

The key contribution of this paper is the development of the game-theoretic security scheduler ARMOR for improving security at the Los Angeles International Airport. The novelty of our work lies in modeling the security problem as a Bayesian Stackelberg game (Fudenberg & Tirole 1997; Parachuri et al. 2007) and applying the efficient DOBSS algorithm to find the optimal security schedule. In previous work, it has been shown that finding an optimal solution for a Bayesian Stackelberg game with multiple follower types is NP-hard (Conitzer & Sandholm 2006). Two different approaches to find solutions to Bayesian Stackelberg games efficiently have been presented previously. The first is an exact approach named the Multiple LPs method (Conitzer & Sandholm 2006). This approach needs the conversion of the Bayesian game into a normal-form game using the Harsanyi transformation (Harsanyi & Selten 1972); thus, it loses its compact structure. The second approach, named ASAP, does not need the Harsanyi transformation (Parachuri et al. 2007), but it provides only an approximate solution. DOBSS outperforms the Multiple LPs method because it does not need the Harsanyi transformation, thus gaining exponential speedups. DOBSS is also superior to the ASAP approach because it provides an exact solution by optimally solving the problem at hand. We provide an experimental comparison of these algorithms in Section 6; note that these algorithms had earlier been investigated outside the context of a specific infrastructure security application, as we describe in this paper. In contrast, Brown et al. (2006) do specifically apply Stackelberg games for defending critical infrastructure. However, they consider a single adversary type (not a Bayesian game), and with ARMOR, we have taken the extra step of actually solving and deploying the solutions to the created Bayesian Stackelberg games at LAX.

The patrolling problem itself has received significant attention in multi-agent literature because of its wide variety of applications, ranging from robot patrol to the border patrolling of large areas (Ruan et al., 2005; Billante, 2003). The key idea behind the policies provided by these techniques is randomization, which decreases the amount of information given to an adversary. However, no specific algorithm/procedure has been provided for the generation of randomized policies; hence, they can lead to highly suboptimal policies. One exception is the early work of Paruchuri et al. (2006), which provides algorithms for analyzing randomization-reward trade-offs; however, they do not model any adversaries. On the other hand, DOBSS provides policies whose randomization is determined by the payoff structure of game matrices; thus DOBSS provides us with optimal randomized policies while accounting for multiple adversary models.

While ARMOR is a game-theoretic security scheduler, there are many other competing non-game-theoretic tools in use for related applications. For example, the Hypercube Queuing Model (Larson 1974) based on queuing theory depicts the detailed spatial operation of urban police departments and emergency medical services and has found application in police-beat design, allocation of patrolling time, and so on. However, this model does not take specific adversary models into account; ARMOR, on the other hand, tailors policies to combat various potential adversaries.

4.3 Security Domain Description

We now describe the specific security challenges faced by the LAWA police. LAX is the fifth busiest and the largest destination airport in the United States, and serves 60–70 million passengers per year (Stevens et al., 2006; General Description, 2007). LAX is unfortunately also suspected to be a prime terrorist target on the west coast of the United States, and there have been multiple arrests of plotters attempting to attack LAX (General Description, 2007). To protect LAX, LAWA police has designed a security system that utilizes multiple rings of protection. As is evident to anyone traveling through any airport, these rings include vehicular checkpoints, police units patrolling the roads to the terminals and inside the terminals (with canines), and security screening and bag checks for passengers. There are unfortunately not enough resources (police officers) to monitor every single event at LAX; given its size and the number of passengers served, such a level of screening would require considerably more personnel and time and cause greater delays to travelers. Thus, assuming that all checkpoints and terminals are not being monitored at all times, setting up available checkpoints, canine units, or other patrols on deterministic schedules allows adversaries to learn the schedules and plot an attack that avoids the police checkpoints and patrols, which makes deterministic schedules ineffective.

Randomization offers a solution here. In particular, from among all the security measures that randomization could be applied to, LAWA police have so far posed two crucial problems to us. The first, given that there are many roads leading into LAX, is where and when to set up checkpoints for cars driving into LAX. For example, Figure 4.1(a) shows a vehicular checkpoint set up on a road inbound toward LAX. Police officers examine cars that drive by, and if a car appears suspicious, they do a more detailed inspection of that car. LAWA police wished to obtain a randomized schedule for such checkpoints for a particular time frame. For example, if we are to set up two checkpoints, and the time frame of interest is 8 AM to 11 AM, then a candidate schedule may suggest to the police that on Monday, checkpoints should be placed on route 1 and route 2,

Figure 4.1. LAX Security: (a) LAX checkpoint and (b) Canine patrol.

whereas on Tuesday during the same time slot, they should be on route 1 and route 3, and so on. Second, LAWA police wished to obtain an assignment of canines to patrol routes through the terminals inside LAX. For example, if there are three canine units available, a possible assignment may be to place canines on terminals 1, 3, and 6 on the first day, and on terminals 2, 4, and 6 on another day, and so on, based on the available information. Figure 4.1(b) illustrates a canine unit on patrol at LAX.

Given these problems, our analysis revealed the following key challenges: (i) Potential attackers can observe security forces' schedules over time and then choose their attack strategy — the fact that the adversary acts with knowledge of the schedule makes deterministic schedules highly susceptible to attack; (ii) there is unknown and uncertain information regarding the types of adversary we may face; and (iii) although randomization helps eliminate deterministic patterns, it must also account for the different costs and benefits associated with particular targets.

4.4 Approach

We modeled the decisions of where and when to set checkpoints or canine patrol routes as Bayesian Stackelberg games. These games allow us to accomplish three important tasks: (i) They model the fact that an adversary acts with knowledge of security forces' schedules, and thus randomize schedules appropriately; (ii) they allow us to define multiple adversary types, meeting the challenge of our uncertain information about our adversaries; and (iii) they enable us to weigh the significance of different targets differently. Because Bayesian Stackelberg games address the challenges posed by our domain, they are at the heart of generating meaningfully randomized schedules. In the material that follows, we will explain what a Bayesian Stackelberg game consists of and how we use DOBSS to optimally solve the problem at hand. We then explain how an LAX security problem can be mapped on to Bayesian Stackelberg games.

4.4.1 Bayesian Stackelberg Game

In a Stackelberg game, a leader first commits to a strategy, and then a follower selfishly optimizes its reward, *considering the action chosen by the leader.* To see the advantage of being the leader in a Stackelberg game, consider a simple game with the payoff table as shown in Table 4.1. The leader is the row player and the follower is the column player. The only pure-strategy Nash equilibrium for this game is when the leader plays A and the follower plays C, which gives the leader a payoff of 2; in fact, for the leader, playing B is strictly dominated. However, if the leader can commit to playing B before the follower chooses its strategy, then the leader will obtain a payoff of 3 because the follower would then play D to ensure a higher payoff for itself. If the leader commits to a uniform mixed strategy of playing A and B with equal (0.5) probability, then the follower will play D, leading to a payoff of 3.5 for the leader.

We now explain a Bayesian Stackelberg game. A Bayesian game contains a set of N agents, and each agent n must be one of a given set of types θ_n. The Bayesian Stackelberg games we consider in this paper have two agents, the leader and the follower. The set of possible types for the leader is θ_1, and θ_2 is the set of possible types for the follower. For the security games of interest in this paper, we assume that there is only one leader type (e.g., only one police force), although there are multiple follower types (e.g., multiple adversary types trying

Table 4.1. *Payoff table for an*
example normal form game

	C	D
A	2,1	4,0
B	1,0	3,2

to infiltrate security). Therefore, although θ_1 contains only one element, there is no such restriction on θ_2. However, the leader does not know the follower's type. For each agent (leader or follower) n, there is a set of strategies σ_n and a utility function $u_n : \theta_1 \times \theta_2 \times \sigma_1 \times \sigma_2 \to \Re$. Our goal is *to find the optimal mixed strategy* for the leader to commit to, given that the follower may know this mixed strategy when choosing its strategy.

4.4.2 DOBSS

We now briefly describe the DOBSS algorithm to solve Bayesian Stackelberg games (Parachuri et al. 2008). Here we provide a brief description of the model and how it relates to a security domain. As mentioned earlier, the concrete novel contribution of this paper is mapping our real-world security problem into a Bayesian Stackelberg game, applying DOBSS to this real-world airport security domain, and, finally, embedding DOBSS in the overall ARMOR system, which provides many features to allow smooth operationalization.

As noted, one key advantage of the DOBSS approach is that it operates directly on the Bayesian representation, without requiring the Harsanyi transformation. In particular, DOBSS obtains a decomposition scheme by exploiting the property that follower types are independent of each other. The key to the DOBSS decomposition is the observation that evaluating the leader strategy against a Harsanyi-transformed game matrix is equivalent to evaluating against each of the game matrices for the individual follower types.

We first present DOBSS in its most intuitive form as a mixed-integer quadratic program (MIQP); we then present a linearized equivalent mixed-integer linear program (MILP). The model we propose explicitly represents the actions by the leader and the optimal actions for the follower types in the problem solved by the agent. Note that we need to consider only the reward-maximizing pure strategies of the follower types because for a given fixed mixed strategy x of the leader's, each follower type faces a problem with fixed linear rewards. If a mixed strategy is optimal for the follower, then so are all the pure strategies in support of that mixed strategy.

We denote by x the leader's policy, which consists of a vector of probability distributions over the leader's pure strategies. Hence, the value x_i is the proportion of times in which pure strategy i is used in the policy. We denote by q^l the vector of strategies of follower type $l \in L$. We also denote by X and Q the index sets of the leader and follower l's pure strategies, respectively. We also index the payoff matrices of the leader and each of the follower types l by the matrices R^l and C^l. Let M be a large positive number. Given a priori probabilities p^l, with $l \in L$, of facing each follower type, the leader solves the following:

$$\max_{x,q,a} \quad \sum_{i \in X} \sum_{l \in L} \sum_{j \in Q} p^l R_{ij}^l x_i q_j^l$$

$$\text{s.t.} \quad \sum_{i \in X} x_i = 1$$

$$\sum_{j \in Q} q_j^l = 1$$

$$0 \le (a^l - \sum_{i \in X} C_{ij}^l x_i) \le (1 - q_j^l)M \tag{4.1}$$

$$x_i \in [0 \ldots 1]$$

$$q_j^l \in \{0, 1\}$$

$$a \in \Re$$

Here, for a set of leader's actions x and actions for each follower q^l, the objective represents the expected reward for the agent considering the a priori distribution over different follower types p^l. The first and the fourth constraints define the set of feasible solutions x as a probability distribution over the set of actions X. Constraints 2 and 5 limit the vector of actions of follower type l, q^l to be a pure distribution over the set Q (i.e., each q^l has exactly one coordinate equal to one, and the rest are equal to zero). The two inequalities in constraint 3 ensure that $q_j^l = 1$ only for a strategy j that is optimal for follower type l. Indeed, this is a linearized form of the optimality conditions for the linear programming problem solved by each follower type. We explain these constraints as follows: Note that the leftmost inequality ensures that for all $j \in Q$, $a^l \ge \sum_{i \in X} C_{ij}^l x_i$. This means that, given the leader's vector x, a^l is an upper bound on follower type l's reward for any action. The rightmost inequality is inactive for every action where $q_j^l = 0$ because M is a large positive quantity. For the action that has $q_j^l = 1$, this inequality states that the adversary's payoff for this action must be $\ge a^l$, which, combined with the previous inequality, shows that this action must be optimal for follower type l.

We can linearize the quadratic programming problem 4.1 through the change of variables $z_{ij}^l = x_i q_j^l$, thus obtaining the following mixed-integer linear programming problem:

$$\max_{q,z,a} \quad \sum_{i \in X} \sum_{l \in L} \sum_{j \in Q} p^l R_{ij}^l z_{ij}^l$$

$$\text{s.t.} \quad \sum_{i \in X} \sum_{j \in Q} z_{ij}^l = 1$$

$$\sum_{j \in Q} z_{ij}^l \le 1$$

$$q_j^l \le \sum_{i \in X} z_{ij}^l \le 1$$

$$\sum_{j \in Q} q_j^l = 1$$

$$0 \le (a^l - \sum_{i \in X} C_{ij}^l (\sum_{h \in Q} z_{ih}^l)) \le (1 - q_j^l) M \qquad (4.2)$$

$$\sum_{j \in Q} z_{ij}^l = \sum_{j \in Q} z_{ij}^1$$

$$z_{ij}^l \in [0 \dots 1]$$

$$q_j^l \in \{0, 1\}$$

$$a \in \Re$$

DOBSS refers to this equivalent mixed-integer linear program, which can be solved with efficient integer programming packages.

4.4.3 Bayesian Stackelberg Game for the Los Angeles International Airport

We now illustrate how the security problems set forth by LAWA police, that is, where and when to deploy checkpoints and canines, can be cast in terms of a Bayesian Stackelberg game. We focus on the checkpoint problem for illustration, but the canine problem is similar. At LAX, there are a specific number of inbound roads on which to set up checkpoints, say, roads 1 through n, and LAWA police have to pick a subset of those roads on which to place checkpoints prior to adversaries selecting which roads to attack. We assume that there are m different types of adversaries, each with different attack capabilities, planning constraints, and financial ability. Each adversary type observes the LAWA-police checkpoint policy and then decides where to attack. Since adversaries can observe the LAWA police policy before deciding their actions, this situation can be modeled via a Stackelberg game, with the police as the leader.

In this setting, the set X of possible actions for LAWA police is the set of possible checkpoint combinations. If, for instance, LAWA police set up one checkpoint, then $X = \{1, \dots, n\}$. If LAWA police set up a combination of two checkpoints, then $X = \{(1,2), (1,3) \dots (n-1, n)\}$, that is, all combinations of two checkpoints. Each adversary type $l \in L = \{1, \dots, m\}$ can decide to attack one of the n roads or maybe to not attack at all (none), so its set of actions is $Q = \{1, \dots, n, none\}$. If LAWA police select road i to place a checkpoint on, and adversary type $l \in L$ selects road j to attack, then the agent receives a reward R_{ij}^l, and the adversary receives a reward C_{ij}^l. These reward values vary based on three considerations: (i) the chance that the LAWA police checkpoint will catch the adversary on a particular inbound road; (ii) the damage the adversary will cause if it attacks via a particular inbound road; and (iii) type of adversary, that is; adversary capability. If LAWA police catch the adversary when $i = j$, we make R_{ij}^l a large positive value and C_{ij}^l a large negative value. However, the probability of catching the adversary at a given checkpoint is based on the volume of traffic through the checkpoint (significant traffic increases the difficulty of catching the adversary), which is an input to the system. If the LAWA police are unable to catch the adversary, then the adversary may succeed, that is, we make R_{ij}^l a large negative value and C_{ij}^l a large positive value. Certainly, if the adversary attacks via an inbound road where no checkpoint was set up, there is no chance that the police will catch the adversary. The magnitude of R_{ij}^l and of C_{ij}^l varies based on the adversary's potential target, given the road from which the adversary attacks. Some roads lead to higher-valued targets for the adversary than others. The game is not a zero-sum game, however, because even if the adversary is caught, it may benefit from the publicity.

The reason we consider a Bayesian Stackelberg game is because LAWA police face multiple adversary types. Thus, differing values of the reward matrices across the different adversary types $l \in L$ represent the different objectives and valuations of the different attackers (e.g., smugglers, criminals, terrorists). For example, a hard-core, well-financed adversary could inflict significant damage on LAX; thus, the negative rewards to the LAWA police are much higher in magnitude than they would be with an amatuer attacker who may not have sufficient resources to carry out a large-scale attack. If only two types of adversaries are faced, then a 20–80 split of probability implies that, while there is a 20% chance that the LAWA police will face the former type of adversary, there is an 80% chance that they will face an amatuer attacker. Our experimental data provides detailed results about the sensitivity of our algorithms to the probability distributions over these two different adversary types. Although the number of adversary types varied based on our discusssions with LAWA police, for any one adversary type, the largest game we constructed, which was done for canine deployment, consisted of 784 actions for the LAWA police (when multiple canine units were active) for the seven possible terminals within the airport and 8 actions per adversary type (one for a possible attack on each terminal, and one for *none*).

4.5 System Architecture

There are two separate versions of ARMOR: ARMOR-checkpoint and ARMOR-canine. While we focus on ARMOR-checkpoint for illustration, both

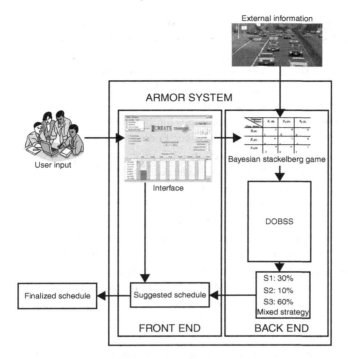

Figure 4.2. ARMOR system flow diagram.

versions use the same underlying architecture, with different inputs. As shown in Figure 4.2, this architecture consists of a front end and a back end, integrating four key components: (i) a front-end interface for user interaction; (ii) a method for creating Bayesian Stackelberg game matrices; (iii) an implementation of DOBSS; and (iv) a method for producing suggested schedules for the user. They also contain two major forms of external input. First, they allow for direct user input into the system through the interface. Second, they allow for file input of relevant information for checkpoints or canines, such as traffic/passenger volume by time of day, which can greatly affect the security measures taken and the value of certain actions. We now discuss in detail what each component consists of and how the components interact with each other.

4.5.1 Interface

The ARMOR interface, seen in Figure 4.3, consists of a file menu, options for local constraints, options to alter the action space, a monthly calendar, and a main spreadsheet to view any day(s) from the calendar. Together these components create a working interface that meets all the requirements set forth by LAWA officers for checkpoint and canine deployment at LAX.

The base of the interface is designed around six possible adjustable options; three of them alter the action space, and three impose local constraints. The three options to alter the action space are the following: (i) number of checkpoints allowed during a particular times lot; (ii) time interval of each time slot; and (iii) number of days to schedule over. For each given time slot, we construct a new game. As discussed in Section 4.4.3, given knowledge of the total number of inbound roads, the number of checkpoints allowed during that time slot determines the available actions for the LAWA police, whereas the action space of the adversary is determined, as discussed in Section 4.4.3 by the number of inbound roads. Thus, we can set up the foundation for the Bayesian Stackelberg game by providing all the actions possible in the game. Once the action space has been generated, it can be sent to the back end to be set up as a Bayesian Stackelberg game, solved, and returned as a suggested schedule, which is displayed to the user via the spreadsheet. The third option determines how many iterations of the game will be played (since it determines the number of days to schedule over).

Once the game is solved, three options serve to restrict certain actions in the generated schedule: (i) forced checkpoint; (ii) forbidden checkpoint; and (iii) at least one checkpoint. These constraints are intended to be used sparingly to accommodate situations in which a user, faced with exceptional circumstances and extra knowledge, wishes to modify the output of the game. The user may impose these restrictions by forcing specific actions in the schedule. In particular, the "forced checkpoint" option schedules a checkpoint at a specific time on a specific day. The "forbidden checkpoint" option designates a specific time on a specific day when a checkpoint should not be scheduled. Finally, the "at least one checkpoint" option designates a set of time slots and ensures that a checkpoint is scheduled in at least one of the slots. We return to these constraints in Section 4.5.3.

The spreadsheet in the interface serves as the main mechanism for viewing, altering, and constraining schedules. The columns correspond to the possible checkpoints, and the rows correspond to the time frames in which to schedule them. Up to a full week can be viewed within the spreadsheet at a single time, with each day marked as shown in Figure 4.3. Once a particular day is in view, the user can assign to that day any constraints they desire. Each constraint is represented by a specific color on the spreadsheet, namely, green, red, and yellow for forced, forbidden, and at-least constraints, respectively.

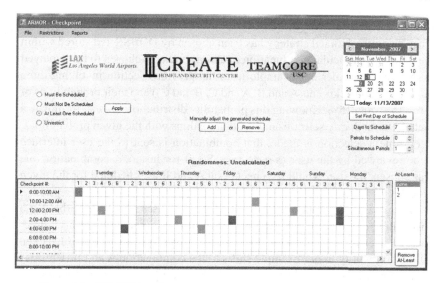

Figure 4.3. ARMOR interface.

4.5.2 Matrix Generation and DOBSS

Given the submitted user information, the system must create a meaningful Bayesian Stackelberg game matrix as suggested in Section 4.4.3. The previous section illustrates the generation of the action space in this game. Based on the prespecified rewards, we can, as discussed in Section 4.3, provide the rewards for the LAWA police and for the adversaries to generate a game matrix for each adversary type. After the final game matrices are constructed for each adversary type, they are sent to the DOBSS implementation, which chooses the optimal mixed strategy over the current action space.

To demonstrate the process, assume there are three possible inbound roads or checkpoint locations (A, B, C), one possible timeslot to schedule over, and two checkpoints available for scheduling. Given this scenario, the unique combinations possible include scheduling checkpoints A and B, A and C, and B and C, over the given time frame. We will assume that checkpoints A and B are highly valuable, whereas C, although not completely invaluable, has a very low value. Based on this information, a likely mixed strategy generated by DOBSS would be to assign a high probability to choosing action A and B, say 70%, and a low probability to both the other actions, say 15% each. Whatever the mixed strategy actually comes out to be, it is the optimal strategy a user could employ to maximize security based on the given information. This mixed strategy is then stored and used for the actual schedule generation.

4.5.3 Mixed Strategy and Schedule Generation

Once an optimal mixed strategy has been chosen by DOBSS and stored within the system, a particular combination of actions must be chosen to be displayed to the user. Consider our example from the previous section involving three possibilities (checkpoints A and B, A and C, B and C)) and their probabilities of 70%, 15%, and 15%. Knowing this probability distribution, we can formulate a method to randomly select from the combinations with the given probabilities. Each time a selection is made, that combination is sent to the user interface to be reviewed by the user as necessary. So, if for instance, combination one was chosen, the user would see checkpoint A and B as scheduled for the given timeslot.

In rare cases, as mentioned in Section 4.5.1, a user may have forbidden a checkpoint, or required a checkpoint. ARMOR accommodates such user directives when creating its schedule, for example, if checkpoint C is forbidden, then all the probability in our example shifts to the combination A and B. Unfortunately, by using this capability frequently (e.g., frequent use of forbidden and required checkpoints), a user can completely alter the mixed strategy produced as the output of DOBSS, defeating DOBSS's guarantee of optimality. To avoid such a possibility, ARMOR incorporates certain alerts (warnings) to encourage noninterference in its schedule generation. For example, if a combination has zero or very low probability of being chosen and the user has forced that checkpoint combination to occur, ARMOR will alert the user. Similarly, if a combination has a very high likelihood and the user has forbidden that event, ARMOR will again alert the user. However, ARMOR only alerts the user; it does not autonomously remove the user's constraints. Resolving more subtle interactions between the user-imposed constraints and DOBSS's output strategy remains an issue for future work.

When a schedule is presented to the user with alerts as we have described, the user may alter the schedule by altering the forbidden/required checkpoints, or possibly by directly altering the schedule. Both possibilities are accomodated in ARMOR. If the user simply adds or removes constraints, ARMOR can create a new schedule. Once the schedule is finalized, it can be saved for actual use, thus completing the system cycle. This full process was designed to specifically meet the requirements at LAX for checkpoint and canine allocation.

4.6 Design Challenges

Designing and deploying the ARMOR software on a trial basis at LAX posed numerous challenges and problems to our research group. We outline some key lessons learned during the design and deployment of ARMOR:

- *Importance of tools for randomization:* There is a critical need for randomization in security operations. Security officials are aware that requiring humans to generate randomized schedules is unsatisfactory because, as psychological studies have often shown (Wagenaar, 1972), humans have difficulty randomizing, and also they can fall into predictable patterns. Instead, mathematical randomization that appropriately weighs the costs and benefits of different actions, and randomizes with appropriate weights leads to improved results. Security officials were therefore extremely enthusiastic in their reception of our research, and eager to apply it to their domain.
- *Importance of manual schedule overrides:* While ARMOR incorporates all the knowledge that we could obtain from LAWA police and provides the best output possible, it may not be aware of dynamic developments on the ground. For example, police officers may have very specific intelligence requiring a checkpoint on a particular inbound road. Hence, it was crucial to allow LAWA police officers (in rare instances when it is necessary) to manually override the schedule provided.
- *Importance of providing police officers with operational flexibility:* When initially generating schedules for canine patrols, we created a very detailed schedule, micromanaging the patrols. This did not get as positive a reception from the officers. Instead, an abstract schedule that gave them the flexibility to respond to dynamic situations on the ground was better received.

4.7 Experimental Results

Our experimental results explore the runtime efficiency of DOBSS (in Section 4.7.1) and evaluate the solution quality and implementation of the ARMOR system (in Section 4.7.2).

4.7.1 Runtime Analysis

Here, we compare the runtime results of DOBSS versus Multiple LPs, described in Section 4.2, given the specific domain used for canine deployment at LAX. The aim of this analysis is to show that DOBSS is indeed the most suitable procedure for application to real domains, such as the LAX canine and checkpoint allocation. To that end, we used the data from a full week of canine deployment to analyze the time necessary to generate a schedule given the DOBSS method and the multiple-LPs method. For completeness, we show the results given one to four adversary types where four adversary types is the actual number LAWA has set forth as necessary.

In Figure 4.4 we summarize the runtime results for our Bayesian games using DOBSS and Multiple LPs. We tested our results on the Bayesian games provided from the canine domain with number of adversary types varying between one to four. Each game between the agent (LAWA) and one adversary type is modeled as a normals-form game. Thus, there are four normal-form games designed for the game between the agent (LAWA) and the various adversary types for the base case. The size of each of these normal-form games is (784,8), corresponding to 784 strategies for the agent (LAWA) and 8 for the adversary. We then used the seven generated instances, taken from an arbitrary week of canine deployment, of this base case to obtain averaged results.

The x-axis in Figure 4.4 shows the number of follower types the leader faces starting from 1 to 4 adversary types, and the y-axis of the graph shows the runtime in seconds ranging from 0 to 1200 seconds. All the experiments that were not concluded in 20 minutes (1200 seconds) were cut off. From the graph we summarize that DOBSS outperforms the multiple-LPs method by a significant margin given our real canine domain. In the graph, while Multiple LPs could solve the problem only till two adversary types, DOBSS could solve for all four adversary types within 80s.

Hence, we can conclude that the DOBSS method is faster than the multiple-LPs method, and consequently, that DOBSS is the algorithm of choice for Bayesian Stackelberg games (Paruchuri et al., 2008), especially given the particular games created by real security domains like the canine patrolling problem presented in this paper.

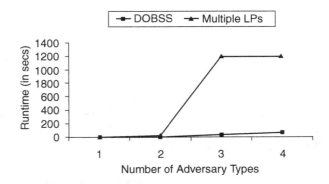

Figure 4.4. Runtimes: DOBSS and multiple-LP methods.

4.7.2 Evaluation of ARMOR

We now evaluate the solution quality obtained when DOBSS is applied to the LAX security domain. We offer three types of evaluation. While our first evaluation is "in the lab," ARMOR is a deployed assistant, and hence, our remaining two evaluations are of its deployment "in the field." With respect to our first evaluation, we conducted four experiments. The first three compared ARMOR's randomization with other randomization techniques, in particular a uniform randomization technique that does not use ARMOR's weights in randomization. The uniformly random strategy gives equal probabilities to all possible actions.

The results of the first experiment are shown in Figures 4.5(a), (b) and (c). The *x*-axis represents the probabilities of occurrence type 1 and type 2 adversaries. Since the actual number of adversary types used for LAX is secure information, we use two adversary types for the sake of simplicity in this analysis. The *x*-axis shows the probability p of adversary type 2 (the probability of adversary type 1 is then obtained on 1-p). The *y*-axis represents the reward obtained. Figure 4.5(a) shows the comparison when one checkpoint is placed. For example, when adversary of type 1 occurs with a probability of 0.1 and type 2 occurs with a probability of 0.9, the reward obtained by the DOBSS strategy is -1.72, whereas the reward obtained by a uniform random strategy is -2.112. It is important to note that the reward of the DOBSS strategy is strictly greater than the reward of the uniform random strategy for all probabilities of occurrence of the adversaries.

Figure 4.5(b) also has the probability distribution on the *x*-axis and the reward obtained on the *y*-axis. It shows the difference in the obtained reward when two checkpoints are placed. Here also, the reward in the case of the DOBSS strategy is greater than the reward of the uniform random strategy. When we have two checkpoints, the type 2 adversary chooses the action *none* (to not attack). This leads to the observation that the rewards of the DOBSS strategy and the reward of the uniform strategy are the same when only the type 2 adversary is present. Figure 4.5(c) presents the case of three checkpoints. Here, the reward values obtained by DOBSS in the three checkpoint case are always positive — this is because the chances of catching the adversary of type 1 improve significantly with 3 checkpoints. This also leads to the reward of DOBSS decreasing with the decrease in the probability of occurrence of the adversary of type 1. Note that the type 2 adversary as with the case of two checkpoints, decides *none*; hence, the reward of the DOBSS strategy and the uniformly random strategy are the same when only type 2 adversary is present.

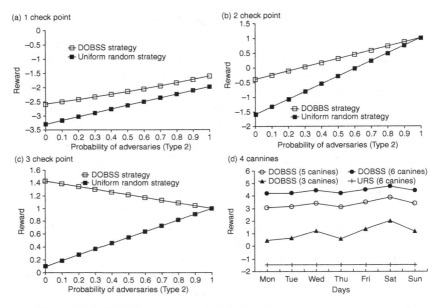

Figure 4.5. DOBSS Strategy versus uniformly random strategy.

The three experiments reported above allow us to conclude that DOBSS weighted randomization provides significant improvements over uniform randomization in the same domain, thus illustrating the utility of our algorithms. We continue these results in the following fourth experiment, focusing now on canine units. Figure 4.5(d) shows the comparison of the reward obtained between scheduling canine units with DOBSS and scheduling them with a uniform random strategy (denoted *URS*). In the uniform random strategy, canines are randomly assigned to terminals, with equal probability. The x-axis represents the weekday and the y-axis represents the reward obtained. We can see that DOBSS performs better even with three canine units as compared to six canine units being scheduled using the uniform random strategy. For example, on Friday, the reward of a uniformly random strategy with six canine units is -1.47 whereas the reward of three, five, and six canines with DOBSS is 1.37, 3.50, and 4.50, respectively. These results show that DOBSS weighted randomization with even three canines provides better results against uniform randomization in the same domain with six canines. Thus our algorithm provides better rewards and can help in reducing the cost of resources needed.

Now, we analyze the performance of ARMOR as it is deployed in the field. In the next evaluation, we examine ARMOR's setting of checkpoints at LAX.

Table 4.2. *Variation in usage percentage*

Checkpoint Number	1	2	3	4	5
Week 1	33.33	4.76	33.33	0	28.57
Week 2	19.04	23.80	23.80	14.28	19.05

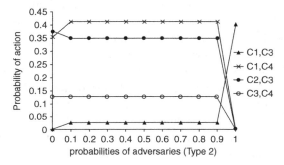

Figure 4.6. Sensitivy analysis.

The first experiment examines the change in checkpoint deployment during a fixed shift (i.e., keeping the time fixed) over two weeks. The results are shown in Table 4.2. The numbers 1 to 5 in the table denote the checkpoint number (we have assigned arbitrary identification numbers to all checkpoints for the purpose of this experiment), and the values of the table show the percentage of times this checkpoint was used. For example, in week 1, checkpoint 2 was used just less than 5% of times, whereas checkpoint 2 was used about 25% of the times in week 2. We can make two observations based on these two weeks: (i) We do not have uniform randomization of these checkpoints, i.e., there is great variance in the percentage of times checkpoints are deployed; and (ii) the checkpoint deployment varies from week to week, for example, checkpoint 4 was not used in week 1, but it was used 15% of the times in week 2.

The goal of the next experiment was to provide results on the sensitivity analysis, specifically, how the probabilities of different actions will change if we change the proportion of adversary types. Figure 4.6 shows the variation in strategy for placing two checkpoints together when the occurrence probability of the adversary changes. The x-axis shows the variation in the occurrence probability of the adversary types, whereas the y-axis shows the variation in the probabilities in the DOBSS strategy. For example, when a type 1 adversary occurs with a probability of 1, the probability of placing both checkpoints 1 and

4 is 0.353; when the adversaries 1 and 2 occur with probabilities of 0.4 and 0.6 respectively, then the probability of placing checkpoints 3 and 4 is 0.127. We can observe that there is very little to no variation in the probabilities in the DOBSS strategies when the probabilities of occurrence of the two adversary types vary from .1 to .9. This indicates that our results are not particularly sensitive to variations in probabilities of opponents except at the very extremes.

Our final evaluation is a more informal one based on feedback from the LAWA police. First, they have provided very positive feedback about the deployment. They suggest that the technique they had previously used was not one of randomization, but one of alternating checkpoints (e.g., if checkpoint 1 is active today, it will be inactive tomorrow); such a routine can bring about determinism in the scheduling, which we have avoided. Second, ARMOR has eliminated the burden for creating schedules, thus reducing routine work and allowing LAWA police to focus on more important tasks. Third, several arrests have been made at checkpoints scheduled by ARMOR. Typically these involved cars attempting to carry weapons into LAX. This does not necessarily suggest that ARMOR's schedule was responsible because this is not a controlled experiment per se. Nonetheless, it illustrates that the first line of defense at the outer airport perimeter is helping to alleviate the threat of violence at the airport.

4.8 Summary

Establishing security around airports, ports, or other infrastructure of economic or political importance is a challenge that is faced today by police forces around the world. Although randomized monitoring (patrolling, checking, searching) is important — as adversaries can observe and exploit any predictability in launching an attack — randomization must use different weighing functions to reflect the complex costs and benefits of different police actions. This paper describes a *deployed agent assistant* called ARMOR that casts the monitoring problem as a Bayesian Stackelberg game, where randomized schedule generation for police forces can appropriately weigh the costs and benefits as well as the uncertainty over adversary types. ARMOR combines three key features: (i) It uses the fastest known solver for Bayesian Stackelberg games called DOBSS, where the dominant mixed strategies provide schedule randomization; (ii) its mixed-initiative-based interface allows users to occasionally adjust or override the automated schedule based on their local constraints; and (iii) it alerts the users in case mixed-initiative overrides appear to degrade the overall desired randomization. ARMOR has been successfully deployed at the Los Angeles International Airport, randomizing allocation of checkpoints since August 2007 and canine deployment since November 2007. ARMOR thus represents a successful transition of multi-agent algorithmic advances that represent the culmination of research published in AAMAS (Paruchuri et al., 2006, 2007, 2008) for the past two years into the real-world.

Acknowledgments

ARMOR's deployment at LAX has only been possible due to the exceptional effort by LAWA police to strike a collaboration. This research was supported by the United States Department of Homeland Security through the Center for Risk and Economic Analysis of Terrorism Events (CREATE) under grant number 2007-ST-061-000001. However, any opinions, findings, and conclusions or recommendations in this document are those of the authors and do not necessarily reflect views of the United States Department of Homeland Security. We would also like to thank the National Science Foundation for their contributions under grant number IS0705587.

5

IRIS – A Tool for Strategic Security Allocation in Transportation Networks

Jason Tsai, Shyamsunder Rathi, Christopher Kiekintveld,
Fernando Ordóñez, and Milind Tambe

5.1 Introduction

Transportation networks such as buses, trains, and airplanes carry millions of people per day and from to their destinations, making them a prime target for terrorists and extremely difficult for law enforcement agencies to protect. In 2001, the 9/11 attack on the World Trade Center in New York City with commercial airliners resulted in $27.2 billion of direct short term costs (Looney 2002) as well as a government-reported 2,974 lives lost. The 2004 Madrid commuter train bombings resulted in 191 lives lost, 1755 people wounded, and an estimated cost of 212 million Euros (Blanco et al., 2007). Finally, in the 2005 London subway and bus bombings, 52 innocent lives were lost, 700 others were injured, and the estimated economic cost was 2 billion pounds (Thornton, 2005).

In addition to preboarding security checkpoints patrols aboard the vehicles are another key defensive measure used by many organizations in these domains (Billante, 2003; Kenney, 1989). In all these networks, there are hundreds or thousands of vehicles to protect, making it difficult to create patrol schedules. Furthermore, since motivated aggressors will attempt to observe law-enforcement patterns and try to exploit the schedule, law-enforcement organizations have embraced the use of randomization in their scheduling practices. Also, in all these networks, it is not possible to simply assign law-enforcement personnel to vehicles in isolation, without considering the route the vehicle takes as well as departure and arrival times. As a simple example, we cannot ask an officer to board and protect a 10:00 AM flight from New York to Los Angeles as well as a 10:30 AM flight from London to Chicago.

Previously published in *Proc. of 8th Int. Conf. on Autonomous Agents and Multiagent Systems (AAMAS 2009)*, Decker, Sichman, Sierra and Castelfranchi (eds.), May, 10–15, 2009, Budapest, Hungary. Copyright © 2009, International Foundation for Autonomous Agents and Multiagent Systems (www.ifaamas.org). All rights reserved.

Thus, three primary challenges must be overcome by any method of randomizing law enforcement in transportation networks: (i) the runtime of solution methods is often prohibitive because of the scale of the problems; (ii) the number of inputs required under many solution methods is also often prohibitive for the same reasons; (iii) the scheduling constraints of a transportation network must be obeyed in any schedule created.

One obvious method of randomization is a dice-roll approach, where we protect each target with the same probability. However, in a realistic situation, some targets are valued more highly than others. If a security organization patrols every target with equal probability, an intelligent attacker will undoubtedly choose the target with the highest value because this has the highest expected payoff. Knowing this, defenders should place more emphasis on protecting the high-value target to decrease the expected value to the attacker of attacking it. Indeed, we could randomize based on the target values instead of uniformly. This strategy, which we show to be superior to a uniform random strategy, fails to account for how the attacker will update his strategy based on knowledge of the defender's strategy.

An alternative methodology would be to use a non-game-theoretic approach to modeling and solving the problem, such as learning and MDP's as done by Ruan et al. (2005). As part of this work, the authors model the patrolling problem with locations and varying incident rates in each location and solve for optimal routes using a MDP framework. Such a framework could account for the differing values of targets in the transportation-network problem and their use of multiple patrol routes to introduce unpredictability to insurgents seems to address the majority of issues we face. However, their strategy still fails to account for attackers' updating their strategy after observing the defender's strategy.

This presents a problem for the security policy because it was generated based on a given frequency of attacker appearances in each of the locations. When the security policy is enacted, however, an intelligent attacker that observes the policy will adjust his behavior and begin to attack locations that were weighted for less security because of the relative infrequency of attacks there previously.

To alleviate this problem, another method would be to have a human create randomized schedules and weight his coverage of the targets based on their value as well as on beliefs about attacker-response behavior. However, studies have shown that humans are poor randomizers and can fall into predictable patterns (Wagenaar 1972). Furthermore, in large domains like transportation networks, the manhours of labor that must be spent to perform a randomization that factors varying target values and attacker behavior by hand would likely be prohibitively large.

Another possibility would be to use a game-theoretic method. The ARMOR program that is currently deployed at Los Angeles International Airport is one possible tool (Pita et al 2008). ARMOR randomizes checkpoints and canine patrols using a Bayesian Stackelberg game model and solves the optimal randomized strategy for the defender. When we model the security game as a Bayesian Stackelberg game, we are able to input different payoff values for each of the targets, which allows us to account for varying target values in the real domain. The use of a set distribution of coverage probabilities prevents human predictability from compromising the system. Finally, the Stackelberg framework inherently accounts for the attacker's response to the defender's policy.

However, while the approach provides a starting point for addressing the transportation-network problem, the three challenges unique to this domain remain. The DOBSS algorithm at the heart of ARMOR does not scale well and would not be able to handle the size of transportation-network problems in a reasonable time frame (Kiekintveld et al., 2009). Scale also presents an issue for inputing values. In the ARMOR system, domain experts individually specified payoff values for each of the targets directly. In a transportation network, this could come to tens of thousands of values versus the tens of values that we had at LAX. Also, the method of game modeling we used in ARMOR will not realistically be able to handle the hard scheduling constraints that we must account for. We outline the primary differences between the LAX domain and the FAMS domain in more detail in Section 5.2.

We provide three key contributions in the implementation of IRIS that revolve around the application of new representations and algorithms to the transportation-network domain that allow us to generate randomized schedules in reasonable time frames. First, we use a new, more efficient MILP for modeling the Stackelberg games to overcome runtime issues that arise due to scale. Second, we introduce an attribute-based preference elicitation system for the risk/reward assessment of potential targets that allows us to avoid requiring user inputs for every individual target (Chen and Pu 2004). Finally, we model the game with defender actions that incorporate the scheduling constraints, which allows us to accurately model and resolve the scheduling constraints issue without combinatorially exploding the actionspace.

Our work is an application of recent advances in multi-agent research in security/patrolling problems and optimal equilibrium algorithms for solving games to a major security problem in the real world (Kiekintveld et al. 2009). Patrolling problems in general have received much attention in multi-agent research because of the variety of applicable domains such as robot patrol and the border patrolling of large areas (Billante 2003; Wagenaar 1972). Game-theoretic advances, specifically in solving Stackelberg games (Conitzer and Sandholm 2006; Sandholm, Gilpin and Conitzer 2005), have ultimately led to successful work in security-policy randomization using a multi-agent systems framework and the recent deployment of the ARMOR system at LAX (Paruchuri et al. 2008, 2007). As we develop more sophisticated techniques for solving these games, we will be able to address larger and more difficult problems in the real world that we could not previously handle. The creation of IRIS for the FAMS is an example of new advances in multi-agent research allowing us to solve a real-world problem that could not realistically be solved with previous techniques.

5.2 Federal Air Marshal Service

The Federal Air Marshal Service (FAMS) domain is a particular instance of a transportation network security problem. The FAMS places undercover law enforcement personnel aboard flights originating in and departing from the United States to dissuade potential aggressors and prevent an attack (TSA, 2008). Strategic randomization based on game-theoretic principles provides a possible method for creating a coverage schedule that avoids the pitfalls of a deterministic strategy.

Variation in target risk and value is extremely apparent in the FAMS domain. While many flights are overbooked, there are some flights with no passengers that are simply flying to a destination for a subsequent flight. Similarly, while some flights fly over densely populated areas, others do not. Also, while a particular subset of flights might be low risk at one point in time, they could become high risk at another time due to a special event (FAMS 2008). We must somehow account for these variations between flights in our randomization of law enforcement forces if we hope to utilize resources effectively. We model this as a Stackelberg game, as in ARMOR (Pita et al. 2008).

However, the three problems unique to transportation networks remain and cannot be handled by the ARMOR system. Whereas ARMOR handles ten terminals at LAX, the FAMS must protect tens of thousands of commercial flights per day. As shown in Kiekintveld et al. (2009), the DOBSS algorithm at the heart of ARMOR cannot handle problems of this magnitude. Also, in ARMOR, domain experts have to enter four payoff values for each of the ten targets in the domain. Asking the same thing of the FAMS would require tens of thousands of values to be entered by hand, likely introducing user error and a potentially prohibitive time burden for each scheduling cycle. Finally, at LAX, we randomize fixed checkpoint locations and canine patrols that only need to be given a set of times and locations to be. The only constraints on resources is the number of checkpoints and canines available to the system. In the FAMS domain, we have hard scheduling constraints due to the fact that they are patrolling moving vehicles and not fixed locations. For example, asking law enforcement personnel to cover a flight from El Paso to New York might not be possible without someone first flying to El Paso from somewhere else if there are simply no personnel that normally reside in El Paso. In generating a schedule for coverage, we need to be mindful of such constraints.

Thus, the FAMS domain presents all three challenges that must be overcome in a practical implementation of a randomized scheduling assistant for a transportation network: (i) runtime issues due to scale; (ii) preference elicitation issues due to scale; (iii) scheduling constraints.

5.3 Background

The primary contribution of this work is in the application of game-theoretic methods to the FAMS domain and overcoming challenges encountered during implementation. Here, we lay the groundwork for our decision to use Stackelberg games in this effort. In Section 5.5 detail how we map the FAMS domain into a Stackelberg game and the challenges we encountered during the process.

A Stackelberg game allows us to create a randomized schedule while taking into account varying values of the targets and the fact that adversaries act with prior knowledge of a security force's policies. Since these are the basic challenges we must overcome in solving security games, Stackelberg games form the basis of our approach. First, we describe Stackelberg games and the subtleties introduced by the leader/follower paradigm. Next, we outline their application to the security domain. Finally, we give a brief overview of the ERASER-C algorithm that we use to solve these games.

5.3.1 Stackelberg Games

Stackelberg games were first introduced to study duopoly competition (von Stackelberg 1934), but they have since been recognized as a general model of leadership and commitment. In Stackelberg games, there are two players: a leader and a follower. The leader commits to a strategy first, after which the follower makes his strategy choice. Although this may appear completely detrimental to the leader, since the follower can act with full knowledge of the leader's strategy, the leader actually has a signficant advantage as well. To see this, consider a game with the payoff table as shown in Table 5.1. If we played this as a simultaneous game, the only pure-strategy Nash equilibrium is when

Table 5.1. *Payoff table for an example normal form game*

	C	D
A	2,1	4,0
B	1,0	3,2

the row player plays A and the column player plays C, giving the row player a payoff of 2. However, if the row player was the leader, and the column player, the follower in a Stackelberg game, the leader can commit to a uniform mixed strategy of playing each A and B half the time. This will force the optimizing follower to choose action D, giving the leader an expected payoff of 3.5.

The fact that the leader is able to force the follower into a specific subset of the actionspace potentially gives the leader an advantage in Stackelberg games. Indeed, it has been shown that being able to commit to a randomized mixed strategy always weakly increases the leader's payoff in equilibrium profiles of the game (von Stengel and Zamir 2004).

5.3.2 Stackelberg Security Games

We now discuss how we map security games onto this framework. In a security game, there exist two players: an attacker and a defender that may have multiple types. As stated before, a defender must perpetually defend the site in question; whereas, the attacker is able to observe the defender's strategy and attack when success seems most likely. This fits neatly into the description of a Stackelberg game if we map the attacker to the follower's role and the defender to the leader's role (Avenhaus et al. 2002; Brown et al. 2006).

We can define the actions for the defender as the set of targets that he chooses to defend. So, as shown in Table 5.2, action "1" might actually represent a decision to protect sites 1, 2, and 3. We refer to this as a coverage set. For the attacker, the actions represent which site to attack. Payoffs can be calculated based on the action choices. If the attacker attacks a target that is in the defender's coverage set, then the attacker receives a negative payoff, and the defender receives a positive payoff in which the magnitudes depend on the value of the target. If the attacker attacks a target outside the defender's coverage set, then the attacker receives a positive payoff and the defender receives a negative payoff. This is the approach used in the ARMOR program at LAX (Pita et al. 2008). ARMOR used the DOBSS algorithm (Paruchuri et al. 2008) to solve the resulting game for an optimal mixed strategy for the defender, which would assign each coverage set a probability of being used.

Table 5.2. *DOBSS*

Action	Targets	Prob.
1	1,2,3	p_1
2	1,2,4	p_2
3	1,2,5	p_3
...	...	...
120	8,9,10	p_{120}

Table 5.3. *ERASER*

Action	Targets	Prob.
1	1	p_1
2	2	p_2
3	3	p_3
...	...	...
10	10	p_{10}

5.3.3 ERASER/ERASER-C

We briefly describe the ERASER (Efficient Randomized Allocation of SEcurity Resources) and ERASER-C (Constrained) methods for modeling these Stackelberg security games. Like DOBSS, ERASER is a mixed-integer linear program. However, the additional insight that ERASER exploits is the fact that the payoffs in these games do not depend on the coverage set being implemented, but simply on whether or not the attacked target is in it. For example, while we might have different types of defenders, the particular type of defender that protects a target does not impact the payoff achieved. Also, whether or not an unattacked target is covered has no impact on the payoff either. This means that from a payoff perspective, many coverage sets are actually identical and we can represent the actions in terms of targets instead of coverage sets.

In the previous representation which DOBSS operates on, if we had 3 guards that could defend any of 10 sites, we would have $\binom{10}{3} = 120$ actions. In the new representation, we simply have 10 actions, one for each target, and a probability distribution across the targets that indicates how we distribute the three guards across them. In Tables 5.2 and 5.3, we show the actionspaces for the example outlined with DOBSS and then with ERASER.

The first line of Table 5.2 indicates that, in the DOBSS representation, the first action has the three guards protecting targets 1, 2, and 3 and we use the first

Table 5.4. *DOBSS*

Action	Targets	Probability
1	(1,2),(3,4),(5,6)	p_1
2	(1,2),(3,4),(7,8)	p_2
3	(1,2),(3,4),(9,10)	p_3
...	...	...
120	(15,16),(17,18),(19,20)	p_{120}

Table 5.5. *ERASER-C*

Action	Targets	Probability
1	(1,2)	p_1
2	(3,4)	p_2
3	(5,6)	p_3
...	...	...
10	(19,20)	p_{10}

action with a probability of p_1. The first line of Table 5.3 indicates that, in the ERASER representation, the first action has a guard protecting target 1 with a probability of p_1. As can be seen, this compact representation idea combinatorially shrinks the actionspace of the game, providing tremendous speed increases in solving these games. Although ERASER requires some postprocessing to obtain a solution in the same form as the DOBSS game, the postprocessing is compartively cheap.

ERASER-C takes this idea into a domain with scheduling constraints. Suppose we have 20 targets and 3 guards and the requirement that targets must be guarded as pairs in the set $S = \{(1,2),(3,4),...,(19,20)\}$. In DOBSS, we would need to generate actions that represented all combinations of all valid schedules instead of combinations of all valid targets as in the previous example. In ERASER-C, we perform a similar aggregation to ERASER and also include a mapping of schedules to targets. We then define a defender's strategy as an assignment of resources to schedules instead of an assignment of resources to individual targets as in the previous case. In Tables 5.4 and 5.5, we show the actionspaces for the example outlined with DOBSS and then with ERASER-C.

This exponentially more compact representation allows ERASER-C to solve this class of security games with scheduling constraints exponentially faster than DOBSS and is discussed in more detail in Kiekintveld et al. (2009). This makes it possible for us to solve these large transportation-network games in reasonable time frames, which we evaluate in Section 5.7.1.

5.4 System Architecture

The IRIS system consists of an input module, a back-end module, a display/output module, and a project management module. Figure 5.1 shows a generic diagram of the system, with grey boxes representing modules and white boxes within them representing the components of the modules. We now describe the modules as well as the particular instantiations of these modules in the FAMS domain.

The input module is composed of four classes of inputs that are required by the system in order to generate a representative Stackelberg game and create an optimal schedule. The first input is the resource data. In the FAMS domain, this is the coverage ability and number of FAMs, which we have chosen to model as locations, where each location has a specific number of FAMs who can cover some subset of flights. The second input is the target data. In this case, this is the flight data and includes all the relevant information about flights that the user considers during scheduling, such as flight number, carrier, origin, destination, and aircraft type. The third input is the data required for risk assessment, which will be used by our attribute-based risk analysis engine that we discuss in Section 5.5.1. Figures such as number of passengers, flight path, city of origin, and city of destination are examples of relevant risk data in the FAMS domain. Finally, we allow inputs for data that can be used in the GUI to aid the user's navigation

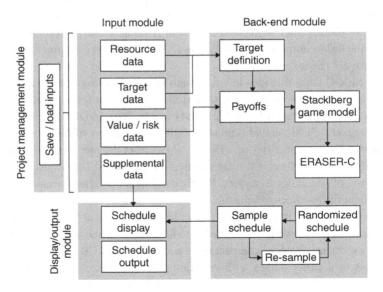

Figure 5.1. Generic diagram of IRIS system.

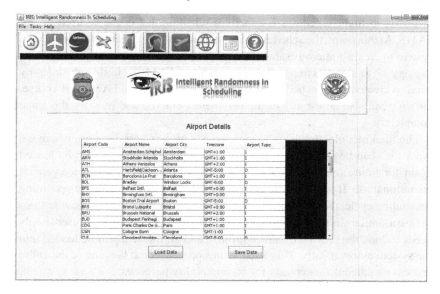

Figure 5.2. Example input screen: Airport details.

and understanding of the system's output. This might include alternative naming schemes for airports and airlines, for example. A sample input screen is shown in Figure 5.2.

The back-end module has six primary components. First, as we describe later in Section 5.5, we have a preprocessing engine that uses the flight and resource information to create the set of all valid flight schedules that serve as the defender's targets in our system. Along with the flight data, this forms the target definition for the game. Second, we have a payoff-generation process that combines the target definition information with the risk data. Third, we translate the payoff information into a Stackelberg game, represented as an MILP. Fourth, we include a generic MILP solver to solve the MILP created via the ERASER-C model. Fifth, we produce a randomized schedule of probability weights for each target based on the solution created by ERASER-C. Finally, we use the randomized schedule to create actual sample schedules that can be implemented by the FAMS.

This information is presented to the user via the display/output module. The schedule created is shown in the interface with pop-up windows as the user's mouse moves over the targets, showing more detailed information about each target. The user is also able to output the schedule to a file that he can then use to analyze the schedule in more detail, as desired. The sample assignment of FAMs to flight schedules is exactly a schedule that could be used by the FAMS. At this point, the scheduling assistant allows the expert who is using the system to create numerous sample schedules based on the same optimal mixed strategy or to simply change the assignment of FAMs to flight schedules by hand to create a final schedule that meets the needs of the FAMS. Of course, the user can also adjust any of the parameters entered and re-solve the game completely.

The final module, the project manager, is a project-based system where the input files can be stored as a "state-of-the-world," which can then be loaded again for future use. The user can then specify a default project for general operational use. If additional security risks are known to exist for the upcoming scheduling cycle, the user can alter the default project and save the new settings in case a similar situation arises again in the future. If this occurs, the user simply needs to load the previously saved project, and all the data will be loaded into the system automatically. This also ensures proper record keeping of the entire process of schedule generation for accountability purposes.

5.5 Major Challenges

Now we describe the process of mapping the FAMS domain into a Stackelberg security game and the challenges we encounter and address during the process.

5.5.1 Describing the game

Although we have decided to cast the FAMS domain as a Stackelberg game, we still have not determined what to use as targets or their payoffs. For this, we must consult with the experts in the domain, such as the current scheduler and/or field personnel, to understand what risks and potential damages they see in their domain. In addition to understanding the current scheduling practices, the answers to the key questions of this phase will be used to determine the structure of the game, such as target definition, resource capabilities and constraints, and risk evaluation for the targets. These answers will allow us to determine the data required as inputs to the IRIS system.

The first two items are much more straightforward to understand. The difficulty that remains with defining the game is efficiently gathering the risk data. While we could simply ask the user to enter each of these risk numbers for every single flight, the attribute-based nature of the problem lends itself to a much easier method. Here we introduce an attribute-based preference elicitation system for aggregating the risk data associated with targets.

We create a preference elicitation system based on the threat, vulnerability, and consequence (TVC) model for estimating terrorism risk (Willis et al. 2005). In TVC, the risk of terrorism is broken down into more easily estimated components, and a formula is created to combine them into an aggregate risk value. Thus, instead of asking the user to calculate and input each flight's overall risk values, we can simply ask the user to input the risk/value numbers for each component of risk that he would use to make the calculation. From here we can create a vector of attributes for each flight by automatically pulling in values that pertain to a flight. Using each of these vectors, we can specify a combination formula to aggregate the information into payoff values for use in our Stackelberg game model. Since a given flight's payoff value may be based on a large number of attributes, we also allow the user to bypass this system and directly edit the payoff value if required. This allows the user to make quick corrections or changes if special situations arise for individual flights.

During a restricted test run on real data, the attribute-based approach called for a total of 114 values to input regardless of the number of flights. By contrast, there were 2,571 valid flights over a week, each requiring four payoff values, summing to 10,284 user-entered values without the attribute-based preference elicitation system. The attribute-based approach clearly requires far fewer inputs and remains constant as the number of flights increases, allowing for excellent scalability as we deal with larger and larger sets of flights. Equally importantly, attribute-based risk assessment is an intuitive and highly scalable method that can be used in any problem in which people must distill numerous attributes of a situation into a single value for a large number of situations that share the same attributes.

5.5.2 Solving the game

We now describe in more detail the considerations involved in addressing the scheduling-constraint challenge mentioned in Section 5.2 that we use ERASER-C to resolve.

Recall that we have a number of hard scheduling constraints that are inherent in the FAMS domain, such as not being able to schedule a FAM on a pair of flights from City A to City B and back if the return flight leaves before the arrival flight lands. These hard scheduling constraints in the FAMS domain make the naïve formulation of modeling every combination of possible schedules difficult to implement. With tens of thousands of flights per day to consider, the number of combinations of possible schedules explodes prohibitively quickly as is discussed in detail in Kiekintveld et al. (2009).

One reasonable approach to this issue would be to model the problem with each "target" representing a possible "schedule" of flights and simply preprocessing the flights into valid schedules before creating the game model. Thus, instead of a possible coverage being "Flight 22 from City A to City B," it might be "Flight 22 from City A to City B and Flight 12 from City B to City A," where each flight schedule is a realistic sequence of flights that a FAM could take that would also bring him home at the end of the schedule. The defender would now simply need to determine an optimal coverage strategy over the universe of flight schedules. The attacker would do the same. However, this is no longer a true representation of the domain. In reality, a potential attacker can actually choose to attack individual flights, not only a sequence of flights, and restricting him to only attacking flight sequences changes the problem we are solving.

An example that illustrates this problem can be constructed as follows. Suppose there are four flights, A,B,C, and D, where flights A and B are medium value, C is extremely high value, and D has extremely low value. After constructing flight schedules, we find that flights must be paired as A/B and C/D. Suppose that in our valuation, the two medium-value flights come to the same overall value assessment as the high-value flight paired with the low-value flight. Thus, our strategy would be to defend both pairs with equal probability, since an attacker evaluating the options would see the same two equal-value options and be indifferent between the two.

However, an attacker might actually view the flights individually because they may not have scheduling constraints. With defenders spread evenly across all four flights, the attackers best choice is to attack the highly valued flight C. This should alter our strategy so that we place more emphasis on the C/D flight pair than we did previously to lower their expected payoff. Thus, the model of flight schedules for attackers and defenders does not properly represent the game and can lead to suboptimal strategies.

Instead, we model the scheduling constraints explicitly by preprocessing the flights into valid flight schedules and incorporating these in a compact way as described in Section 5.3.3. This alleviates the problem of an exploding actionspace and allows us to solve much larger games in reasonable time frames. Thus, we are able to simultaneously overcome the complexity introduced by scheduling constraints and to solve these games much more quickly than we could have using the DOBSS method.

5.6 Organizational Acceptance

In real-world deployment of cutting-edge research, overcoming organizational doubt and resistance is a critical and easily overlooked aspect of the project. For example, if a new methodology has too steep a learning curve or is too dramatic a change from the current methodology, it is very difficult for people to adopt to. If the new program requires significant infrastructure change to incorporate it into other routines, it may simply not be cost-effective to do so. Also, if people have trouble convincing themselves that the new solution performs at least as well as the existing solution, we cannot reasonably expect them to use it. We now discuss three key points that contributed to our successful collaboration with the FAMS: adhering to current practices, ease of incorporation, and error checking.

In creating solutions for people, we must be cognizant of how difficult it will be for a user to adopt our solution. Each deviation from existing methodology is a step away from the familiar that we must convince the user to accept. Instead of asking people to make numerous and sometimes unnecessary changes, minimizing these differences and complexities can help pave the way towards a successful implementation. For example, we spent months fine-tuning IRIS's interface until we achieved a look and feel that FAMS was familiar and comfortable with. Changes included such things as what information to display in the schedule, how to output the finalized schedule, how to format the flight number and carrier name, terminology to use, colors to use, and logos. While it is true that these changes were all cosmetic and thus as researchers, we may be tempted to dismiss them, their importance cannot be stressed enough in real-world implementation.

Similarly, because infrastructure changes are often costly and time-consuming, ease of incorporating our work into the user's daily routine is essential. In our case, the FAMS had a system from which they could extract flight information in the same way as for their current schedule-generation practices and then a set of tools for analyzing the schedules that were created. While the specific format of inputs/ouputs is not of theoretical interest, we recognized that incorporating IRIS into FAMS's scheduling practices would probably require a significant effort on their put and asking them to further change other processes to accommodate us would be very inconsiderate. Allowing IRIS to use inputs and create outputs that were in the same format as existing their protocols minimized the additional work that our assistant would create for them.

Another aspect of organizational acceptance is making error checking your implementation easy. Existing practices have a proven track record, and users are inevitably wary of new methods until they have convinced themselves of their quality. Instead of attempting to convince users that the solution is correct, we found that giving them tools to check, compare, and alter the solution's output was just as effective. For example, in IRIS, we output schedules in a manner that easily allows for external reporting tools to be run on them. This makes it that much simpler to convince users that schedules are "random" and that we are not modeling their problem incorrectly. Also, due to the size of the problem, error checking helps identify errors in the process that could lead to incorrect outputs. Instead of asking people to unreasonably assume the correctness of our solution, we simply include tools for them to check the results directly.

Although it is not strictly a part of most academic research, organizational acceptance is a very real problem that must be tackled with every application of theory into practice. Recognizing and working through these situations is crucial and oftentimes proves to be quite simple to achieve.

5.7 Experimental Results

Two primary concerns can be raised regarding the IRIS system: (i) the time required to develop a randomized schedule; (ii) evidence supporting the quality of the schedules generated. To address these, we conduct experiments exploring these two issues. All of our experiments were run on a machine with dual Xeon 3.2Ghz processors and 2GB of RAM, running RHEL 3. We use CPLEX 9.0.0 with default parameter settings to solve the MILPs.

5.7.1 Runtime Analysis

In creating the system, practical application was the primary goal. If the system was not fast enough for feasible use, then it could not be useful to the FAMS. Thus, we set an initial goal of creating a week's schedule for all flights between the United States and a Region A within a reasonable time frame and include tools to manage the effects of scheduling for successive periods to allow for schedule creation for longer periods. In Figure 5.3, we show the results of creating randomized schedules for subsets of the FAMS problem.

The experiments were run using one week of real flight data for the subregions of Region A and three separate sets of hypothetical FAMS home-city data that vary the number of FAMs available to explore its impact upon runtime. Region A and the countries within it are actual places for which we have used real flight data, but for security reasons we have disguised them here. Region A is composed of five larger countries which we have designated 1–5, as well as a few small countries that are only included in the full region tests. We created random values for the other inputs and held them constant throughout the experiments.

In Figure 5.3, the y-axis represents the time required for generating a schedule in minutes, and the x-axis shows which countries are included in the game being

Table 5.6. *Game sizes for experiments that were run*

Region	Flights	Flight schedules
1	873	1,181
1,2	1,147	1,403
1,2,3	1,528	1,660
1,2,3,4	1,845	1,975
1,2,3,4,5	2,033	2,114
Region A	2,571	2,416

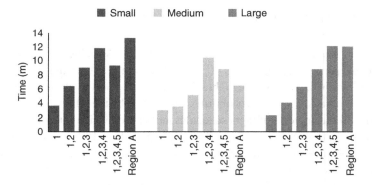

Figure 5.3. Runtimes for scheduling one-week subregions of region A.

run. The x-axis is grouped in three separate sets that represent, from left to right, a small number of FAMs, a medium number of FAMs, and a large number of FAMs distributed through the same set of home cities. For example, the first bar on the left represents an average runtime of 3.65 minutes to create a schedule for all flights to Country 1 within a one week period over twenty trials. In light grey, the first bar on the left represents the exact same experiment, but run with a medium number of FAMs. In Table 5.6, we show the exact size of the game for each of the subregions. As can be seen, all tested game instances could be completed within fifteen minutes.

5.7.2 Evaluation

In evaluating our method, we compare the schedules generated using IRIS against a uniform random policy as well as a naïve weighting policy. In the

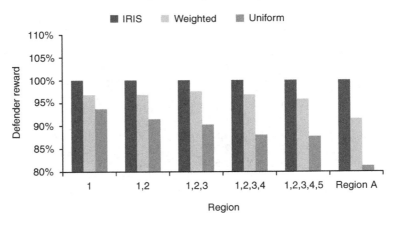

Figure 5.4. Maximum expected defender reward by strategy.

uniform random policy, each location covers all of its reachable flight schedules with equal probability regardless of payoff. In the naïve weighting policy, each location randomizes across the flight schedules based solely on the payoff attainable by the attacker, where probabilities are dictated by the relative payoffs. For example, if the universe of flight schedules included eleven flights, of which ten flights had a payoff of ten and one flight had a payoff of 100, and the defender had two resources available, the naïve weighting policy would assign a probability of 100 percent to the high-value flight and 10 percent each to the low-value flights. As the benchmark of quality, we calculate the highest expected payoff attainable by the defender, assuming that the attacker chooses the target with the highest payoff for him.

In Figure 5.4, the y-axis represents the normalized payoff return for each of the three strategies, with all payoffs normalized to the maximum expected defender's payoff achievable under the strategy generated by IRIS. Across the x-axis, each of the regions are labeled as before. Thus, the rightmost group of bars, from left to right, represents the maximum expected defender's payoff achievable under IRIS as 100 percent; under the weighted randomization strategy as 9 percent worse than IRIS's; and under the uniform randomization strategy as 19 percent worse than IRIS. As can be seen, IRIS's solution is superior to the other two strategies in every region tested.

5.8 Summary

Onboard patrols are a key component of law enforcement in transportation networks. In generating schedules for these patrols, it is important to account for the varying weights of the vehicles being protected, as well as for the fact that potential attackers can often observe the procedures being used. This paper describes IRIS, a scheduling assistant for FAMS, which provides a game-theoretic solution to this problem. Although IRIS is similar in spirit to the ARMOR system deployed at LAX, the inherent challenges of transportation networks evident in the FAMS domain necessitate major additions and advances to the existing methodologies.

In particularly, IRIS combines three key advancements: (i) It uses the fastest known solver for this class of security games, ERASER-C, which exploits symmetries in the payoff structure; (ii) it models the problem using action definitions for defenders and attackers, which allows us to efficiently handle the scheduling constraints inherent in the domain; and (iii) it includes an attribute-based preference elicitation system for calculating the risk values of targets, eliminating the need for users to enter risk values for each target individually.

IRIS makes use of algorithmic advances in multi-agent systems research to solve the class of massive security games with complex constraints that were not previously solvable in realistic timeframes. Thus, although our work on IRIS thus far has been restricted to the FAMS, it provides a general framework for solving patrolling scheduling problems in other transportation networks as well.

One example of another transportation network that resembles the FAMS domain is the New York City subway system. The NYC subway includes tens of subway routes, thousands of subway cars, and a daily weekday ridership of a few million people. Although there are only a few subway routes compared to the number of commercial flights in the FAMS domain, once we consider that a patrolling officer can start and end his patrol route at any two subway stops and must also choose which subway cars to protect while aboard the train, the number of potential patrol "actions" explodes extremely quickly. Similarly to the FAMS domain, we also have scheduling constraints on the sequence of subway routes a law enforcement officer can patrol. Other transportation networks that share similar challenges include bus systems and commuter rail systems as well.

IRIS has been in use since October 2009, and we are working to expand our methods to other applicable domains in the near future.

Acknowledgments

IRIS's development has only been so successful due to the exceptional collaboration with the United States Federal Air Marshal Service. This research was supported by the United States Department of Homeland Security through the

Center for Risk and Economic Analysis of Terrorism Events (CREATE) under grant number 2007-ST-061-000001. However, any opinions, findings, and conclusions or recommendations in this document are those of the authors and do not necessarily reflect views of the United States Department of Homeland Security.

6

GUARDS: Game-Theoretic Security Allocation on a National Scale

James Pita, Milind Tambe, Christopher Kiekintveld,
Shane Cullen, and Erin Steigerwald

6.1 Introduction

The United States Transportation Security Administration (TSA) is tasked with protecting the nation's transportation systems. These systems are often large in scale and protecting them requires many personnel and security activities. One set of systems in particular is the over 400 airports. These airports serve approximately 28,000 commercial flights per day and up to approximately 87,000 total flights [Air Traffic Control]. To protect this large transportation network, the TSA employs approximately 48,000 Transportation Security Officers (TSA); who are responsible for implementing security activities at each.

Many people are aware of the common security activities, especially individual passenger screening. However, this is just one of many security layers TSA personnel implement to help prevent potential threats (TSA). These layers can involve hundreds of heterogeneous security activities executed by limited TSA personnel, leading to a complex resource-allocation challenge. Unfortunately, TSA cannot possibly run every security activity all the time and thus must decide how to appropriately allocate its resources among the layers of security activities.

To aid the TSA in scheduling resources in a risk-based manner, we take a multi-agent game-theoretic approach. Motivated by advantages of such an approach reported at AAMAS conferences (see Section 6.2.2), we utilize Stackelberg games, in which one agent (the leader) must commit to some strategy first and a second agent (the follower) can make his decision with knowledge of this commitment. Here, the TSA acts as a defender (i.e., the leader) who

Previously published in *Proc. of 10th Int. Conf. on Autonomous Agents and Multiagent Systems – Innovative Applications Track (AAMAS 2011)*, Tumer, Yolum, Sonenberg, and Stone (eds.), May, 2–6, 2011, Taipei, Taiwan.

has a set of targets to protect, a number of security activities they can utilize to protect each target, and a limited number of resources to assign to these security activities. This approach then models a motivated attacker's ability to observe the TSA's resource allocations before choosing to execute a potential threat in an attempt to attack an airport target. The advantage of our approach is in finding the optimal mixed strategy for the TSA to commit to that will provide them with a risk-based, randomized schedule for allocating their limited resources. From the perspective of the underlying game-theoretic model, a crucial difference between our novel approach and previous approaches is that we allow for both heterogeneous security activities and threats; whereas, previous "security games" approaches reported at AAMAS (Pita et al., 2008; Tsai et al., 2009) are only able to consider homogeneous security activities and threats, leading to a new game model called "security circumvention games" (SCGs).

In conjunction with TSA subject-matter experts, we developed a software system, Game-theoretic Unpredictable and Randomly Deployed Security (GUARDS), which utilizes a Stackelberg framework to aid in protecting the airport transportation network. From an application perspective, the fundamental novelty in GUARDS, compared to previous applications (Pita et al., 2008; Tsai et al., 2009) of such game-theoretic approaches, is the potential for national-scale deployment at over 400 airports. Given that previous approaches only dealt with a single, stand-alone location, this scale raises three new issues. The first issue involves appropriately modeling the TSA's security challenges to achieve the best security policies (mixed strategy). Due to the complex nature of TSA's security challenges, traditional models of security games (Yin et al., 2010) are no longer appropriate models. Specifically, the TSA's domain has the following additional features that is, beyond traditional security games: (i) heterogeneous security activities for each potential target; and (ii) heterogeneous threats for each potential target; and (iii) unique security activities for individual airports. The second issue has to do with efficiently solving the model we developed in which, because we are considering a national deployment, a special-purpose solver may not be appropriate. In fact, previous solution techniques (Jain et al., 2010; Kickintveld et al., 2009) for traditional security games are no longer directly applicable. The third issue concerns knowledge acquisition for the many variables involved in TSA's security challenges.

In consideration of national deployment for TSA, we face two unique constraints. First, headquarters cannot do the kind of centralized planning in which they create a single, optimal security policy (mixed strategy) that will be applicable to all airports. Each airport is unique, and thus requires its own individual security policy. Second, TSA wants to maintain a common standard of security among airports. This precludes an entirely decentralized approach in which each individual airport is completely in charge of creating its own security policy. Even so, because of the possibility that there will be over 400 end-users, it is not practical to sit down with each location and tailor the system to their individual needs. This presents a challenge in acquiring the necessary domain knowledge to appropriately model the security challenge for such a large network of airports.

To address these issues, we developed both a new, formal model of security games and techniques to solve this class of games. We also had to incorporate a new methodology for knowledge acquisition. To appropriately model the TSA's security challenges, we created a novel game-theoretic model, SCGs, and cast the TSA's challenges within it. In creating SCGs we provide the following contributions: (i) the ability for defenders to guard targets with more than one type of security activity (heterogeneous activities); and (ii) the ability for attackers to choose threats designed to circumvent specific security activities. Given our new model, we designed an efficient solution technique in which we create a compact representation of SCGs. This allows us to avoid using a tailored Stackelberg solver and instead to utilize a general purpose Stackelberg solver to compute solutions efficiently. Finally, we took a partially centralized approach to knowledge acquisition for the TSA domain. We integrated a two-phase knowledge-acquisition process in which we acquire common information, standards, and practices directly from TSA headquarters, and then developed the GUARDS system itself to acquire the necessary information that is unique to individual airports.

These key issues present a novel and exciting problem in transitioning years of research from the AAMAS conference to a highly complex domain (Kickintveld et al., 2009; Paruchuri et al., 2008; Pita et al., 2008; Tsai et al., 2009; Yin et al., 2010). GUARDS is currently under evaluation by the TSA with the goal of incorporating its scheduling practices into their unpredictable security programs across airports nationwide.

6.2 Background

Game theory is well known to be a useful foundation in multiagent systems to reason about multiple agents each pursuing their own interests (Fudenberg and Tirole, 1991). Game-theoretic approaches, specifically based on Stackelberg games, have recently become popular for addressing security problems (e.g., assigning checkpoints, air marshals, or canine patrols). These approaches reason about two agents pursuing opposing interests (i.e., a security force and an adversary) in an attempt to optimize the security force's goals. Specifically, they model the commitment a security force must make in providing security and the attacker's capability of observing this commitment before attacking. The objective is to find the optimal mixed strategy to commit to, given that an attacker will optimize his reward after observing this strategy. Now we describe how security games, as defined in Yin et al. (2010), fit into the Stackelberg paradigm. In Section 6.3.1 we will define SCGs to account for the challenges the TSA faces.

6.2.1 Security Games

In a security game there are two agents – the defender (security force) and an attacker – who act as the leader and the follower in a Stackelberg game. There is also a set of targets, which the defender is trying to protect. Each of these targets has a unique reward and penalty to both the defender and attacker. Thus, some targets may be more valuable to the defender than others. To protect these targets, the defender has a number, K, of resources at her disposal. There is a single security activity being considered, and these resources can be allocated to execute this activity on any target. Once a resource is allocated to a target, it is marked as covered; otherwise, it is marked as uncovered. If the attacker attacks an uncovered target he gets his reward, and the defender gets her corresponding penalty, or vice versa. The defender's goal is to maximize her reward given that the attacker will attack with knowledge of the defensive strategy the defender has chosen. In most cases, the defender's optimal strategy is a randomized one in which she chooses a mixed strategy over all her possible resource assignments.

There exist a number of algorithms and techniques for solving security games (Conitzer and Sandholm, 2006; Jain et al., 2010; Kickintveld et al., 2009; Paruchuri et al., 2008). DOBSS, a mixed-integer linear program, and the MLPs methods are the most general and are capable of solving any Stackelberg game optimally (Conitzer and Sandholm, 2006; Paruchuri et al., 2008). The other algorithms are tailored to security games specifically and in practice are much faster for these games.

6.2.2 Assistants for Security Games

A number of tools have been designed to assist in security problems that fall under the security game paradigm. ARMOR and IRIS are two such tools which take a game-theoretic approach in scheduling checkpoints and canine patrols (ARMOR) and Federal Air Marshals (IRIS). In fact, ARMOR and IRIS have been deployed to aid with security operations for the Los Angeles World Airport Police at LAY and at LAX for the FAMS, respectively (Pita et al., 2008; Tsai et al., 2009). These systems offer two sets of advantages. The first deals with solution quality: (i) they provide an optimal mixed strategy for the single security activity they consider, such as assigning checkpoints or air marshals; (ii) the randomized solutions that are produced both avoid deterministic strategies, which are easily exploitable, and remove the human element in randomization since humans are well known to be poor randomizers (Wagenaar, 1972); and (iii) they reason over difficult problems that are often impossible for humans to reason over optimally. These advantages are useful for any tool being utilized in the field to help with randomized resource allocation in security problems, and we incorporate them into GUARDS as well.

The second set of advantages is specific to the problems they address: (i) they develop unique and useful preference elicitation systems and knowledge acquisition techniques for the specific problem they address; (ii) based on practical requirements, they apply state of the art algorithms tailored to efficiently solving the Stackelberg games they consider. Unfortunately, previous methods are too specific to the stand-alone location they consider and thus cannot directly be applied in GUARDS; indeed, GUARDS requires us to address a novel set of challenges, as we describe in the next section.

6.3 National Deployment Challenges

We now describe in detail the three major issues involved in potentially deploying game-theoretic randomization for airport security on a national scale, including modeling, computational, and knowledge acquisition challenges, and our solutions to them.

6.3.1 Modeling the TSA Resource Allocation challenges

While we are motivated by an existing model of security games (Yin et al., 2010), there are three critical aspects of the new TSA domain that raise new challenges. First, the defender now reasons over heterogeneous security activities for each potential area within an airport.[1] For example, airports have ticketing areas, waiting areas, and cargo-holding areas. Within each of these areas, TSA has a number of security activities to choose from, such as running perimeter patrols, screening cargo, screening employees, and many others. Second, given the multiple possible security activities, the defender may allocate more than one resource per area (i.e., areas are no longer covered or uncovered). Finally, the defender now considers an adversary who can execute heterogeneous attacks on an area. The TSA must reason about a large number of potential threats in each area, such as chemical weapons, active shooters, and bombs. The key

---

[1] Because of the nature of the TSA's security challenge, we will refer to targets in the TSA's domain as "areas" henceforth.

challenge, then, is how to allocate limited TSA security resources to specific activities in particular areas, taking into account an attacker's response.

To address this challenge, it is necessary to create a more expressive model than was outlined in security games, one that is able to reason over the numerous areas, security activities, and threats within an individual airport. We refer to this new class of security games as security circumvention games (SCGs). SCGs are more expressive than traditional security games and thus can represent both traditional security games and the games we considered for the TSA. In SCGs, the TSA must choose some combination of security activities to execute within each area, and the attacker must reason over both what area to attack and what method of attack to execute based on the defender's strategy. Now we elaborate on the defender's and attacker's possible strategies.

6.3.1.1 Defender Strategies

We denote the defender by Θ, and the set of defender's pure strategies by $\sigma_\Theta \in \Sigma_\Theta$. The TSA is able to execute a variety of security activities, which we denote by $S = \{s_1, \ldots, s_m\}$. Each security activity has two components. The first is the type of activity it represents, and the second is the area in which the activity is performed. We denote the set of areas by $A = \{a_1, \ldots, a_n\}$.

The defender has K resources available and thus can run any K security activities. The TSA's task is to consider how to allocate these resources among security activities to provide the optimal protection to their potential areas. An assignment of K resources to K security activities represents a single strategy $\sigma_\Theta \in \Sigma_\Theta$. For example, if there are three security activities, $S = \{s_1, s_2, s_3\}$ and two resources available, one possible pure strategy for the defender is to assign these two resources to s_1 and s_3. Given that the number of possible combinations of K security activities at an airport can be on the order of 10^{13} or greater for the TSA, we develop a compact representation of the possible strategies that we present in (Section 6.3.2). The defender's mixed strategies $\delta_\Theta \in \Delta_\Theta$ are the possible probability distributions over Σ_Θ. Similarly to previous work, a mixed strategy (randomized solution) is typically the optimal strategy.

6.3.1.2 Attacker Actions

Defending a target against terrorist attacks is complicated by the diversity of the potential threats. For example, in any given area an attacker may try to use a vehicle-borne explosive device, an active shooter, or a suitcase bomb, among others. Not all methods of attack would make sense in all areas. For example, in some airport configurations using a vehicle-borne explosive device in the checked baggage screening area would not be a viable method of attack. We denote the attacker by Ψ, and the set of pure strategies for the attacker is given by $\sigma_\Psi \in \Sigma_\Psi$. Each pure strategy for the attacker corresponds to selecting a single area $a_i \in A$ to attack, and a specific mode of attack. However, given that each airport considers its own potential threats, enumerating all threats for each individual airport through the software may not be practical. To handle the national deployment challenge we face and avoid this difficulty, we developed a novel way to represent threats for TSA's domain that we describe in Section 6.3.2.1.

6.3.2 Compact Representation for Efficiency

Although we have developed a model that appropriately captures the TSA's security challenge, there is one issue with this model namely, that both the attacker- and the defender-strategy spaces grow combinatorially as the number of defender security activities increases. Also, listing such a large number of potential threats may lead to extreme memory and runtime inefficiencies. Furthermore, existing solution techniques that have been developed for security games (Jain et al., 2010; Kickintveld et al., 2009) are not directly applicable to SCGs.

With this in mind, we looked at an alternate approach to finding optimal solutions efficiently. Specifically, we looked at representing threats in a more intelligent manner and creating a compact representation for the defender-strategy space. By utilizing both of these techniques, we achieved large reductions in runtime. We utilized the general Stackelberg solver known as DOBSS (Paruchuri et al., 2008) to solve our compact representation and avoided creating a tailored algorithm for each specific airport. Now we explain both how we model threats and how we achieve a compact representation of the defender's full strategy space.

6.3.2.1 Threat Modeling for TSA

While it is important that we reason over all the security activities that are available to an individual airport, enumerating all potential threats can lead to severe memory and runtime inefficiencies. Thus, the problem we face is how to model attack methods in a way that limits the number of threats that GUARDS needs to reason over but appropriately captures both an attacker's capabilities and his goals. In particular, we automatically generate attack methods for the adversary that capture two key goals: (i) an attacker wanting to avoid the security activities that are in place; (ii) an attacker wanting to cause maximal damage with minimum cost.

To achieve these goals, an intelligent adversary will observe a defender's security activities over time and design his attack method based on his observations. The attacker's plan will be designed to avoid security activities that he believes will be in place. We refer to this as "circumventing security activities". For example, imagine there is a single area with three security activities, such as passenger screening, luggage screening, and perimeter patrol. In this example, TSA only has one resource available and thus can only execute one of these activities at a time. While passenger screening may have the highest probability of success, if TSA never screens luggage or patrols the perimeter, the adversary can choose an attack path that avoids passenger screening, for example, utilizing a suitcase bomb or attacking from the perimeter.

On the defender side, we know that dedicating more resources to security activities in an area increases the security afforded to that area. However, even with more resources, we want to avoid being predictable since attackers can exploit this predictability; avoiding the security activities they know will be in place. Thus, we needed to represent threats in a way that accounts for the attacker's ability to observe security in advance and avoid specific security activities, but still represents the benefit of dedicating more resources.

A naïve approach is to represent only a single threat per area and to decrease the likelihood that the threat will be successful because more security activities are put in place. This captures the increase in security for additional security activities; however, it does not account for the attacker's ability to circumvent security activities. With this method you would simply choose security activities in the order of their relative success, making the defender's strategy predictable and exploitable.

The alternative that we chose is to create a list of potential threats that circumvent different combinations of specific security activities. By basing threats on circumventing particular combinations of security activities, we avoid the issue of enumerating all the possible potential threats. Instead, the threats are automatically created based on the security activities in an area. However, we also incorporate a cost to the attacker for circumventing more activities to capture the idea of causing maximal damage at minimal cost. Each individual activity is associated with a specific circumvention cost, and a higher number of activities circumvented leads to a higher circumvention cost. This cost reflects the additional difficulty of executing an attack against increased security. This difficulty could be due to the need for additional resources, time, and other factors in executing an attack. Since attackers can now actively circumvent specific security activities, randomization becomes a key factor in the solutions that are produced because any deterministic strategies can be circumvented.

6.3.2.2 Compact Representation

We introduce a compact representation that exploits similarities in defender security activities to reduce the number of strategies that must be enumerated and considered when finding an optimal solution to SCGs. First, we identify security activities that provide coverage to the same areas, and have the same circumvention costs (i.e., have identical properties). Let $\gamma_i \in \Gamma$ represent the sets of security activities that can be grouped together because they have identical properties. Now, instead of reasoning over individual security activities, we reason about groups of identical security activities $\gamma_i \in \Gamma$. A strategy $\sigma_\Theta \in \Sigma_\Theta$ is represented by the number of resources assigned to each set of identical security activities γ_i.

To illustrate this new representation, we provide a concrete example of the full representation versus the compact representation in Tables 6.1 and 6.2. In this example there are 4 security activities and 2 resources. Here, s_1 and s_2 have identical circumvention costs and affect a_1 while s_3 and s_4 have identical circumvention costs and affect a_2. Table 6.1 presents the full representation with corresponding payoffs and Table 6.2 represents the compact form of the same where γ_1 represents the group s_1 and s_2 and γ_2 represents the group s_3 and s_4. In both tables, each row represents a single pure strategy for the defender and each column the same for the attacker. Notice in Table 6.1 each strategy $\sigma_\Theta \in \Sigma_\Theta$ is represented by the exact security activities being executed while in Table 6.2, it is only which set $\gamma_i \in \Gamma$ each resource has been allocated to.

The key to the compact representation is that each of the security activities from a set $\gamma_i \in \Gamma$ will have the same effect on the payoffs. Therefore, it is optimal for the defender to distribute probability uniformly at random across all security activities within a set γ_i, so that all security activities are chosen with equal probability in the solution. Given that the defender strategy uniformly distributes resources among all security activities $s_j \in \gamma_i$, we also know that it does not matter which specific security activities the attacker chooses to circumvent from the set γ_i. For any given number of security activities circumvented, the expected payoff to the attacker is identical, regardless of which specific activities within the set are chosen. This is because we are selecting security activities uniformly at random within the set γ_i. Therefore, we can use a similar compact representation for the attacker strategy space as for the defender space, reasoning only over the aggregate number of each type of security activity rather than over specific security activities.

Given this, we only need to know how many security activities are selected from each set in order to compute the expected payoffs for each player in the compact representation. For example, examining the second row and second

Table 6.1. *Example payoffs for a sample game*

	$a_1 : \emptyset$	$a_1 : s_1$	$a_1 : s_2$	$a_2 : \emptyset$	$a_2 : s_3$	$a_2 : s_4$
s_1, s_2	2, −1	4, −3	4, −3	−20, 10	−17, 7	−17, 7
s_1, s_3	2, −1	−8, 3	4, −3	5, −5	−17, 7	8, −8
s_1, s_4	2, −1	−8, 3	4, −3	5, −5	8, −8	−17, 7
s_2, s_3	2, −1	4, −3	−8, 3	5, −5	−17, 7	8, −8
s_2, s_4	2, −1	4, −3	−8, 3	5, −5	8, −8	−17, 7
s_3, s_4	−10, 5	−8, 3	−8, 3	5, −5	8, −8	8, −8

Table 6.2. *Example compact version of sample game*

	$a_1 : \emptyset$	$a_1 : \gamma_1$	$a_2 : \emptyset$	$a_2 : \gamma_2$
γ_1, γ_1	2, −1	4, −3	−20, 10	−17, 7
γ_1, γ_2	2, −1	−2, 0	5, −5	−4.5, −5
γ_2, γ_2	−10, 5	−8, 3	5, −5	8, −8

column of Table 6.2 we see that the reward to the defender is −2 and the reward to the attacker is 0. In this case, the defender strategy is to assign one resource to activities in γ_1 and one resource to activities in γ_2. Given that the defender is uniformly distributing these resources, it follows that she will execute s_1 half of the time and s_2 the other half. On the attacker side, we know that the attacker is circumventing one security activity from the set γ_1. If he circumvents either s_1 or s_2 he will only succeed half of the time. Thus, half of the time the defender receives 4 and the other half −8 for an expectation of −2 $(4 * .5 + (−8) * .5)$. We compute the attacker's reward in the same manner.

Given this compact representation for both the defender and attacker, we can compute an optimal mixed strategy of assigning resources over Γ. Once we have this mixed strategy, we will need to determine an actual strategy for the TSA to execute by sampling one of the possible strategies from the mixed strategy we have determined for our compact representation (e.g., one sample may be $\gamma_2 \gamma_2$). Once sampled, we will know exactly how many resources are available to each set $\gamma_i \in \Gamma$. Given this resource assignment, we can then sample security activities by selecting k uniformly at random, where k is the number of resources assigned to $\gamma_i \in \Gamma$. This specific set of security activities for each area under the current resource assignment is a full strategy for the TSA to execute.

6.3.3 Knowledge Acquisition

One of the most difficult issues we faced from a potential national-deployment perspective was acquiring the appropriate knowledge for the security challenge being considered. In the past, tools such as ARMOR and IRIS (Pita et al. 2008, Tsai et al., 2009) were developed for reasoning about a single security activity in a stand-alone location. That approach gave the advantage of being able to sit down with domain experts who will be using the system and develop a knowledge-acquisition process for the specific domain at hand. Unfortunately, with hundreds of airports to consider, it is not possible to sit down at each location and learn its exact needs. To overcome this obstacle, we worked in close collaboration with TSA headquarters to develop a two-phase knowledge-acquisition process.

In phase one, we took an approach similar to previous centralized approaches. In particular, we met with domain experts to acquire knowledge that is common among all airports. This included area definitions, defining security activities, and determining resource capabilities. In collaboration with headquarters, we then decided how individual airports can customize these components in their individual games while maintaining standards set forth by headquarters (as we discuss later). Additionally, we collaborated with headquarters to limit the amount of customization inputs so that users at individual airports are not overwhelmed – a key to organizational acceptance discussed in Section 6.6.

In phase two of our knowledge acquisition, we took a decentralized approach in which it is the responsibility of individual airports to input customized information. For this phase we could not create a rigid system designed with one specific game instance in mind for a single airport. Instead, we relied on SCGs and developed a system in collaboration with headquarters that allows individual airports to manipulate specific components within this framework to create unique game instances. These inputs are designed to ensure that individual airports maintain standards set forth by headquarters in phase one. For example, individual airports are responsible for determining the unique reward and penalty for the defender and attacker associated with each area, given a successful or unsuccessful attack. However, TSA headquarters requires a standardized method for determining these values to ensure that resources are being appropriately distributed. To this end, we designed an input module within GUARDS to reflect a risk-evaluation process developed by the TSA in which a series of quantifiable questions are answered for each area by individual airports. For example, questions might include the number of fatalities that may result from an attack in an area or whether the area has access control. The answers to these question are then combined in a mathematical formula to decide the values for a particular area for both the defender and attacker.[2] This input process ensures that airports are appropriately valuing the areas they protect within an airport

---

[2] Previous work by Pita et al. (2008), Tsai et al. (2009), and Wagenaar (1972) has shown that security problems are not necessarily zero-sum for a number of potential reasons. In GUARDS, for similar reasons, games are not necessarily zero-sum.

according to headquarters guidelines. In general, using the customizable input that airports generate, we can then create the unique game instance for that particular airport.

Our two-phase knowledge-acquisition process follows a partially centralized approach and provides the following advantages: (i) it allows domain experts from TSA headquarters to assure that the system meets the required needs of the challenge being considered; (ii) it focuses on creating customizable inputs instead of a system that is tailored to a highly specific problem instance; and (iii) it allows TSA headquarters to have control while still enabling individual airports to customize the system to meet their individual needs. With this third advantage, there is an important trade-off between system customization and standardization among airports. Determining this trade-off is an important part of the first phase in this two-phase knowledge-acquisition process.

6.4 System Architecture

The GUARDS system consists of three modules. First, there is an input module designed to acquire the necessary information for a unique instance of the complex security game we consider. Second, there is a back-end module that is designed to both create and solve the unique game instance based on the inputs. Finally, there is a display/output module that presents a sample schedule to TSA officials based on the optimal solution. We now describe each individual module and its operations in TSA's airport domain.

Input Module: The input module consists of three classes of inputs that the system requires to generate a representative Stackelberg game and create an optimal allocation of resources. All inputs are quantifiable and tangible so that headquarters is able to maintain standards and guidelines on the way security policies are created. The first input is the area data. First, airports must input each of their potential areas. Second, for each area the airport must go through the risk-evaluation process (see Section 6.3.3), which involves answering a series of quantifiable questions. The second set of inputs is the security-activities data. For each area the airport must list all of the security activities that are available to execute in that area. There is a standard list of activities airports can select from, but they can also input new security activities that may be unique to that airport. The third input is the resource data. This includes the number of days needed to create a schedule for and the number of resources available each day.

Back-end Module: The back-end module has three primary components: generating the game, solving the game, and returning one sample schedule for TSA's use. First, based on the inputs from the input module, there is a component that creates a compact representation of the specific game instance

Locations	8/15	8/16	8/17	8/18	8/19	8/20	8/21
A1	1	3	1	1	3	0	0
A2	0	2	1	0	0	0	0
A3	2	2	0	1	0	3	1
A4	1	0	3	2	0	1	2
...	...	...	...	...	...	...	...
Total	10	10	10	10	10	10	10

Figure 6.1. Summary of sample schedule.

the system is considering. This game instance is based on the compact form of the model we presented in Section 6.3.1. Second, we compute the solution to the Stackelberg game model using DOBSS, a general Stackelberg solver (Paruchuri et al., 2008). This produces a solution, which is a mixed strategy over the possible action space, as defined in Section 6.3.2. Finally, using the optimal mixed strategy, we sample one possible resource assignment that can be implemented by TSA.

Display/Output Module: The actual resource assignment selected is presented to the user via the display/output module. The schedule that was created is shown in the interface first, as a summary of the number of resources assigned to each area similar that is to the mockup in Figure 6.1.[3] Once the schedule is created, TSA personnel can proceed to a more in-depth report of the schedule. This report lists each of the specific security activities that were chosen for each location, along with specific details of these security activities. After reviewing the report, TSA personnel can also choose to examine the distribution of resources over areas that the optimal mixed strategy provides, as is shown in Figure 6.2.

6.5 Evaluation

When evaluating a system like GUARDS there are two important issues that are raised. The first issue is with scalability and run-times. To be useful in practice, the system needs to be able to solve real world challenges. The second issue is evaluating the value of the security policies generated against alternative approaches. In the following sections we present each of these evaluations.

---

[3] We are unable to show actual screen shots from our system for security reasons. For the remainder of this paper we show only basic visual representations of what GUARDS displays.

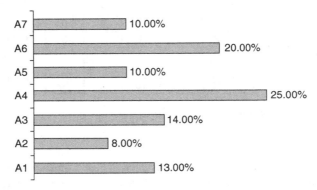

Figure 6.2. Summary of probability distribution over areas.

6.5.1 Runtime Analysis

We present simulation results, focusing on the computational efficiency of our compact method versus the full representation. All experiments are run on a system with an Intel 2 GHz processor and 1 GB of RAM. We used a publicly available linear programming package called GLPK to solve optimization problems, as specified in the original DOBSS procedure. For the compact version we use a slightly altered version of DOBSS that is designed specifically for efficiency in the compact representation. The solver was allowed to use up to 700 MB of memory during the solution process. For larger game instances, solving the problem with the full representation uses up all the memory and solutions cannot be found. In the results presented below we exclude results in cases in which the full representation was not able to produce a result using the allotted memory. We also note that in all experiments both the solution found by the full representation and the solution found by the compact representation are optimal.

To test the solution methods, we generated random game instances by randomly selecting payoff values from 1 to 50 and circumvention costs from 1 to 5 for each area. For each experiment we generated twenty random game instances and averaged the results (there is little variance in the runtimes for different problem instances). We considered three different scenarios. The first presents results for when there is an increasing number of areas, and there are three security activities associated with each area. There are five resources available for the defender, and each security activity has identical properties (i.e. no security activity has a higher cost for circumvention or higher probability of success) for the area it is associated with. Given the M possible areas, for the full representation there are $\binom{3*M}{5}$ possible defender pure strategies and $8 * M$ possible attacker pure strategies. Thus, in the ten-area case there are 142,506 defender pure strategies and 80 attacker pure strategies. Examining Figure 6.3(a), we show the improvement in runtime of our compact representation over the full representation. For more than four areas, the full representation failed to achieve a solution within the memory bounds. For four areas, the compact representation runs much faster than the full representation, with a runtime of less than 1 second versus the 177 seconds required by the full representation. In fact, for ten areas, the compact representation has an average run-time of approximately 1 second, which is still much faster than the full representation for only four areas. Even if the number of security activities associated with each area is a relatively small constant, our compact representation provides substantial benefits. As the number of similar security activities associated with an area increases, this advantage grows.

In our second scenario, we considered a situation in which security activities are distributed randomly across possible areas. The total number of security activities is set similarly to the previous experiment, in that the total number of security activities is three times the number of areas. However, we randomly assigned security activities to areas (with each area having at least one security activity), so the number is no longer uniform across areas. Once again, the defender has five resources available, and security activities have identical properties within an area. It follows that in the full representation, the number of defender pure strategies and of attacker pure strategies are identical to the previous scenario. However, the number of strategies in the compact representation for both the defender and attacker may vary. Looking at Figure 6.3 (b), we see benefits for the compact representation case that are similar to the previous experiment with a uniform distribution of activities.

In the final scenario, we considered a situation in which there are ten areas to protect, each area has three identical security activities, and we increased the number of resources available to distribute among these areas. Thus, in the full representation, assuming there are K resources available, the defender has $\binom{30}{K}$ possible pure strategies and the attacker has eighty possible pure strategies. In Figure 6.4, we increase the number of resources available along the x-axis and show the time to compute a solution in seconds on the y-axis. The full representation is unable to compute a solution for more than four resources under these conditions within the allotted memory. On the other hand, the compact representation is able to arrive at a solution for ten available resources in less than 30 seconds.

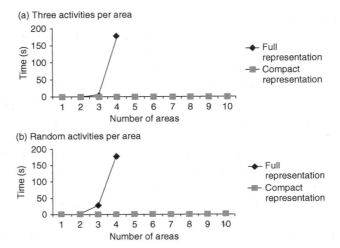

Figure 6.3. X-axis: Areas, Y-axis: Runtime.

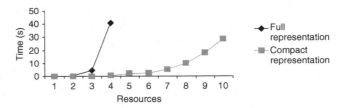

Figure 6.4. Run-time: increasing resources for ten areas with three security activities per area.

These results show the benefits of our compact representation in terms of efficiency. We obtained further efficiency gains by caching results: Specifically, the inputs into the game do not change on a daily basis. Thus, we can cache the resulting mixed strategy and present the results from sampling this mixed strategy, as long as the program users have not changed the inputs. When they do change inputs, we resolve the game using our compact representation.

6.5.2 Security Policy Analysis

For this analysis we examined the security policies generated by our game representation against two other possible solution strategies. The first strategy is a solution concept in which resources are distributed uniformly among areas (uniformly random), an approach that is sometimes used in lieu of a game-theoretic approach. The second strategy uses our new representation, however, it does not allow attackers to circumvent security activities (SCGs without circumvention). That is, we allow the attacker only a single attack strategy per area and simply reduce the value of that strategy as the number of security activities increases. This is a simplified model of an attacker as mentioned in Section 6.3.2.1. Finally, we included our new representation and allow an intelligent attacker to circumvent specific security activities when planning his mode of attack (SCGs).

We generated twenty random game instances with ten areas and three security activities per area. In each game instance, the payoff value of each area for both the defender and the attacker are randomly selected from 1 to 50, and the circumvention costs are similarly selected from 1 to 5. We then calculated the optimal solution under the current solution strategy (i.e. uniformly random, SCGs without circumvention, and SCGs). After finding the optimal solution, we determined the expected reward for each solution, given the assumptions made in SCGs (i.e., attackers are allowed to circumvent specific security activities when planning their attack). For each game instance, we computed the optimal solution, varying the number of resources available from 1 to 10 as seen on the x-axis of Figure 6.5. On the y-axis, we present the average expected reward obtained by each solution strategy across all twenty game instances. In Figure 6.5 we see that the uniform policy is outperformed by both game-theoretic approaches, with the approach that accounts for circumvention strategies performing the best. In fact, an approach that accounts for circumvention strategies was the only one that was able to obtain a positive reward for the defender in the twenty randomly generated game instances, and in the ten-resource case obtains

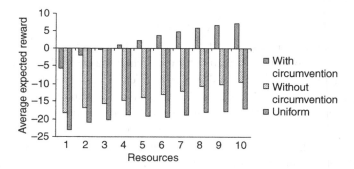

Figure 6.5. Policy analysis: increasing resources for ten areas with three security activities per area.

a 200 percent improvement in reward over any other strategy. This shows the benefits of reasoning about an intelligent attacker who will research and exploit deterministic security activities.

6.6 Lessons in Transitioning Research into Practice

GUARDS is the result of a unique collaboration wherein university researchers worked directly with a security agency for the purpose of creating a useful product to potentially deploy the outcomes of research on a national scale. This collaboration that transitioned research to such a large-scale deployment has provided valuable lessons. In this section we outline the three areas of insights we gained during the process: (i) acceptance of GUARDS at headquarters; (ii) acceptance of GUARDS by a variety of end-users at numerous airports; (iii) obtaining correct input from users. Some of these insights are contrary to accepted wisdom in the research community.

In a large organization like the TSA, it is important that they are able to provide quality guarantees. A key implication is that a system such as GUARDS must be very clear-cut in terms of its assumptions and in terms of the solution quality guarantees it makes based on these assumptions. Researchers often assume that speedy heuristic solutions that are high quality on average may be adequate "in the field," but we have learned from our dealings with security agencies that it is important that we provide guarantees on solution quality. More importantly, these guarantees may even have to be optimal (i.e., even if we can guarantee solutions within some bound of the optimal solution, it may not be enough). Without such guarantees, the TSA may be unable to justify the use of any particular security strategy. In accordance with this requirement, we use DOBSS, which provides game-theoretic optimal solutions in Stackelberg games.

With respect to the acceptance of GUARDS at individual airports, one major lesson we learned is helping to bridge the culture gap between academic research and real-world operations. Indeed, what researchers may consider small, uninteresting issues may nullify all their major research advances. For example, in an initial version of GUARDS, we displayed the final probabilities of our mixed strategies, but truncated the presentation of real numbers (i.e., by truncating all decimal values). Unfortunately, this single display issue turned out to be a major headache for users who had assumed that GUARDS was incorrect when the distribution of resources appeared to be less than 100%. Specifically, instead of considering the truncation of all real values, users might assume that some resources were not being utilized. A second major lesson learned is the continued need for the efficiency of game-theoretic algorithms. Although significant research has gone into speeding up these algorithms, we are still not able to get off-the-shelf algorithms and deploy; GUARDS required the use of new compact representations. We outline our key advances in this regard in Section 6.5.1; including the need for caching.

A third lesson learned concerning user acceptance is the need for careful design of the user interface so as to reduce the amount of user workload to provide inputs: This must be kept at a manageable level. For instance, if users are required to enter values directly into the generated game matrix, it can require thousands of inputs. Instead, it is important to provide a user-friendly method of conveying the necessary information. We used a simple interface in which users are only required to input the base information that is then used to generate the larger game matrix. By base information, we mean such things as the areas and the security activities. Users have direct access to this information, which can easily be input by the individual airports.

Finally, in any collaboration, it is important that researchers receive appropriate input from their collaborators. This includes understanding what information is available versus what is not, and accounting for this in modeling the problem. Regarding available information, end-users often do not understand the techniques that are being applied and thus are prone to providing vague or incorrect information. For example, if a security agency such as the TSA is asked to provide a utility for an attacker and for themselves as the defender on a successful attack, the agency may always say that it is very bad for themselves and very good for the attacker. Specifically, if there are five areas, and the agency provides a utility for each on a ten-point scale, they may always claim that it is -10 for the defender and 10 for the attacker. In practice, this feedback may not be useful because attacks on different areas may actually have very different impacts in terms of economic damage, casualties, and many other factors. To help prevent this scenario, it is important to convey the impact that the inputs will have on outputs, aiding their understanding of how their input affects results.

6.7 Related Work and Summary

To the best of our knowledge, this paper presents the first-ever effort to transition any research reported at AAMAS conferences to an application designed for potential national deployment to hundreds of locations. This contrasts with previous efforts, including efforts that focus on application of game-theoretic approaches such as ARMOR and IRIS (Pita et al., 2008; Tsai et al., 2009), as detailed earlier in the paper. It also contrasts alternative models based on Markov decision problems (MDPs), queuing theory, or game-theoretic approaches that would enumerate all possible defender actions and attacker threats (Larson, 1974). To accomplish this transition, we outlined novel contributions to game modeling and the compact representations of games because of the scale-up in defender and attacker strategies. This research complements other solution techniques for Stackelberg games (Basilico et al., 2009; Korzhyk et al., 2010), which have not traditionally focused on this kind of scale-up. Our work also complements research that has actually been applied to randomize patrolling strategies in robot patrol (Agmon, 2010, Agmon et al., 2009), given our emphasis on modeling adversaries in a game-theoretic setting.

TSA is charged with protecting over 400 airports in the United States. The key challenge is figuring out how to intelligently deploy limited security resources in unpredictable airport security activities in a risk-based manner so as to provide the maximum possible protection. These decisions may be made on a daily basis, based on the local information available at each airport.

This paper describes a scheduling assistant for TSA, GUARDS, which takes a game-theoretic approach to this task of resource allocation. In creating GUARDS, we addressed three key issues that arise from a potential national deployment case. These issues are: (i) knowledge acquisition for hundreds of end-users within one organization; (ii) appropriately modeling TSA's security challenge to achieve the best security policies; (iii) efficiently finding solutions to the problem we were considering. We addressed the first challenge by using a two-phase knowledge-acquisition process in which we acquire common information, standards, and practices directly from TSA headquarters. We then constructed the GUARDS system itself to reflect a risk-evaluation process designed by TSA to acquire the necessary information that is unique to individual airports. To address the second challenge, we developed a novel game-theoretic model, which we refer to as security circumvention games (SCGs), and cast TSA's security challenge within this model. This model has made the following contributions: (i) it gives defenders the ability to guard targets with more than one type of security activity (heterogeneous activities); (ii) it gives attackers the ability to choose threats designed to mitigate specific security activities. Finally, we designed an efficient solution technique for reasoning over our new game model in which we rely on creating a compact representation of each game instance and solving it using a general purpose Stackelberg solver. This is in contrast to the tailored algorithms of the past which are designed for specific problem instances for stand-alone locations. To conclude, we present results that demonstrate the benefits of our contributions, along with the lessons we learned in creating GUARDS. The scheduling assistant has been delivered to the TSA and is currently under evaluation and testing for unpredictable scheduling practices at an undisclosed airport.

Acknowledgments

The development of GUARDS has only been possible because of our exceptional collaboration with the Transportation Security Administration. This research was supported by the United States Department of Homeland Security through the Center for Risk and Economic Analysis of Terrorism Events (CREATE) under grant number 2007-ST-061-000001. However, any opinions, findings, conclusions, or recommendations in this document are the authors and do not necessarily reflect views of the United States Department of Homeland Security.

PART III

Efficient Algorithms for Massive Security Games

7

Coordinating Randomized Policies for Increasing the Security of Agent Systems

Praveen Paruchuri, Jonathan P. Pearce, Janusz Marecki,
Milind Tambe, Fernando Ordóñez, and Sarit Kraus

7.1 Introduction

Security, commonly defined as the ability to deal with intentional threats from other agents, is a major challenge for agents deployed in adversarial environments (Paruchuri et al., 2006). In this paper, we focus on adversarial domains in which the agents have limited information about the adversaries. Such adversarial scenarios arise in a wide variety of situations that are becoming increasingly important, such as patrol agents providing security for a group of houses or regions (Carroll et al., 2005; Paruchuri et al., 2007), UAVs monitoring a humanitarian mission (Beard and Mclain, 2003; Paruchuri et al., 2006), agents assisting in routine security checks at airports (Poole and Passantino, 2003), agents providing privacy in sensor network routing (Ozturk, Zhang, and Trappe, 2004), and agents maintaining anonymity in peer-to-peer networks (Borisov and Waddle, 2005).

This paper brings together some of our recent work on how to plan for agents acting in uncertain environments in the presence of adversaries (Paruchuri et al., 2006, 2007, 2008). This research has introduced two very different approaches to increasing security in agent systems and has lead to the ARMOR (Assistant for Randomized Monitoring over Routes) system, which has been deployed for security scheduling at the LAX airport since August 2007 (Murr, 2007; Paruchuri et al., 2008; Pita et al., 2008). Here we will present the main results and algorithms proposed in these two approaches and highlight the relationship between them. The common assumption in these security domains is that the agent commits to a plan or policy first, while the adversary observes the agent's actions and hence knows its plan/policy. The adversary can then exploit

Previously published in P. Paruchuri, J. Pearce, J. Marecki, M. Tambe, F. Ordóñez, and S. Kraus, Coordinating randomized policies for increasing security of agent systems. In *Journal of Information Technology and Management* (ITM), 10:67–79, 2009.

the plan or policy the agent committed to. In addition, the agent might have only incomplete information when deciding on its strategy. For example, in a typical security domain, such as in the patrolling agents example, agents provide security for a group of houses or regions via patrolling. The patrol agents commit to a plan or policy while the adversaries can observe the patrol routes, learn the patrolling pattern and exploit it to their advantage. Furthermore, the agents might not know which adversaries they face or what exactly their objectives are. To solve this problem with incomplete information about the adversaries, we provide efficient algorithms for improving security broadly considering two realistic situations: First, when the agents have no model of their adversaries, our objective is to obtain strategies for a Markov decision process (MDP) that balance the agent's reward with the amount of information the adversary has gained about the agent. Second, when the agents have partial model of their adversary, we use a game theoretic framework to obtain maximal reward strategies that take into account the uncertainty over adversary types.

When agents have no model of their adversaries, we briefly present efficient algorithms, as introduced in Paruchuri et al. (2006), for generating randomized plans or policies for agents that minimize the information that adversaries can gain. Such randomized policies that attempt to minimize the opponent's information gain are referred to as *secure policies*. However, arbitrary randomization can violate such quality constraints as increasing resource usage, frequency of patrols in key areas. To that end, we developed algorithms for efficient policy randomization with quality guarantees using MDPs (Puterman, 1994). We measure randomization via an entropy-based metric. In particular, we illustrate that simply maximizing entropy-based metrics introduces a nonlinear program that has nonpolynomial runtime. Hence, we introduce our CRLP (convex combination for randomization) and BRLP (binary search for randomization) linear programming (LP) techniques that randomize policies in polynomial time with different tradeoffs as explained later.

When agents have a partial model of their adversary, we model the security domain as a Bayesian Stackelberg game (Parichuri et al., 2007; Conitzer and Sandholm, 2006). A Bayesian game is a game in which agents may belong to one or more types; the type of agent determines its possible actions and payoffs. The assumption made here is that the agent knows the adversary's actions and payoffs but does not know which adversary is active at a given time. Usually, these games are analyzed according to the concept of Bayes-Nash equilibrium, an extension of Nash equilibrium for Bayesian games in which it is assumed that all agents choose their strategies simultaneously. However, the main feature of the security games we consider is that one player must commit first to a strategy before the other players choose their strategies. In the patrol domain, the patrol agent commits to a strategy first, and the adversaries get to observe the agent's strategy and choose a course of action. These scenarios are known as Stackelberg games (Fudenberg and Tirole, 1991). More precisely, we model our security domains as Bayesian Stackelberg games to take into account that the leader must plan for potentially many different types of adversaries. The solution concept for these games is that the security agent has to pick the optimal strategy considering the actions, payoffs, and probability distribution over the adversaries. In Parichuri et al. (2007) and (2008), we introduced efficient techniques for generating optimal leader strategies with controlled and optimal randomization for Bayesian Stackelberg games, named ASAP (Agent Security via Approximate Policies) and DOBSS (Decomposed Optimal Bayesian Stackelberg Solver), respectively. Furthermore, DOBSS is at the heart of the ARMOR (Parichuri et al., 2008; Pita et al., 2008) system that is currently deployed for security scheduling at LAX, which has been described in popular scientific magazines and news media such as *Newsweek* (Murr, 2007).

The ARMOR software is a general-purpose security scheduler built over the DOBSS algorithm. In particular, it is being used for randomizing police checkpoints and canine patrols to improve security at LAX. For example, airports cannot afford to have checkpoints on all roads at all times because they have limited security personnel. Potential adversaries can monitor the checkpoints regularly and learn weaknesses/patterns. ARMOR accounts for various factors, including number of checkpoints, their operation times, traffic patterns, the cost to the adversary of getting caught, and the adversary estimated target priority, to calculate the optimal randomized solution. In most security domains, police/canine units commit first to a security policy while our adversaries observe and exploit that policy. This key observation is mapped to a Bayesian Stackelberg game and is solved using the DOBSS algorithm.[1]

The rest of this paper is organized as follows: In Section 7.2 we present related work. Section 7.3 introduces the classic Markov decision approach for planning and the LP solution to solve it. We then present a nonlinear program and two approximate linear programming alternatives called the CRLP and the BRLP algorithms for efficient randomized policy generation in the presence of an unmodeled adversary. Section 7.4 briefly presents the DOBSS procedure for generating optimal randomized strategies, for non-Bayesian games first, for clarity; then it shows how DOBSS can be adapted for Bayesian games with partial adversary information. We then provide a brief description of the ASAP algorithm that generates policies with controlled randomization using the framework developed for DOBSS. Section 7.5 provides experimental results for both techniques developed in this paper. Section 7.6 pressents our conclusions and discusses the policy implications of the methods presented in the paper.

---

[1] The ARMOR software has been developed in close interaction with the LAWA (Los Angeles World Airports) police, and has been in use at LAX since August 2007.

7.2 Related Work

We follow two main methodological directions in this work: decision-theoretic and game-theoretic models. We point to related work in both these areas and show how it pertains to randomizing in security domains.

Decision-theoretic frameworks like MDPs are extremely useful and powerful modeling tools that are increasingly being applied to build agents and agent teams that can be deployed in real world. The main advantages of modeling agent and agent teams using these tools are the following:

- The real world is uncertain, and the decision-theoretic frameworks can model such real-world environmental uncertainty. In particular, the MDP (Puterman, 1994) framework can model stochastic actions and hence can handle transition uncertainty.
- Efficient algorithms have been devised for generating optimal plans for the agents and agent teams that are modeled using these frameworks (Puterman, 1994).

However, these optimal policy-generation algorithms have focused on maximizing the total expected reward while taking the environmental uncertainties into account. These optimal policies are deterministic and are therefore useful when the agents are in environments in which acting in a predictable manner is not problematic. As agents are increasingly deployed into the real world, they will have to act in adversarial domains, often without any adversary model available. Hence, the randomization of policies becomes critical. The randomization of policies using decision-theoretic frameworks as a goal has received little attention, primarily being seen as a side effect in attaining other objectives, as in constrained MDPs (Dolgov and Durfce, 2003; Paruchuri et al., 2004).

Stackelberg games (Stackelberg, 1934; Roughgarden, 2001) are commonly used to model attacker-defender scenarios in security domains (Brown et al., 2006). In particular Brown et al. develop algorithms to make critical infrastructure more resilient against terrorist attacks by modeling the scenario as a Stackelberg game. However, they do not address the issue of incomplete information about adversaries; whereas, agents acting in the real world quite frequently are uncertain, or do not have complete information, about the adversary they face. Bayesian games have been a popular choice for modeling such incomplete information games (Brynielsson and Arnborg, 2004; Conitzer and Sandholm, 2006), and the solution concept is called the Bayes-Nash equilibrium (Fudenberg and Tirole, 1991). The problem of choosing an optimal strategy for the leader to commit to in a Stackelberg game is analyzed in Conitzer and Sandholm (2006), and found to be NP-hard in the case of a Bayesian game with multiple types of followers. Methods for finding optimal leader strategies for non-Bayesian games (Conitzer and Sandholm, 2006) can be applied to this problem by converting the Bayesian game into a normal-form game using the Harsanyi transformation (Harsanyi and Selten, 1972). However, in transforming the game, the compact structure of the Bayesian game is lost. In addition, the method by Conitzer and Sandholm (2006) (called the multiple-LPs method) requires solving many linear programs, some of which may be infeasible. If, on the other hand, we wish to compute the highest-reward Nash equilibrium, new methods using mixed-integer linear programs (MILPs) (Sandholm, Gilpin, and Conitzer, 2005) may be used, since the highest-reward Bayes-Nash equilibrium is equivalent to the corresponding Nash equilibrium in the transformed game. Furthermore, since the Nash equilibrium assumes a simultaneous choice of strategies, the advantages of being the leader are not considered. Our work proposes an efficient and compact technique for choosing optimal strategies in Bayesian-Stackelberg games.

7.3 Randomization with No Adversary Model

In this section, we first describe MDPs, followed by our approaches to randomization of MDP policies. An MDP is a tuple, $\langle S, A, P, R \rangle$, that consists of world states $\{s_1, \ldots, s_m\}$, actions $\{a_1, \ldots, a_k\}$, transition function which is a set of tuples $p(s, a, j)$ and immediate reward denoted by tuples $r(s, a)$. If $x(s, a)$ represents the number of times the MDP visits state s and takes action a, and α_j represents the number of times the MDP starts in each state $j \in S$, then the optimal policy, maximizing expected reward, is derived via the following linear program (Dolgov and Durfee, 2003):

$$\max \quad \sum_{s \in S} \sum_{a \in A} r(s, a) x(s, a)$$

$$\text{s.t.} \quad \sum_{a \in A} x(j, a) - \sum_{s \in S} \sum_{a \in A} p(s, a, j) x(s, a) = \alpha_j, \forall j \in S \qquad (7.1)$$

$$x(s, a) \geq 0 \qquad\qquad \forall s \in S, a \in A$$

If x^* is the optimal solution to (7.1), the optimal policy π^* is given by (7.2) (following), where $\pi^*(s, a)$ is the probability of taking action a in state s and is deterministic that is, $\pi^*(s, a)$ has a value of either 0 or 1. However, such deterministic policies are undesirable in security domains.

$$\pi^*(s, a) = \frac{x^*(s, a)}{\sum_{\hat{a} \in A} x^*(s, \hat{a})} . \qquad (7.2)$$

7.3.1 Maximal Entropy Solution

We aim to randomize these optimal deterministic policies, where randomness is quantified using some entropy measure. The notion of entropy for probability distributions is introduced by Shannon (1948). Entropy for a discrete distribution $p_1, \ldots, p_n$ is defined by $H = -\sum_{i=1}^{n} p_i \log p_i$. For an MDP we introduce the *weighted entropy* function, borrowing from the classic entropy definition. The weighted entropy is defined by adding the entropy for the distributions at every state weighted by the likelihood that the MDP visits that state, namely,

$$
\begin{aligned}
H_W(x) &= -\sum_{s \in S} \frac{\sum_{\hat{a} \in A} x(s, \hat{a})}{\sum_{j \in S} \alpha_j} \sum_{a \in A} \pi(s, a) \log \pi(s, a) \\
&= -\frac{1}{\sum_{j \in S} \alpha_j} \sum_{s \in S} \sum_{a \in A} x(s, a) \log \left(\frac{x(s, a)}{\sum_{\hat{a} \in A} x(s, \hat{a})} \right).
\end{aligned}
$$

Note that when all states have an equal weight of 1, we call the above function as additive entropy denoted by $H_A(x)$. The maximal entropy solution for MDP can be defined as:

$$
\begin{aligned}
\max \quad &-\frac{1}{\sum_{j \in S} \alpha_j} \sum_{s \in S} \sum_{a \in A} x(s, a) \log \left(\frac{x(s, a)}{\sum_{\hat{a} \in A} x(s, \hat{a})} \right) \\
\text{s.t.} \quad &\sum_{a \in A} x(j, a) - \sum_{s \in S} \sum_{a \in A} p(s, a, j) x(s, a) = \alpha_j \\
&\hspace{6cm} \forall j \in S \hspace{1cm} (7.3) \\
&\sum_{s \in S} \sum_{a \in A} r(s, a) x(s, a) \geq E_{\min} \\
&x(s, a) \geq 0 \hspace{3cm} \forall s \in S, a \in A
\end{aligned}
$$

Here, $E_{\min}$ is the reward threshold and is an input domain parameter. Note that for $E_{\min} = 0$ the above problem finds the maximum weighted entropy policy, and for $E_{\min} = E^*$, Problem (7.3) returns the maximum expected reward policy with largest entropy, where E^* is the maximum possible expected reward. Unfortunately, the function $H_W(x)$ is neither convex nor concave in x; hence, there are no complexity guarantees in solving Problem (7.3), even for local optima. This negative complexity motivates the polynomial methods presented in the next section.

7.3.2 Efficient Single-Agent Randomization

Note that while entropy calculation is a nonlinear function, entropy maximization is a convex problem. The nonconvexity in the functions just described arises from the way probabilities are calculated, that is, as a ratio of the flow variables in the (MDP) network. We now present two polynomial time algorithms to obtain policies for an MDP that balance reward and randomness. The algorithms that we introduce consider two inputs: a minimal expected reward value $E_{\min}$ and a randomized solution $\bar{x}$ (or policy $\bar{\pi}$). The input $\bar{x}$ can be any solution with high entropy and is used to enforce some level of randomness on the high expected reward output, through linear constraints. One such high entropy input for MDP-based problems is the uniform policy, where $\bar{\pi}(s,a) = 1/|A|$. We enforce the amount of randomness in the high expected reward solution that is output through a parameter $\beta \in [0,1]$. For a given β and a high entropy solution $\bar{x}$, we output a maximum expected reward solution that has a certain level of randomness by solving (7.4).

$$
\begin{aligned}
\max \quad & \sum_{s \in S} \sum_{a \in A} r(s,a) x(s,a) \\
\text{s.t.} \quad & \sum_{a \in A} x(j,a) - \sum_{s \in S} \sum_{a \in A} p(s,a,j) x(s,a) = \alpha_j \qquad (7.4) \\
& \hspace{5cm} \forall j \in S \\
& x(s,a) \geq \beta \bar{x}(s,a) \qquad \forall s \in S, a \in A,
\end{aligned}
$$

which can be expressed in matrix notation. Let $x = (x(s,a))_{s \in S, a \in A}$ be an $|S||A|$ dimensional variable vector, α a vector in $\Re^{|S|}$, r a vector in $\Re^{|S||A|}$, and M a matrix with $|S|$ rows and $|S||A|$ columns. The matrix shorthand would then be

$$
\begin{aligned}
\max \quad & r^T x \\
\text{s.t.} \quad & Mx = \alpha \\
& x \geq \beta \bar{x} .
\end{aligned}
$$

As the parameter β is increased, the randomness requirements of the solution become stricter, and hence the solution to (7.4) would have smaller expected reward and higher entropy. For $\beta = 0$, the above problem reduces to (7.1), returning the maximum expected reward solution E^*; and for $\beta = 1$, the problem obtains the maximal expected reward (denoted $\overline{E}$) out of all solutions with as much randomness as $\bar{x}$.

Theorem 7.1. *If $\bar{x}$ is a feasible solution to (7.1) (i.e., $M\bar{x} = \alpha, \bar{x} \geq 0$), and E^* is finite, then $\bar{x}$ is an optimal solution to (7.4) when $\beta = 1$ and $\overline{E} = \sum_{s \in S} \sum_{a \in A} r(s,a) \bar{x}(s,a) = r^T \bar{x}$.*

Proof. If E^* is finite, then for any x such that $Mx = 0, x \geq 0$ we must have that $r^T x \leq 0$. By construction, $\bar{x}$ is feasible for (7.4) with $\beta = 1$. Consider a solution $\tilde{x}$ feasible for (7.4) with $\beta = 1$. Then $\tilde{x} - \bar{x} \geq 0$ and $M(\tilde{x} - \bar{x}) = 0$; therefore, since E^* is finite, we have $r^T(\tilde{x} - \bar{x}) \leq 0$, which shows that $\bar{x}$ is optimal for (7.4). ∎

Our new algorithm to obtain an efficient solution with a expected reward requirement of E_{min} is based on the following result, which shows that the solution to (7.4) is a convex combination of the deterministic and the random input solutions.

Theorem 7.2. ((Paruchuri et al., 2006), Theorem 1) *Consider a solution* $\bar{x}$, *which satisfies* $M\bar{x} = \alpha$ *and* $\bar{x} \geq 0$. *Let* x^* *be the solution to (7.1) and* $\beta \in [0, 1]$. *If* x_β *is the solution to (7.4), then* $x_\beta = (1 - \beta)x^* + \beta\bar{x}$.

Proof. We reformulate problem (7.4) in terms of the slack $z = x - \beta\bar{x}$ of the solution x over $\beta\bar{x}$, leading to the following problem:

$$\beta r^T \bar{x} + \quad \max \quad r^T z$$
$$\text{s.t.} \quad Mz = (1 - \beta)\alpha$$
$$z \geq 0,$$

The foregoing problem is equivalent to (7.4), where we used the fact that $M\bar{x} = \alpha$. Let z^* be the solution to this problem, which shows that $x_\beta = z^* + \beta\bar{x}$. Dividing the linear equation $Mz = (1 - \beta)\alpha$, by $(1 - \beta)$, and substituting $u = z/(1 - \beta)$, we recover the deterministic Problem (7.1) in terms of u, with u^* as the optimal deterministic solution. Renaming variable u to x, we obtain $\frac{1}{1-\beta}z^* = x^*$, which concludes the proof. ∎

Since $x_\beta = (1 - \beta)x^* + \beta\bar{x}$, we can directly find a randomized solution that obtains a target expected reward of E_{min}. Due to the linearity in the relationship between x_β and β, a linear relationship exists between the expected reward obtained by x_β (i.e $r^T x_\beta$) and β. In fact, setting $\beta = \frac{r^T x^* - E_{min}}{r^T x^* - r^T \bar{x}}$ makes $r^T x_\beta = E_{min}$. Using the theorem, we now present algorithm CRLP based on the observations made about β and x_β.

Algorithm 1 CRLP$(E_{min}, \bar{x})$

1: Solve Problem (7.1), let x^* be the optimal solution
2: Set $\beta = \frac{r^T x^* - E_{min}}{r^T x^* - r^T \bar{x}}$
3: Set $x_\beta = (1 - \beta)x^* + \beta\bar{x}$
4: **return** x_β (expected reward $= E_{min}$, entropy based on $\beta\bar{x}$)

Algorithm CRLP is based on a linear program and thus obtains, in polynomial time, solutions to Problem(7.4) with expected reward values $E_{min} \in [\overline{E}, E^*]$. Note that Algorithm CRLP might unnecessarily constrain the solution set because Problem (7.4) implies that at least $\beta \sum_{a \in A} \bar{x}(s, a)$ flow has to reach each state s. This restriction may negatively impact the entropy it attains, as we experimentally verified in Section 7.5. This concern is addressed by a reformulation of Problem (7.4) that replaces the flow constraints with policy constraints at each stage. For a given $\beta \in [0,1]$ and a solution $\bar{\pi}$ (policy calculated from $\bar{x}$), this replacement leads to the following linear program:

$$
\begin{aligned}
\max \quad & \sum_{s \in S} \sum_{a \in A} r(s,a)x(s,a) \\
\text{s.t.} \quad & \sum_{a \in A} x(j,a) - \sum_{s \in S} \sum_{a \in A} p(s,a,j)x(s,a) = \alpha_j, \quad \forall j \in S \\
& x(s,a) \geq \beta \bar{\pi}(s,a) \sum_{b \in A} x(s,b), \quad \forall s \in S, a \in A .
\end{aligned}
\tag{7.5}
$$

For $\beta = 0$ this problem reduces to (7.1) returning E^*, for $\beta = 1$ it returns a maximal expected reward solution with the same policy as $\bar{\pi}$. This means that for β, at values 0 and 1, Problems (7.4) and (7.5) obtain the same solution if policy $\bar{\pi}$ is the policy obtained from the flow function $\bar{x}$. However, in the intermediate range of 0 to 1 for β, the policy obtained by problems (7.4) and (7.5) are different, even if $\bar{\pi}$ is obtained from $\bar{x}$. Thus, Theorem 7.2 holds for problem (7.4) but not for (7.5). We now present our BRLP algorithm 2.

Algorithm 2 BRLP($E_{\min}, \bar{x}$)

1: Set $\beta_l = 0$, $\beta_u = 1$, and $\beta = 1/2$.
2: Obtain $\bar{\pi}$ from $\bar{x}$
3: Solve Problem (7.5), let x_β and $E(\beta)$ be the optimal solution and expected reward
   value returned
4: **while** $|E(\beta) - E_{\min}| > \epsilon$ **do**
5:    **if** $E(\beta) > E_{\min}$, **then**
6:       Set $\beta_l = \beta$
7:    **else**
8:       Set $\beta_u = \beta$
9:    $\beta = \frac{\beta_u + \beta_l}{2}$
10:   Solve Problem (7.5); let x_β and $E(\beta)$ be the optimal solution and expected
   reward value returned
11: **return** x_β (expected reward $= E_{\min} \pm \epsilon$, entropy related to $\beta \bar{x}$)

Given input $\bar{x}$, algorithm BRLP runs in polynomial time, since at each iteration it solves an LP and for tolerance of ϵ, it takes at most $O\left(\frac{E(0) - E(1)}{\epsilon}\right)$ iterations to converge (E(0) and E(1) expected rewards correspond to 0 and 1 values of β).

Throughout this paper, we set $\bar{x}$ based on uniform randomization $\bar{\pi} = 1/|A|$. By manipulating $\bar{x}$, we can accommodate the knowledge of the adversary's behavior. For instance, if the agent knows that a specific state s cannot be targeted by the adversary, then $\bar{x}$ for that state can have all values 0, implying that no entropy constraint is necessary. In such cases, $\bar{x}$ will not be a complete solution for the MDP but rather concentrates on the sets of states and actions that are under risk of attack. For $\bar{x}$ that do not solve the MDP, Theorem 7.2 does not hold and therefore Algorithm CRLP is not valid. In this case, a high-entropy solution that meets a target expected reward can still be obtained via Algorithm BRLP.

7.4 Randomization Using a Partial Adversary Model

In this section, we first describe the Bayesian Stackelberg games, followed by our efficient approaches to obtain optimal randomized policies. As mentioned in Section 7.1, in the case that the leader has a partial model of the adversary, we use a Bayesian Stackelberg game to represent the interaction between players. In a Stackelberg game, a leader commits to a strategy first, and then a follower (or group of followers) selfishly optimize their own rewards, *considering the action chosen by the leader.* To see the advantage of being the leader in a Stackelberg game, consider a simple game with the following payoff table. The leader is the row player and the follower is the column player.

	1	2
1	2, 1	4, 0
2	1, 0	3, 2

If we consider the above problem to be a simultaneous move game, then the only pure-strategy Nash equilibrium for this game is when the leader plays 1 and the follower plays 1, which gives the leader a payoff of 2; in fact, for the leader, playing 2 is strictly dominated. However, if the leader can commit to playing 2 before the follower chooses its strategy, then the leader will obtain a payoff of 3, since the follower would then play 2 to ensure a higher payoff for itself. If the leader commits to a uniform mixed strategy of playing 1 and 2 with equal (0.5) probability, then the follower will play 2, leading to a payoff for the leader of 3.5.

7.4.1 *Exact Solution: DOBSS*

We developed an efficient exact procedure to generate an optimal leader strategy for DOBSS security domains. This method has two key advantages. First, it directly searches for an optimal strategy, rather than a Nash (or Bayes-Nash) equilibrium, which allows it to find high-reward nonequilibrium strategies. Second, the method expresses the Bayes-Nash game compactly without requiring conversion to a normal-form game.

The DOBSS procedure we propose operates directly on the compact Bayesian representation, without requiring the Harsanyi transformation. This is achieved because the different follower (robber) types are independent of each other. Hence, evaluating the leader strategy against a Harsanyi-transformed game matrix is equivalent to evaluating against each of the game matrices for the individual follower types. This independence property is exploited in DOBSS to yield a decomposition scheme. Also, note that DOBSS requires the solution of one optimization problem, rather than solving a series of problems as in the multiple-LPs method (Conitzer and Sandholm, 2006).

Note that for a single follower type, we simply take the mixed strategy for the leader that gives the highest payoff when the follower plays a reward-maximizing strategy. We need only to consider the reward-maximizing pure strategies of the followers, since for a given fixed strategy x of the leader, each follower type faces a problem with fixed linear rewards. If a mixed strategy is optimal for the follower, then so are all the pure strategies in support of that mixed strategy.

We begin with the case of a single follower. Let the leader be the row player and the follower the column player. We denote by x the leader's policy, which consists of a vector of the leader's pure strategies. The value x_i is the proportion of times in which pure strategy i is used in the policy. Similarly, q denotes the vector of strategies of the follower. We also denote X and Q as the index sets of the leader's and follower's pure strategies, respectively. The payoff matrices R and C are defined such that R_{ij} is the reward of the leader and C_{ij} is the reward of the follower when the leader takes pure strategy i and the follower takes pure strategy j.

We first fix the policy of the leader to some policy x. We formulate the optimization problem the follower solves to find its optimal response to x as the following linear program:

$$\max_q \quad \sum_{j \in Q} \sum_{i \in X} C_{ij} x_i q_j$$
$$\text{s.t.} \quad \sum_{j \in Q} q_j = 1 \qquad (7.6)$$
$$q \geq 0.$$

Thus, given the leader's strategy x, the follower's optimal response, $q(x)$, satisfies the LP optimality conditions:

$$a \geq \sum_{i \in X} C_{ij} x_i, \ j \in Q$$

$$q_j \left(a - \sum_{i \in X} C_{ij} x_i \right) = 0 \ j \in Q$$

$$\sum_{j \in Q} q_j = 1$$

$$q \geq 0.$$

Therefore, the leader solves the following integer problem to maximize its own payoff, given the follower's optimal response $q(x)$:

$$\begin{aligned}
\max_x \quad & \sum_{i \in X} \sum_{j \in Q} R_{ij} q(x)_j x_i \\
\text{s.t.} \quad & \sum_{i \in X} x_i = 1 \\
& x_i \in [0 \dots 1].
\end{aligned} \tag{7.7}$$

Problem (7.7) maximizes the leader's reward with follower's best response, denoted by vector $q(x)$ for every leader strategy x. We complete this problem by including the characterization of q(x) through linear programming optimality conditions. The leader's problem becomes

$$\begin{aligned}
\max_{x,q,a} \quad & \sum_{i \in X} \sum_{j \in Q} R_{ij} x_i q_j \\
\text{s.t.} \quad & \sum_i x_i = 1 \\
& \sum_{j \in Q} q_j = 1 \\
& 0 \leq (a - \sum_{i \in X} C_{ij} x_i) \leq (1 - q_j) M \\
& x_i \in [0 \dots 1] \\
& q_j \in \{0, 1\} \\
& a \in \Re.
\end{aligned} \tag{7.8}$$

Here, M is some large constant, and a is the follower's maximum reward value. The first and fourth constraints enforce a feasible mixed policy for the leader, and the second and fifth constraints enforce a feasible pure strategy for the follower. The third constraint enforces the dual feasibility of the follower's problem (leftmost inequality) and the complementary slackness constraint for an optimal pure strategy q for the follower (rightmost inequality).

We now show how we can apply our decomposition technique on the MIQP to obtain significant speedups for Bayesian games with multiple follower types.

To admit multiple adversaries in our framework, we modify the notation defined in the previous section to reason about multiple follower types. We denote by x the vector of strategies of the leader; and by q^l, the vector of strategies of follower l, with L denoting the index set of follower types. We also denote by X and Q the index sets of leader and follower l's pure strategies, respectively. We also index the payoff matrices on each follower l, considering the matrices R^l and C^l.

Given *a priori* probabilities p^l, with $l \in L$ of facing each follower, the leader now faces the decomposed problem:

$$\max_{x,q,a} \sum_{i \in X} \sum_{l \in L} \sum_{j \in Q} p^l R^l_{ij} x_i q^l_j$$

$$\text{s.t.} \quad \sum_i x_i = 1$$
$$\sum_{j \in Q} q^l_j = 1$$
$$0 \le (a^l - \sum_{i \in X} C^l_{ij} x_i) \le (1 - q^l_j) M \qquad (7.9)$$
$$x_i \in [0 \ldots 1]$$
$$q^l_j \in \{0, 1\}$$
$$a \in \Re$$

Proposition 7.1. *Problem (7.9) for a Bayesian game with multiple follower types is equivalent to Problem (7.8) on the payoff matrices given by the Harsanyi transformation.*

Proof. To show the equivalence, we show that a feasible solution to (7.9) leads to a feasible solution to (7.8) with same objective value or better, and vice versa. This implies equality in the optimal objective value and correspondence between optimal solutions.

Consider x, q^l, a^l, with $l \in L$ being a feasible solution to Problem (7.9). We now construct a feasible solution to (7.8). From its second constraint and the integrality of q, we have that for every l there is exactly one j_l such that $q^l_{j_l} = 1$. Let j be the Harsanyi action that corresponds to $(j_1, \ldots, j_{|L|})$, and let q be its pure strategy (i.e., q is a strategy in the transformed game where $q_j = 1$, and $q_h = 0$ for all other $h \ne j$). We now show that the objective of (7.9) equals that of (7.8), exploiting these corresponding actions. In particular,

$$\sum_{i \in X} \sum_{l \in L} p^l x_i \sum_{h \in Q} R^l_{ih} q^l_h = \sum_{i \in X} x_i \sum_{l \in L} p^l R^l_{ij_l}$$

$$= \sum_{i \in X} x_i R_{ij} = \sum_{i \in X} \sum_{h \in Q} x_i R_{ih} q_h.$$

So, now we just have to show that x, q, and $a = \sum_{l \in L} p^l a^l$ are feasible for Problem (7.8). Constraints 1, 2, 4, and 5 in (7.8) are easily satisfied by the proposed solution. Constraint 3 in (7.9) means that $\sum_{i\in X} x_i C_{ijl}^l \geq \sum_{i\in X} x_i C_{ih}^l$, for every $h \in Q$ and $l \in L$, leading to

$$\sum_{i\in X} x_i C_{ij} = \sum_{l\in L} p^l \sum_{i\in X} x_i C_{ijl}^l \geq \sum_{l\in L} p^l \sum_{i\in X} x_i C_{ih_l}^l = \sum_{i\in X} x_i C_{ih'},$$

for any pure strategy $h_1,\ldots,h_{|L|}$ for each of the followers and h' its corresponding pure strategy in the Harsanyi game. We conclude this part by showing that

$$\sum_{i\in X} x_i C_{ij} = \sum_{l\in L} p^l \sum_{i\in X} x_i C_{ijl}^l = \sum_{l\in L} p^l a^l = a .$$

Now, we start with (x,q,a) feasible for (7.8). This means that $q_j = 1$ for some pure action j. Let $(j_1,\ldots,j_{|L|})$ be the corresponding actions for each follower l. We show that x, q^l with $q_{j_l}^l = 1$ and $q_h^l = 0$ for $h \neq j_l$, and $a^l = \sum_{i\in X} x_i C_{ijl}^l$ with $l \in L$ is feasible for (7.9). By construction, this solution satisfies constraints 1, 2, 4, 5 and has a matching objective function. We now show that constraint 3 holds by showing that $\sum_{i\in X} x_i C_{ijl}^l \geq \sum_{i\in X} x_i C_{ih}^l$ for all $h \in Q$ and $l \in L$. Let us assume it does not. That is, there is an $\hat{l} \in L$ and $\hat{h} \in Q$ such that $\sum_{i\in X} x_i C_{ij_{\hat{l}}}^{\hat{l}} < \sum_{i\in X} x_i C_{i\hat{h}}^{\hat{l}}$. Then, by multiplying by $p^{\hat{l}}$ and adding $\sum_{l\neq\hat{l}} p^l \sum_{i\in X} x_i C_{ijl}^l$ to both sides of the inequality we obtain

$$\sum_{i\in X} x_i C_{ij} < \sum_{i\in X} x_i \left(\sum_{l\neq\hat{l}} p^l C_{ijl}^l + p^{\hat{l}} C_{i\hat{h}}^{\hat{l}} \right) .$$

The right-hand side equals $\sum_{i\in X} x_i C_{ih}$ for the pure strategy h that corresponds to $(j_1,\ldots,\hat{h},\ldots,j_{|L|})$, which is a contradiction since constraint 3 of (7.8) implies that $\sum_{i\in X} x_i C_{ij} \geq \sum_{i\in X} x_i C_{ih}$ for all h. ∎

We can then linearize the quadratic programming problem (7.9) through the change of variables $z_{ij}^l = x_i q_j^l$, obtaining the following problem:

$$
\begin{aligned}
\max_{q,z,a} \quad & \sum_{i\in X} \sum_{l\in L} \sum_{j\in Q} p^l R_{ij}^l z_{ij}^l \\
\text{s.t.} \quad & \sum_{i\in X} \sum_{j\in Q} z_{ij}^l = 1 \\
& \sum_{j\in Q} z_{ij}^l \leq 1 \\
& q_j^l \leq \sum_{i\in X} z_{ij}^l \leq 1 \\
& \sum_{j\in Q} q_j^l = 1 \\
& 0 \leq (a^l - \sum_{i\in X} C_{ij}^l (\sum_{h\in Q} z_{ih}^l)) \leq (1 - q_j^l) M \\
& \sum_{j\in Q} z_{ij}^l = \sum_{j\in Q} z_{ij}^1 \\
& z_{ij}^l \in [0\ldots1] \\
& q_j^l \in \{0,1\} \\
& a \in \Re
\end{aligned}
\tag{7.10}
$$

Theorem 7.3. *Problems (7.9) and (7.10) are equivalent.*

Proof. Consider x, q^l, a^l with $l \in L$ a feasible solution of (7.9). We will show that $q^l, a^l, z_{ij}^l = x_i q_j^l$ is a feasible solution of (7.10) with same objective function value. The equivalence of the objective functions and constraints 4, 7, and 8 of (7.10) are satisfied by construction. The fact that $\sum_{j \in Q} z_{ij}^l = x_i$ as $\sum_{j \in Q} q_j^l = 1$ explains constraints 1, 2, 5, and 6 of (7.10). Constraint 3 of (7.10) is satisfied because $\sum_{i \in X} z_{ij}^l = q_j^l$.

Lets now consider q^l, z^l, a^l to be feasible for (7.10). We will show that q^l, a^l, and $x_i = \sum_{j \in Q} z_{ij}^l$ are feasible for (7.9) with the same objective value. In fact, all constraints of (7.9) are readily satisfied by construction. To see that the objectives match, notice for each l one q_j^l must equal 1, and the rest equal 0. Let us say that $q_{j_l}^l = 1$, then the third constraint in (7.10) implies that $\sum_{i \in X} z_{ij_l}^l = 1$. This condition and the first constraint in (7.7) give that $z_{ij}^l = 0$ for all $i \in X$ and all $j \neq j_l$. In particular, this implies that

$$x_i = \sum_{j \in Q} z_{ij}^1 = z_{ij_1}^1 = z_{ij_l}^l,$$

the last equality from constraint 6 of (7.10). Therefore, $x_i q_j^l = z_{ij_l}^l q_j^l = z_{ij}^l$. This last equality is because both are 0 when $j \neq j_l$ (and $q_j^l = 1$ when $j = j_l$). This shows that the transformation preserves the objective function value, completing the proof. ∎

We can therefore solve this equivalent linear integer program with efficient integer programming packages that can handle problems with thousands of integer variables. We implemented the decomposed MILP, and the results are shown in Section 7.4.

We now provide a brief intuition into the computational savings provided by our approach. We compare the work done by DOBSS and by the other exact solution approach to Bayesian Stackelberg games, namely the multiple-LPs method by Conitzer and Sandholm (2006). The DOBSS method achieves an exponential reduction in the problem that must be solved over the multiple-LPs approach for the following reasons: The multiple-LPs method solves an LP over the exponentially blown Harsanyi-transformed matrix for each of the adversaries joint strategies (also exponential in number). By contrast, DOBSS solves a problem that has one integer variable per strategy for every adversary.

To be more precise, let X be the number of agent actions, Q the number of adversary actions, and L the number of adversary types. The DOBSS procedure solves a MILP with XQL continuous variables, QL binary variables, and 4QL+2XL+2L constraints. We note that this MILP has Q^L feasible integer solutions, due to constraint 4 in (7.10). Solving this problem with a judicious branch and bound procedure will lead in the worst case to a tree with $O(Q^L)$ nodes, each requiring the solution of an LP of size $O(XQL)$. Here, the size of an LP is the number of variables + number of constraints.

On the other hand, the multiple-LPs method needs the Harsanyi transformation. This transformation leads to a game in which the agent can take X actions, and the joint adversary can take Q^L actions. This method then solves exactly Q^L different LPs, each with X variables and Q^L constraints, that is, each LP is of size $O(X + Q^L)$.

In summary, both methods require the solution to about $O(Q^L)$ linear programs; however, these are of size $O(XQL)$ for DOBSS; whereas, they are of size $O(X + Q^L)$ for multiple LPs. This exponential increase in the problem size would lead to a much higher computational burden for multiple LPs as the number of adversaries increases. We note also that the branch-and-bound procedure seldom explores the entire tree as it uses the bounding procedures to discard sections of the tree which are provably non optimal. The multiple-LPs method, on the other hand, must solve all Q^L problems.

7.4.2 Approximate Solution: ASAP

We now present our limited randomization approach introduced by Parachuri et al. (2007), where we limit the leader's possible mixed strategies to select actions with probabilities that are integer multiples of 1/k for a predetermined integer k. One advantage of such strategies is that they are compact to represent (as fractions) and simple to understand; therefore, they can potentially be efficiently implemented in real patrolling applications. Thus, for example, when k = 3, we can have a mixed strategy where strategy 1 is picked twice, that is, probability = 2/3, and strategy 2 is picked once, with probability = 1/3. We now present our ASAP algorithm using the mathematical framework developed in the previous section. In particular, we start with Problem 7.9 and convert x from a continuous to an integer variable that varies between 0 and k, thus obtaining the following problem:

$$\max_{x,q,a} \quad \sum_{i \in X} \sum_{l \in L} \sum_{j \in Q} \frac{p^l}{k} R_{ij}^l x_i q_j^l$$

$$\text{s.t.} \quad \sum_i x_i = k$$
$$\sum_{j \in Q} q_j^l = 1$$
$$0 \leq (a^l - \sum_{i \in X} \frac{1}{k} C_{ij}^l x_i) \leq (1 - q_j^l)M \qquad (7.11)$$
$$x_i \in \{0, 1, ..., k\}$$
$$q_j^l \in \{0, 1\}$$
$$a^l \in \Re$$

We then linearize problem (7.11) through the change of variables $z_{ij}^l = x_i q_j^l$, obtaining the following equivalent MILP:

$$\max_{q,z,a} \quad \sum_{i \in X} \sum_{l \in L} \sum_{j \in Q} \frac{p^l}{k} R_{ij}^l z_{ij}^l$$

$$\text{s.t.} \quad \sum_{i \in X} \sum_{j \in Q} z_{ij}^l = k$$
$$\sum_{j \in Q} z_{ij}^l \leq k$$
$$kq_j^l \leq \sum_{i \in X} z_{ij}^l \leq k$$
$$\sum_{j \in Q} q_j^l = 1 \tag{7.12}$$
$$0 \leq (a^l - \sum_{i \in X} \frac{1}{k} C_{ij}^l (\sum_{h \in Q} z_{ih}^l)) \leq (1 - q_j^l) M$$
$$\sum_{j \in Q} z_{ij}^l = \sum_{j \in Q} z_{ij}^1$$
$$z_{ij}^l \in \{0, 1, \ldots, k\}$$
$$q_j^l \in \{0, 1\}$$
$$a^l \in \Re$$

Unfortunately, although ASAP was designed to generate simple policies, the fact that it has so many more integer variables makes it a more challenging problem than DOBSS. In fact, as we present in the next section, our computational results show that solution times for DOBSS and ASAP are comparable when ASAP finds an optimal solution. However, ASAP can experience difficulty in finding a feasible solution for large problems. This added difficulty makes DOBSS the method of choice.

7.5 Experimental Results

7.5.1 No Adversary Model

Our first set of experiments examine the trade-offs in runtime, expected reward, and entropy for single-agent problems. Figure 7.1(a) shows the results based on the generation of MDP policies for ten MDPs. These experiments compare the performance of our four randomization methods for single-agent policies. In the figures, *CRLP* refers to algorithm 1 and *BRLP* refers to algorithm 2; whereas $H_W(x)$ and $H_A(x)$ refer to Problem 7.3 with these objective functions. The top graph (a) examines the trade off between entropy and expected-reward thresholds. It shows the average weighted entropy on the y-axis and the reward threshold percent on the x-axis. The average maximally obtainable entropy for these MDPs is 8.89 (shown by the line at the top) and three of our four methods (except CRLP) attain it at about 50% threshold, that is, an agent can attain maximum entropy if it is satisfied with 50% of the maximum expected reward. However, if no reward can be sacrificed (100% threshold), the policy returned is deterministic.

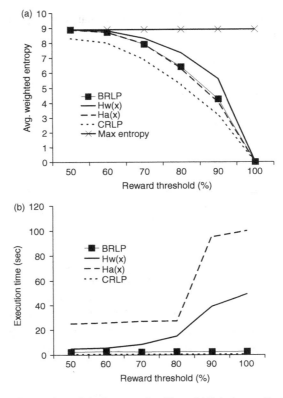

Figure 7.1. Comparison of single-agent algorithms. (a) Solution quality (measured using Average Weighted Entropy) comparison graph. (b) Run time (measured in seconds) comparison graph.

Figure 7.1(b) also shows the runtimes, plotting the execution time in seconds on the y-axis, and expected reward threshold percent on the x-axis. These numbers represent averages over the same ten MDPs. Algorithm CRLP is the fastest, and its runtime is very small and remains constant over the whole range of threshold rewards, as can be seen from the plot. Algorithm BRLP also has a fairly constant run-time and is slightly slower than CRLP. Both CRLP and BRLP are based on LPs, hence, their small and fairly constant run-times. Problem 7.3, for both the $H_A(x)$ and $H_W(x)$ objectives, exhibits an increase in the run-time as the expected reward threshold increases. This trend can be attributed to the fact that maximizing a nonconcave objective while simultaneously attaining feasibility becomes more difficult as the feasible region shrinks.

We conclude the following from Figure 7.1: (i) CRLP is the fastest but provides lowest entropy; (ii) BRLP is significantly faster than Problem (7.3), providing seven-fold average speedup over the ten MDPs over the entire threshold range; and (iii) Problem (7.3) with $H_W(x)$ provides the highest entropy among our methods, but the average gain in entropy is only 10% over BRLP. (iv) CRLP provides a four-fold speedup on an average over BRLP but with a significant entropy loss of about 18%. In fact, CRLP is unable to reach maximal possible entropy for the threshold range considered in the plot.

7.5.2 Partial Adversary Model

We performed experiments on a patrolling domain in which the police patrol various numbers of houses, as presented in Paruchuri et al. (2008). The domain is then modeled as a Bayesian Stackelberg game consisting of two players: the security agent (i.e., the patrolling robot or the leader) and the robber (the follower) in a world consisting of m houses, $1 \ldots m$. The security agent's set of pure strategies consists of possible routes of d houses to patrol (in some order). The security agent can choose a mixed strategy so that the robber will be unsure of exactly where the security agent may patrol, but the robber will know the mixed strategy the security agent has chosen. With this knowledge, the robber must choose a single house to rob, although the robber generally takes a long time to rob a house. If the house chosen by the robber is not on the security agent's route, then the robber successfully robs the house. Otherwise, if it is on the security agent's route, then the earlier the house is on the route, the easier it is for the security agent to catch the robber before he finishes robbing it.

The payoffs are modeled with the following variables:

- $v_{y,x}$: value of the goods in house y to the security agent
- $v_{y,q}$: value of the goods in house y to the robber
- c_x: reward to the security agent of catching the robber
- c_q: cost to the robber of getting caught
- p_y: probability that the security agent can catch the robber at the yth house in the patrol ($p_y < p_{y'} \iff y' < y$)

The security agent's set of possible pure strategies (patrol routes) is denoted by X and includes all d-tuples $i = < w_1, w_2, ..., w_d >$. Each of $w_1 \ldots w_d$ may take values 1 through m (different houses); however, no two elements of the d-tuple are allowed to be equal (the agent is not allowed to return to the same house). The robber's set of possible pure strategies (houses to rob) is denoted by Q and includes all integers $j = 1 \ldots m$. The payoffs (security agent, robber) for pure strategies i, j are

- $-v_{y,x}, v_{y,q}$, for $j = l \notin i$.
- $p_y c_x + (1 - p_y)(-v_{y,x}), -p_y c_q + (1 - p_y)(v_{y,q})$, for $j = y \in i$.

With this structure it is possible to model many different types of robbers who have differing motivations; for example, one robber may have a lower cost of getting caught than another or may value the goods in the various houses differently. We performed our experiments using four methods for generating the security agent's strategy: DOBSS for finding the optimal solution (Paruchuri et al. 2008); the ASAP procedure, which provides best policies with limited randomization (Paruchuri et al. 2007); the multiple-LPs method presented in Conitzer and Sandholm (2006), which provides optimal policies, and the MIP-Nash procedure (Sandholm, Gilpin, and Conitzer, 2005) for finding the best Bayes-Nash equilibrium. The multiple-LPs method and the MIP-Nash procedure require a normal-form game as input, and so the Harsanyi transformation is required as an initial step. We do not record this preprocessing time here, thus giving those other methods an advantage.

Figure 7.2 shows the run-time results for all four methods for two, three, and four houses. Each run-time value in the graph(s) corresponds to an average of over twenty randomly generated scenarios. The x-axis shows the number of follower types the leader faces, starting from 1 to 14 adversary types, and the y-axis of the graph shows the run-time in seconds on a log scale ranging from .01 to 10000 seconds. The choice of .01 to 10000 is made for the convenience of representation of the log scale(with base 10). All the experiments that were not concluded in 30 minutes (1800 seconds) were cut off.

From the run-time graphs we conclude that the DOBSS and ASAP methods outperform the multiple-LPs and MIP-Nash methods with respect to run-time. We modeled a maximum of fourteen adversary types for all our domains. For the domain with two houses, whereas the MIP-Nash and multiple-LPs methods, needed about 1000s for solving the problem with fourteen adversary types, both the DOBSS and ASAP provided solutions in less than 0.1's. Note that DOBSS provided the optimal solution while ASAP provided the best possible solution with randomization constraints. These randomization constraints also sometimes cause ASAP to *incorrectly* claim that solutions are infeasible, the details of which we present later on in this section. The runtime for ASAP in all our results is taken as either the time needed to generate an optimal solution or the time needed to determine that no feasible solution exists.

The first graph in Figure 7.2 shows the trends for all four methods for the domain with two houses. While the run-times of DOBSS and ASAP show a linear increase in runtimes, the other two show an exponential trend. The runtimes of DOBSS and ASAP are themselves exponential since they show a

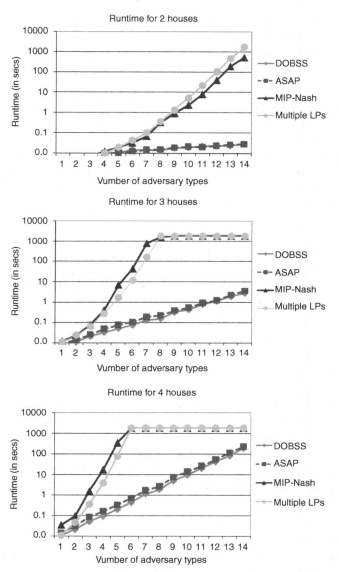

Figure 7.2. Runtimes (plotted on a log scale): DOBSS, ASAP, MIP-Nash and multiple-LP methods.

linear increase when plotted on a log-scale graph. Furthermore, they have an exponential speedup over the other two procedures as seen in the graph.

The second graph in Figure 7.2 presents results for the domain having three houses. Both the MIP-Nash and multiple-LPs methods could solve this problem only till seven adversary types within the cutoff time of 1800s; whereas DOBSS and ASAP could solve the problem for all the fourteen adversary types modeled under 10s. (The cutoff of 1800s is also the reason MIP-Nash and multiple LPs appear to have a constant run-time beyond seven adversary types.) Similar trends can be observed in the third graph, which has a domain of four houses where MIP-Nash and multiple-LPs could solve only till five adversary types; whereas, DOBSS and ASAP could solve till fourteen adversary types within 400s for DOBSS and 500s for ASAP. From this set of three graphs, we conclude that DOBSS and ASAP outperform the other two procedures, by an exponential margin.

Between DOBSS and ASAP, DOBSS is our procedure of choice since ASAP suffers from problems of infeasibility. Therefore, we present our second set of experimental results in Figure 7.3 to highlight the infeasibility issue of the ASAP procedure. In this experiment, the same settings as described above were used. The number of houses was varied between two to seven(columns in the table) and the number of adversary types was varied between one to fourteen(rows in the table). For each fixed number of houses and follower types, twenty scenarios were randomly generated. We ran the ASAP procedure and presented the number of infeasible solutions obtained, as a percentage of all the scenarios tested for each of the fixed number of houses and adversary types. For example, with the eight-adversary type (the row numbered 8) and four houses (the column numbered 4) scenario, ASAP generates 15% infeasible solutions. Note that for the values marked with a star the percentage presented in the table represents an upper bound on the number of infeasible scenarios. In these starred scenarios the ASAP procedure ran out of time in many instances. When ASAP ran out of time, it either indicated infeasibility, in which case it was classified as an infeasible solution, making it an upper bound (since there might be a feasible solution when sufficient time is provided) or it indicated that there was a feasible solution even though it has not found the optimal yet, in which case it was obviously not marked as infeasible.

We make the following conclusions about ASAP from the table in Figure 7.3: (a) In general, given a fixed number of houses, as the number of adversary types increases (i.e., from 1 to 14), the percentage of infeasible solutions increases (as we go down the columns); (b) given a fixed number of adversary types, as the number of houses increases, the percentage of infeasible solutions increases (as we go across the rows). Although there are exceptions to both the conclusions,

	2	3	4	5	6	7
1	0	0	0	0	0	10
2	0	0	0	0	5	0
3	0	5	5	15	5	10
4	0	10	15	20	20	20
5	0	10	10	10	5	10
6	0	10	10	10	15	15
7	0	15	20	15	10	20
8	0	5	15	10	30	45
9	0	5	10	15	20	30*
10	5	10	20	5	35*	35*
11	0	5	20	10	35*	40*
12	0	10	20	10	30*	30*
13	0	20	20	25*	25*	0
14	0	20	20	30*	20*	20*

Figure 7.3. Percent of infeasible solutions for ASAP. Rows represent the number of adversary types (1–14), columns represent the number of houses (2–7).

the general trend is that as the problem size increases (due to increase in houses or adversary types or both) ASAP tends to generate more infeasible solutions, making it unsuitable for bigger problems. From the table we obtain that more than 12.5% of the solutions are infeasible for the five house problem when averaged over all the adversary scenarios. This number increases to as high as 18% and 20% on an average for the six and seven house problems. If we perform similar calculations over the last five adversary scenarios, that is, when the number of adversary types are varied from 10 to 14, we obtain 16%, 29%, and 25%, respectively, for the five, six and seven house scenarios. This shows that the ASAP produces more infeasible solutions as the problem size increases. Furthermore, there is no procedure to determine if ASAP will generate a infeasible solution until runtime, making the ASAP approach impractical.

7.6 Conclusions and Policy Implications

In this paper we present our recent work on algorithms for secure patrols in adversarial domains. We follow two different approaches based on what is known about the adversary. When there is no information about the adversary, we provide for random policy generation using MDPs. When there is partial information available about the adversary, we model our domain as a Bayesian Stackelberg game and provide efficient MIP formulations for it. We also present experimental results to show that our techniques provide optimal, secure policies. Thus, this work represents a significant advance in the state of the art in addressing security domains.

We note that these two types of models are related. In fact, the idea of randomizing to reduce the information made available to the adversary can be the optimal Stackelberg strategy for the leader when the adversary's reward matrix is balanced over the different actions. Let us illustrate this with the following simple example. Consider a zero-sum square game in which the payoff matrix for the agent gives 1 in the diagonal and -1 everywhere else. We can show that the uniform strategy is also the optimal Stackelberg solution. Note that when the agent must decide among a set of actions, the maximum entropy solution is also the uniform strategy. Given a strategy x for the leader in this example, the payoff the leader gets if the adversary chooses action j is $x_j - (x_1 + \ldots + x_{j-1} + x_{j+1} + \ldots + x_n) = 2x_j - 1$ since x adds up to 1. Since the adversary receives a payoff $= 1 - 2x_j$ (a zero-sum game) for this action, the adversary will select the action that does the following: $\max_{j=1\ldots n} 1 - 2x_j$, giving the leader a reward of $\min_{j=1\ldots n} 2x_j - 1$. The leader therefore must maximize $\min_{j=1\ldots n} 2x_j - 1$ when selecting x, which is done for the uniform x. Thus, we conclude that the uniform randomization approach can be represented as a Stackelberg game with appropriate payoffs for the agent and adversary.

There are number of different conclusions and policy implications we can draw from this work, for example: (a) Randomization decreases predictability and the amount of information given out to the adversary and hence increases security for many problems. The increase security comes at the expense of the efficiency of the solution, where a patrol's efficiency refers to the value of some alternate measure, such as resources consumed, cost, or coverage. (b) When there is no model of the adversary or when there is great uncertainty about the adversary information, the rational choice for the agent is to patrol following the maximally random solution while ensuring that some efficiency constraints are met. (c) When security planners have a reasonable, possibly partial model of the adversaries actions and rewards, it is natural to represent the relation between security and adversaries using game-theoretic formulations. (d) Both the decision-theoretic and game-theoretic approaches return a probability distribution over a set of actions, which in the case of MDPs can depend on the state. Actual patrolling schedules are obtained by sampling from these optimal probability distributions. This procedure will in the long run will generate a patrolling policy that approximates the optimal probability distributions over actions. (e) We assume the optimal probability distributions are known for the adversaries because they could observe samples over time to estimate it. In addition we assume that the adversaries respond optimally to this information, either maximizing their reward (in the game-theoretic approach) or by some unspecified means (in the decision-theoretic approach). The realistic situation in which adversaries do not have all the information or do not behave rationally is the topic of current research. (f) The algorithms presented here are general purpose and can be tailored to improve security at many real-world targets, such as airports, dams, museums, and stadiums. In fact, the DOBSS formulation is used in the real-world security scheduler ARMOR, which has been in deployment at the LAX airport since August 2007 (Murr, 2007; Pita, 2008). The implementation of this methodology to other domains is the subject of ongoing work.

Acknowledgments

This research is supported by the United States Department of Homeland Security through the Center for Risk and Economic Analysis of Terrorism Events (CREATE). Sarit Kraus is also affiliated with the University of Maryland Institute for Advanced Computer Studies (UMIACS).

8

Computing Optimal Randomized Resource Allocations for Massive Security Games

Christopher Kiekintveld, Manish Jain, Jason Tsai, James Pita,
Fernando Ordóñez, and Milind Tambe

8.1 Introduction

Providing security for transportation systems, computer networks, and other critical infrastructure is a large and growing problem. Central to many of these security problems is a resource allocation task. For example, a police force may have limited personnel to conduct patrols, operate checkpoints, and conduct random searches. Other scarce resources including bomb-sniffing canines, vehicles, and security cameras. The key question is how to efficiently allocate these resources to protect against a wide variety of potential threats.

The adversarial aspect of security domains poses unique challenges for resource allocation. A motivated attacker can gather information about security measures using surveillance and plan more effective attacks. Predictable resource allocations may be exploited by an attacker, greatly reducing resource effectiveness. A better approach for deploying security resources is to use *randomization* to increase the uncertainty of potential attackers. We develop new computational methods that use game-theoretic analysis to generate optimal randomized resource allocations for security domains.

Game theory offers a more sophisticated approach to randomization than simply "rolling dice." It allows the analyst to factor differential risks and values into the game model, and incorporates game-theoretic predictions of how the attacker will respond to a given security policy. Recent work by Paruchuri et al. uses a game-theoretic approach to create randomized security policies for traffic checkpoints and canine patrols at the Los Angeles International Airport (LAX), which are deployed in the daily airport-security operations (Paruchuri et al., 2008; Pita et al., 2008). They build on recent advances in solution algorithms

Previously published in *Proc. of 8th Int. Conf. on Autonomous Agents and Multiagent Systems (AAMAS 2009)*, Decker, Sichman, Sierra and Castelfranchi (eds.), May, 10–15, 2009, Budapest, Hungary. Copyright © 2009, International Foundation for Autonomous Agents and Multiagent Systems (www.ifaamas.org). All rights reserved.

for Bayesian Stackelberg games, which capture the surveillance aspect of the domain.

A significant limitation of existing solution methods is that they handle multiple security by enumerating all possible combinations of resource assignments. This grows combinatorially in the number of resources, which makes it computationally infeasible to solve large problems. Enumeration was feasible in the LAX application due to the relatively small size of the domain (on the order of ten resources). We are interested in application domains with thousands of attack targets and hundreds of resources. Section 8.3 describes one such domain – the problem of assigning federal air marshals (FAMs) to flights.

We introduce new techniques for randomized security resource allocation that scale to problems orders of magnitude larger than existing methods. The first algorithm introduces a compact representation to dramatically reduce both space and time requirements for the multiple-resource case. Two additional algorithms further improve performance by exploiting payoff regularities in a restricted class of security games. Finally, we extend the first algorithm to incorporate additional scheduling and resource constraints into the model. We demonstrate compelling performance improvements in both memory and runtime on random problem instances and realistic data from the LAX and FAMS domains.

8.2 Game-Theoretic Modeling of Security Games

Security problems are increasingly studied using game-theoretic analysis, ranging from computer network security (Wei Lye and Wing, 2005; Srivastava et al., 2005) to terrorism (Sandler and D.G.A.M., 2003). We model the security resource allocation problem as a Stackelberg game. Stackelberg games were introduced to study duopoly competition (von Stackelberg, 1934) and are now widely used to model leadership and commitment. A related family of Stackelberg games called inspection games includes models of arms inspections and border patrolling (Avenhaus, von Stengel, and Zamir, 2002). Stackelberg games have also been applied to resource allocation in a computer job-scheduling domain (Roughgarden, 2004). The most directly related work applies Stackelberg games to security patrolling, both in a generic "police and robbers" scenario (Gatti, 2008) and in a fielded application at LAX (Pita et al., 2008).

Motivated by these and other applications, there have been several recent algorithmic advances for Stackelberg games. Conitzer and Sandholm give complexity results and algorithms for computing optimal commitment strategies, including both pure and mixed-strategy commitments and a Bayesian case (Conitzer and Sandholm, 2006). A new algorithm for solving Bayesian Stackelberg games (DOBSS) is central to the LAX application (Parachuri et al., 2008). We consider cases with multiple resources, which can be solved using the existing algorithms only by exhaustively enumerating an exponential number of joint assignments. Our algorithms use compact representations to dramatically reduce the time and space requirements to compute solutions for common classes of Stackelberg security games with multiple resources.

8.2.1 Stackelberg Security Games

We begin by defining a generic security problem as a normal-form Stackelberg game. A security game has two players, a *defender*, Θ, and an *attacker*, Ψ. These players need not represent individuals, but can also be groups that cooperate to execute a joint strategy, such as a police force or a terrorist organization. Each player has a set of possible *pure strategies*, denoted $\sigma_\Theta \in \Sigma_\Theta$ and $\sigma_\Psi \in \Sigma_\Psi$. A *mixed strategy* allows a player to play a probability distribution over pure strategies, denoted $\delta_\Theta \in \Delta_\Theta$ and $\delta_\Psi \in \Delta_\Psi$. Payoffs for each player are defined over all possible joint pure-strategy outcomes: $\Omega_\Theta : \Sigma_\Psi \times \Sigma_\Theta \to \mathcal{R}$ for the defender, and similarly for the attacker. The payoff functions are extended to mixed strategies in the standard way by taking the expectation over pure-strategy outcomes.

So far, our game description follows the standard normal-form game. Stackelberg games introduce a distinction between the players: a "leader" moves first, and the "follower" observes the leader's strategy before acting. In our security games, the defender is a Stackelberg leader, and the attacker is a follower. This models the capability of malicious attackers to employ surveillance in planning attacks. In this model, predictable defense strategies are vulnerable to exploitation by a determined adversary. Formally, the attacker's strategy in a Stackelberg security game is a function that selects a strategy in response to each leader strategy: $F_\Psi : \Delta_\Theta \to \Delta_\Psi$.

8.2.2 Stackelberg Equilibrium

The standard solution concept in game theory is a *Nash equilibrium*: a strategy profile (strategy for each player) such that no player can gain by unilaterally deviating to another strategy (Osbourne and Rubinstein, 1994). Stackelberg equilibrium is a refinement of Nash equilibrium that is specific to Stackelberg games. It is a form of subgame perfect equilibrium, in that each player chooses a best-response in any subgame of the original (where subgames correspond to partial sequences of actions). This eliminates Nash equilibrium profiles supported by noncredible threats off the equilibrium path. Subgame perfection alone does not guarantee a unique solution for Stackelberg games since the follower can be indifferent among a set of strategies. There are two types of unique Stackelberg equilibria, first proposed by Leitmann (1978), and 'typically called "strong" and "weak" after Breton et. al. (1988). The strong form assumes that the follower will always choose the optimal strategy for the leader in cases of indifference, while the weak form assumes that the follower will choose the worst strategy for the leader. A strong Stackelberg equilibrium exists in all Stackelberg games, but a weak Stackelberg equilibrium may not (Basar and Olsder, 1995). In addition, the leader can often induce the favorable strong equilibrium by selecting a strategy arbitrarily close to the equilibrium that causes the the follower to strictly prefer the desired strategy (von Stengel and Zamir, 2004). We adopt strong Stackelberg equilibrium (SSE) here due to the key existence result and because it is the most commonly adopted concept in the related literature (Conitzer and Sandholm, 2006; Osbourne and Rubinstein, 1994; Parachuri et al., 2008).

Definition 8.1. *A pair of strategies* (δ_Θ, F_Ψ) *form an SSE if they satisfy the following:*

1. *The leader plays a best-response:*
   $\Omega_\Theta(\delta_\Theta, F_\Psi(\delta_\Theta)) \geq \Omega_\Theta(\delta'_\Theta, F_\Psi(\delta'_\Theta)) \, \forall \, \delta'_\Theta \in \Delta_\Theta.$
2. *The follower play a best-response:*
   $\Omega_\Psi(\delta_\Theta, F_\Psi(\delta_\Theta)) \geq \Omega_\Psi(\delta_\Theta, \delta_\Psi) \, \forall \, \delta_\Theta \in \Delta_\Theta, \delta_\Psi \in \Delta_\Psi.$
3. *The follower breaks ties optimally for the leader:*
   $\Omega_\Theta(\delta_\Theta, F_\Psi(\delta_\Theta)) \geq \Omega_\Theta(\delta_\Theta, \delta_\Psi) \, \forall \, \delta_\Theta \in \Delta_\Theta, \delta_\Psi \in \Delta_\Psi^*(\delta_\Theta),$ *where* $\Delta_\Psi^*(\delta_\Theta)$ *is the set of follower best-responses, as in number 2.*

Whether or not the Stackelberg leader benefits from the ability to commit depends on whether commitment to mixed strategies is allowed. Committing to a pure strategy can be either good or bad for the leader; for example, in the "rock, paper, and scissors" game, committing to a pure strategy guarantees a loss. However, the ability to commit to a mixed strategy always weakly increases the leader's payoffs in the game's equilibrium profiles (von Stengel and Zamir, 2004). In the context of a Stackelberg security game, a deterministic policy is a liability for the defender (the leader), but a credible randomized security policy is an advantage. Our model allows commitment to mixed strategies by the defender.

8.3 Motivating Domains

The primary problem we address in this work is combinatorial explosion in the game representation for security games with multiple resources. Many security domains feature multiple resources, including the LAX application described previously (Pita et al., 2008). In this case, multiple canine units (resources) are assigned to cover multiple targets (airport terminals). The authors solved this problem by enumerating all possible assignments of canines to terminals – roughly 800 possible assignments. We are interested in applications with thousands of resources and targets, such as subway systems, random baggage screening, container inspections at ports, and scheduling for the Federal Air Marshals Service (FAMS). By way of comparison, even 100 targets and 10 resources yields a problem with 1.7×10^{13} assignments; a massive increase from the LAX problem.

The Federal Air Marshal Service (FAMS) has law enforcement authority for commercial air transportation.[1] One important activity of the service is to deploy armed federal air marshals (FAMs) on commercial flights, where they are able to detect, deter, and defeat terrorist/criminal attempts to gain control of the aircraft. As U.S. commercial airlines fly 27,000 domestic flights and over 2000 international flight each day, FAMS lacks the resources to cover all flights and deployments must be risk-based. However, even the *possibility* that a FAM could be on any given flight is a powerful deterrent for terrorist activities. The effectiveness of this deterrence depends on the ability of the FAMS to randomize the flight schedules for air marshals. If a terrorist adversary were able to reliably predict which flights will not have marshals, the deterrence effect would be reduced.

Flights should not necessarily have equal weighting in a randomized schedule. Information about how flight risks are evaluated is not public, but it is easy to imagine that many factors contribute to the evaluation, ranging from specific intelligence to general risk factors. A game-theoretic approach is ideal for creating a randomized schedule that incorporates these risk factors. However, creating such a schedule is significantly more daunting than even the LAX problem. There are thousands of flights each day, departing from hundreds of airports worldwide, and a multiplicity of air marshals to schedule. Moreover, there are scheduling constraints that must be considered in generating an allocation. An individual air marshal's potential departures are constrained by his current location, and schedules must account for flight and transition times. The algorithms we develop in the sequel are motivated by these challenges.

---

[1] See the TSA websites http://www.tsa.dhs.gov/lawenforcement/programs/fams.shtm and http://www.tsa.dhs.gov/lawenforcement/programs/fams.shtm for additional information.

Table 8.1. *Example payoffs for an attack on a target*

	Covered	Uncovered
Defender	5	−20
Attacker	−10	30

8.4 A Compact Representation for Multiple Resources

Many security domains – including both LAX and FAMS – involve allocating multiple resources to cover many potential targets. They can be represented in normal form, but only at the cost of a combinatorial explosion in the size of the strategy space and payoff representation. We develop a compact representation for multiple resources and introduce an algorithm that exploits this representation. Our approach is similar in spirit to other compact representations for games (Koller and Milch, 2003; Jiang and Leyton-Brown, 2006) is but tailored to security domains.

8.4.1 Compact Security Game Model

Let $T = \{t_1, \ldots, t_n\}$ be a set of *targets* that may be attacked, corresponding to pure strategies for the attacker. The defender has a set of resources available to *cover* these targets, $R = \{r_1, \ldots, r_m\}$ (e.g., in the FAMS domain targets could be flights and air marshals modeled as resources). Here, we assume that all resources are identical and may be assigned to any target, but we relax these assumptions in Section 8.6. Associated with each target are four payoffs defining the possible outcomes for an attack on the target, as shown in Table 8.1. There are two cases, depending on whether or not the target is covered by the defender. The defender's payoff for an uncovered attack is denoted $U_\Theta^u(t)$, and $U_\Theta^c(t)$ for a covered attack. Similarly, $U_\Psi^u(t)$ and $U_\Psi^c(t)$ are the attacker's payoffs.

A crucial feature of the model is that payoffs depend only on the identity of the attacked target and whether or not it is covered by the defender. For example, it does not matter whether or not any unattacked target is covered or not. From a payoff perspective, many resource allocations are identical. We exploit this by summarizing the payoff-relevant aspects of the defender's strategy in a *coverage* vector, C, that gives the probability that each target is covered, c_t. The analogous attack vector A gives the probability of attacking a target, which in the sequel we restrict to attack a single target with probability 1 (without loss of generality because a SSE solution still exists). The defender's expected payoff given attack and coverage vectors is shown in Equation 8.1. Equation 8.2 gives the expected payoff for an attack on target t, given C. The same notation applies for the follower, replacing Θ with Ψ. We also define the useful notion of the *attack set*, $\Gamma(C)$, which contains all targets that yield the maximum expected payoff for the attacker given coverage C.

$$U_\Theta(C, A) = \sum_{t \in T} a_t \cdot (c_t \cdot U_\Theta^c(t) + (1 - c_t)U_\Theta^u(t)) \tag{8.1}$$

$$U_\Theta(t, C) = c_t U_\Theta^c(t) + (1 - c_t)U_\Theta^u(t) \tag{8.2}$$

$$\Gamma(C) = \{t : U_\Psi(t, C) \geq U_\Psi(t', C) \, \forall t' \in T\}. \tag{8.3}$$

In an SSE, the attacker selects the target in the attack set with maximum payoff for the defender. Let t^* denote this optimal target. Then the expected SSE payoff for the defender is $\hat{U}_\Theta(C) = U_\Theta(t^*, C)$, and for the attacker is $\hat{U}_\Psi(C) = U_\Psi(t^*, C)$.

8.4.2 Compact versus Normal Form

Any security game represented in this compact form can also be represented in normal form. The attack vector A maps directly to the attacker's pure strategies, with one strategy per target. For the defender, each possible allocation of resources corresponds to a pure strategy in the normal form. A resource allocation maps each available resource to a target, so there are n *Choose* m ways to allocate m resources to n targets (assuming at most one resource is assigned to a target). Equation 4 set gives an example of how a coverage vector corresponds to a mixed strategy, for two resources and four targets. The probability assigned to a pure strategy covering targets i and j is $\delta_\Theta^{i,j}$. The first row states that the probability of covering target 1 is the sum of the probability assigned to pure strategies that cover 1.

$$\delta_\Theta^{1,2} + \delta_\Theta^{1,3} + \delta_\Theta^{1,4} = c_1$$
$$\delta_\Theta^{1,2} + \delta_\Theta^{2,3} + \delta_\Theta^{2,4} = c_2$$
$$\delta_\Theta^{1,3} + \delta_\Theta^{2,3} + \delta_\Theta^{3,4} = c_3$$
$$\delta_\Theta^{1,4} + \delta_\Theta^{2,4} + \delta_\Theta^{3,4} = c_4 \tag{8.4}$$

The payoff function Ω_Θ for the defender defines a payoff for each combination of a resource allocation schedule and target. If the target is covered by the allocation, the value is U_Θ^c, and if not it is U_Θ^u. The attacker payoff function is defined similarly. Comparing the size of the strategies and payoff functions in these alternative representations is striking. In the compact form, each strategy is represented by n continuous variables, and the payoff function by $4n$ variables. In contrast, the defender's strategy in normal form requires n *Choose* m variables, while the attacker strategy remains the same. The payoff function is of size $n \cdot (n\,Choose\,m)$.

8.4.3 ERASER Solution Algorithm

The ERASER (Efficient Randomized Allocation of Security Resources) algorithm takes as input a security game in compact form and solves for an optimal coverage vector corresponding to a SSE strategy for the defender. The algorithm is an MILP, presented in Equations 8.5 through 8.11. Equations 8.6 and 8.7 force the attack vector to assign a single target probability 1. Equation 8.8 restricts the coverage vector to probabilities in the range $[0, 1]$, and Equation 8.9 constrains the coverage by the number of available resources.

In Equations 8.10 and 8.11, Z is a large constant relative to the maximum payoff value. Equation 8.10 defines the defender's expected payoff, contingent on the target attacked in A. The constraint places an upper bound of $U_\Theta(t, C)$ on d, but only for the attacked target. For all other targets, the right-hand side is arbitrarily large. Since the objective maximizes d, for any optimal solution $d = U_\Theta(C, A)$. This also implies that C is maximal, given A for any optimal solution, since d is maximized.

In a similar way, Equation 8.11 forces the attacker to select a strategy in the attack set of C. The first part of the constraint specifies that $k - U_\Psi(t, C) \geq 0$, which implies that k must be at least as large as the maximal payoff for attacking any target. The second part forces $k - U_\Psi(t, C) \leq 0$ for any target that is attacked in A. If the attack vector specifies a target that is not maximal, this constraint is violated. Taken together, the objective and Equations 8.10 through 8.11 imply that C and A are mutual best responses in any optimal solution.

$$\max \quad d \tag{8.5}$$

$$a_t \in \quad \{0, 1\} \quad \forall t \in T \tag{8.6}$$

$$\sum_{t \in T} a_t = \quad 1 \tag{8.7}$$

$$c_t \in \quad [0, 1] \quad \forall t \in T \tag{8.8}$$

$$\sum_{t \in T} c_t \leq \quad m \tag{8.9}$$

$$d - U_\Theta(t, C) \leq (1 - a_t) \cdot Z \quad \forall t \in T \tag{8.10}$$

$$0 \leq k - U_\Psi(t, C) \leq (1 - a_t) \cdot Z \quad \forall t \in T \tag{8.11}$$

We now show that an optimal solution to the ERASER MILP corresponds to an SSE of the security game. First, we show that the legal coverage vectors can be implemented by mixed strategies, and then we show how full a full SSE can be constructed from an optimal ERASER solution.

Theorem 8.1. *For any feasible ERASER coverage vector, there is a corresponding mixed strategy δ_Θ that implements the desired coverage probabilities.*

Proof sketch: Translating C into a mixed strategy involves solving a set of n linear equations with $\binom{n}{m}$ variables; in practice, we use a linear program. The claim is trivial when $m = 1$, since each pure strategy maps directly to a target. In the general case, we must map the feasible set of ERASER coverage vectors to the feasible set of the mixed strategies Δ_Θ. We provide the intuition for this mapping here. Each pure strategy σ_Θ can be represented by an m-dimensional indicator vector that selects m out of the possible n targets. The full set of pure strategies Σ_Θ consists of the $\binom{n}{m}$ indicator vectors of this form. The set of possible mixed strategies for the normal-form game is Δ_Θ, defined by valid probability distributions over Σ_Θ.

Now, let P_E be the polyhedron defined by the solution space of the ERASER coverage vector. We show that all extreme points of P_E are in Δ_Θ, which implies that P_E is a subset of the polyhedron defined over Δ_Θ. The extreme points of P_E are defined by n linearly independent equality constraints. Since they have to satisfy $\sum_{i=1}^{n} c_i = m$, $n - 1$ of the constraints $0 \leq c_i \leq 1$ must be tight, so $n - 1$ of the c_i variables are either 0 or 1. Since m is an integer, the other variable must also be either 0 or 1. This implies that exactly m of the $c_i = 1$ and the rest of $c_i = 0$ for any extreme point of P_E. This c vector is therefore one of the pure strategies σ_Θ that define the extreme points of Δ_Θ, proving the inclusion. We can similarly argue the other direction, proving equivalence of the feasibility sets. If ERASER has a valid solution, we will be able to find a corresponding mixed strategy.

Theorem 8.2. *A pair of attack and coverage vectors (C, A) is optimal for the ERASER MILP correspond to at least one SSE of the game.*

Proof. We claim above that C corresponds to a mixed strategy for the defender, but A is an incomplete description of the attacker's Stackelberg strategy F_Ψ; it does not specify choices for any coverage other than C. Here, we show that the conditions of the MILP imply the existence of a function F_Ψ extending A such that C and F_Ψ satisfy the conditions of SSE given in Definition 8.1. We have already shown above that C and A are mutual best-responses for an optimal MILP solution. It remains to describe the attacker's behavior off the equilibrium path, for any other feasible coverage vectors $C' \neq C$. Let $t^* \in \Gamma(C')$

be a target in the attack set for C' with maximal payoff for the defender, and let A' be the attack vector that places probability 1 on t^*. By construction, A' is feasible in the MILP and satisfies conditions 2 and 3 for a SSE. Since (C', A') is a feasible solution in the MILP, $U_\Theta(C', A') \leq U_\Theta(C, A)$ since (C, A) is optimal for the MILP. Let F_Ψ be a function constructed using this method for every possible $C' \neq C$. Then C is a best-response to F_Ψ since $U_\Theta(C', A') \leq U_\Theta(C, A)$, satisfying condition 1 of the SSE. ∎

8.5 Exploiting Payoff Structure

We now consider a class of security games in which the defender always benefits by having additional resources covering an attacked target, while the attacker is always worse off attacking a more heavily defended target. These assumptions are quite reasonable in many security games. Formally, we restrict payoff functions so that $U_\Theta^u(t) < U_\Theta^c(t)$ and $U_\Psi^u(t) > U_\Psi^c(t)$ for all t (note the strict inequalities). This is similar in spirit to a zero-sum assumption, but somewhat less restrictive. It is well-known that zero-sum games often admit more efficient solution algorithms, such as Luce's polynomial method for two-player, zero-sum games (Luce and Raiffa, 1989). We introduce two algorithms that compute extremely fast solutions for security games with this restriction on payoffs by exploiting structural properties of the optimal solution. We begin with three observations about the properties of the optimal solution for this class of games.

Observation 8.1. *All else equal, increasing c_t for any target not in $\Gamma(C)$ has no effect on $\hat{U}_\Theta(C)$ or $\hat{U}_\Psi(C)$.*

Increasing c_t can only decrease $U_\Psi(t, C)$ (due to the payoff assumption), and cannot affect the payoffs for any other target. Since t was not in $\Gamma(C)$ before, decreasing the payoff cannot result in a change to $\Gamma(C)$, and therefore cannot influence the SSE payoffs.

Observation 8.2. *If $\Gamma(C) \subset \Gamma(C')$ and $c_t = c'_t$ for all $t \in \Gamma(C)$ then $\hat{U}_\Theta(C) \leq \hat{U}_\Theta(C')$.*

In other words, adding an additional target to the attack set cannot hurt the defender. This is a straightforward consequence of the SSE assumption that the defender receives the optimal payoff among targets in the attack set.

Observation 8.3. *If $\hat{U}_\Psi(C) = x$, then $c_t \geq \frac{x - U_\Psi^u(t)}{U_\Psi^c(t) - U_\Psi^u(t)}$ for every target t with $U_\Psi^u(t) > x$.*

The inequality comes from setting the expected payoff for the target equal to the payoff for targets in the attack set: $x = c_t(U_\psi^c) + (1 - c_t)U_\psi^u$. Solving for c_t gives the coverage probability necessary to induce indifference between attacking t and any target in the attack set. If this condition is not satisfied for some t with $U_\psi^u(t) > x$, then the attacker strictly prefers an attack on t instead of the attack set, contradicting the definition of the attack set (or x).

Algorithm 1 ORIGAMI

---

targets $\leftarrow T$ sorted by $U_\psi^u(t)$
payoff[t] $\leftarrow U_\psi^u(t)$, coverage[t] $\leftarrow 0$
left $\leftarrow m$, next $\leftarrow 2$
covBound $\leftarrow -\infty$
while next $\leq n$ **do**
    addedCov[t] $\leftarrow \frac{payoff[next] - U_\psi^u(t)}{U_\psi^c(t) - U_\psi^u(t)}$ - coverage[t]
    if coverage[t] + addedCov[t] ≥ 1 **then**
        covBound $\leftarrow$ Max(covBound, $U_\psi^c(t)$)
    end if
    if covBound $\geq -\infty$ OR $\sum_{t \in T}$ addedCov[t] $\leq$ left **then**
        BREAK
    end if
    coverage[t] += addedCov[t]
    left -= $\sum_{t \in T}$ addedCov[t]
    next++
end while
ratio[t] $\leftarrow \frac{1}{U_\psi^u(t) - U_\psi^c(t)}$
coverage[t] += $\frac{ratio[t] \cdot left}{\sum_{t \in T} ratio[t]}$
ifcoverage[t] ≥ 1 **then**
    covBound $\leftarrow$ Max(covBound, $U_\psi^c(t)$)
end if
if covBound $\geq -\infty$ **then**
    coverage[t] $\leftarrow \frac{covBound - U_\psi^u(t)}{U_\psi^c(t) - U_\psi^u(t)}$
end if

We exploit these observations in the ORIGAMI (Optimizing Resources in Games Using Maximal Indifference) algorithm, which we present pseudocode for in Algorithm 8.5. The idea is to directly compute the attack set for the attacker, using the indifference equation in Observation 8.3. Starting with a target that has maximal $U_\psi^u(t)$, the attack set is expanded at each iteration in order of decreasing $U_\psi^u(t)$.[2] Each time the attack set is expanded, the coverage

---

[2] It is not strictly necessary to start from the maximal value and expand the set in order. A faster but slightly more complicated variation of the algorithm could be implemented using a binary

of each target is updates to maintain the indifference of attacker payoffs within the attack set.

There are two termination conditions. The first occurs when adding the next target to the attack set requires more total coverage probability than the defender has resources available. At this point, the size of the attack set cannot be increased further, but additional probability can still be added to the targets in the attack set in the specific ratio necessary to maintain indifference. The second termination condition occurs when any target t is covered with probability 1. The expected value for an attack on this target cannot be reduced below $U^c_\psi(t)$, so this defines the final expected payoffs for the attack set. The final coverage probabilities are computed setting the coverages so that as many targets as possible have an expected payoff of $U^c_\psi(t)$. In both cases, the solution maximizes the number of targets in the final attack set. Within the attack set, it maximizes the total coverage probability assigned while maintaining the attacker's indifference between the targets. The coverage probability for all targets outside of the attack set is 0. We show below that these properties suffice to identify a coverage vector that is an SSE of the security game.

Theorem 8.3. *ORIGAMI computes a coverage vector C that is optimal for the ERASER MILP, and is therefore consistent with an SSE of the security game.*

Proof. Let (C, A) be an optimal solution for ERASER MILP and C' be a coverage vector generated by ORIGAMI. C' is feasible in the MILP by construction. We first show that A must attack a target in $\Gamma(C')$, or it violates the optimality constraint for the attacker. Suppose ORIGAMI terminates because a target t is assigned $c'_t = 1$. By construction, $t \in \Gamma(C')$, and $U^c_\psi(t) \geq U^u_\psi(t')$ for any t' outside of $\Gamma(C')$. Since $c'_t = 1$ it cannot be greater in any coverage vector, and $c'_{t'} = 0$ so it cannot be smaller. Therefore, t' cannot be part of $\Gamma(C)$ for any feasible C. Now, suppose ORIGAMI terminates because all resources are assigned. Since maximal coverage is assigned to targets in $\Gamma(C')$, in any coverage vector C, $c'_t \leq c_t$ for at least one, t, or C violates the constraint on total resources available. Now, let t' be any target not in $\Gamma(C')$. We know that $U_\psi(t, C') > U_\psi(t', C')$, and since $c'_t \leq c_t$, then $U_\psi(t, C) > U_\psi(t', C)$ and t' is not in $\Gamma(C)$.

Having established that $\Gamma(C) \subset \Gamma(C')$ for any feasible C, we now consider whether any feasible C can improve the defender's payoff for an attack within $\Gamma(C')$. By Observation 8.1, we need to consider only changes in coverage probability within $\Gamma(C')$. To improve the defenders payoff over $\hat{U}_\Theta(C')$,

---

search to find the attack set of maximal size that can be induced using the available coverage resources.

the coverage probability for the new attack target t must increase. Otherwise, $\hat{U}_{\Theta}(C')$ would already achieve at least the payoff for t. First, take the case where C' assigns maximal coverage. It is not possible to have $c_t > c'_t$ for some t without having $c_{t'} < c'_{t'}$ for at least one other t', since the sum of c'_t is already maximal. Since $U_{\Psi}(t, C') = U_{\Psi}(t', C')$, an attack on t' is strictly preferred and the target t with higher coverage is no longer in the attack set. Similarly, in the case where a target is assigned coverage probability 1, it is not possible to increase the coverage of that target. Increasing the coverage of any other target reduces the attacker's payoff and removes it from the attack set.   ■

$$\min \quad k \tag{8.12}$$

$$\gamma_t \in \quad \{0, 1\} \quad \forall t \in T \tag{8.13}$$

$$c_t \in \quad [0, 1] \quad \forall t \in T \tag{8.14}$$

$$\sum_{t \in T} c_t \leq \quad m \tag{8.15}$$

$$U_{\Psi}(t, C) \leq \quad k \quad \forall t \in T \tag{8.16}$$

$$k - U_{\Psi}(t, C) \leq (1 - \gamma_t) \cdot Z \,\forall t \in T \tag{8.17}$$

$$c_t \leq \quad \gamma_t \quad \forall t \in T \tag{8.18}$$

We have also implemented an MILP that applies the same principles as ORIGAMI, which we call ORIGAMI-MILP. It is presented in Equations 8.12 through 8.18. The vector γ represents the attack set, and replaces A in ERASER. γ_t is 1 for targets in the attack set, and 0 for all other targets. ORIGAMI-MILP is similar to ERASER, but does not optimize the defender's payoff. Instead, it minimizes the attacker's payoff, and adds a constraint that restricts c_t for any t not in $\Gamma(C)$ to 0, consistent with Observation 8.1. This constraint forces the attack set to include the maximal number of targets.

Theorem 8.4. *ORIGAMI-MILP generates an optimal solution for the ERASER MILP.*

Proof sketch: ORIGAMI-MILP generates solutions with the same properties as ORIGAMI. In particular, no coverage probability is assigned to targets outside of the attack set. This implies that any target in the attack set is assigned exactly the coverage probability necessary to induce indifference with all other targets in the attack set, as in Observation 8.3. The objective of minimizing the attacker's payoff forces an attack set with the lowest expected payoff for the attacker. Any target with an uncovered payoff higher than this value must be included in the attack set, which forces the attack set to be maximal. This in turn maximizes the defender's SSE payoff.

8.6 Scheduling and Resource Constraints

We now introduce ERASER-C ("Constrained"), an extension of ERASER which adds the capability to represent certain kinds of resource and scheduling constraints, motivated by the real example domains described previously. We demonstrate that the basic idea of using a compact representation of the defender's strategy space and of the payoff functions for both players is still useful in this setting when resources are heterogeneous.

The first extension allows resources to be assigned to *schedules* covering multiple targets. The set of legal schedules $S = \{s_1 \ldots s_l\}$ is a subset of the power set of the targets, with restrictions on this set representing scheduling constraints. We define the relationship between targets and schedules with the function $M : S \times T \rightarrow \{0, 1\}$, which evaluates to 1 if and only if t is covered in s.[3] The defender's strategy is an assignment of resources to schedules, rather than targets. A second extension introduces *resource types*, $\Omega = \{\omega_1, \ldots, \omega_v\}$, each with the capability to cover a different subset of S. The number of available resources of each type is given by the function $\mathcal{R}(\omega)$. Coverage capabilities for each type are given by the function $Ca : S \times \Omega \rightarrow \{0, 1\}$, which is 1 if the type is able to cover the given schedule, and 0 otherwise.[4]

The combination of schedules and resource types captures key elements of the FAMS domain. Suppose we model air marshals as resources, flights as targets, and defined payoffs by expert risk analysis. A single marshal cannot be on all possible flights due to location and timing constraints. We could use legal schedules to define the set of feasible flights for a particular air marshal. Resource types can be used to specify different sets of legal schedules for each resource (e.g., based on initial location). Adding these constraints effectively reduces the space of feasible coverage vectors. Consider an example with a single resource defending three targets. There are two legal schedules, covering targets $\{1, 2\}$ and $\{2, 3\}$. Given only these schedules, it is not possible to implement a coverage vector that places 50% probability on both targets 1 and 3, with no coverage of target 2.

An MILP implementing ERASER-C is presented in Equations 8.19 through 8.30. The MILP is very similar to the original ERASER, but it enforces additional constraints on the legal schedules and coverage for each resource type. The q variables represent the total probability assigned to each schedule by all resource types, and the h variables are the probability assigned to a schedule

---

[3] For the purposes of the FAMS domain and the version of ERASER-C presented here, all schedules are of size 2 and there are no odd cycles in the graph where targets are vertices and edges are schedules.

[4] Our implementation uses complete matrices for M and Ca, but sparse representations could improve performance.

by a specific type of resource. In Equations 8.29 and 8.30, Z is a large constant relative to the maximum payoff.

Constraint 8.20 restricts the attack vector to binary variables, which correspond to pure strategies for the attacker. Constraints 8.21 through 8.23 restrict the defender's strategy so that no target is assigned probability greater than 1. The coverage of each schedule must sum to the contributions of the individual resource types, specified in Equation 8.25. The mapping between the coverage of schedules and coverage of targets is enforced in Constraint 8.26. Constraint 8.27 restricts the schedule so that only the available number of resources of each type are used. No probability may be assigned to disallowed schedules for each resource type, which is explicitly enforced by Constraint 8.28. The final three constraints specify the maximization performed by both the attacker and defender, exactly as in the ERASER (see Section 8.4.3).

$$\max \quad d \tag{8.19}$$

$$a_t \in \quad \{0,1\} \quad \forall t \in T \tag{8.20}$$

$$c_t \in \quad [0,1] \quad \forall t \in T \tag{8.21}$$

$$q_s \in \quad [0,1] \quad \forall s \in S \tag{8.22}$$

$$h_{s,\omega} \in \quad [0,1] \quad \forall s, \omega \in S \times \Omega \tag{8.23}$$

$$\sum_{t \in T} a_t = \quad 1 \tag{8.24}$$

$$\sum_{\omega \in \Omega} h_{s,\omega} = \quad q_s \quad \forall s \in S \tag{8.25}$$

$$\sum_{s \in S} q_s M(s,t) = \quad c_t \quad \forall t \in T \tag{8.26}$$

$$\sum_{s \in S} h_{s,\omega} Ca(s,\omega) \leq \quad \mathcal{R}(\omega) \quad \forall \omega \in \Omega \tag{8.27}$$

$$h_{s,\omega} \leq \quad Ca(s,\omega) \quad \forall s, \omega \in S \times \Omega \tag{8.28}$$

$$d - U_\Theta(t,C) \leq (1 - a_t) \cdot Z \,\, \forall t \in T \tag{8.29}$$

$$0 \leq k - U_\Psi(t,C) \leq (1 - a_t) \cdot Z \,\, \forall t \in T \tag{8.30}$$

An optimal coverage vector of ERASER-C meets the equilibrium conditions, following the same line of reasoning as Theorem 8.2. However, the MILP as written can result in coverage vectors that cannot be implemented by mixed strategies in the original solution space if arbitrary schedules are allowed (as noted above, in the FAMS domain schedules have a restricted form). In particular, additional constraints are necessary if odd cycles are possible in the schedules. We defer full analysis and discussion of this issue to future work, but note that in empirical testing with realistic data even simple heuristic methods are able to generate sample joint assignments that closely approximate the optimal coverage probabilities identified by this MILP.

8.7 Experimental Evaluation

We evaluate the four algorithms using both randomly generated security games and real examples from the LAX and FAMS domains. Our baseline for comparing with existing methods is DOBSS (Paruchuri et al., 2008), which is the fastest known algorithm for general Bayesian Stackelberg games. While we do not consider the Bayesian case here, DOBSS is also comparable to other methods (notably [189]) for the non-Bayesian case. All of our algorithms generate optimal SSE solutions, so the primary metrics of comparison are the computational requirements to compute solutions, in both time and memory. We note that the algorithms are applicable to different classes of games, with faster algorithms generally able to solve a smaller class of games. The ordering of the algorithms in terms of the size of the class of games is given by ORIGAMI/ORIGAMI-MILP $\subset$ ERASER $\subset$ ERASER-C $\subset$ DOBSS.

All of our experiments were run on a machine with dual Xeon 3.2Ghz processors and 2GB of RAM, running RHEL 3. We use CPLEX 9.0.0 with default parameter settings to solve MILPs. All data points are based on twenty sample game instances, except when explicitly stated otherwise. Our first set of experiments compares the performance of DOBSS, ERASER, and ERASER-C on random game instances. We next compare ERASER, ORIGAMI, and ORIGAMI-MILP on much larger instances that DOBSS is unable to solve, given memory limitations. The final experiment compares the algorithms on relevant example games for the LAX and FAMS domains described in Section 8.3.

For the first set of tests we generate random instances of compact security games of the form used by ERASER (see Section 8.4.1). To generate a game with a given number of targets and resources, we independently randomly draw four integer payoffs for each target. Thus, U_Θ^c and U_Ψ^u are drawn from $Uniform[0, 100]$, while U_Θ^u and U_Ψ^c are drawn from $Uniform[-100, 0]$. We use a value of five resources for this set of results and vary the number of targets. The generated game instances are translated into the representations used by DOBSS and ERASER-C.

Figure 8.1a compares runtime performance of DOBSS, ERASER and ERASER-C on this set of games. The x-axis is the size of the game (in targets),

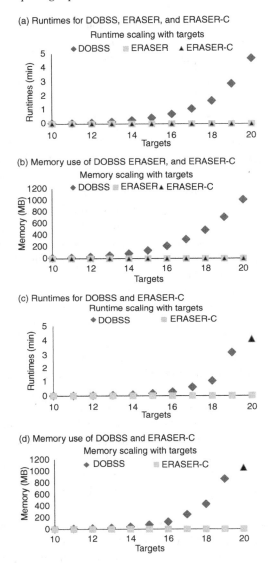

Figure 8.1. Runtime and memory scaling.

and the y-axis is runtime in minutes. For example, the point (20, 4.68) indicates that DOBSS has an average runtime of 4.68 m on problems with twenty targets; ERASER and ERASER-C each run for 0.002s for twenty targets. The data show an exponential increase in time necessary to compute DOBSS solutions, and essentially no change in runtimes for ERASER and ERASER-C up to 20 targets. The differences between both variants of ERASER and DOBSS are statistically significant (using Yuen's test) for the larger games, while there is no significant difference between ERASER and ERASER-C for games of this size. Figure 8.1b compares the memory performance on the same set of games; there the y-axis represents the memory usage of AMPL in MB. Runtime performance roughly tracks memory performance, and the same exponential behavior is observed for DOBSS. Memory limitations become prohibitive for DOBSS before runtimes become extremely long (though the growth trend is already clear); we were unable to successfully complete game instances beyond roughly 1GB on the memory measure.

We also compare the performance of ERASER-C and DOBSS on games that require the additional capabilities of ERASER-C; ERASER is not included in this test because it cannot solve the relevant games. Our random game instances now include schedules, resource types, and the schedule and coverage mappings, as described in Section 8.6. We test games with three resource types, and availability of $[3,3,2]$ for each type. There are twice as many schedules as targets, and each schedule covers a randomly selected set of two targets (we also ensure that each target is covered in at least one schedule). Each resource type covers approximately 33% of the legal schedules, again selected randomly.

Figures 8.1c and 8.1d compare the performance of DOBSS and ERASER-C on this set of games, using the same metrics as the previous set of results. DOBSS was unable to complete all games with twenty targets due to memory limitations; the black triangle gives the result for the three complete trials (which are likely biased low). All comparisons are statistically significant for large games. We observe the same patterns of performance for both DOBSS and ERASER-C for this set of games as in the more restricted class solvable by ERASER. ERASER-C adds representational power, and retains substantial performance improvements over the baseline DOBSS algorithm.

We now compare the performance of ERASER, ORIGAMI, and ORIGAMI-MILP on very large games well beyond the limits of DOBSS. Random game instances are generated as before for the experiment including ERASER; the random payoffs generated already meet the restrictions of the ORIGAMI algorithms. Figure 8.2 compares the runtimes of the three algorithms on games with 25 resources and up to 3000 targets. Figure 8.2b extends the data out to 1,000 resources and 40,000 targets for the two ORIGAMI algorithms. In both figures, the x-axis is the number of targets, and the y-axis is runtime, as before.

The ERASER algorithm was able to solve games of 3000 targets in 13.30 minutes, which is quite impressive. The ORIGAMI algorithms were even

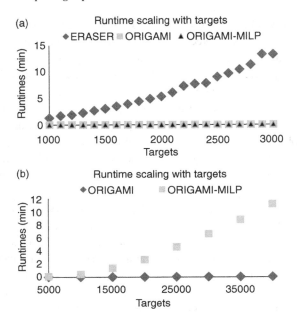

Figure 8.2. Runtime scaling of ERASER, ORIGAMI, and ORIGAMI-MILP.

more impressive, solving these games in seconds. Yuen's test confirms that the ORIGAMI times for large games are significantly different than the ERASER times. As a further point of comparison, for the 3000 target, 25 resource game, the size of the defender's strategy space in normal form is roughly 10^{60} – clearly infeasible to represent, let alone solve. The results for the two ORIGAMI algorithms given in Figure 8.2b show that as the size of the game scales to very large instances, ORIGAMI outperforms ORIGAMI-MILP. To test the ultimate scalability of ORIGAMI, we ran a single trial of a game with 1,000,000 targets and 10,000 resources. ORIGAMI successfully computed a solution in 1.51 hours.

In the final set of experiments we test the algorithms on real data acquired for both the LAX canine and FAMS scheduling domains. The LAX data consists of a single game instance with six resources (canine units) and eight targets (terminals). For FAMS we generated two hypothetical examples using real (public) flight information and hypothetical information about resources and coverage capabilities, and hypothetical payoffs. Both examples cover a one week period, but they cover different foreign and domestic airports to generate "small" and "large" tests.

Table 8.2. *Runtimes on real data*

	Actions	DOBSS	ERASER (-C)
LAX (6 canines)	784	0.94s	0.23s
FAMS (small)	~6,000	4.74s	0.09s
FAMS (large)	~85,000	435.6s*	1.57s

Table 8.2 shows runtimes and DOBSS action space size for these problem instances, averaged over twenty trials of the same game instance. The first line compares DOBSS and ERASER for the LAX security domain. The second and third lines compare DOBSS and ERASER-C on the two instances of the FAMS domain (ERASER is not capable of representing these problems). DOBSS did not complete the large problem instance, reaching a memory limit after 435.6s of runtime. All differences in means are statistically significant (though we emphasize that these are repeated trials on the same game instance). Our algorithms show dramatic performance improvements over DOBSS on these real data sets, in addition to the randomly generated data sets presented previously.

8.8 Conclusion

Allocating limited resources is an important problem in many security domains. Airport security, the federal air marshals, screening incoming shipments at ports, patrolling subway systems, and random checks at customs are all examples of this. Increasingly, game-theoretic analysis is seen as a valuable tool for analyzing these problems, and especially for determining effective randomization strategies. We apply the theory of Stackelberg games to this problem, following the successful application of similar technology at the LAX airport by Pita et al. (2008).

We contribute new algorithms for computing optimal solutions to security games that scale to massive games with many resources and many targets. While the best existing algorithm was unable to solve games larger than twenty targets because of memory limitations, our algorithms scale to thousands – and in some cases *millions* – of targets. The first method, ERASER, introduces a compact representation for security games with multiple resources, avoiding a combinatorial explosion in representation size of the normal-form game. We present two algorithm which offer even more dramatic performance improvements for a class of games with plausible restrictions on the payoff functions for the players. These algorithms exploit structural properties of optimal solutions under the payoff restrictions. Finally, we extend the ERASER algorithm to incorporate scheduling and resource constraints motivated by the FAMS domain. The resulting ERASER-C algorithm is more expressive than ERASER, but still improves performance over the existing baseline methods. Together, these four algorithms offer a powerful set of computational tools for solving massive security games. In many cases, they offer improvements of several orders of magnitude in computational scalability.

Acknowledgment

This research was supported by the United States Department of Homeland Security through the Center for Risk and Economic Analysis of Terrorism Events (CREATE) under grant number 2007-ST-061-000001. We are also grateful to the United States Federal Air Marshal Service for their exceptional collaboration. However, any opinions, conclusions or recommendations herein are solely those of the authors and do not necessarily reflect views of the Department of Homeland Security or Federal Air Marshal Service.

9

Security Games with Arbitrary Schedules: A Branch-and-Price Approach

Manish Jain, Erim Kardeş, Christopher Kiekintveld,
Milind Tambe, and Fernando Ordóñez

9.1 Introduction

Algorithms for attacker-defender Stackelberg games, resulting in random-ized schedules for deploying limited security resources at airports, subways, ports, and other critical infrastructure have garnered significant research inter-est (Parachuri et al. 2008; Kiekintveld et al. 2009). Indeed, two important deployed security applications are using such algorithms: ARMOR and IRIS. ARMOR has been in use for over two years by Los Angeles International Airport police to generate canine-patrol and vehicle-checkpoint schedules (Pita et al., 2009). IRIS was recently deployed by the Federal Air Marshals Service (FAMS) to create flight schedules for air marshals (Tsai et al., 2009). These applications use efficient algorithms that solve large-scale games (Parachuri et al., 2008; Conitzer and Sandholm, 2006; Basilico, Gatti, and Amigoni, 2009), the latest being ERASER-C, the algorithm used in IRIS.

Unfortunately, current state-of-the art algorithms for Stackelberg games are inadequate for many applications. For example, U.S. carriers fly over 27,000 domestic and 2,000 international flights daily, presenting a massive schedul-ing challenge for FAMS. IRIS addresses an important part of this space – the international sector – but only considers schedules with a single departure and return flight. The ERASER-C algorithm used in this application does not provide correct solutions for longer and more complex tours (which are com-mon in the domestic sector). In fact, recent complexity results show that the problem of finding Stackelberg equibria with general scheduling constraints is NP-hard (Korzhyk, Conitzer, and Parr, 2010) and can be solved in polynomial time only for restricted cases. This is due to the exponential explosion in the size of the defender's strategy space caused by large, arbitrary schedules.

Despite the discouraging complexity results, arbitrary schedules are an important element of security scheduling problems for FAMS, border security, and many other applications. We develop algorithms for SPARS (Security Problems with Arbitrary Schedules), drawing on techniques used to solve very large mixed-integer programs. Our main contribution is ASPEN (Accelerated SPARS Engine), which is based on the branch and price framework. The first novel feature of ASPEN is that it uses column generation to avoid representing the full (exponential) strategy space for the defender. To this end, we provide a novel decomposition of SPARS into a master problem and a network-flow subproblem. Second, ASPEN uses a novel branch-and-bound method for searching the space of attacker strategies, achieving significant performance improvements by integrating branching criteria and bounds generated with ORIGAMI algorithm (Kiekintveld et al. 2009). We evaluate ASPEN empirically on SPARS, illustrating that this is the first known method for efficiently solving real-world-sized security games with arbitrary schedules.

9.2 SPARS

A security game (Kiekintveld et al. 2009) is a two-player game between a defender and an attacker. The attacker's pure strategy space $\mathcal{A}$ is the set of targets T that could be attacked, $T = \{t_1, t_2, \ldots, t_n\}$. The corresponding mixed strategy $\mathbf{a} = \langle a_i \rangle$ is a vector where a_i represents the probability of attacking t_i. The defender allocates resources of different types $\lambda \in \Lambda$ to protect targets, with the number of available resources given by $R = \{r_1, r_2, \ldots, r_{|\Lambda|}\}$. Each resource can be assigned to a *schedule* covering multiple targets, $s \subseteq T$, so the set of all legal schedules $S \subseteq \mathcal{P}(T)$. There is a set of legal schedules for each λ, $S_\lambda \subseteq S$.

The defender's pure strategies are the set of *joint schedules* that assign each resource to at most one schedule. Additionally, we assume that a target may be covered by at most one resource in a joint schedule (though this can be generalized). A joint schedule $\mathbf{j}$ can be represented by the vector $\mathbf{P_j} = \langle P_{jt} \rangle \in \{0, 1\}^n$, where P_{jt} represents whether or not target t is covered in joint schedule $\mathbf{j}$. The set of all feasible joint schedules is denoted by $\mathbf{J}$. We define a mapping M from $\mathbf{j}$ to $\mathbf{P_j}$ as: $M(\mathbf{j}) = \langle P_{jt} \rangle$, where $P_{jt} = 1$ if $t \in \bigcup_{s \in \mathbf{j}} s$; 0 otherwise. The defender's mixed strategy $\mathbf{x}$ specifies the probabilities of playing each $\mathbf{j} \in \mathbf{J}$, where each individual probability is denoted by x_j. Let $\mathbf{c} = \langle c_t \rangle$ be the vector of coverage probabilities corresponding to $\mathbf{x}$, where $c_t = \sum_{\mathbf{j} \in \mathbf{J}} P_{jt} x_j$ is the marginal probability of covering t.

Payoffs depend on the target attacked and whether or not a defender resource is covering the target. Then $U_d^c(t)$ denotes the defender's utility if t is attacked when it is covered by a resource of any type. If t is not covered, the defender gets $U_d^u(t)$. Likewise, the attacker's utilities are denoted by $U_a^c(t)$ and $U_a^u(t)$. We assume that adding coverage to target t is strictly better for the defender and worse for the attacker: $U_d^c(t) > U_d^u(t)$ and $U_a^c(t) < U_a^u(t)$, however, not necessarily zero-sum. For a strategy profile $\langle \mathbf{c}, \mathbf{a} \rangle$, the expected utilities for the defender and attacker are given by:

$$U_d(\mathbf{c}, \mathbf{a}) = \sum_{t \in T} a_t \left(c_t U_d^c(t) + (1 - c_t) U_d^u(t) \right) \tag{9.1}$$

$$U_a(\mathbf{c}, \mathbf{a}) = \sum_{t \in T} a_t \left(c_t U_a^c(t) + (1 - c_t) U_a^u(t) \right) \tag{9.2}$$

We adopt a Stackelberg model in which the defender acts first and the attacker chooses a strategy after observing the defender's mixed strategy. Stackelberg games are common in security domains in which attackers can surveil the defender strategy (Paruchuri et al., 2008). The standard solution concept is strong stackelberg equilibrium (SSE) (Leitmann, 1978; Breton, Alg, and Haurie, 1988; von Stengel and Zamir, 2004), in which the leader selects an optimal mixed strategy based on the assumption that the follower will choose an optimal response, breaking ties in favor of the leader.[1] There always exists an optimal pure-strategy response for the attacker, so we restrict our attention to this set in this paper.

Example: Consider a FAMS game with five targets (flights), $T = \{t_1, \ldots, t_5\}$, and three marshals of the same type, $r_1 = 3$. Let the set of feasible schedules be $S_1 = \{\{t_1, t_2\}, \{t_2, t_3\}, \{t_3, t_4\}, \{t_4, t_5\}, \{t_1, t_5\}\}$. The set of feasible joint schedules, in which column $\mathbf{J}_1$ represents the joint schedule $\{\{t_1, t_2\}, \{t_3, t_4\}\}$ is as follows:

$$\mathbf{P} = \begin{array}{c} \\ t_1 : \\ t_2 : \\ t_3 : \\ t_4 : \\ t_5 : \end{array} \begin{array}{c} \mathbf{J}_1 \ \mathbf{J}_2 \ \mathbf{J}_3 \ \mathbf{J}_4 \ \mathbf{J}_5 \\ \begin{bmatrix} 1 & 1 & 1 & 1 & 0 \\ 1 & 1 & 1 & 0 & 1 \\ 1 & 1 & 0 & 1 & 1 \\ 1 & 0 & 1 & 1 & 1 \\ 0 & 1 & 1 & 1 & 1 \end{bmatrix} \end{array}$$

Each joint schedule in $\mathbf{J}$ assigns only two air marshals in this example, since no more than one FAM is allowed on any flight. Thus, the third air marshal will remain unused. Suppose all the targets have identical payoffs $U_d^c(t) = 1$, $U_d^u(t) = -5$, $U_a^c(t) = -1$ and $U_a^u(t) = 5$. In this case, the optimal strategy for the defender randomizes uniformly across the joint schedules, $\mathbf{x} = \langle .2, .2, .2, .2, .2 \rangle$, resulting in coverage $\mathbf{c} = \langle .8, .8, .8, .8, .8 \rangle$. All pure strategies have equal payoffs for the attacker, given this coverage vector.

---

[1] This tie-breaking rule is counterintuitive, but the defender can make this response strictly optimal for the attacker by playing a strategy an infinitesimal ϵ away from the SSE strategy.

9.3 ASPEN Solution Approach and Related Work

The ERASER-C mixed-integer linear program (MIP) (Kiekintveld et al., 2009) is the most recent algorithm developed for larger and more complex Stackelberg security games.Whereas previous work has focused on patrolling arbitrary topologies using Stackelberg games (Basilico, Gatti, and Amigoni 2009; Parachuri et al., 2008), it has typically focused on a single defender. In contrast, ASPEN and ERASER-C focus on games with large numbers of defenders of different types, handling the combinatorial explosion in the defender's joint schedules. Unfortunately, as the authors note, ERASER-C may fail to generate a correct solution in cases in which arbitrary schedules with more than two flights (i.e., multicity tours) are allowed in the input, or when the set of flights cannot be partitioned into distinct sets for departure and arrival flights. For instance, ERASER-C incorrectly outputs the coverage vector $\mathbf{c} = \langle 1, 1, 1, 1, 1 \rangle$ for the example above. ERASER-C, avoids enumerating joint schedules to gain efficiency, but loses the ability to correctly model arbitrary schedules. Furthermore, ERASER-C only outputs a coverage vector $\mathbf{c}$, and not the distribution $\mathbf{x}$ over joint schedules $\mathbf{J}$ necessary to implement the coverage in practice.

SPARS problems can be formulated as mixed-integer programs in which adversary strategies are represented by integer variables $\mathbf{a}$ with $a_t = 1$ if target t is attacked, and 0 otherwise. Two key computational challenges arise in this formulation. First, the space of possible strategies (joint schedules) for the defender suffers from combinatorial explosion: A FAMS problem with 100 flights, schedules with 3 flights, and 10 air marshals has up to 100,000 schedules and $\binom{100000}{10}$ joint schedules. Second, integer variables are a well-known challenge for optimization. Branch and Price (Barnhart et al., 1994) is a framework for solving very large optimization problems that combines branch-and-bound search with column generation to mitigate both of these problems. This method operates on joint schedules (and not marginal probabilities, like ERASER-C), so it is able to handle arbitrary scheduling constraints directly.

An example of branch and price for our problem is shown in Figure 9.1, with the root representing the original problem. Branches to the left (gray nodes) set exactly one variable t_i in $\mathbf{a}$ to 1, and the rest to zero, resulting in a linear program that gives a lower bound on the overall solution quality. Branches to the right fix variable t_i to zero, leaving the remaining variables unconstrained. An upper bound on solution quality computed for each white node can be used to terminate execution without exploring all the possible integer assignments. Solving the linear programs in each gray node normally requires enumerating all joint schedules for the defender. Column generation (i.e., pricing) is a technique that avoids this by iteratively solving a restricted *master problem*,

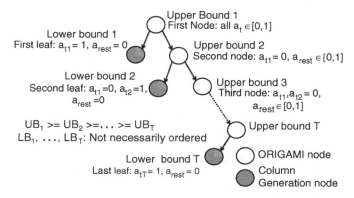

Figure 9.1. Working of branch and price.

which includes only a small subset of the variables, and a *slave problem*, which identifies new variables to include in the master problem that can improve the solution.

Unfortunately, branch and price is not an "out-of-the-box approach" and it has only recently begun to be applied in game-theoretic settings (Halvorson, Conitzer, and Parr, 2009). We introduce a novel master-slave decomposition to facilitate column generation for SPARS, including a network flow formulation of the slave problem. We also show experimentally that conventional linear programming relaxations used for branch and bound perform poorly in this domain, and we replace them with novel techniques that are based on fast algorithms for security games without scheduling constraints.

9.4 ASPEN Column Generation

The linear programs at each leaf in Figure 9.1 are decomposed into *master* and *slave* problems for column generation (see Algorithm 9.1). The master solves for the defender strategy $\mathbf{x}$, given a restricted set of columns (i.e., joint schedules) $\mathbf{P}$. The objective function for the slave is updated based on the solution of the master, and the slave is solved to identify the best new column to add to the master problem, using *reduced costs* (explained later). If no column can improve the solution, the algorithm terminates.

Master Problem: The master problem (Equations 9.3 through 9.8) solves for the probability vector $\mathbf{x}$ that maximizes the defender reward (Table 9.1 describes the notation). This master problem operates directly on columns of $\mathbf{P}$, and the coverage vector $\mathbf{c}$ is computed from these columns as $\mathbf{Px}$. Constraints 9.4

Table 9.1. *Notation*

Variable	Definition	Dimension
$\mathbf{P}$	Mapping between T and J	$|T| \times |J|$
$\mathbf{x}$	Probability distribution over J	$|J| \times 1$
$\mathbf{a}$	Attack vector	$|T| \times 1$
d	Defender reward	−
k	Adversary reward	−
$\mathbf{d}$	Column vector of d	$|T| \times 1$
$\mathbf{k}$	Column vector of k	$|T| \times 1$
$\mathbf{D}$	Diag. matrix of $U_d^c(t) - U_d^u(t)$	$|T| \times |T|$
$\mathbf{A}$	Diag. matrix of $U_a^c(t) - U_a^u(t)$	$|T| \times |T|$
$\mathbf{U}_d^u$	Vector of values $U_d^u(t)$	$|T| \times 1$
$\mathbf{U}_a^u$	Vector of values $U_a^u(t)$	$|T| \times 1$
M	Huge positive constant	-

Algorithm 9.1 Column generation

1. Initialize P
2. Solve Master Problem
3. Calculate reduced cost coefficients from solution
4. Update objective of slave problem with coefficients
5. Solve Slave Problem
if Optimal solution obtained, **then**
    6. Return $(\mathbf{x}, \mathbf{P})$
else
7. Extract new column and add to $\mathbf{P}$
8. Repeat from Step 2

---

through 9.6 enforce the SSE conditions that the players choose mutual best-responses, mirroring similar constraints in ERASER-C. The defender expected payoff (Equation 9.1) for target t is given by the tth component of the column vector $\mathbf{DPx} + \mathbf{U}_d^u$ and denoted $(\mathbf{DPx} + \mathbf{U}_d^u)_t$. Similarly, the attacker payoff for target t is given by $(\mathbf{APx} + \mathbf{U}_a^u)_t$. Constraints 9.4 and 9.5 are active only for the single target t^* attacked ($a_{t^*} = 1$). This target must be a best-response, due to Constraint 9.6.

$$\max \quad d \tag{9.3}$$

$$\text{s.t.} \quad \mathbf{d} - \mathbf{DPx} - \mathbf{U}_d^u \leq (\mathbf{1} - \mathbf{a})M \tag{9.4}$$

$$\mathbf{k} - \mathbf{APx} - \mathbf{U}_a^u \le (1 - \mathbf{a})M \tag{9.5}$$

$$\mathbf{APx} + \mathbf{U}_a^u \le \mathbf{k} \tag{9.6}$$

$$\sum_{j \in J} x_j = 1 \tag{9.7}$$

$$\mathbf{x}, \mathbf{a} \ge 0 \tag{9.8}$$

Slave Problem: The slave problem finds the best column to add to the current columns in **P**. This is done using *reduced cost*, which captures the total change in the defender payoff if a candidate column is added to **P**. The candidate column with minimum reduced cost improves the objective value the most (Bertsimas and Tsitsiklis, 1994). The reduced cost $\bar{c}_j$ of variable x_j, associated with column $\mathbf{P_j}$, is given in Equation 9.9, where $\mathbf{w}, \mathbf{y}, \mathbf{z}$, and h are dual variables of master constraints 9.4 through 9.7, respectively. The dual variable measures the influence of the associated constraint on the objective, and can be calculated using standard techniques.

$$\bar{c}_j = \mathbf{w}^T (\mathbf{DP_j}) + \mathbf{y}^T (\mathbf{AP_j}) - \mathbf{z}^T (\mathbf{AP_j}) - h \tag{9.9}$$

An inefficient approach would be to iterate through all the columns and calculate each reduced cost to identify the best column to add. Instead, we formulate a minimum cost network flow (MCNF) problem that efficiently finds the optimal column. Feasible flows in the network map to feasible joint schedules in the SPARS problem, so the scheduling constraints are captured by this formulation. For a SPARS instance we construct the MCNF graph G as follows.

A source node source$_\lambda$ with supply r_λ is created for each defender type $\lambda \in \Lambda$. A single sink node has demand $\sum_{\lambda \in \Lambda} r_\lambda$. Targets in schedule s for resource λ are represented by pairs of nodes $(a_{s_\lambda,t}, b_{s_\lambda,t})$ that have a connecting link (so each target corresponds to many nodes). For every schedule $s_\lambda \in S_\lambda$, we add a path from the source to the sink: $\langle \text{source}_\lambda, a_{s,t_{i_1}}, b_{s,t_{i_1}}, a_{s,t_{i_2}}, \ldots, b_{s,t_{i_L}}, \text{sink} \rangle$. The capacities on all links are set to 1, and the default costs to 0. A dummy flow with infinite capacity is added to represent the possibility that some resources are unassigned. The number of resources assigned to t in a column $\mathbf{P_j}$ is computed as: $\text{assigned}(t) = \sum_{s \in S} \text{flow}[\text{link}(a_{s,t}, b_{s,t})]$. Constraints are added to G, so $\text{assigned}(t) \le 1$ for all targets t.

A partial graph G for our earlier example is shown in Figure 9.2, showing paths for three of the five schedules. The paths correspond to schedules $\{t_1, t_2\}$, $\{t_2, t_3\}$ and $\{t_1, t_5\}$. The supply and demand are both 3, corresponding to the number of available FAMS. Double-bordered boxes mark the flows used to compute $\text{assigned}(t_1)$ and $\text{assigned}(t_2)$. Every joint schedule corresponds to a feasible flow in G. For example, the joint schedule $\{\{t_2, t_3\}, \{t_1, t_5\}\}$ has a flow

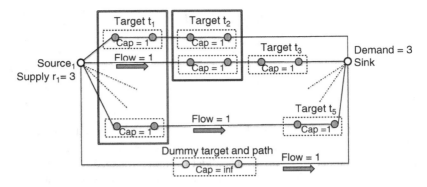

Figure 9.2. Example network graph.

of 1 unit each through the paths corresponding to schedules $\{t_2, t_3\}$ and $\{t_1, t_5\}$, and a flow of 1 through the dummy. Similarly, any feasible flow through the graph G corresponds to a feasible joint schedule, since all resource constraints are satisfied.

It remains to define link costs such that the cost of a flow is the reduced cost for the joint schedule. We decompose $\bar{c}_j$ into a sum of cost coefficients per target, $\hat{c}_t$, so that $\hat{c}_t$ can be placed on links $(a_{s,t}, b_{s,t})$ for all targets t. Then $\hat{c}_t$ is defined as $w_t.D_t + y_t.A_t - z_t.A_t$, where w_t, y_t and z_t are t^{th} components of $\mathbf{w}, \mathbf{y}$ and $\mathbf{z}$. D_t is equal to $U_d^c(t) - U_d^u(t)$ and $A_t = U_a^c(t) - U_a^u(t)$. The overall objective given below for the MCNF problem sums the contributions of the reduced cost from each individual flow and subtracts the dual variable h. If this is nonnegative, no column can improve the master solution, otherwise the optimal column (identified by the flow) is added to the master and the process iterates.

$$\min_{\text{flow}} \sum_{(a_{s,t}, b_{s,t})} \hat{c}_t.\text{flow}[(a_{s,t}, b_{s,t})] - h$$

9.5 Improving Branching and Bounds

ASPEN uses branch and bound to search over the space of possible attacker strategies. A standard technique in branch and price is to use LP relaxation, that is, to allow the integer variables to take on arbitrary values, to give an optimistic bound on the objective value of the original MIP for each internal node. Unfortunately, our experimental results show that this generic method is ineffective in our domain. We introduce ORIGAMI-S, a novel branch and bound heuristic for SPARS based on ORIGAMI (Kiekintveld et al., 2009), which is an efficient solution method for security games without scheduling constraints and heterogeneous resources. We use ORIGAMI-S to solve a relaxed version of SPARS, and integrate this in ASPEN to give bounds and select branches.

$$\min \quad k \tag{9.10}$$

$$\mathbf{U}_a(\mathbf{c}) = \quad \mathbf{Ac} + \mathbf{U}_a^u \tag{9.11}$$

$$\mathbf{0} \leq \mathbf{k} - \mathbf{U}_a(\mathbf{c}) \leq \quad (\mathbf{1} - \mathbf{q}) \cdot M \tag{9.12}$$

$$c_t = \quad \sum_{s \in S} \tilde{c}_{t,s} \quad \forall t \in T \tag{9.13}$$

$$\sum_{s \in S_\lambda} \tilde{c}_{T_\lambda(s),s} \leq \quad r_\lambda \quad \forall \lambda \in \Lambda \tag{9.14}$$

$$\sum_{t \in T} c_t \leq \quad L \cdot \sum_{\lambda \in \Lambda} r_\lambda \tag{9.15}$$

$$\mathbf{c} \leq \quad \mathbf{q} \tag{9.16}$$

$$\mathbf{q} \in \{0, 1\}, \quad \mathbf{c}, c_{t,s} \in [0, 1] \quad \forall t \in T, s \in S \tag{9.17}$$

The ORIGAMI-S model is given in Equations 9.10 through 9.17. It minimizes the attacker's maximum payoff (Equations 9.10 through 9.12). The vector $\mathbf{q}$ represents the *attack set*, and is 1 for every target that gives the attacker maximal expected payoff (Equation 9.12). The remaining nontrivial constraints restrict the coverage probabilities. ORIGAMI-S defines a set of probabilities $\tilde{c}_{t,s}$ that represent the coverage of each target t in each schedule $s \in S_\lambda$. The total coverage c_t of target t is the sum of coverage on t across individual schedules (Equation 9.13). We define a set T_λ which contains one target from each schedule $s \in S_\lambda$. The total coverage assigned by resource type λ is upper-bounded by r_λ (Equation 9.14), analogous to the constraint that the total flow from a source in a network flow graph cannot be greater than the available supply. Total coverage is also bounded by multiplying the number of resources by the *maximum* size of any schedule (L) in Equation 9.15. The defender can never benefit by assigning coverage to nodes outside the attack set, so these are constrained to 0 (Equation 9.16).

ORIGAMI-S is solved once at the beginning of ASPEN, and targets in the attack set are sorted by expected defender reward. The maximum value is an initial upper bound on the defender reward. The first leaf node that ASPEN evaluates corresponds to this maximum valued target (i.e, setting its attack value to 1), and a solution is found using column generation. This solution is a lower bound of the optimal solution, and the algorithm stops if this lower bound meets the ORIGAMI-S upper bound. Otherwise, a new upper bound from the ORIGAMI-S solution is obtained by choosing the second-highest defender payoff from targets in the attack set, and ASPEN evaluates the corresponding leaf node. This process continues until the upper bound is met or the available nodes in the search tree are exhausted.

Theorem 9.1. *The defender payoff, computed by ORIGAMI-S, is an upper bound on the defender's payoff for the corresponding SPARS problem. For any target not in the attack set of ORIGAMI-S, the restricted SPARS problem in which this target is attacked is infeasible.*

Proof Sketch: ORIGAMI and ORIGAMI-S both minimize the maximum attacker payoff over a set of feasible coverage vectors. If there are no scheduling constraints, this also maximizes the defender's policy (Kiekintveld et al., 2009). Briefly, the size of the attack set in the solution is maximized, and the coverage probability on each target in the attack set is also maximal. Both of these weakly improve the defender's payoff because adding coverage to a target is strictly better for the defender and worse for the adversary.

ORIGAMI-S makes optimistic assumptions about the coverage probability the defender can allocate by taking the maximum that could be achieved by *any* legal joint schedule and allowing it to be distributed arbitrarily across the targets, ignoring the scheduling constraints. To see this, consider the marginal probabilities $\mathbf{c}^*$ of any legal defender strategy for SPARS. There is at least one feasible coverage strategy for ORIGAMI that gives the same payoff for the defender. Constraints 9.13 and 9.17 are satisfied by $\mathbf{c}^*$ because they are also constraints of SPARS. Each variable $\tilde{c}_{T_\lambda(s),s}$ in the set defined for Constraint 9.14 belongs to a single schedule associated with resource type λ, and at most r_λ of these can be selected in any feasible joint schedule, so this constraint must also hold for $\mathbf{c}^*$. Constraint 9.15 must be satisfied because it assumes that each available resource covers the largest possible schedule, so it generally allows excess coverage probability to be assigned. Finally, Constraint 9.16 may be violated by $\mathbf{c}^*$ for some target t. However, the coverage vector with coverage identical to $\mathbf{c}^*$ for all targets in the ORIGAMI-S attack set, and 0 coverage outside the attack set has identical payoffs (since these targets are never attacked).

9.6 Experimental Results

Comparison on FAMS domain: We compare the runtime performance of ASPEN, branch and price without the ORIGAMI-S heuristic (BnP), and ERASER-C. For this experiment we generate random instances of FAMS problems (Kiekintveld et al., 2009) with schedules of size two, with one departure

Table 9.2. *Number of columns:* 200 *targets,* 600 *schedules*

Resources	ASPEN	ERASER-C	BnP (max. 30 mins)
10	126	204	1532
20	214	308	1679
30	263	314	1976
40	227	508	1510
50	327	426	1393

Table 9.3. *Number of columns:* 200 *targets,* 1000 *schedules*

Resources	3 Tar. / sch.	4 Tar. / sch.	5 Tar. / sch.
5	456	518	658
10	510	733	941
15	649	920	1092
20	937	1114	1124

flight and one arrival flight drawn from disjoint sets (for correct operation of ERASER-C). We vary the number of targets, defender resources, and schedules.

ERASER-C outputs a coverage vector $\mathbf{c}$, so to obtain a probability distribution $\mathbf{x}$ over joint schedules $\mathbf{J}$, we need an additional method. Instead, we modify our column-generation approach, using a revised master problem with the objective of minimizing the difference $\mathbf{Px} - \mathbf{c}$. The slave problem remains unchanged. In our results, we present runtimes for ERASER-C that include the generation of a joint distribution in order to provide a fair comparison with ASPEN.

All experiments were based on fifteen sample games, and problem instances that took longer than thirty minutes to run were terminated. Results varying the number of defender resources are shown in Figure 9.3(a). The y-axis shows the runtime in seconds on the *logarithmic scale*. The x-axis shows the number of resources. ASPEN is the fastest of the three algorithms. The effectiveness of the ORIGAMI-S bounds and branching are clear in the comparison with standard BnP method. Since ASPEN solves a far more general set of security games (SPARS), we would not expect it to be competitive with ERASER-C in its specialized domain. However, ASPEN was six times faster than ERASER-C in some instances. This improvement over ERASER-C was an unexpected trend, and can be attributed to the number of columns generated by the two approaches (see Table 9.2). We observe similar results in the second and third data sets presented in Figures 9.3b and 9.3c.

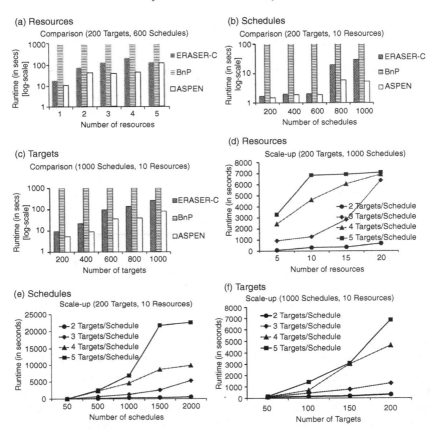

Figure 9.3.   Run-time Results.

ASPEN on Large SPARS Instances: We also evaluate the performance of ASPEN on arbitrary scheduling problems as the size of the problem is varied to include very large instances. No comparisons could be made because ERASER-C does not handle arbitrary schedules and the only correct algorithms known, DOBSS (Paruchuri et al., 2008) and BnP, do not scale to these problem sizes. We vary the number of resources, schedules, and targets as before. In addition, we vary the number of targets per schedule for each of the three cases to test more complex scheduling problems. Figure 9.3d shows the run-time results with 1000 feasible schedules and 200 targets, averaged over ten samples. The x-axis shows the number of resources, and the y-axis shows the run-time in seconds. Each line represents a different number of schedules per target. The number of joint schedules in these instances can be as large as 10^{23} ($\binom{1000}{10} \approx 2.6 \times 10^{23}$). Interestingly, the run-time does not increase much when the number of resources is increased from 10 to 20 when there are 5 targets per schedules. Column 4 of Table 9.2 illustrates that the key reason for constant run-time is that the average number of generated columns remains similar. Similarly, for a fixed number of resources, we observe an increase in runtime for more complex schedules that corresponds with an increase in the number of columns generated. The other two experiments, Figure 9.3e and f also show similar trends.

9.7 Conclusion

We present a branch-and-price method, ASPEN, for solving large-scale Stackelberg security games with arbitrary constraints. ASPEN incorporates several novel contributions, including a decomposition of SPARS to enable column generation and the integration of ORIGAMI-S, to substantially speed up the branch and bound search. Experimental results show that ASPEN is competitive with ERASER-C for the restricted class of games where ERASER-C is applicable. More importantly, ASPEN solves far more general instances of scheduling problems where ERASER-C and other existing techniques fail. ASPEN is also substantially faster than a standard implementation of branch and price for this domain. This work contributes to a very new area of work that applies techniques used in large-scale optimization to game-theoretic problems – an exciting new avenue with the potential to greatly expand the reach of game theory.

Acknowledgments

We would also like to thank Jason Tsai and the reviewers for their comments and suggestions. This research was supported by the United States Department of Homeland Security through the Center for Risk and Economic Analysis of Terrorism Events (CREATE) under grant number 2007-ST-061-000001. F. Ordóñez would also like to acknowledge the support of Fondecyt, through Grant No. 1090630.

PART IV

Future Research

10

Effective Solutions for Real-World Stackelberg Games: When Agents Must Deal with Human Uncertainties

James Pita, Manish Jain, Fernando Ordóñez, Milind Tambe, Sarit Kraus, and Reuma Magori-Cohen

10.1 Introduction

In Stackelberg games, one player, the leader, commits to a strategy publicly before the remaining players, the followers, make their decisions (Fudenberg and Tirole, 1991). There are many multi-agent security domains, such as attacker-defender scenarios and patrolling, for which these types of commitments by the security agent are necessary (Agmon et al., 2008; Brown et al., 2006; Kiekintveld et al., 2009; Paruchuri et al., 2006), and it has been shown that Stackelberg games appropriately model these commitments (Paruchuri et al., 2008; Pita et al., 2008). For example, security personnel patrolling an infrastructure decide on a patrolling strategy first, before their adversaries act taking this committed strategy into account. Indeed, Stackelberg games are at the heart of the ARMOR system, deployed at LAX since 2007 to schedule security personnel (Paruchuri et al., 2008; Pita et al., 2008), and they have recently been applied to federal air marshals (Kiekintveld et al., 2009). Moreover, these games have potential applications for network routing and pricing in transportation systems, among many others possibilities (Cardinal et al., 2005; Korilis, Lazar, and Orda, 1997).

Existing algorithms for Bayesian Stackelberg games find optimal solutions considering an a priori probability distribution over possible follower types (Conitzer and Sandholm, 2006; Paruchuri et al., 2008). Unfortunately, to guarantee optimality, these algorithms make strict assumptions on the underlying games; namely, that players are perfectly rational and that followers perfectly observe the leader's strategy. However, these assumptions rarely hold in real-world domains, particularly those involving human actors. Of specific

Previously published in *Proc. of 8th Int. Conf. on Autonomous Agents and Multiagent Systems (AAMAS 2009)*, Decker, Sichman, Sierra and Castelfranchi (eds.), May, 10–15, 2009, Budapest, Hungary. Copyright © 2009, International Foundation for Autonomous Agents and Multiagent Systems (www.ifaamas.org). All rights reserved.

interest are the security domains mentioned earlier (e.g., LAX). Even though an automated program may determine an optimal leader (security personnel) strategy, it must take into account a human follower (adversary). Such human adversaries may not be utility maximizers, computing optimal decisions. Instead, their decisions may be governed by their bounded rationality (Simon, 1956), which causes them to deviate from their expected optimal. Humans may also suffer from limited ability to observe the security personnel's strategy, giving them a false impression of that strategy. Thus, a human adversary may not respond with the game-theoretic optimal choice, causing the leader uncertainty over the gamut of adversary's actions. Therefore, in general, the leader in a Stackelberg game must commit to a strategy considering three different types of uncertainty: (i) adversary response uncertainty due to his bounded rationality, that is, the adversary may not choose the utility maximizing optimal strategy; (ii) adversary response uncertainty due to limitations in his ability to appropriately observe the leader's, strategy; and (iii) adversary reward uncertainty modeled as different reward matrices with a Bayesian a priori distribution assumption, i.e., a Bayesian Stackelberg game. Although existing algorithms handle the third type of uncertainty (Conitzer and Sandholm, 2006; Paruchuri et al., 2008), these models can give a severely underperforming strategy when the adversary deviates because of the first two types of uncertainty. This degradation in leader rewards may be unacceptable in certain domains.

To overcome this limitation, this paper proposes three new algorithms based on MILPs. The major contribution of these new MILPs is that they provide a fundamentally novel integration of key ideas from: (i) previous best-known algorithms from the multi-agent literature for solving Bayesian Stackelberg games; (ii) robustness approaches from robust optimization literature (Aghassi and Berlsimas, 2006; Ordóñez and Stier-Moses, 2007); and (iii) anchoring theories on human perception of probability distributions from psychology (See, Fox, and Rottenstreich, 2006). Although the robustness approach addresses human response imprecision, anchoring, which is an expansion of general support theory (Tversky and Koehler, 1994) on how humans attribute probabilities to a discrete set of events, addresses limited observational capabilities. To the best of our knowledge, the effectiveness of the combination of these ideas has not been explored in the context of Stackelberg games (or any other games). By uniquely incorporating these ideas our goal is to defend against the suboptimal choices that humans may make due to bounded rationality or observational limitations. These new MILPs complement the prior algorithms for Bayesian Stackelberg games, handling all three of the types of uncertainty mentioned.

Since these algorithms are centered on addressing nonoptimal and uncertain human responses, traditional proofs of correctness and optimality are insufficient: It is necessary to experimentally test these new approaches against existing approaches. Experimental analysis against human subjects allows us to show how these algorithms are expected to perform against human adversaries compared to previous approaches. To that end, we experimentally tested our new approaches to determine their success by considering two settings based on real, deployed security systems. In both settings, six different approaches were compared (three new approaches, one existing approach, and two baseline approaches), in four different observability conditions. These experiments involved ninety-eight human subjects playing 1360 games in total and yielded statistically significant results showing that one of our new algorithms substantially outperformed existing methods when dealing with human adversaries. Runtime results were also gathered from our new algorithms against previous approaches showing that their solution speeds are equivalent to or faster than previous approaches. Based on these results we concluded that, although they are theoretically optimal, existing algorithms for Bayesian Stackelberg games may need to be significantly modified for real-world security domains. They are not only outperformed by one of our new algorithms, which incorporates both robustness approaches and anchoring theories, but also may be outperformed by simple baseline algorithms in certain cases. This is an important conclusion since existing algorithms have seen real deployment, such as at LAX (Pita et al., 2008). Indeed, our new algorithms for addressing human adversaries in Stackelberg games suggest significant potential improvements whenever, existing algorithms are deployed in real-world domains and leaders are facing human adversaries.

10.2 Background

Stackelberg Game: In a Stackelberg game, a leader commits to a strategy first, and then a follower optimizes his reward, *considering the action chosen by the leader.* To see the advantage of being the leader in a Stackelberg game, consider the game with the payoff shown in Table 10.1. The leader is the row player and the follower is the column player. If this were a simultaneous move game, the pure-strategy Nash equilibrium for this game is when the leader plays *a* and the follower plays *c*, which gives the leader a payoff of 2. However, in this Stackelberg game, if the leader commits to a mixed strategy of playing *a* and *b* with equal (0.5) probability, then the follower will play *d*, leading to a higher expected payoff for the leader of 3.5.

Table 10.1. *Payoff table for example Stackelberg game*

	c	d
a	2,1	4,0
b	1,0	3,2

Bayesian Stackelberg Game: In a Bayesian game of N agents, each agent n must be one of a given set of types. This paper considers a Bayesian Stackelberg game that was inspired by a security domain presented for LAX (Pita et al., 2008). This game has two agents, the leader and the follower. It is assumed there is only one leader type (e.g., only one police force enforcing security), although there are multiple follower types (e.g., multiple types of adversaries), denoted by $l \in L$. However, the leader does not know the follower's type. For each agent (leader or follower) n, there is a set of strategies σ_n and a utility function $u_n : L \times \sigma_1 \times \sigma_2 \to \Re$. The goal is *to find the optimal mixed strategy* for the leader given that the follower knows this strategy when choosing his own strategy.

DOBSS: Although the problem of choosing an optimal strategy for the leader in a Stackelberg game is NP-hard for a Bayesian game with multiple follower types (Conitzer and Sandholm, 2006), researchers have continued to provide practical improvements. DOBSS is currently the most efficient algorithm for such games (Paruchuri et al., 2008) and is in use for security scheduling at LAX. It operates directly on the compact Bayesian representation, giving speedups over the multiple-linear programs method (Conitzer and Sandholm, 2006) which requires conversion of the Bayesian game into a normal-form game by the Harsanyi transformation (Harsanyi and Selten, 1972).

We now discuss DOBSS, which provides the optimal mixed strategy for the leader while considering an *optimal* follower response for this leader strategy. Note that it needs to consider only the reward-maximizing pure strategies of the followers, since if a mixed strategy is optimal for the follower, then so are all the pure strategies in the support of that mixed strategy. The leader's mixed strategy is denoted by x, a probability distribution over the vector of the leader's pure strategies. The value x_i is the proportion of times in which pure strategy i is used in the strategy. The vector of strategies of follower $l \in L$ is denoted by q^l. The index sets of leader and follower type l's pure strategies are denoted by X and Q respectively. The payoff matrices of the leader and each of the followers l is indexed by the matrices R^l and C^l. DOBSS assumes a priori probabilities p^l, with $l \in L$ of facing each follower type. Considering auxiliary variable $z_{ij}^l = x_i q_j^l$, DOBSS computes the leader's optimal decision problem using the following MILP formulation (Paruchuri et al., 2008):

$$
\begin{aligned}
\max_{q,z,a} \quad & \sum_{i \in X} \sum_{l \in L} \sum_{j \in Q} p^l R_{ij}^l z_{ij}^l \\
\text{s.t.} \quad & \sum_{i \in X} \sum_{j \in Q} z_{ij}^l = 1 \\
& \sum_{j \in Q} z_{ij}^l \le 1 \\
& q_j^l \le \sum_{i \in X} z_{ij}^l \le 1 \\
& \sum_{j \in Q} q_j^l = 1 \\
& 0 \le (a^l - \sum_{i \in X} C_{ij}^l (\sum_{h \in Q} z_{ih}^l)) \le (1 - q_j^l) M \\
& \sum_{j \in Q} z_{ij}^l = \sum_{j \in Q} z_{ij}^1 \\
& z_{ij}^l \in [0 \dots 1] \\
& q_j^l \in \{0, 1\} \\
& a \in \Re
\end{aligned}
\tag{10.1}
$$

For future discussion it is important to understand the following set of constraints. The fourth and eighth constraints limit the vector q^l of follower type l's actions to be a pure distribution over the set Q (i.e., each q^l has exactly one coordinate equal to one and the rest equal to zero). The two inequalities in the fifth constraint ensure that $q_j^l = 1$ only for a strategy j that is optimal for follower type l. Therefore, in the current formulation each follower type l is allowed to choose exactly one optimal action from his set of possible actions.

Baseline Algorithms: For completeness this paper includes both a uniformly random strategy and a MAXIMIN strategy against human opponents as a baseline against the performance of both existing algorithms, such as DOBSS, and our new algorithms. Algorithms must outperform the two baseline algorithms to provide benefits.

UNIFORM: UNIFORM is the most basic method of randomization that just assigns an equal probability of taking each action $i \in X$ (a uniform distribution).

MAXIMIN: MAXIMIN is a traditional approach that assumes the follower may take any of the available actions. The objective of the following LP is to maximize the minimum reward γ the leader will obtain irrespective of the follower's action.

$$
\begin{aligned}
\max \quad & \sum_{l \in L} p^l \gamma_l \\
\text{s.t.} \quad & \sum_{i \in X} x_i = 1 \\
& \sum_{i \in X} R_{ij}^l x_i \ge \gamma_l \\
& x_i \in [0 \dots 1]
\end{aligned}
\tag{10.2}
$$

10.3 Robust Algorithms

There are two fundamental assumptions underlying current algorithms for Stackelberg games, including DOBSS. First, the follower is assumed to act with infallible utility-maximizing rationality, choosing the absolute optimal among his strategies. Second, if the follower faces a tie in his strategies' rewards, it will break in favor of the leader, choosing the one that gives a higher reward to the leader. This standard assumption is also shown to follow from the follower's rationality and optimal response under some conditions (von Stengel and Zamir, 2004). Unfortunately, in many real-world domains, agents may face human followers who do not respond optimally: This may be caused by their bounded rationality or by their uncertainty about leader strategy. In essence, the leader faces uncertainty over follower responses – the follower may not choose the optimal response but from a range of possible responses – potentially significantly degrading leader rewards. No a priori probability distributions are available or assumed for this follower response uncertainty.

To remedy this situation, we draw inspiration from robust optimization methodology in which the decision maker optimizes against the worst outcome over the uncertainty (Aghassi and Bertsimas, 2006; Nilim and Ghaoui, 2004), as well as psychological support theory for human decision making when they are given a discrete set of actions and an unknown probability function over those actions (See et al., 2006; Tversky and Koehler 1994). In the presented Stackelberg problem, the leader will make a robust decision by considering that the boundedly rational follower could choose a strategy from his range of possible responses that most degrades the leader rewards or that he could choose a strategy based on limited observations. This approach differs from standard robust optimization methodology in that it makes predictions about how and why the human adversary's response will deviate and robustly guards against those predictions, as opposed to considering arbitrary deviations in the responses. This paper introduces three MILPs to that end. The first MILP, BRASS (Bounded Rationality Assumption in Stackelberg Solver) addresses the uncertainty that may arise from human imprecision in choosing the expected optimal strategy due to bounded rationality. The second MILP, GUARD (Guarding Using Alpha Ranges in DOBSS) utilizes the anchoring biases to protect against limited observation conditions. The third MILP, COBRA (Combined Observability and Rationality Assumption), provides a robust response for all three types of uncertainty previously mentioned. We first describe in depth the key ideas behind our new approaches and then define the MILPs that use them.

Bounded Rationality: Some of our new algorithms assume that the follower is boundedly rational and may not strictly maximize utility. As a result, the follower may select an ε-optimal response strategy, That is, the follower may choose any of the responses within ε-reward of the optimal strategy. Given multiple ε-optimal responses, the robust approach is to assume that the follower could choose the one that provides the leader the worst reward – not necessarily because the follower attends to the leader reward, but to robustly guard against the worst case outcome. This worst-case assumption contrasts with those of other Stackelberg solvers that, given a tie, the follower will choose a strategy that favors the leader (Conitzer and Sandholm, 2006; Paruchuri et al., 2008), making this new approach novel for human followers.

Anchoring Theory: Support theory is a theory of subjective probability (Tversky and Koehler, 1994) and has been used to introduce anchoring biases (See et al., 2006). An anchoring bias is when, given a lack of information about the occurrence of a discrete set of events, humans assign equal weight to the occurrence of each event (a uniform distribution). It has been shown that humans are particularly susceptible to anchoring on the uniform distribution before they have information and that, once they are given information, they are slow to update away from this assumption (See et al., 2006). Thus they leave some weight, $\alpha \in [0 \dots 1]$, on the uniform distribution and the rest, $1 - \alpha$, on the occurrence they have actually viewed. As humans become more confident in what they are viewing, this bias begins to diminish, decreasing the value of α. Models have been proposed to address this bias and predict what probability a human will assign to a particular event x from a set of events X. One proposed model is written in odds form as $R(x, X \backslash x) = (|x|/|X \backslash x|)^\alpha * (P(x)/P(X \backslash x))^{1-\alpha}$; however, a linear model is also possible (Fox, personal communication; Tversky and Koehler, 1994). The linear model introduces a new term $P(x')$, which is the probability the human assigns to event x as opposed to the real probability of event x occurring: $P(x') = (1/|X|) * (\alpha) + (1 - \alpha) * P(x)$. The parameter α dictates how much support the human will give to the uniform probability distribution and how much support he will give to the real probability ($P(x)$). The end result is the predicted probability the human will assign to event x. We commandeer this anchoring bias for Stackelberg games to determine how a human follower may perceive the leader strategy. For example, in the game shown in Table 10.1, suppose the leader strategy was to play a with a probability of 0.8 and b with 0.2. Anchoring bias would predict that in the absence of any information ($\alpha = 1$), humans will assign a probability of 0.5 to each of a and b, and will only update this belief (alter the value of α) after observing the leader strategy for some time.

10.3.1 Brass

BRASS considers the case of a boundedly rational follower in which BRASS maximizes the minimum reward it obtains from any ε-optimal response. In the following MILP, we use the same variable notation as in DOBSS. In addition, the variables h_j^l identify the optimal strategy for follower type l with a value of a^l in the third and fourth constraints. Variables q_j^l represent all ε-optimal strategies for follower type l; the second constraint now allows selection of more than one strategy per follower type. The fifth constraint ensures that $q_j^l = 1$ for every action j such that $a^l - \sum_{i \in X} C_{ij}^l < \varepsilon$ because in this case the middle term in the inequality is less than ε and the left inequality is then only satisfied if $q_j^l = 1$. This robust approach required the design of a new objective and additional constraint. The sixth constraint helps define the objective value against follower type l, γ_l, which must be lower than any leader reward for all actions $q_j^l = 1$, as opposed to the DOBSS formulation which has only one action $q_j^l = 1$. Setting γ_l to the minimum leader reward allows BRASS to robustly guard against the worst-case scenario. The new MILP is as follows:

$$\max_{x,q,h,a,\gamma} \quad \sum_{l \in L} p^l \gamma_l$$

$$\text{s.t.} \quad \sum_{i \in X} x_i = 1$$

$$\sum_{j \in Q} q_j^l \geq 1$$

$$\sum_{j \in Q} h_j^l = 1$$

$$0 \leq (a^l - \sum_{i \in X} C_{ij}^l x_i) \leq (1 - h_j^l)M$$

$$\varepsilon(1 - q_j^l) \leq a^l - \sum_{i \in X} C_{ij}^l x_i \leq \varepsilon + (1 - q_j^l)M \qquad (10.3)$$

$$M(1 - q_j^l) + \sum_{i \in X} R_{ij}^l x_i \geq \gamma_l$$

$$h_j^l \leq q_j^l$$

$$x_i \in [0 \ldots 1]$$

$$q_j^l, h_j^l \in \{0, 1\}$$

$$a \in \Re$$

10.3.2 Guard

GUARD considers the case in which the human follower is perfectly rational, but faces limited observations. GUARD draws upon the theory of anchoring biases to help address the human uncertainty that arises from such limited observation. It deals with two strategies: (i) the real leader strategy (x) and (ii) the leader strategy the follower believes (x'), in which x' is defined by the linear model presented earlier. Given the follower's belief strategy, x_i is replaced in the third constraint with x_i' and x_i' is accordingly defined as $x_i' = (1/|X|) * (\alpha) + (1 - \alpha) * x_i$. The justification for this replacement is as follows: First, this particular constraint ensures that the follower maximizes his reward.

Since the follower believes x_i' to be the leader strategy, he will choose his
strategy according to x_i', and not x_i. Second, given this knowledge, the leader
can find the follower's responses based on x_i' and optimize his actual strategy
x_i against this strategy. Since x_i' is a combination of x_i and the bias toward the
uniform probability distribution GUARD is able to find a strategy x_i that will
maximize the leader's reward based on how the follower will update his beliefs,
the new MILP is as follows:

$$\max_l \quad \sum_{l \in L} p^l \gamma_l$$

$$\text{s.t.} \quad \sum_{i \in X} x_i = 1$$

$$\sum_{j \in Q} q_j^l = 1$$

$$0 \le (a^l - \sum_{i \in X} C_{ij}^l * x_i') \le (1 - q_j^l)M$$

$$M(1 - q_j^l) + \sum_{i \in X} R_{ij}^l x_i \ge \gamma_l \qquad\qquad (10.4)$$

$$x_i \in [0 \dots 1]$$

$$q_j^l \in \{0, 1\}$$

$$a \in \Re$$

$$x_i' = (1/|X|) * (\alpha) + (1 - \alpha) * x_i$$

10.3.3 Cobra

COBRA is an MILP that combines both a bounded rationality assumption and
an observational uncertainty assumption. This is achieved by incorporating the
alterations made in BRASS and GUARD into a single MILP. Namely, COBRA
includes both the ε parameter and the α parameter from MILP (10.3) and MILP
(10.4) respectively. The MILP that follows is identical to MILP (10.3) except
that in the fourth and fifth constraints, x_i is replaced with x_i' as it is in MILP
(10.4). The justification for this replacement is the same as in MILP (10.4). The
new MILP then is as follows:

$$\max_{x,q,h,a,\gamma} \quad \sum_{l \in L} p^l \gamma_l$$

$$\text{s.t.} \quad \sum_{i \in X} x_i = 1$$

$$\sum_{j \in Q} q_j^l \ge 1$$

$$\sum_{j \in Q} h_j^l = 1$$

$$0 \le (a^l - \sum_{i \in X} C_{ij}^l * x_i') \le (1 - h_j^l)M$$

$$\varepsilon(1 - q_j^l) \le a^l - \sum_{i \in X} C_{ij}^l * x_i' \le \varepsilon + (1 - q_j^l)M$$

$$M(1 - q_j^l) + \sum_{i \in X} R_{ij}^l x_i \ge \gamma_l$$

$$h^l_j \leq q^l_j$$
$$x_i \in [0 \ldots 1]$$
$$q^l_j, h^l_j \in \{0, 1\} \tag{10.5}$$
$$a \in \Re$$
$$x'_i = (1/|X|) * (\alpha) + (1 - \alpha) * x_i$$

Proposition 10.1. *When $\varepsilon = 0$ and $\alpha = 0$ then MILPs (10.1) and (10.5) are equivalent.*

Proof sketch: It follows from the definition of x'_i that when $\alpha = 0$ then $x'_i = x_i$ since the follower is assumed to once again perfectly observe and believe the leader strategy x_i. Note that if $\varepsilon = 0$ the inequality in the fifth constraint of (10.5) is the same expression as the inequality in the fourth constraint with q^l_j substituted for h^l_j. We will show that the two problems attain the same optimal objective function value.

To show that solution to (10.5) $\geq$ solution to (10.1), consider (q, z, a) a feasible solution for (10.1). We define $\bar{x}_i = \sum_{j \in Q} z^l_{ij}$, $\bar{q} = \bar{h} = q$, $\bar{a} = a$, and $\bar{\gamma}_l = \sum_{i \in X} \sum_{j \in Q} R^l_{ij} z^l_{ij}$. From the first through third constraints and the sixth constraint in (10.1) we can show that $z^l_{ij} = 0$ for all j such that $q^l_j = 0$, and thus that $\bar{x}_i = z^l_{ij}$ for all j such that $q^l_j = 1$. This implies that $\bar{\gamma}_l = \sum_{i \in X} R^l_{ij} \bar{x}_i$ for the j such that $q^l_j = 1$, and it is then easy to verify that $(\bar{x}, \bar{q}, \bar{h}, \bar{a}, \bar{\gamma})$ is feasible for (10.5) with the same objective function value of (q, z, a) in (10.1).

For solution to (10.1) $\geq$ solution to (10.5), consider (x, q, h, a, γ) feasible for (10.5). Define $\bar{q} = h$, $\bar{z}^l_{ij} = x_i h^l_j$, and $\bar{a} = a$. Then we can show that $(\bar{q}, \bar{z}, \bar{a})$ is feasible for (10.1) by construction. Since $h^l_j \leq q^l_j$, it follows that $\gamma_l \leq \sum_{i \in X} R^l_{ij} x_i$ for the j such that $h^l_j = 1$. This implies that $\gamma_l \leq \sum_{i \in X} \sum_{j \in Q} R^l_{ij} \bar{z}^l_{ij}$ and that the objective function value of $(\bar{q}, \bar{z}, \bar{a})$ in (10.1) greater than or equal to the objective value of (x, q, h, a, γ) in (10.5). ∎

The key implication of the above proposition is that when $\varepsilon = 0$, COBRA loses its robustness feature so that, once again, when the follower faces a tie, it selects a strategy favoring the leader, as in DOBSS. Based on this proposition, the following few observations surrounding the COBRA algorithm can be made: (i) if $\alpha = 0$, COBRA is equivalent to BRASS; (ii) if $\varepsilon = 0$, COBRA is equivalent to GUARD and; (iii) if both $\alpha = 0$ and $\varepsilon = 0$, COBRA is equivalent to DOBSS. Based on these observations, the propositions presented in this paper can be generalized to the other three algorithms (DOBSS, GUARD, and BRASS) accordingly.

Proposition 10.2. *When α is held constant, the optimal reward COBRA can obtain is decreasing in ε.*

Proof sketch: Since the fifth constraint in (10.5) makes $q^l_j = 1$ when that action has a follower reward between $(a^l - \varepsilon, a^l]$, increasing ε would increase the number of follower strategies set to 1. Having more active follower actions in the sixth constraint can only decrease the minimum value γ_l. ∎

Proposition 10.3. *Regardless of α, if $\frac{1}{3}\varepsilon \geq C \geq |C^l_{ij}|$ for all i, j, l, then COBRA is equivalent to MAXIMIN.*

Proof sketch: Note that $|a^l|$ in (10.5) $\leq C$. The leftmost inequality of the fifth constraint in (10.5) shows that all q^l_j must equal 1, which makes COBRA equivalent to MAXIMIN. Suppose some $q^l_j = 0$, then that inequality states that $-C \leq \sum_{i \in X} C^l_{ij} x_i \leq a^l - \varepsilon < C - 3C = -2C$ a contradiction. ∎

Deciding α and ε: To decide the value of ε we employed a heuristic in which ε is decided based on how close to the optimal response the follower is expected to come, e.g., if we expect human followers to play within 20% of the optimal, we set ε to 20% of the optimal reward. We try two different techniques to determine α, leading to two different versions of COBRA. The first approach is to vary α based on the number of observations that human followers are anticipated to have. This standard version of COBRA implies that when deploying it, α is adjusted per anticipated observation capability. In this case, if a human follower has had zero observations, we assume that he would be entirely guided by the anchoring bias to uniform probability, and hence set $\alpha = 1$, i.e., $x' = 1/|X|$. In contrast, if a follower has infinite observations, he would correctly determine the actual leader strategy, i.e., $x' = x$, and hence $\alpha = 0$. When a follower has only a limited number of observations, we heuristically select α, decreasing it with increasing number of follower's observations – choosing the right α remains an issue for future work. The second approach is to assume a constant α, leading to a version of COBRA that we will refer to as COBRA-C (COBRA with constant α). We discuss the choice of α for COBRA-C in Section 10.4.1

Complexity: DOBSS, BRASS, GUARD, and COBRA require the solution of a MILP, whereas MAXIMIN is a linear programming problem. Therefore, the complexity of MAXIMIN is polynomial, whereas DOBSS, BRASS, GUARD and COBRA face an NP-hard problem (Conitzer and Sandholm, 2006). A number of effective solution packages for MILPs can be used, but their performance depends on the number of integer variables. DOBSS and GUARD consider $|Q||L|$ integer variables, while BRASS and COBRA double that. Thus we anticipated MAXIMIN will have the lowest running time per problem instance, followed by DOBSS and GUARD with BRASS and COBRA close behind. However, as shown in runtime results, this was not the final result.

10.4 Experiments

We now present results comparing the quality and runtime of strategies introduced in the previous two sections. The goal of our new algorithms was to improve interactions between agents and humans by addressing the bounded rationality that humans may exhibit and the limited observations they may experience in real-world settings. To that end, experiments were set up to play against human subjects as followers (adversaries), with varying observability conditions.

First, we constructed a domain inspired by the security domain at LAX (Paruchuri et al., 2008; Pita et al., 2008), but converted it into a pirate-and-treasure theme. The domain had three pirates – jointly acting as the leader – guarding eight doors, and each individual subject acted as an adversary. The subject's goal was to steal treasure from behind a door without getting caught. Each of the eight doors would have a unique reward and penalty associated with it for both the subjects as well as the pirates – a non-zero-sum game. If a subject chose a door that a pirate was guarding, the subject would incur the unique subject penalty for that door and the pirate would receive the unique pirate reward for that door, else vice versa. This setup led to a Stackelberg game with $\binom{8}{3} = 56$ leader actions, and eight follower actions.

10.4.1 Quality Comparison

Experimental Structure and Setup: Given the eight-door three-pirate domain described, we constructed two unique reward structures corresponding to the eight doors. The second reward structure increased the penalty structure for the leader – to test its effect on our robust algorithms. For each reward structure the subjects were also exposed to four separate observability conditions. The subject observed the pirates' strategy under the current observability condition and reward structure, and then was allowed to make his decision. A single observation consisted of seeing where the three pirates were stationed behind the eight doors, having the doors close, and then having the pirates restation themselves according to their mixed strategy. The four different observation conditions tested were: (i) The subject does not get any observations; (ii) the subject gets five observations; (iii) the subject gets twenty observations; and (iv) the subject gets infinite observations – simulated by revealing the exact mixed strategy of the pirate to the subject. Subjects were given full knowledge of their rewards and penalties and those of the pirates in all situations.

Algorithms: These experiments only compare DOBSS, BRASS, COBRA, MAXIMIN, and UNIFORM. We reiterate that GUARD refers to a special case of COBRA, wherein ε is set to zero. On closer examination, it is clear that

GUARD is dominated by COBRA. GUARD is equivalent to DOBSS when $\alpha = 0$; thus, when $\alpha = 0$, our results will show that COBRA is superior to DOBSS and consequently to GUARD. On the other extreme, when $\alpha = 1$ in the unobserved observation condition it has also been concluded by experimental tests that GUARD once again performs worse than COBRA, obtaining an expected reward of $-.65$ in reward structure one and -2.15 in reward structure two compared to the expected reward $.205$ and $.7$ obtained by COBRA. Furthermore, in both cases these results were statistically significant. Since at both extremes GUARD is dominated by COBRA, we do not include GUARD in our experimental analysis and results. We could make a similar argument for not including BRASS; however, it is important to include either BRASS or GUARD to demonstrate that the results obtained by COBRA are not only due to handling human bounded rationality but to handling both human bounded rationality and limited observation conditions.

For these experiments ε was set to 2.5. This choice for ε was made because the follower's reward for each door ranged from 1 to 10, and we wanted to robustly guard against boundedly rational strategies within 25% of the optimal strategy. We employed our heuristic for deciding the α parameters of COBRA, which was explained in Section 10.3. For COBRA-C α was set to the same α value as the five observation cases from the two reward structures with the expectation that it would perform poorly in higher observation conditions since it was not appropriately adjusted.

Experiments: Each of our 48 game settings (two reward structures, six algorithms, and four observability conditions) were played by 40 subjects, that is, in total there were 1360 total trials. Notice that the unobserved case only needed to be played by one set of 40 subjects as the choices made without any observation would be similar regardless of the algorithm. This follows from the fact that the subject had no information about the strategy he was facing, and thus his decisions for this particular condition were solely based on the reward structure. Given this setup, each subject played a total of 14 unique games and the games were presented in random orderings to avoid any order bias. In total, there were 98 different subjects that played. For a given algorithm we computed the expected leader reward for each follower action, that is, for each choice of door by subject. We then found the average expected reward for a given algorithm using the actual door selections from the 40 subject trials. For each game, the subject's objective was to earn as many points as possible by choosing the highest value door he thought would be unguarded; and once a door was chosen that game was over and the subject played the next game. Starting with a base of eight dollars, each reward point within the game was worth fifteen cents for the subject; and each penalty point deducted, 15 cents.

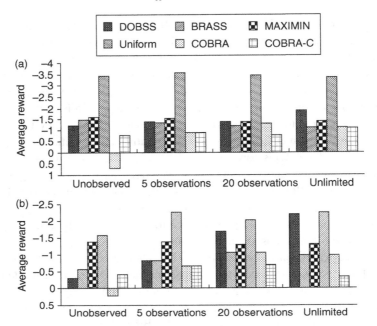

Figure 10.1. Expected average reward: (a) reward structure one and (b) reward structure two.

This was incorporated to give the subjects incentive to play as optimally as possible. On average, subjects earned $13.13.

Results: Figure 10.1a shows the average expected leader reward for our first reward structure, with each data-point averaged over 40 human responses. Figure 10.1b shows the same for the second reward structure. Notice that *a lower bar is better* since all strategies have a negative average, with the exception of COBRA in the unobserved case. In both figures, the x-axis shows the observation condition for each strategy, and the y-axis shows the average expected reward each strategy obtained. For example, examining Figure 10.1b in the unlimited observation case, COBRA-C scores an average expected leader reward of -0.33, whereas DOBSS suffers a 663% degradation of reward, obtaining an average score of -2.19.

Statistical Significance: Since our results critically depend on significant differences among DOBSS, BRASS, COBRA, MAXIMIN, and UNIFORM, we ran the Friedman test for repeated observations (Friedman, 1937) in the unobserved case and Yuen's test for comparing trimmed means (Yuen, 1974) for the five-, twenty-, and infinite-observation cases[1]. For our tests we used a standard 20% trimmed mean to test for significant differences in group means. The maximum p-value obtained for COBRA-C versus any other strategy was .033, showing that under all conditions the results obtained for COBRA-C are statistically significantly different than the results obtained by other strategies. COBRA also obtained statistical significance in all cases against other strategies except the twenty-observation case with a maximum p-value of .029. It is evident from these values and the results presented that COBRA-C is statistically significantly better than all other strategies in every observation condition except the unobserved case.

Conclusions and Analysis: Analysis of the reported results yields the following conclusions: (i) COBRA, which adjusts its strategy based on observations, performs significantly better than DOBSS with humans. The main implication being that if we know approximately how many observations the adversary will obtain, then we can exploit the variable α in COBRA to our advantage. (ii) Dealing with both bounded rationality and limited observations is important when designing an algorithm that performs well against humans. Our results demonstrate that only utilizing α or ε is not enough, but rather the combination of the two is necessary for superior performance under all observation conditions. (iii) COBRA-C surprisingly performs better than COBRA under high-observation conditions. This finding is particularly important since in many real-world domains the observational limitations may be unknown making it difficult to decide α. Finally, (iv) COBRA and COBRA-C both perform better than our baseline algorithms, making the extra computation worthwhile.

Next we discuss the key implications of these conclusions and why they were reached. We include two tables (Tables 10.2 and 10.3) for reference. Table 10.2 shows the percentage of times the follower chose a response that the current algorithm predicted he would choose for different observation conditions in reward structure one, which we will refer to as a *predicted response*. The predicted responses are the ones the leader optimized against. Table 10.3 shows the expected rewards (for a subset of the algorithms tested) the leader should obtain for each door selection by the follower in reward structure one. For instance, if the follower selected Door 2 when playing against DOBSS the leader would expect to obtain a reward of $-.97$.

Why does COBRA perform better than DOBSS? The simple answer is that by incorporating a bounded rationality assumption along with anchoring theory for limited observation conditions COBRA more accurately predicts human

---

[1] Yuen's test was run on the combined data from both reward structures since a two-way Friedman test reveals that structure is insignificant to the results.

Table 10.2. *Percentage of times follower chose a*
leader predicted response in reward structure one

Structure One	Unobserved	5	20	Infinite
DOBSS	20%	7.5%	17.5%	12.5%
BRASS	65%	65%	65%	70%
COBRA	57.5%	92.5%	72.5%	70%
COBRA-C	92.5%	92.5%	87.5%	95%
MAXIMIN	100%	100%	100%	100%

Table 10.3. *Leader expected rewards for reward structure one*

	DOBSS	BRASS	MAXIMIN	COBRA-C COBRA-5	COBRA-20
Door 1	−5	−4.58	−1.63	−5	−4.61
Door 2	−.97	−.42	−1.63	−.30	−.37
Door 3	−.36	−.36	−1	−.30	−.37
Door 4	−1.38	−.79	−1.63	−.30	−.73
Door 5	−.06	−.36	−1.63	−.30	−.37
Door 6	−1	−.86	−1	−1	−.87
Door 7	−.39	−.36	−1.63	−.30	−.37
Door 8	−4.57	−3.69	−1.63	−3.32	−3.67

responses. If followers played according to the expectations of DOBSS, it would be the superior strategy, however, they do not. Looking at Table 10.2 for instance, we see that in the five observation case of DOBSS the follower chooses a predicted response only 7.5% of the time; whereas in COBRA he chose a predicted response 92.5% of the time. The predicted response by DOBSS is that the follower plays door 7; and for COBRA it is all doors where it obtains −.3. Notice in Table 10.3 if the human follower had played the predicted response of Door 7 100% of the time, then DOBSS would have obtained a reward of .39 whereas COBRA in the five-observation case can only obtain a meager −.30. Further examination of Table 10.3, however, reveals that DOBSS can suffer tremendously depending on what nonoptimal response is chosen. In Door 1 for example, DOBSS can obtain a reward of −5. This shows why DOBSS can suffer if followers stray from the predicted response. Since followers rarely stray from the predicted response in COBRA, we expect to obtain a reward around the predicted reward of −.30, and indeed COBRA in the five-observation condition gives an expected reward of −.65, lower than expected, but much better than the −.81 that DOBSS obtained compared to the predicted reward of .39.

In fact, under high-observation conditions, DOBSS is seen performing even worse than our simple baseline of MAXIMIN.

Now, we examine why dealing with both bounded rationality and observational limitations is necessary for performance. BRASS is equivalent to COBRA with $\alpha = 0$, showing how COBRA performs without an α parameter. As shown in Figure 10.1a, BRASS is outperformed by COBRA (obtains lower expected rewards) in the unobserved and five-observation cases. This demonstrates that by varying α, COBRA has significantly improved its strategies and expected rewards in limited observation conditions. Of course when observation is perfect, COBRA and BRASS are equivalent and both outperform DOBSS in the infinite-observation conditions. This demonstrates that ε is also important, even when α is not present (since $\alpha = 0$ in this case). These results clearly show that dealing with both bounded rationality and observational limitations is necessary to achieve a superior performing algorithm.

Why does COBRA-C outperform COBRA? The simple answer is that COBRA-C utilizes its resources better, by being better able to predict human responses. Looking at Table 10.2, COBRA-C accurately predicts human responses 87.5% of the time in the worse case. COBRA-C makes use of the concept that even though the human follower may not have seen a guard on a particular door, he will still attribute some probability, even if it is low, that a guard may appear on that door at some point. Although the strategies are not presented here, in the twenty-observation case COBRA assigns a guard to Doors 1 and 6 each 7% of the time. COBRA-C, on the other hand, uses this 14% total and distributes it among other choices, assuming the follower will assign some probability to these doors regardless of what the actual strategy is. Thus, COBRA-C increases the expected value of other doors ($-.3$ rather than $-.37$ for COBRA-20). Even in the infinite-observation case, COBRA-C is found to be a better predictor of human responses, with followers choosing a predicted response 95% of the time, as opposed to the 70% against COBRA. Although this was not expected, it was a welcome surprise.

Why do COBRA and COBRA-C perform better than our baseline algorithms? The main reason is they make more intelligent use of the available resources. UNIFORM is a naive strategy that does not make use of the reward structure, and MAXIMIN is too defensive, trying to make all doors of equal value so the defender can be safe regardless of the follower's choice. COBRA and COBRA-C exploit game-theoretic reasoning to solve the problem at hand, utilizing their resources to better deal with the imprecise decisions of humans, but not trivially wasting resources as in MAXIMIN and UNIFORM.

Given this analysis, COBRA and COBRA-C, with appropriately chosen α values, appear to be the best performing among our new algorithms. The performance of DOBSS in these experiments also illustrates the need for the novel approaches presented in this paper for dealing with humans. Indeed, with DOBSS having been deployed since 2007 at LAX (Pita et al., 2008), these results show that security at LAX could potentially be improved by incorporating our new methods for dealing with human adversaries.

10.4.2 Runtime Results

For our runtime results, in addition to the original eight-door game, we constructed a ten-door game with $\binom{10}{3} = 120$ leader actions, and ten follower actions. To average our runtimes over multiple instances, we created nineteen additional reward structures for each of the eight-door and ten-door games. Furthermore, since our algorithms handle Bayesian games, we created eight variations of each of the resulting twenty games to test scaleup in number of follower types. We assume that each follower occurs with a 10% probability except the last, which occurs with $1 - .10 * (n - 1)$ where n is the number of follower types. Experiments were run using CPLEX 8.1 on an Intel(R) Xeon(TM) CPU 3.20 GHz processor with 2 GB RDRAM.

In Figure 10.2, we summarize the runtime results for our Bayesian game using DOBSS, BRASS, COBRA, and MAXIMIN. The eight-door results are marked with solid figures and the ten-door results are marked with open figures. The value of α was varied to show the impact on solution speed. We include $\alpha = .25$ and $\alpha = .75$, in the graph, denoted by COBRA_25 and COBRA_75, respectively. The x-axis in Figure 10.2 varies the number of follower types from one to eight. The y-axis of the graph shows the runtime of each algorithm in seconds. All experiments that were not concluded in 1200 seconds were cut off. As expected, MAXIMIN is the fastest among the algorithms with a maximum

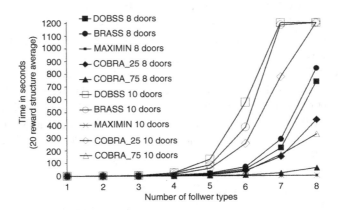

Figure 10.2. Comparing runtimes.

runtime of 0.054 seconds on average in the ten-door case. Not anticipated was the approximately equivalent runtime of DOBSS and BRASS and even more surprising were the significant speedups of COBRA over DOBSS and BRASS depending on the value of α. As shown in Figure 10.2, as α increases, the runtime of COBRA decreases. For example, in the ten-door, eight-follower type case when $\alpha = .25$ COBRA is unable to reach a solution within 1200 on average. However, when we increase α to .75, COBRA is able to find a solution in 327.5 seconds on average. In fact, every strategy except MAXIMIN and COBRA with $\alpha = .75$ reached the maximum runtime in the ten-door, eight-follower-type domain.

10.5 Summary and Related Work

Stackelberg games are crucial in many multi-agent applications, and particularly for security applications (Brown et al., 2006; Paruchuri et al., 2008); the DOBSS algorithm, for instance, is applied for security scheduling at LAX (Pita et al., 2008). In such applications automated Stackelberg solvers may create an optimal leader strategy. Unfortunately, the bounded rationality and limited observations of human followers challenge a critical assumption – that followers will act optimally – in DOBSS or any other existing Stackelberg solver, which may lead to a severely underperforming strategy when the follower deviates from the optimal strategy. To apply Stackelberg games to any setting involving people, this limitation must be addressed. This paper provides the following key contributions. First, it provides three new robust algorithms, BRASS, GUARD and COBRA, based on two key ideas: (i) Human anchoring biases drawn from support theory and (ii) robust approaches for MILPs to address human imprecision. To the best of our knowledge, the effectiveness of each of these key ideas against human adversaries had not been explored in the context of Stackelberg games. These algorithms take a robust approach to solving Stackelberg games according to predictions on how and why human adversaries' responses deviate from the optimal. Second, this paper provides experimental evidence that these new algorithms, in particular COBRA, perform statistically significantly better than existing algorithms and baseline algorithms when human adversaries are followers. These conclusions are drawn from experiments done on two settings based on real, deployed security systems, in four different observability conditions, involving 98 human subjects playing 1360 games in total. These results show that COBRA is likely better suited for real-world applications involving human adversaries. Lastly, runtime analysis is provided for these algorithms, showing that they maintain equivalent solution speeds compared to existing approaches.

In terms of related work, other non-game-theoretic models for security have also been explored. The patrolling problem itself has received significant attention in multi-agent literature because of its wide variety of applications, ranging from robot patrol to border patrolling of large areas (Agmon et al., 2008; Kiekintveld et al., 2009; Paruchuri et al., 2006). We complement these works by applying Bayesian Stackelberg games to these domains. In particular, we turn to robust game theory, which was first introduced for Nash equilibria (Aghassi and Bertsimas, 2006) and adapted to Wardrop network equilibria (Ordóñez and Stier-Moses, 2007). These prior works show that an equilibrium exists and how to compute it when players act robustly to parameter uncertainty. We also draw inspiration from approaches to bounded rationality in game theory (Rubinstein, 1998) – the key question remains how to precisely model it in game-theoretic settings. Limited observability provides a different challenge which we addressed via support theory (Tversky and Koehler, 1994). Related work in support theory has shown that people exhibit anchoring biases and are slow to update away from these biases (See et al., 2006). Combining these concepts in a novel context (Stackelberg games), we are able to address human adversaries as followers.

Acknowledgments

This research was supported by the United States Department of Homeland Security through the Center for Risk and Economic Analysis of Terrorism Events (CREATE) under grant number 2007-ST-061-000001. However, any opinions, findings, and conclusions or recommendations in this document are those of the authors and do not necessarily reflect views of the United States Department of Homeland Security. This work was also supported in part by the National Science Foundation grant number IIS0705587 and the Israel Science Foundation.

11

Approximation Methods for Infinite Bayesian Stackelberg Games: Modeling Distributional Payoff Uncertainty

Christopher Kiekintveld, Janusz Marecki, and Milind Tambe

11.1 Introduction

Stackelberg games are increasingly important for informing real-world decision making, including a growing body of work that applies these techniques in security domains such as critical infrastructure protection (Bier, 2007; Sandler and D. G. A. M., 2003), computer networks (Alpcan and Basar, 2003; Nguyen and Basar 2009), and robot patrolling strategies (Agmon et al., 2009; Basilico, Gatti, and Amigoni, 2009; Gatti, 2008). Two software systems that use this type of game modeling are in use by the the Los Angeles International Airport (LAX) (Pita et al., 2008) and the Federal Air Marshals Service (FAMS) (Tsai et al., 2009) to assist with resource allocation decision. A key issue that has arisen in these applications is whether the models can accurately represent the uncertainty that domain experts have about the inputs used to construct the game models, including the preferences and capabilities of terrorist adversaries.

To apply game-theoretic reasoning, the first step in the analysis is to construct a precise game model. The typical approach (e.g., in the LAX and FAMS applications) is to construct a model using a combination of the available data and expert opinions. Unfortunately, the data is often limited or imprecise, especially in regard to information about the terrorist adversaries. For example, it can be difficult to predict precisely how attackers will weigh casualties, economic consequences, media exposure, and other factors when selecting targets. Our focus in this paper is on developing techniques to more accurately model the uncertainty about the parameters of the model to avoid poor decisions due to overconfidence.

Previously published in *Proc. of 10th Int. Conf. on Autonomous Agents and Multiagent Systems (AAMAS 2011)*, Tumer, Yolum, Sonenberg and Stone (eds.) May 2–6, 2011, Taipei, Taiwan.

213

Bayesian games (Harsanyi, 1967–8) are the most common framework for reasoning about uncertainty in game-theoretic settings. Unfortunately, it is known that finding equilibria of finite Bayesian Stackelberg games is NP-hard (Conitzer and Sandholm, 2006). The DOBSS algorithm (Paruchuri et al., 2008) used in the ARMOR system at LAX is able to solve games with roughly ten attacker types and up to five actions for each player. Until very recently, with the development of HBGS (Jain, Kiekintveld, and Tambe, 2011), DOBSS was the fastest known algorithm for finite Bayesian Stackelberg games. Both DOBSS and HBGS are too slow to scale to domains such as FAMS with its thousands of actions, and we show in our experimental results that restricting the model to a small number of attacker types generally leads to poor solution quality.

In this chapter we introduce a general model of infinite Bayesian Stackelberg security games that allows payoffs to be represented using continuous payoff distributions (e.g., Gaussian or uniform distributions). This model allows for a richer and more natural expression of uncertainty about the input parameters, leading to higher-quality and more robust solutions than finite Bayesian models. Our analysis of the model shows that finding exact analytic solutions is infeasible (and efficient algorithms are unlikely in any case, given the complexity results for the finite case). We focus instead on developing approximate solution methods that employ numerical methods, Monte Carlo sampling, and approximate optimization. Our experiments show that even approximate solutions for the infinite case offer dramatic benefits in both solution quality and scalability over the existing approaches based on perfect information or small numbers of attacker types.

11.2 Related Work

Stackelberg games have important applications in security domains. These include fielded applications at LAX (Pita et al., 2008) and FAMS (Tsai et al., 2009), work on patrolling strategies for robots and unmanned vehicles (Agmon et al., 2009; Basiloco et al., 2009; Gatti, 2008), applications of game theory in network security (Alpcan and Basar, 2003; Nguyen and Basar, 2009; Wei Lye and Wing, 2005), and research that provides policy recommendations for the allocation of security resources at a national level (Bier, 2007; Sandler and D G. A. M, 2003). Bayesian games (Harsanyi, 1967–8) are a standard approach for modeling uncertainty, and there are many specific examples of infinite Bayesian games that have been solved analytically, including many types of auctions (Krishna, 2002).

However, relatively little work has been done on general algorithms for solving large and infinite Bayesian games. Recent interest in this class of games focuses on developing approximation algorithms (Armantier, Florens, and Richard, 2008; Ceppi, Gatti, and Basilico, 2009; Reeves and Wellman, 2004). Monte Carlo sampling approaches similar to those we describe have been applied to some kinds of auctions (Cai and Wurman, 2005). In addition, the literature on stochastic choice (Luce and Raiffa, 1989) studies problems that are simplified versions of the choice problem attackers face in our model. Closed-form solutions exist only for special cases with specific types of uncertainty, even in the single-agent stochastic choice literature. A alternative to Bayesian games that has been developed recently is robust equilibrium (Aghassi and Bertsimas, 2006), which takes a worst-case approach inspired by the robust optimization literature.

11.3 Bayesian Security Games

We define a new class of infinite Bayesian security games, extending the model in Kiekintveld et al. (2009) to include uncertainty about the attacker's payoffs. The key difference between our model and existing approaches (such as in Paruchuri et al. 2008) is that we allow the defender to have a continuous distribution over the possible payoffs of the attacker. Previous models have restricted this uncertainty to a small, finite number of possible attacker types, limiting the kinds of uncertainty that can be modeled.

A security game has two players, a *defender*, Θ, and an *attacker*, Ψ; a set of *targets* $T = \{t_1, \ldots, t_n\}$ that the defender wants to protect (the attacker wants to attack); and a set of *resources* $R = \{r_1, \ldots, r_m\}$ (e.g., police officers) that the defender may deploy to protect the targets. Resources are identical in that any resource can be deployed to protect any target, and any resource provides equivalent protection. A defender's pure strategy, denoted σ_Θ, is a subset of targets from T with size less than or equal to m. An attacker's pure strategy, σ_Ψ, is exactly one target from T. The set of all defender's pure strategies is denoted by Σ_Θ, and Σ_Ψ is the set of all attacker's pure strategies. We model the game as a Stackelberg game (von Stackelberg, 1934) that unfolds as follows: (1) The defender commits to a mixed strategy δ_Θ that is a probability distribution over the pure strategies from Σ_Θ; (2) nature chooses a random attacker type $\omega \in \Omega$ with probability $Pb(\omega)$; (3) the attacker observes the defender's mixed strategy δ_Θ; and (4) the attacker responds to δ_Θ with a best-response strategy from Σ_Ψ that provides the attacker (of type ω) with the highest *expected* payoff given δ_Θ.

The payoffs for the defender depend on which target is attacked and whether the target is protected (covered) or not. Specifically, for an attack on target t, the defender receives a payoff $U_\Theta^u(t)$ if the target is uncovered, and $U_\Theta^c(t)$ if the target is covered. The payoffs for an attacker of type $\omega \in \Omega$ is

$U_\psi^u(t,\omega)$ for an attack on an uncovered target, and $U_\psi^c(t,\omega)$ for an attack on a covered target. We assume that both the defender and the attacker know the above payoff structure exactly. However, the defender is uncertain about the attacker's type, and can only estimate the expected payoffs for the attacker. We do not to model uncertainty that the attacker has about the defender's payoffs because we assume that the attacker is able to directly observe the defender's strategy.

11.3.1 Bayesian Stackelberg Equilibrium

A Bayesian Stackelberg equilibrium (BSE) for a security game consists of a strategy profile in which every attacker type is playing a best response to the defender strategy, and the defender is playing a best response to the distribution of actions chosen by the attacker types. We first define the equilibrium condition for the attacker and for the defender. We represent the defender's mixed strategy δ_Θ by the compact *coverage vector* $C = (c_t)_{t \in T}$ that gives the probabilities c_t that each target $t \in T$ is covered by at least one resource. Note that $\sum_{t \in T} c_t \leq m$ because the defender has m resources available. In equilibrium, each attacker type ω best-responds to the coverage C with a pure strategy $\sigma_\psi^*(C,\omega)$ given by:

$$\sigma_\psi^*(C,\omega) = \arg\max_{t \in T}(c_t \cdot U_\psi^c(t,\omega) + (1 - c_t) \cdot U_\psi^u(t,\omega)) \qquad (11.1)$$

To define the equilibrium condition for the defender, we first define the *attacker response function* $A(C) = (a_t(C))_{t \in T}$ that returns the probabilities $a_t(C)$ that each target $t \in T$ will be attacked, given the distribution of attacker types and a coverage vector C. Specifically:

$$a_t(C) = \int_{\omega \in \Omega} Pb(\omega)\mathbf{1}_t(\sigma_\psi^*(C,\omega))d\omega \qquad (11.2)$$

where $\mathbf{1}_t(\sigma_\psi^*(C,\omega))$ is the indicator function that returns 0 if $t = \sigma_\psi^*(C,\omega)$ and 0 otherwise. Given the attacker response function $A(\cdot)$ and a set of all possible defender coverage vectors $\mathcal{C}$, the equilibrium condition for the defender is to execute its best-response mixed strategy $\delta_\Theta^* \equiv C^*$ given by:

$$\delta_\Theta^* = \arg\max_C \sum_{t \in T} a_t(C)(c_t \cdot U_\Theta^c(t) + (1 - c_t) \cdot U_\Theta^u(t)). \qquad (11.3)$$

11.3.2 Attacker Payoff Distributions

When the set of attacker types is infinite, calculating the attacker response function directly from Equation (11.2) is impractical. For this case, we instead replace each payoff in the original model with a continuous distribution over possible payoffs. Formally, for each target $t \in T$ we replace values $U^c_\psi(t,\omega)$, $U^u_\psi(t,\omega)$ over all $\omega \in \Omega$ with two continuous probability density functions:

$$f^c_\psi(t,r) = \int\limits_{\omega \in \Omega} Pb(\omega)U^c_\psi(t,\omega)d\omega \tag{11.4}$$

$$f^u_\psi(t,r) = \int\limits_{\omega \in \Omega} Pb(\omega)U^u_\psi(t,\omega)d\omega \tag{11.5}$$

that represent the defender's *beliefs* about the attacker payoffs. For example, the defender expects, with probability $f^c_\psi(t,r)$, that the attacker receives payoff r for attacking target t when it is covered. This provides a convenient and general way for domain experts to express uncertainty about payoffs in the game model, whether based on their own beliefs or on uncertain evidence from intelligence reports. Given this representation, we can now derive an alternative formula for the attacker response function. For some coverage vector C, let $X_t(C)$ be a random variable that describes the *expected* attacker payoffs for attacking target t, given C. It then holds for each target $t \in T$ that:

$$a_t(C) = Pb[X_t(C) > X_{t'}(C) \text{ for all } t' \in T \setminus t] \tag{11.6}$$

because the attacker acts rationally. Equation (11.6) can be rewritten as:

$$a_t(C) = \int\limits_{r=-\infty}^{r=+\infty} Pb[X_t(C) = r] \cdot \prod_{t' \in T \setminus t} Pb[X_{t'}(C) < r]dr \tag{11.7}$$

$$= \int\limits_{r=-\infty}^{r=+\infty} Pb[X_t(C) = r] \cdot \prod_{t' \in T \setminus t} \int\limits_{r'=-\infty}^{r'=r} Pb[X_{t'}(C) = r']dr' \, dr.$$

Hence, we now show how to determine the random variables $X_t(C)$ used in Equation (11.7). That is, we provide a derivation of values $Pb[X_t(C) = r]$ for all $t \in T$ and $-\infty < r < +\infty$. To this end, we represent each $X_t(C)$ using two random variables, $X^-_t(C)$ and $X^+_t(C)$. Now, $X^-_t(C)$ describes the expected attacker payoffs for *being caught* when attacking target t while $X^+_t(C)$ describes the expected attacker payoffs for *not being caught* when attacking target t, given coverage vector C. It then holds that $X_t(C) = r$ if $X^-_t(C) = x$ and $X^+_t(C) = r - x$ for some $-\infty < x < +\infty$. (Note, that in a trivial case where $c_t = 1$ it holds that $Pb[X^+_t(C) = 0] = 1$ and consequently $X^-_t(C) = X_t(C)$. Similarly, if $c_t = 0$ then $Pb[X^-_t(C) = 0] = 1$ and $X^+_t(C) = X_t(C)$.) We can then derive $Pb[X_t(C) = r]$ as follows:

$$Pb[X_t(C) = r] = \int\limits_{x=-\infty}^{x=+\infty} Pb[X_t^-(C) = x] \cdot Pb[X_t^+(C) = r - x]dx$$

$$= \int\limits_{x=-\infty}^{x=+\infty} \frac{Pb[X_t^-(C) = x]dx \cdot Pb[X_t^+(C) = r - x]dx}{dx}$$

$$= \int\limits_{x=-\infty}^{x=+\infty} \frac{Pb[x \le X_t^-(C) \le x + dx] \cdot Pb[r - x \le X_t^+(C) \le r - x + dx]}{dx}.$$

If a random event provides payoff $y := \frac{x}{c_t}$ with probability c_t, the expected payoff of that event is $y \cdot c_t = x$. Therefore:

$$= \int\limits_{x=-\infty}^{x=+\infty} \frac{1}{dx} \int\limits_{y=\frac{x}{c_t}}^{y=\frac{(x+dx)}{c_t}} f_\psi^c(t,y)dy \int\limits_{y=\frac{r-x}{1-c_t}}^{y=\frac{r-x+dx}{1-c_t}} f_\psi^u(t,y)dy$$

Substituting $u := c_t y$, $v := (1 - c_t)y$ in the inner integrals we get:

$$= \int\limits_{x=-\infty}^{x=+\infty} \frac{1}{dx} \int\limits_{u=x}^{u=x+dx} f_\psi^c\left(t,\frac{u}{c_t}\right)\frac{1}{c_t}du \int\limits_{v=r-x}^{v=r-x+dx} f_\psi^u\left(t,\frac{v}{1-c_t}\right)\frac{1}{1-c_t}dv$$

$$= \int\limits_{x=-\infty}^{x=+\infty} \frac{1}{dx} f_\psi^c\left(t,\frac{x}{c_t}\right)\frac{1}{c_t}dx \cdot f_\psi^u\left(t,\frac{r-x}{1-c_t}\right)\frac{1}{1-c_t}dx$$

$$= \int\limits_{x=-\infty}^{x=+\infty} \frac{1}{c_t} f_\psi^c\left(t,\frac{x}{c_t}\right) \cdot \frac{1}{1-c_t} f_\phi^u\left(t,\frac{r-x}{1-c_t}\right)dx.$$

Using this derived formula for $Pb[X_t(C) = r]$ in (11.7) we obtain:

$$a_t(C) = \int\limits_{r=-\infty}^{r=+\infty}\int\limits_{x=-\infty}^{x=+\infty} \frac{1}{c_t} f_\psi^c\left(t,\frac{x}{c_t}\right) \cdot \frac{1}{1-c_t} f_\phi^u\left(t,\frac{r-x}{1-c_t}\right)dx\,dr$$

$$\cdot \prod\limits_{t' \in T \setminus t} \int\limits_{r'=-\infty}^{r'=r}\int\limits_{x=-\infty}^{x=+\infty} \frac{1}{c_{t'}} f_\psi^c\left(t',\frac{x}{c_{t'}}\right) \cdot \frac{1}{1-c_{t'}} f_\phi^u\left(t',\frac{r'-x}{1-c_{t'}}\right)dx\,dr'$$

Also written as $a_t(C) = \int g_t \prod_{t' \in T \setminus t} G_{t'}$ where $G_t := \int g_t$ and

$$g_t(r) := \int\limits_{x=-\infty}^{x=+\infty} \frac{1}{c_t} f_\psi^c \left(t, \frac{x}{c_t} \right) \cdot \frac{1}{1-c_t} f_\phi^u \left(t, \frac{r-x}{1-c_t} \right) dx$$

While a direct analytic solution of these equations is not tractable, we can use numerical techniques to compute g_t, G_t, and $a_t(C)$. In our experiments we test two methods, one using straightforward Monte Carlo simulation and the second using piecewise-constant functions to approximate f_ϕ^u and f_ϕ^u. The argument-wise multiplication $f_\phi^u \cdot f_\phi^u$ still results in a piecewise-constant function that, after the integration operation, results in a piecewise-linear function $g_t(r)$. We then re-approximate $g_t(r)$ with a piecewise-constant function, integrate $g_t(r)$ to obtain a piecewise-linear function $G_t(r)$, and again re-approximate $G_t(r)$ with a piecewise-constant function. Each product $g_t \prod_{t' \in T \setminus t} G_{t'}$ is then a piecewise-constant function that, after the integration operation, is represented as a piecewise-linear function. The value of that last function approaches $a_t(C)$ as the number of segments approaches infinity. By varying the accuracy of these computations, one can trade off optimality for speed, as is shown in our experiments.

11.4 Solution Methods

To solve the model described in the previous section, we need to find a BSE that gives an optimal coverage strategy for the defender and an optimal response for every attacker type. If there are a finite number of attacker types, an optimal defender strategy can be found using DOBSS (Paruchuri et al., 2008). Unfortunately, there are no known methods for finding exact equilibrium solutions for infinite Bayesian Stackelberg games, and DOBSS only scales to small numbers of types. Here, we focus on methods for approximating solutions to infinite Bayesian Stackelberg games. The problem can be broken down into two parts:

1. Computing/estimating the attacker response function (Equation 11.7)
2. Optimizing over the space of defender strategies, given the attacker response function

In the previous section we were able to derive the form of the attacker response function, but we lack any means to compute this function analytically. As described above, we explore both brute-force Monte Carlo sampling and a piecewise-constant-function approximation method to approximate this function. In addition, we explore a variety of different approaches for optimizing the defender strategy. Overall, we describe five different approximate solution methods.

11.4.1 Sampled Bayesian ERASER

Our first method combines Monte Carlo sampling from the space of attacker types with an exact optimization over the space of defender strategies. This approach is based on the DOBSS solver (Paruchuri et al., 2008) for finite Bayesian Stackelberg games. However, we also incorporate several improvements from the ERASER solver (Kiekintveld et al., 2009) that offer faster solutions for the restricted class of security games. The resulting method can be encoded as a mixed-integer linear program (MIP), which we call *Bayesian ERASER* (not presented here because of space constraints).

To use Bayesian ERASER to approximate a solution for an infinite game, we draw a finite number of sample attacker types from the type distribution, assuming that each occurs with equal probability. The payoffs for each type are determined by drawing from the payoff distributions specified in Equations 11.4 and 11.5. This results in a constrained, finite version of the infinite game that can be solved using the Bayesian ERASER MIP. We refer to this method as *sampled Bayesian ERASER* (SBE) and use SBE-x to denote this method with x sample attacker types. Armantier et al. [2008] develop an approach for approximating general infinite Bayesian games that relies on solving constrained versions of the original game. Given certain technical conditions, a sequence of equilibria of constrained games will converge to the equilibrium of the original game. Here, increasing the number of sample types corresponds to such a sequence of constrained games, so in the limit as the number of samples goes to infinity the equilibrium of SBE-∞ will converge to the true Bayesian Nash equilibrium.

11.4.2 Sampled Replicator Dynamics

The second algorithm uses a local search method (replicator dynamics) to approximate the defender's optimal strategy, given the attacker response function. Given that we are already using numerical techniques to estimate the attacker response, it is sensible to explore approximations for the defender's optimization problem as well. This allows us to trade off whether to use additional computational resources to improve the attacker response estimation or the defender strategy optimization.

Sampled replicator dynamics (SRD) is based on replicator dynamics (Taylor and Jonker, 1978). Since this is a form of local search, we require only a black-box method to estimate the attacker response function. We could use either

Monte Carlo sampling or piecewise-constant approximation, but use Monte Carlo in our experiments. As above, we use SRD-x to denote SRD with x sample attacker types. SRD proceeds in a sequence of iterations. At each step the current coverage strategy $C^n = (c_t^n)_{t \in T}$ is used to estimate the attacker response function, which in turn is used to estimate the expected payoffs for both players. A new coverage strategy $C^{n+1} = (c_t^{n+1})_{t \in T}$ is computed according to the replicator equation:

$$c_t^{n+1} \propto c_t^n \cdot (E_t(C) - U_\Theta^{min}), \tag{11.8}$$

where U_Θ^{min} represents the minimum possible payoff for the defender, and $E_t(C)$ is the expected payoff the defender gets for covering target t with probability 1 and all other targets with probability 0, given the estimated attacker response to C^n. The search runs for a fixed number of iterations, and returns the coverage vector with the highest expected payoff. We introduce a learning rate parameter α that interpolates between C^n and C^{n+1}, with C^{n+1} receiving weight α in the next population and C^n having weight $1 - \alpha$. Finally, we introduce random restarts to avoid becoming stuck in local optima. After initial experiments, we settled on a learning rate of $\alpha = 0.8$ and random restarts every fifteen iterations, which generally yielded good results (though the solution quality was not highly sensitive to these settings).

11.4.3 Greedy Monte Carlo

Our next algorithm combines a greedy heuristic for allocating defender resources with a very fast method for updating the attacker response function that was estimated using Monte-Carlo type sampling. We call this algorithm Greedy Monte Carlo (GMC). The idea of the greedy heuristic is to start from a coverage vector that assigns 0 probability to every target. At each iteration, the algorithm evaluates the prospect of adding some small increment (Δ) of coverage probability to each target. The algorithm computes the difference between the defender's expected payoff for the current coverage vector C and the new coverage vector that differs only in the coverage for a single target t such that $c_t' = c_t + \Delta$. The target with the maximum payoff gain for the defender is selected, Δ is added to the coverage for that target, and the algorithm proceeds to the next iteration. It terminates when all the available resources have been allocated.

The idea of using a greedy heuristic for allocating coverage probability is motivated in part by the ORIGAMI algorithm (Kiekintveld et al., 2009) that is known to be optimal for cases without uncertainty about attacker payoffs. That algorithm proceeds by sequentially allocating coverage probability to the set of targets that give the attacker the maximal expected payoff. In the Bayesian case there is no well-defined set of targets with maximal payoff for the attacker since each type may have a different optimal target to attack, so we choose instead to base the allocation strategy on the defender's payoff.

In principle, any method for estimating the attacker response function could be used to implement this greedy algorithm. However, we take advantage of the fact that the algorithm only requires adding coverage to a single target at a time to implement a very fast method for estimating the attacker response function. We begin by using Monte Carlo sampling to generate a large number of sample attacker types. For each target we maintain a list containing the individual attacker types that will attack that target, given the current coverage vector. For each type ω we track the current expected payoff for each target, the *best* target to attack, and the *second* best target to attack. These can be used to calculate the minimum amount of coverage δ that would need to be added to current coverage c_{best} of the *best* target to induce type ω to switch to attacking the *second* best target instead. Formally, the target switching condition:

$$(c_{best} + \delta)U_\psi^c(best, \omega) + (1 - (c_{best} + \delta))U_\psi^u(best, \omega)$$
$$= (c_{second})U_\psi^c(second, \omega) + (1 - c_{second})U_\psi^u(second, \omega)$$

allows us to derive:

$$\delta = \frac{(c_{second})U_\psi^c(second, \omega) + (1 - c_{second})U_\psi^u(second, \omega)}{U_\psi^c(best, \omega) - U_\psi^u(best, \omega)}$$
$$- \frac{(c_{best})U_\psi^c(best, \omega) - (c_{best})U_\psi^u(best, \omega)}{U_\psi^c(best, \omega) - U_\psi^u(best, \omega)}. \tag{11.9}$$

Using this data structure we can quickly compute the change in the defender's expected payoff for adding Δ coverage to a target t. There are three factors to account for:

1. The defender's expected payoff for an attack on t increases.
2. The probability that the attacker will choose t may decrease, as some types may no longer have t as a best response.
3. The probability that other targets are attacked may increase if types that were attacking t choose different targets instead.

For every type in the list for target t, we determine whether or not the type will change using Equation 11.9. If the type changes, we update the payoff against that type to be the expected defender payoff associated with the second best target for that type. If not, the payoff against that type is the new defender expected payoff for target t with coverage $c_t + \Delta$. After adjusting the payoffs for every type that was attacking target t in this way, we have the change in the defender expected payoff for adding Δ for target t.

After computing the potential change for each target we select the target with the maximum gain for the defender and add the Δ coverage units to that target. We update the data structure containing the types by updating the expected value for the changed target for every type (regardless of which target it is currently attacking). If the updated target was either the best or second best target for a type, we recompute the best and second best targets and, if necessary, move the type to the list for the new best target.

Based on our initial experiences with the GMC method we added two modifications to prevent the algorithm from becoming stuck in local optima in specific cases. First, we placed a lower bound of 1% on the Δ used during the calculations to compute the value of adding coverage to each target, even through the actual amount of coverage added once the best target is selected may be much smaller. In practice, this smoothes out the estimated impact of types changing to attack different targets by averaging over a larger number of types. Second, for cases with a very small numbers of types we use an "optimistic" version of the heuristic in which we assume that the new value for any type that changes to attacking a new target gives the maximum of the current value or the value for the new target (for the defender). The intuition for this heuristic is that it assumes that additional coverage could later be added to the second-best target to make the type to switch back.

11.4.4 Worst-Case Interval Uncertainty

We also consider an approach based on minimizing the worst-case outcome, assuming interval uncertainty over the attacker's payoffs. The BRASS algorithm (Pita et al., 2009) was originally designed to model bounded rationality in humans. Instead of the standard assumption that attackers will choose an optimal response, BRASS assumes that attackers will choose any response in the set of responses that has expected value within ϵ units of the optimal response, where ϵ is a parameter of the algorithm. The algorithm optimizes the defender's optimal payoff for the worst-case selection of the attacker within the set of feasible responses defined by ϵ.

Although this technique was originally motivated as a way to capture deviations from perfect rationality in human decision making, here we reinterpret the method as a worst-case approach for payoff uncertainty. Suppose that the defender does not know the attacker's payoffs with certainty, but knows only that each payoff is within an interval of *mean* $\pm \frac{\epsilon}{2}$. Then, an attacker playing optimally could attack any target within ϵ of the target with the best expected value based on the means (since the "best" value could be up to $\frac{\epsilon}{2}$ too high, and the value for another target could be up to $\frac{\epsilon}{2}$ too low).

11.4.5 Decoupled Target Sets

Our last method for solving infinite Bayesian Stackelberg games is called decoupled target sets (DTS). DTS is an approximate solver, for it assumes that the attacker preference as to which target $t \in D \subset \{1,2,...,T\}$ to attack depends on the probabilities c_t of targets $t \in D$ being covered, but does *not* depend on the probabilities $c_{\bar{t}}$ of targets $\bar{t} \in \overline{D} := \{1,2,...,T\} \setminus D$ being covered. For example, let $D = \{1,2\} \subset \{1,2,3\}$. Here, DTS assumes that when the attacker evaluates whether it is more profitable to attack target 1 than to attack target 2, the attacker needs to know the probabilities c_1, c_2 but does *not* have to reason about the probability c_3 of target 3 being covered. While this attacker strategy appears sound (after all, "Why should the attacker bother about target 3 when it debates whether it is better to attack target 1 than to attack target 2?"), it can be shown that it is not always optimal. In general then, DTS assumes that for any two coverage vectors $C = (c_t)_{t \in D \cup \overline{D}}$, $C' = (c'_t)_{t \in D \cup \overline{D}}$ such that $c_t = c'_t$ for all $t \in D$, it holds that

$$\frac{a_t(C)}{a_{t'}(C)} = \frac{a_t(C')}{a_{t'}(C')} \quad \text{for any } t, t' \in D. \tag{11.10}$$

The immediate consequence of this assumption is that a systematic search for the optimal coverage vector can be performed incrementally, considering larger and larger sets of targets $D \subset \{1,2,...T\}$ (by adding to D a target from $\{1,2,...,T\} \setminus D$ in each algorithm iteration). In particular, to find an optimal coverage vector for targets $\{1,2,...d\}$, DTS reuses the optimal coverage vectors (for coverage probability sums $c_1 + c_2 + ... + c_{d-1}$ ranging from 0 to 1) for targets $\{1,2,...,d-1\}$ alone (found at previous algorithm iteration) while ignoring the targets $\{d+1, d+2,...,T\}$. Assuming that a probability of covering a target is a multiple of ϵ, DTS's search for the optimal—modulo assumption (11.10)—coverage vector can be performed in time $O(\epsilon \cdot T)$. Our implementation of DTS uses the piecewise-constant attacker response approximation method.

11.5 Experimental Evaluation

We present experimental results comparing the solution quality and computational requirements of the different classes of approximation methods introduced previously.

11.5.1 Experimental Setup

Our experiments span three classes of security games, each with a different method for selecting the distributions for attacker payoffs. In every case we first draw both penalty and reward payoffs for both the attacker and defender. All rewards are drawn from $U[6,8]$ and penalties are drawn from $U[2,4]$. We then generate payoff distributions for the attacker's payoffs using the values drawn above as the mean for the distribution. In *uniform games* the attacker's payoff is a uniform distribution around the mean, and we vary the length of the intervals to increase or decrease uncertainty. For *Gaussian games* the distributions are Gaussian around the mean payoff, with varying standard deviation. In both cases, all distributions for a particular game have the same interval size or standard deviation. The final class of games, *Gaussian Variable*, models a situation where some payoffs are more or less certain by using Gaussian distributions with different standard deviations for each payoff. The standard deviations themselves are drawn from either $U[0,0.5]$ or $U[0.2,1.5]$ to generate classes with "low" or "high" uncertainty on average.

Our solution methods generate coverage strategies that must be evaluated based on the attacker response. Since we do not have a way to compute this exactly, we compute the expected payoffs for any particular strategy by finding an extremely accurate estimate of the attacker response using 100000 Monte-Carlo samples. We employ two baseline methods in our experiments. The first simply plays a uniform random coverage strategy, such that each target is covered with equal probability using all available resources. The second uses the mean of each attacker distribution as a point estimate of the payoff. This is a proxy for models in which experts are forced to specify a specific value for each payoff, rather than directly modeling any uncertainty about the payoff. This can be solved using the SBE method, using the mean payoffs to define a single attacker type.

11.5.2 Attacker Response Estimation

We implemented two different methods for estimating the attacker response function. The first uses Monte Carlo sampling to generate a finite set of attacker types. To estimate the response probabilities we calculate the best response for each sample type and use the observed distribution of targets attacked as the estimated probabilities. The second method approximates each distribution using a piecewise constant (PWC) function and directly computes the result of Equation 11.7 for these functions.

Figures 11.1a and b compare the estimation accuracy for these two methods. Results are averaged over 100 sample games, each with 10 targets and

(a) Estimation time vs. accuracy for uniform distribution

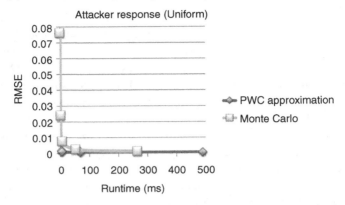

(b) Estimation time vs. accuracy for Gaussian distribution

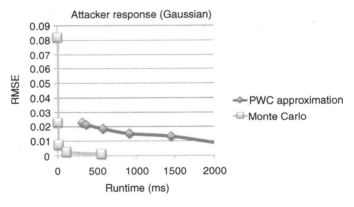

Figure 11.1. Comparison of Monte Carlo and piecewise-constant estimation methods for the attacker response function.

1 defender resource. For each game we draw a random coverage vector uniformly from the space of defender strategies to evaluate. For the uniform case, mean attacker payoffs are drawn from U[5,15] for the covered case and U[25,35] for the uncovered case, and every distribution has a range of 10 centered on the mean. For the Gaussian case, mean payoffs are drawn from U[2.5,3.5] for the covered case and U[5,6] for the uncovered case, with standard deviations for each distribution drawn from U[0,0.5]. Each method has a parameter controlling the tradeoff between solution quality and computation time. For Monte-Carlo sampling this is the number of sample types, and for the PWC approximation it is the absolute difference in function values between two adjacent constant

intervals. To enable easy comparison, we plot the solution time on the x-axis, and the solution quality for each method on the y-axis (rather than the raw parameter settings). Solution quality is measured based on the root mean squared error from an estimate of the true distribution based on 100000 sample attacker types. We see that in the uniform case, PWC approximation generally offers a better tradeoff between solution time and quality. However, for the more complex Gaussian distributions the Monte-Carlo method gives better performance.

11.5.3 Approximation Algorithms

We next compare the performance of the full approximation algorithms, evaluating both the quality of the solutions they produce and the computational properties of the algorithms. The first set of experiments compares all of the algorithms and the two baseline methods (uniform and mean) on small game instances with 5 targets and 1 defender resource. We generated random instances from each of the three classes of games described in Section 11.5.1: Uniform, Gaussian, and Gaussian Variable, varying the level of payoff uncertainty using the parameters described above. We used 100 games instances for every different level of payoff uncertainty in each class of games. The tests are paired, so every algorithm is run on the same set of game instances to improve the reliability of the comparisons.[1]

The first three plots, Figures 11.2a, b, and c show a comparison of the best solution quality achieved by each algorithm in the three classes of games. The y-axis shows the average expected defender reward for the computed strategies, and the x-axis represents the degree of uncertainty about the attacker's payoffs. Each algorithm has parameters that can affect the solution quality and computational costs of generating a solution. We tested a variety of parameter settings for each algorithm, which are listed in Table 11.1. For cases with more than one parameter, we tested all combinations of the parameter settings shown in the table. The first set of results reports the *maximum* solution quality achieved by each algorithm over any of the parameter settings to show the potential quality given under ideal settings. The settings that yield the best performance may differ in the different types of games and level of uncertainty.

The results are remarkably consistent in all of the conditions included in our experiment. First, we observe that the baseline method "mean" that uses point estimates of payoff distributions performs extremely poorly in these games – in many cases it is actually worse than playing a uniform random strategy! SBE

---

[1] In general, there is substantial variance in the overall payoffs due to large differences in the payoffs for each game instance (i.e., some games are inherently more favorable than others). However, the differences in performance between the algorithms on each individual instance are much smaller and very consistent.

Table 11.1. *Parameter settings for the algorithms tested in the first experiment*

Parameter	Values
SBE num types	1, 3, 5, 7
BRASS epsilon	0.1, 0.2, 0.3, 0.5, 1.0
SRD num types	10, 50, 100, 1000
SRD num iterations	1000, 10000
GMC num types	100, 1000, 10000
GMC coverage increment	0.01, 0.001, 0.0001
DTS max error	0.02, 0.002
DTS step size	0.05, 0.02
DTS coverage increment	0.05, 0.02

performs somewhat better, but is severely limited by an exponential growth in solution time required to find an exact optimal defender strategy as the number of sample attacker types increases. The maximum number of types we were able to run in this experiment was only seven (many orders of magnitude smaller than the number of sample types used for the other methods).

All four remaining methods (SRD, BRASS, GMC, and DTS) give much higher solution quality than either of the baselines or the SBE method in all cases. These methods are similar in that all four rely on approximation when computing the defender's strategy, but they use very different approaches. It is therefore quite surprising that the expected payoffs for all four methods are so close for these small games. This is true when we look at the data for individual game instances as well as in aggregate. On any individual instance, the difference between the best and worst solution generated by one of these four is almost always less than 0.05 units. This suggests that the strategies generated by all four algorithms are very close to optimal in these games. Overall, the GMC method does outperform the others by a very small margin. This is also consistent on a game-by-game basis, with GMC generating the best strategy in over 90% of the game instances.

Upto this point we have focused on the the best solution quality possible with each method. We now extend the analysis to include the trade-off of computational speed versus increased solution quality. This is particularly complex because of the large number of potential parameter settings for each algorithm and the fact that these parameters do not have the same interpretation. To analyze this trade-off, we plot the solution quality against the solution time for each of the parameter settings of the different algorithms. The data for Gaussian games with attacker standard deviations of 0.2 is presented in Figure 11.3.

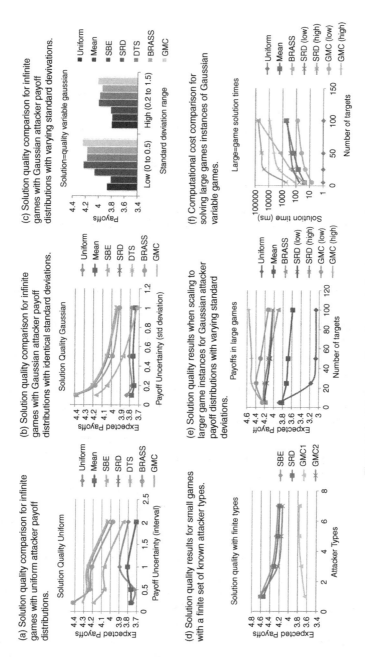

Figure 11.2. Solution quality and computation time comparisons.

229

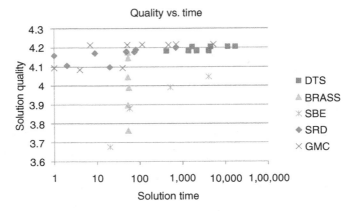

Figure 11.3. Comparison of the trade-off in solution quality and computational cost for each of the algorithms, exploring the effects of different parameter settings.

Other classes of games have similar results. Solution time (in ms) is given on the x-axis in a log scale, and solution quality is reported on the y-axis as before.

The upper-left corner of the plot corresponds to high solution quality and low computational efforts, so it is most desirable. Points from the GMC and SRD methods dominate this part of the figure, indicating that these methods are computationally scalable and give high-quality solutions. In contrast, SBE scales very poorly; even after 10000 ms, SBE still has a lower solution quality than any of the data points for GMC, SRD, or DTS. Although DTS consistently has high solution quality, it takes much longer than GMC or SRD even in the best case. BRASS has a different pattern of performance than the other methods. Every parameter setting takes roughly the same amount of time, they vary dramatically in solution quality. This is because the best setting for the ϵ parameter depends on the amount of uncertainty in the game, and is not directly related to the quality of approximation in the same way as the parameters for the other algorithms. In practice, this is a significant disadvantage, since it is not obvious how to set the value of ϵ for any particular problem. This can be determined empirically (as in our experiments), but it requires running BRASS multiple times with different settings to find a good value.

Our next experiment focuses on the quality of the approximations for SRD and GMC in a situation where an optimal solution can be computed. For finite Bayesian Stackelberg games with a small number of types, we can compute an exact optimal response using SBE. Since both SRD and GMC use Monte Carlo sampling to approximate the attacker-type distribution for infinite games, we can also apply these methods to finite games with known types. In this experiment, we test SBE, SRD, and GMC on finite games with exactly the same types. The games are generated from the Gaussian infinite games with standard deviations of 0.2, but once the types are drawn, these are interpreted as known finite games. Results are shown in Figure 11.2d, with the number of attacker types on the x-axis and solution quality on the y-axis. GMC1 is GMC with the original greedy heuristic, and GMC2 uses the modified optimistic greedy heuristic. We can see in this experiment that SRD and GMC2 both achieve very close to the true optimal defender strategy in these games, but GMC1 performs poorly. In general, GMC1 performs very well in games with large numbers of types (such as when we are approximating the infinite case), but GMC2 is preferable when there is a very small number of types.

The final experiment we report takes the three most scalable methods (SRD, GMC, and BRASS) and tests them on much larger game instances. We run this experiment on the Gaussian variable class of games with standard deviations drawn $U[0, 0.5]$. The number of targets varies between 5 and 100 in this experiment, with the number of resources set to 20% of the number of targets in each case. Because of the increased computational time to run experiments, we use only thirty sample games for each number of targets in this experiment. For SRD and GMC we tested "low" and "high" computational effort parameter settings. Solution quality results are shown in Figure 11.2e, and timing results are presented in Figure 11.2f.

The three approximate methods all clearly outperform both the uniform and mean baselines. As the number of targets increases, the mean method shows some improvement over the uniform random strategy. BRASS and the two variants of SRD both have similar solution quality scores. The most striking result is that both the low- and high-effort version of GMC significantly outperform all of the other methods for larger games and also has relatively faster solution times.

11.6 Conclusion

Developing the capability to solve large game models with rich representations of uncertainty is critical to expanding the reach of game-theoretic solutions to more real-world problems. This cuts to the central concern of ensuring that users have confidence that their knowledge is accurately represented in the model. Our experiments reinforce that experts and game theorists should not be comfortable relying on perfect-information approximations when there is uncertainty in the domain. Relying on a perfect information approximation such as the mean baseline in our experiments resulted in very poor decisions –

closer in quality to the uniform random baseline than to our approximate solvers that account for distributional uncertainty.

In this work we developed and evaluated a wide variety of different approximation techniques for solving infinite Bayesian Stackelberg games. These algorithms have very different properties, but they all show compelling improvements over existing methods. Of the approximate methods, Greedy Monte Carlo (GMC) has the best performance in solution quality and scalability, and Sampled Replicator Dynamics (SRD) also performs very well. As a group, the approximate solvers introduced here constitute the only scalable algorithms for solving a very challenging class of games with important real-world applications.

Acknowledgments

This research was supported by the United States Department of Homeland Security through the Center for Risk and Economic Analysis of Terrorism Events (CREATE) under grant number 2007-ST-061-000001. This research was also sponsored by the U.S. Army Research Laboratory and the U.K. Ministry of Defence under Agreement Number W911NF-06-3-0001. The views and conclusions in this document are those of the author(s) and should not be interpreted as representing the official policies, either expressed or implied, of the U.S. Army Research Laboratory, the U.S. Government, or the U.K. Government. The U.S. and U.K. Governments are authorized to reproduce and distribute reprints for government purposes notwithstanding any copyright notation hereon.

12

Stackelberg versus Nash in Security Games: Interchangeability, Equivalence, and Uniqueness

Zhengyu Yin, Dmytro Korzhyk, Christopher Kiekintveld,
Vincent Conitzer, and Milind Tambe

12.1 Introduction

There has been significant recent research interest in game-theoretic approaches to security at airports, ports, transportation, shipping and other infrastructure (Basilico, Gatti, and Amigoni, 2009; Conitzer and Sandholm, 2006; Kiekintveld et al., 2009; Pita et al., 2008). Much of this work has used a *Stackelberg* game framework to model interactions between the security forces and attackers. That is, the defender (i.e., the security forces) acts first by committing to a patrolling or inspection strategy, and the attacker chooses where to attack after observing the defender's choice. The typical solution concept applied to these games is strong Stackelberg equilibrium (SSE), which assumes that the defender will choose an optimal mixed (randomized) strategy based on the assumption that the attacker will observe this strategy and choose an optimal response. This leader-follower paradigm appears to fit many real-world security situations. Indeed, Stackelberg games are at the heart two major decision-support applications: the ARMOR program in use at the Los Angeles International Airport since 2007 to randomize allocation of checkpoints and canine patrols (Pita et al., 2008), and the IRIS program in use by the U.S. Federal Air Marshals to randomize assignments of air marshals to flights (Tsai et al., 2009).

However, there are legitimate concerns about whether the Stackelberg model is appropriate in all cases. In some situations attackers may choose to act without acquiring costly information about the security strategy, especially if security measures are difficult to observe (e.g., undercover officers) and insiders are unavailable. In such cases, a simultaneous-move game model may be a better

Previously published in *Proc. of 9th Int. Conf. on Autonomous Agents and Multiagent Systems (AAMAS 2010)*, van der Hoek, Kaminka, Luck and Sen (eds.) May 10–14, 2010, Toronto, Canada.

Table 12.1. *Example game where
the Stackelberg equilibrium is* not *a
Nash equilibrium*

	c	d
a	2,1	4,0
b	1,0	3,1

reflection of the real situation. The defender faces an unclear choice about which strategy to adopt: the recommendation of the Stackelberg model, or of the simultaneous-move model, or something else entirely? In general settings, the equilibrium strategy can in fact differ between these models. Consider the following game in normal form (Table 12.1):

If the row player has the ability to commit, the SSE strategy is to play a with .5 and b with .5, so that the best response for the column player is to play d, which gives the row player an expected utility of 3.5[2]. On the other hand, if the players move simultaneously the only Nash equilibrium (NE) of this game is for the row player to play a and the column player c. This can be seen by noticing that b is strictly dominated for the row player. Previous work has failed to resolve the defender's dilemma of choosing which strategy to select when the attacker's observation capability is unclear.

We conduct theoretical and experimental analysis of the leader's dilemma, focusing on *security games* (Kiekintveld, et al., 2009). These are non-zero-sum games motivated by real-world security domains, and they are at the heart of applications such as ARMOR and IRIS (Kiekintveld et al., 2009; Pita et al., 2008; Tsai et al., 2009). We make four primary contributions. First, we show that Nash equilibria are interchangeable in security games, avoiding equilibrium selection problems. Second, if the game satisfies the *SSAS* (Subsets of Schedules are Schedules) property, the defender's set of SSE strategies is a subset of her NE strategies. In this case, the defender is always playing a best response by using an SSE regardless of whether or not the attacker observes the defender's strategy. Third, we provide counter-examples to this (partial) equivalence in two cases: (1) when the *SSAS* property does not hold for defender schedules, and (2) when the attacker can attack multiple targets simultaneously. In these cases, the defender's SSE strategy may not be part of any NE profile. Finally,

---

[2] In these games it is assumed that if the follower is indifferent, he breaks the tie in the leader's favor (otherwise, the optimal solution is not well defined).

our experimental tests show that the fraction of games where the SSE strategy played is not part of any NE profile is vanishingly small. However, when attackers can attack multiple targets a relatively large number of games have distinct SSE and NE strategies.

12.2 Motivating Domains

We study quite general classes of security games in this work, but with assumptions motivated by two real-world applications. The first is the ARMOR security system deployed at the Los Angeles International Airport (LAX) (Pita et al., 2008). In this domain police are able to set up checkpoints on roads leading to particular terminals, and assign canine units (bomb-sniffing dogs) to patrol terminals. Police resources in this domain are homogeneous and do not have significant scheduling constraints.

IRIS is a similar application deployed by the Federal Air Marshals Service (FAMS) (Tsai et al., 2009). Armed marshals are assigned to commercial flights to deter and defeat terrorist attacks. This domain has more complex constraints. In particular, marshals are assigned to tours of flights that return to the same destination, and the tours on which any given marshal is available to fly are limited by the marshal's current location and timing constraints. The types of scheduling and resource constraints we consider in this work are motivated by those necessary to represent this domain.

Additionally, there are many other potential security applications, for example, the Los Angeles Port domain, where port police patrol the docks to ensure the safety and security of all passenger, cargo, and vessel operations.

12.3 Definitions and Notation

A security game (Kiekintveld et al., 2009) is a two-player game between a defender and an attacker. The attacker may choose to attack any target from the set $T = \{t_1, t_2, \ldots, t_n\}$. The defender tries to prevent attacks by covering targets using resources from the set $R = \{r_1, r_2, \ldots, r_K\}$. As shown in Figure 12.1, $U_d^c(t_i)$ is the defender's utility if t_i is attacked while t_i is covered by some defender resource. If t_i is not covered, the defender gets $U_d^u(t_i)$. The attacker's utility is denoted similarly by $U_a^c(t_i)$ and $U_a^u(t_i)$. We use $\Delta U_d(t_i) = U_d^c(t_i) - U_d^u(t_i)$ to denote the difference between defender's covered and uncovered utilities. Similarly, $\Delta U_a(t_i) = U_a^u(t_i) - U_a^c(t_i)$. As a key property of security games, we assume $\Delta U_d(t_i) > 0$ and $\Delta U_a(t_i) > 0$. In other words, adding resources to cover a target helps the defender and hurts the attacker.

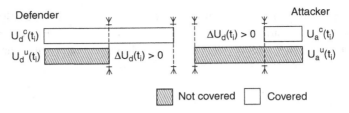

Figure 12.1. Payoff structure of security games.

Motivated by FAMS and similar real-world domains, we introduce resource and scheduling constraints for the defender. Resources may be assigned to *schedules* covering multiple targets, $s \subseteq T$. For each resource r_i, there is a subset S_i of the schedules S that resource r_i can potentially cover. That is, r_i can cover any $s \in S_i$. In the FAMS domain, flights are targets and air marshals are resources. Schedules capture the idea that air marshals fly tours and must return to a particular starting point. Heterogeneous resources can express additional timing and location constraints that limit the tours on which any particular marshal can be assigned to fly. An important subset of the FAMS domain can be modeled using fixed schedules of size 2 (i.e., a pair of departing and returning flights). The LAX domain is also a subclass of security games as defined here, with schedules of size 1 and homogeneous resources.

A security game of the foregoing description can be represented as a normal-form game, as follows. The attacker's pure strategy space $\mathcal{A}$ is the set of targets. The attacker's mixed strategy $\mathbf{a} = \langle a_i \rangle$ is a vector where a_i represents the probability of attacking t_i. The defender's pure strategy is a feasible assignment of resources to schedules, that is, $\langle s_i \rangle \in \prod_{i=1}^{K} S_i$. Since covering a target with one resource is essentially the same as covering it with any positive number of resources, the defender's pure strategy can also be represented by a coverage vector $\mathbf{d} = \langle d_i \rangle \in \{0, 1\}^n$, where d_i represents whether t_i is covered or not. For example, $\langle \{t_1, t_4\}, \{t_2\} \rangle$ can be a possible assignment, and the corresponding coverage vector is $\langle 1, 1, 0, 1 \rangle$. However, not all the coverage vectors are feasible because of resource and schedule constraints. We denote the set of feasible coverage vectors by $\mathcal{D} \subseteq \{0, 1\}^n$.

The defender's mixed strategy $\mathbf{C}$ specifies the probabilities of playing each $\mathbf{d} \in \mathcal{D}$, where each individual probability is denoted by $C_{\mathbf{d}}$. Let $\mathbf{c} = \langle c_i \rangle$ be the vector of coverage probabilities corresponding to $\mathbf{C}$, where $c_i = \sum_{\mathbf{d} \in \mathcal{D}} d_i C_{\mathbf{d}}$ is the marginal probability of covering t_i. For example, suppose the defender has two coverage vectors: $\mathbf{d}_1 = \langle 1, 1, 0 \rangle$ and $\mathbf{d}_2 = \langle 0, 1, 1 \rangle$. Then $\mathbf{C} = \langle .5, .5 \rangle$ is one defender's mixed strategy, and the corresponding $\mathbf{c} = \langle .5, 1, .5 \rangle$. Denote the mapping from $\mathbf{C}$ to $\mathbf{c}$ by φ, so that $\mathbf{c} = \varphi(\mathbf{C})$.

If strategy profile $\langle \mathbf{C}, \mathbf{a} \rangle$ is played, the defender's utility is

$$U_d(\mathbf{C}, \mathbf{a}) = \sum_i^n a_i \left(c_i U_d^c(t_i) + (1 - c_i) U_d^u(t_i) \right),$$

while the attacker's utility is

$$U_a(\mathbf{C}, \mathbf{a}) = \sum_i^n a_i \left(c_i U_a^c(t_i) + (1 - c_i) U_a^u(t_i) \right).$$

If the players move simultaneously, the standard solution concept is Nash equilibrium.

Definition 12.1. *A pair of strategies $\langle \mathbf{C}, \mathbf{a} \rangle$ forms a* Nash equilibrium *(NE) if they satisfy the following:*

1. *The defender plays a best-response:*
   $U_d(\mathbf{C}, \mathbf{a}) \geq U_d(\mathbf{C}', \mathbf{a}) \, \forall \mathbf{C}'.$
2. *The attacker plays a best-response:*
   $U_a(\mathbf{C}, \mathbf{a}) \geq U_a(\mathbf{C}, \mathbf{a}') \, \forall \mathbf{a}'.$

In our Stackelberg model, the defender chooses a mixed strategy first, and the attacker chooses a strategy after observing the defender's choice. The attacker's response function is $g(\mathbf{C}) : \mathbf{C} \to \mathbf{a}$. In this case, the standard solution concept is Strong Stackelberg Equilibrium (Leitmann, 1978; von Stengel and Zamir, 2004).

Definition 12.2. *A pair of strategies $\langle \mathbf{C}, g \rangle$ forms a* strong Stackelberg equilibrium *(SSE) if they satisfy the following:*

1. *The leader (defender) plays a best-response:*
   $U_d(\mathbf{C}, g(\mathbf{C})) \geq U_d(\mathbf{C}', g(\mathbf{C}')), \text{ for all } \mathbf{C}'.$
2. *The follower (attacker) plays a best-response:*
   $U_a(\mathbf{C}, g(\mathbf{C})) \geq U_a(\mathbf{C}, g'(\mathbf{C})), \text{ for all } \mathbf{C}, g'.$
3. *The follower breaks ties optimally for the leader:*
   $U_d(\mathbf{C}, g(\mathbf{C})) \geq U_d(\mathbf{C}, \tau(\mathbf{C})), \text{ for all } \mathbf{C}, \text{ where } \tau(\mathbf{C}) \text{ is the set of follower best-responses to } \mathbf{C}.$

We denote the set of mixed strategies for the defender that are played in some Nash equilibrium by Ω_{NE}, and the corresponding set for strong Stackelberg equilibrium by Ω_{SSE}.

Table 12.2. *A security game that is not strategically zero-sum*

	t_1		t_2		t_3	
	C	U	C	U	C	U
Def	1	0	2	0	3	0
Att	0	1	0	1	0	1

12.4 Equilibria in Security Games

The challenge for us is to understand the fundamental relationships between the SSE and NE strategies in security games. A special case is zero-sum security games, where the defender's utility is the exact opposite of the attacker's utility. For finite two-person, zero-sum games, it is known that the different game theoretic solution concepts of NE, minimax, maximin and SSE all give the same answer. In addition, Nash equilibrium strategies of zero-sum games have a very useful property in that they are *interchangeable*: An equilibrium strategy for one player can be paired with the other player's strategy from *any* equilibrium profile, and the result is an equilibrium, and the payoffs for both players remain the same.

Unfortunately, security games are not necessarily zero-sum (and are not zero-sum in deployed applications). Many properties of zero-sum games do not hold in security games. For instance, a minimax strategy in a security game may not be a maximin strategy. Consider the example in Table 12.2, in which there are three targets and one defender resource. The defender has three actions; each of defender's actions can only cover one target at a time, leaving the other targets uncovered. While all three targets are equally appealing to the attacker, the defender has varying utilities of capturing the attacker at different targets. For the defender, the unique minimax strategy, $\langle 1/3, 1/3, 1/3 \rangle$, is different from the unique maximin strategy, $\langle 6/11, 3/11, 2/11 \rangle$.

Strategically zero-sum games (Moulin and Vial, 1978) are a natural and strict superset of zero-sum games for which most of the desirable properties of zero-sum games still hold. This is exactly the class of games for which no completely mixed Nash equilibrium can be improved upon. Moulin and Vial proved a game (A, B) is strategically zero-sum if and only if there exist $u > 0$ and $v > 0$ such that $uA + vB = U + V$, where U is a matrix with identical columns and V is a matrix with identical rows (Moulin and Vial, 1978). Unfortunately, security games are not even strategically zero-sum. The game in Table 12.2 is a counter-example, because otherwise there must exist $u, v > 0$ such that

$$u \begin{pmatrix} 1 & 0 & 0 \\ 0 & 2 & 0 \\ 0 & 0 & 3 \end{pmatrix} + v \begin{pmatrix} 0 & 1 & 1 \\ 1 & 0 & 1 \\ 1 & 1 & 0 \end{pmatrix}$$

$$= \begin{pmatrix} a & a & a \\ b & b & b \\ c & c & c \end{pmatrix} + \begin{pmatrix} x & y & z \\ x & y & z \\ x & y & z \end{pmatrix}$$

From these equations, $a + y = a + z = b + x = b + z = c + x = c + y = v$, which implies $x = y = z$ and $a = b = c$. We also know $a + x = u$, $b + y = 2u$, $c + z = 3u$. However, since $a + x = b + y = c + z$, u must be 0, which contradicts the assumption $u > 0$.

Nevertheless, we show in the rest of this section that security games still have some important properties. We start by establishing equivalence between the set of defender's minimax strategies and the set of defender's NE strategies. Second, we show that Nash equilibria in security games are interchangeable, resolving the defender's equilibrium strategy selection problem in simultaneous-move games. Third, we show that under a natural restriction on schedules, any SSE strategy for the defender is also a minimax strategy and hence an NE strategy. This resolves the defender's dilemma about whether to play according to SSE or NE when there is uncertainty about attacker's ability to observe the strategy. Finally, for a restricted class of games (including the games from the LAX domain), we find that there is a unique SSE/NE defender strategy and a unique attacker NE strategy.

12.4.1 Equivalence of NE and Minimax

We first prove that any defender's NE strategy is also a minimax strategy. Then for every defender's minimax strategy $\mathbf{C}$ we construct a strategy $\mathbf{a}$ for the attacker such that $\langle \mathbf{C}, \mathbf{a} \rangle$ is an NE profile.

Definition 12.3. *For a defender's mixed strategy $\mathbf{C}$, define the attacker's best response utility by $E(\mathbf{C}) = \max_{i=1}^{n} U_a(\mathbf{C}, t_i)$. Denote the minimum of the attacker's best response utilities over all defender's strategies by $E^* = \min_{\mathbf{C}} E(\mathbf{C})$. The set of defender's minimax strategies is defined as*

$$\Omega_M = \{\mathbf{C} | E(\mathbf{C}) = E^*\}.$$

We define the function f as follows. If $\mathbf{a}$ is an attacker's strategy in which target t_i is attacked with probability a_i, then $f(\mathbf{a}) = \bar{\mathbf{a}}$ is an attacker's strategy such that

$$\bar{a}_i = \lambda a_i \frac{\Delta U_d(t_i)}{\Delta U_a(t_i)}$$

where $\lambda > 0$ is a normalizing constant such that $\sum_i^n \bar{a}_i = 1$. The inverse function $f^{-1}(\bar{\mathbf{a}}) = \mathbf{a}$ is given by the following equation:

$$a_i = \frac{1}{\lambda} \bar{a}_i \frac{\Delta U_a(t_i)}{\Delta U_d(t_i)} \tag{12.1}$$

Lemma 12.1. *Consider a security game $\mathcal{G}$. Construct the corresponding zero-sum security game $\bar{\mathcal{G}}$ in which the defender's utilities are redefined as follows:*

$$U_d^c(t) = -U_a^c(t)$$
$$U_d^u(t) = -U_a^u(t)$$

Then $\langle \mathbf{C}, \mathbf{a} \rangle$ is an NE profile in $\mathcal{G}$ if and only if $\langle \mathbf{C}, f(\mathbf{a}) \rangle$ is an NE profile in $\bar{\mathcal{G}}$.

Proof. Note that the supports of strategies $\mathbf{a}$ and $\bar{\mathbf{a}}$ are the same, and also that the attacker's utility function is the same in games $\mathcal{G}$ and $\bar{\mathcal{G}}$. Thus $\mathbf{a}$ is a best response to $\mathbf{C}$ in $\mathcal{G}$ if and only if $\bar{\mathbf{a}}$ is a best response to $\mathbf{C}$ in $\bar{\mathcal{G}}$.

Denote the utility that the defender gets if profile $\langle \mathbf{C}, \mathbf{a} \rangle$ is played in game $\mathcal{G}$ by $U_d^{\mathcal{G}}(\mathbf{C}, \mathbf{a})$. To show that $\mathbf{C}$ is a best response to $\mathbf{a}$ in game $\mathcal{G}$ if and only if $\mathbf{C}$ is a best response to $\bar{\mathbf{a}}$ in $\bar{\mathcal{G}}$, it is sufficient to show equivalence of the following two inequalities.

$$U_d^{\mathcal{G}}(\mathbf{C}, \mathbf{a}) - U_d^{\mathcal{G}}(\mathbf{C}', \mathbf{a}) \geq 0$$
$$\Leftrightarrow U_d^{\bar{\mathcal{G}}}(\mathbf{C}, \bar{\mathbf{a}}) - U_d^{\bar{\mathcal{G}}}(\mathbf{C}', \bar{\mathbf{a}}) \geq 0$$

We will prove the equivalence by starting from the first inequality and transforming it into the second one. On the one hand, we have

$$U_d^{\mathcal{G}}(\mathbf{C}, \mathbf{a}) - U_d^{\mathcal{G}}(\mathbf{C}', \mathbf{a}) = \sum_i^n a_i(c_i - c_i')\Delta U_d(t_i).$$

Similarly, on the other hand, we have

$$U_d^{\bar{\mathcal{G}}}(\mathbf{C}, \bar{\mathbf{a}}) - U_d^{\bar{\mathcal{G}}}(\mathbf{C}', \bar{\mathbf{a}}) = \sum_i^n \bar{a}_i(c_i - c_i')\Delta U_a(t_i).$$

Given Equation (12.1) and $\lambda > 0$, we have

$$U_d^{\mathcal{G}}(\mathbf{C}, \mathbf{a}) - U_d^{\mathcal{G}}(\mathbf{C}', \mathbf{a}) \geq 0$$

$$\Leftrightarrow \sum_i^n a_i(c_i - c_i')\Delta U_d(t_i) \geq 0$$

$$\Leftrightarrow \sum_i^n \frac{1}{\lambda}\bar{a}_i \frac{\Delta U_a(t_i)}{\Delta U_d(t_i)}(c_i - c_i')\Delta U_d(t_i) \geq 0$$

$$\Leftrightarrow \frac{1}{\lambda}\sum_i^n \bar{a}_i(c_i - c_i')\Delta U_a(t_i) \geq 0$$

$$\Leftrightarrow \frac{1}{\lambda}\left(U_d^{\bar{\mathcal{G}}}(\mathbf{C}, \bar{\mathbf{a}}) - U_d^{\bar{\mathcal{G}}}(\mathbf{C}', \bar{\mathbf{a}})\right) \geq 0$$

$$\Leftrightarrow U_d^{\bar{\mathcal{G}}}(\mathbf{C}, \bar{\mathbf{a}}) - U_d^{\bar{\mathcal{G}}}(\mathbf{C}', \bar{\mathbf{a}}) \geq 0$$

∎

Lemma 12.2. *Suppose* $\mathbf{C}$ *is a defender NE strategy in a security game. Then* $E(\mathbf{C}) = E^*$, *i.e.,* $\Omega_{NE} \subseteq \Omega_M$.

Proof. Suppose $\langle \mathbf{C}, \mathbf{a} \rangle$ is an NE profile in the security game $\mathcal{G}$. According to Lemma 12.1, $\langle \mathbf{C}, f(\mathbf{a}) \rangle$ must be an NE profile in the corresponding zero-sum security game $\bar{\mathcal{G}}$. Since $\mathbf{C}$ is an NE strategy in a zero-sum game, it must also be a minimax strategy (Fudenberg and Tirole, 1991). Thus $E(\mathbf{C}) = E^*$. ∎

Lemma 12.3. *In a security game* $\mathcal{G}$, *any defender's strategy* $\mathbf{C}$ *such that* $E(\mathbf{C}) = E^*$ *is an NE strategy, i.e.,* $\Omega_M \subseteq \Omega_{NE}$.

Proof. $\mathbf{C}$ is a minimax strategy in both $\mathcal{G}$ and the corresponding zero-sum game $\bar{\mathcal{G}}$. Any minimax strategy is also an NE strategy in a zero-sum game (Fudenberg and Tirole, 1991). Then there must exist an NE profile $\langle \mathbf{C}, \bar{\mathbf{a}} \rangle$ in $\bar{\mathcal{G}}$. By Lemma 12.1, $\langle \mathbf{C}, f^{-1}(\bar{\mathbf{a}}) \rangle$ is an NE profile in $\mathcal{G}$. Thus, $\mathbf{C}$ is an NE strategy in $\mathcal{G}$. ∎

Theorem 12.1. *In a security game, the set of defender's minimax strategies is equal to the set of defender's NE strategies, i.e.,* $\Omega_M = \Omega_{NE}$.

Proof. Lemma 12.2 shows that every defender's NE strategy is a minimax strategy, and Lemma 12.3 shows that every defender's minimax strategy is an NE strategy. Thus the sets of defender's NE and minimax strategies must be equal. ∎

12.4.2 Interchangeability of Nash Equilibria

We now show that Nash Equilibria in security games are interchangeable.

Theorem 12.2. *Suppose* $\langle \mathbf{C}, \mathbf{a} \rangle$ *and* $\langle \mathbf{C}', \mathbf{a}' \rangle$ *are two NE profiles in a security game* $\mathcal{G}$. *Then* $\langle \mathbf{C}, \mathbf{a}' \rangle$ *and* $\langle \mathbf{C}', \mathbf{a} \rangle$ *are also NE profiles in* $\mathcal{G}$.

Proof. Consider the corresponding zero-sum game $\bar{\mathcal{G}}$. From Lemma 12.1, both $\langle \mathbf{C}, f(\mathbf{a}) \rangle$ and $\langle \mathbf{C}', f(\mathbf{a}') \rangle$ must be NE profiles in $\bar{\mathcal{G}}$. By the interchange property of NE in zero-sum games (Fudenberg and Tirole, 1991), $\langle \mathbf{C}, f(\mathbf{a}') \rangle$ and $\langle \mathbf{C}', f(\mathbf{a}) \rangle$ must also be NE profiles in $\bar{\mathcal{G}}$. Applying Lemma 12.1 again in the other direction, we get that $\langle \mathbf{C}, \mathbf{a}' \rangle$ and $\langle \mathbf{C}', \mathbf{a} \rangle$ must be NE profiles in $\mathcal{G}$. ∎

By Theorem 12.2, the defender's equilibrium selection problem in a simultaneous-move security game is resolved. The reason is that given the attacker's NE strategy $\mathbf{a}$, the defender must get the same utility by responding with any NE strategy. Next, we give some insights on expected utilities in NE profiles. We first show that the attacker's expected utility is the same in all NE profiles, followed by an example demonstrating that the defender may have varying expected utilities corresponding to different attacker's strategies.

Theorem 12.3. *Suppose* $\langle \mathbf{C}, \mathbf{a} \rangle$ *is an NE profile in a security game. Then,* $U_a(\mathbf{C}, \mathbf{a}) = E^*$.

Proof. From Lemma 12.2, $\mathbf{C}$ is a minimax strategy and $E(\mathbf{C}) = E^*$. On the one hand,

$$U_a(\mathbf{C}, \mathbf{a}) = \sum_i^n a_i U_a(\mathbf{C}, t_i) \leq \sum_i^n a_i E(\mathbf{C}) = E^*.$$

On the other hand, because $\mathbf{a}$ is a best response to $\mathbf{C}$, it should be at least as good as the strategy of attacking $t^* \in \arg\max_t U_a(\mathbf{C}, t)$ with probability 1, that is,

$$U_a(\mathbf{C}, \mathbf{a}) \geq U_a(\mathbf{C}, t^*) = E(\mathbf{C}) = E^*.$$

Therefore we know $U_a(\mathbf{C}, \mathbf{a}) = E^*$. ∎

Unlike the attacker who gets the same utility in all NE profiles, the defender may get varying expected utilities depending on the attacker's strategy selection. Consider the game shown in Table 12.3. The defender can choose to cover one of the two targets at a time. The only defender's NE strategy is to cover t_1 with 100% probability, making the attacker indifferent between attacking t_1 and t_2. One attacker's NE response is always attacking t_1, which gives the defender an expected utility of 1. Another attacker's NE strategy is $\langle 2/3, 1/3 \rangle$, given which the defender is indifferent between defending t_1 and t_2. In this case, the

Table 12.3. *A security game in which the defender's expected utility varies in different NE profiles*

	t_1		t_2	
	C	U	C	U
Def	1	0	2	0
Att	1	2	0	1

Table 12.4. *A schedule-constrained security game where the defender's SSE strategy is not an NE strategy.*

	t_1		t_2		t_3		t_4	
	C	U	C	U	C	U	C	U
Def	10	9	−2	−3	1	0	1	0
Att	2	5	3	4	0	1	0	1

defender's utility decreases to 2/3 because she captures the attacker with a lower probability.

12.4.3 SSE and Minimax/NE

We have already shown that the set of defender's NE strategies coincides with her minimax strategies. If every defender's SSE strategy is also a minimax strategy, then SSE strategies must also be NE strategies. The defender can then safely commit to an SSE strategy; there is no selection problem for the defender. Unfortunately, if a security game has arbitrary scheduling constraints, then an SSE strategy may not be part of any NE profile. For example, consider the game in Table 12.4 with four targets $\{t_1,\ldots,t_4\}$, two schedules $s_1 = \{t_1,t_2\}$, $s_2 = \{t_3,t_4\}$, and a single defender resource. The defender always prefers that t_1 is attacked, and t_3 and t_4 are never appealing to the attacker.

There is a unique SSE strategy for the defender, which places as much coverage probability on s_1 as possible without making t_2 more appealing to the attacker than t_1. The rest of the coverage probability is placed on s_2. The result is that s_1 and s_2 are both covered with probability 0.5. In contrast, in a simultaneous-move game, t_3 and t_4 are dominated for the attacker. Thus, there is no reason for the defender to place resources on targets that are never attacked, so the defender's unique NE strategy covers s_1 with probability 1. That is, the defender's SSE strategy is different from the NE strategy. The difference between the defender's payoffs in these cases can also be arbitrarily large because t_1 is always attacked in an SSE, and t_2 is always attacked in a NE.

The above example restricts the defender to protect t_1 and t_2 together, which makes it impossible for the defender to put more coverage on t_2 without making t_1 less appealing. If the defender could assign resources to any subset of a schedule, this difficulty is resolved. More formally, we assume that for any resource r_i, any subset of a schedule in S_i is also a possible schedule in S_i:

$$\forall 1 \le i \le K : s' \subseteq s \in S_i \Rightarrow s' \in S_i. \tag{12.2}$$

If a security game satisfies Equation (12.2), we say it has the *SSAS* property. This is natural in many security domains since it is often possible to cover *fewer* targets than the maximum number that a resource could possibly cover in a schedule. We find that this property is sufficient to ensure that the defender's SSE strategy must also be an NE strategy.

Lemma 12.4. *Suppose* $\mathbf{C}$ *is a defender strategy in a security game that satisfies the* SSAS *property, and* $\mathbf{c} = \varphi(\mathbf{C})$ *is the corresponding vector of marginal probabilities. Then for any* $\mathbf{c}'$ *such that* $0 \le c_i' \le c_i$ *for all* $t_i \in T$, *there must exist a defender strategy* $\mathbf{C}'$ *such that* $\varphi(\mathbf{C}') = \mathbf{c}'$.

Proof. The proof is by induction on the number of t_i where $c_i' \neq c_i$, as denoted by $\delta(\mathbf{c}, \mathbf{c}')$. As the base case, if there is no i such that $c_i' \neq c_i$, the existence trivially holds because $\varphi(\mathbf{C}) = \mathbf{c}'$. Suppose the existence holds for all $\mathbf{c}, \mathbf{c}'$ such that $\delta(\mathbf{c}, \mathbf{c}') = k$, where $0 \le k \le n-1$. We consider any $\mathbf{c}, \mathbf{c}'$ where $\delta(\mathbf{c}, \mathbf{c}') = k+1$. Then for some j, $c_j' \neq c_j$. Since $c_j' \ge 0$ and $c_j' < c_j$, we have $c_j > 0$. There must be a nonempty set of coverage vectors $\mathcal{D}_j$ that cover t_j and receive positive probability in $\mathbf{C}$. Because the security game satisfies the *SSAS* property, for every $\mathbf{d} \in \mathcal{D}_j$, there is a valid $\mathbf{d}^-$ which covers all targets in $\mathbf{d}$ except for t_j. From the defender strategy $\mathbf{C}$, by shifting $\frac{C_{\mathbf{d}}(c_j - c_j')}{c_j}$ probability from every $\mathbf{d} \in \mathcal{D}_j$ to the corresponding $\mathbf{d}^-$, we get a defender strategy $\mathbf{C}^\dagger$ where $c_i^\dagger = c_i$ for $i \neq j$, and $c_i^\dagger = c_i'$ for $i = j$. Hence, $\delta(\mathbf{c}^\dagger, \mathbf{c}') = k$, implying there exists a $\mathbf{C}'$ such that $\varphi(\mathbf{C}') = \mathbf{c}'$ by the induction assumption. By induction, the existence holds for any $\mathbf{c}, \mathbf{c}'$. ∎

Theorem 12.4. *Suppose* $\mathbf{C}$ *is a defender SSE strategy in a security game that satisfies the* SSAS *property. Then* $E(\mathbf{C}) = E^*$, *i.e.,* $\Omega_{SSE} \subseteq \Omega_M = \Omega_{NE}$.

Proof. The proof is by contradiction. Suppose $\langle \mathbf{C}, g \rangle$ is an SSE profile in a security game which satisfies the *SSAS* property, and $E(\mathbf{C}) > E^*$. Let $T_a = \{t_i | U_a(\mathbf{C}, t_i) = E(\mathbf{C})\}$ be the set of targets that give the attacker the maximum utility given the defender strategy $\mathbf{C}$. By the definition of SSE, we have

$$U_d(\mathbf{C}, g(\mathbf{C})) = \max_{t_i \in T_a} U_d(\mathbf{C}, t_i).$$

Consider a defender mixed strategy $\mathbf{C}^*$ such that $E(\mathbf{C}^*) = E^*$. Then, for any $t_i \in T_a$, $U_a(\mathbf{C}^*, t_i) \leq E^*$. Consider a vector $\mathbf{c}'$:

$$c_i' = \begin{cases} c_i^* - \dfrac{E^* - U_a(\mathbf{C}^*, t_i) + \epsilon}{U_a^u(t_i) - U_a^c(t_i)}, & t_i \in T_a, \quad (12.3a) \\ c_i^*, & t_i \notin T_a, \quad (12.3b) \end{cases}$$

where ϵ is an infinitesimal positive number. Since $E^* - U_a(\mathbf{C}^*, t_i) + \epsilon > 0$, we have $c_i' < c_i^*$ for all $t_i \in T_a$. On the other hand, since for all $t_i \in T_a$,

$$U_a(\mathbf{c}', t_i) = E^* + \epsilon < E(\mathbf{C}) = U_a(\mathbf{C}, t_i),$$

we have $c_i' > c_i \geq 0$. Then for any $t_i \in T$, we have $0 \leq c_i' \leq c_i^*$. From Lemma 12.4, there exists a defender strategy $\mathbf{C}'$ corresponding to $\mathbf{c}'$. The attacker's utility of attacking each target is as follows:

$$U_a(\mathbf{C}', t_i) = \begin{cases} E^* + \epsilon, & t_i \in T_a, \quad (12.4a) \\ U_a(\mathbf{C}^*, t_i) \leq E^*, & t_i \notin T_a. \quad (12.4b) \end{cases}$$

Thus, the attacker's best responses to $\mathbf{C}'$ are still T_a. For all $t_i \in T_a$, since $c_i' > c_i$, it must be the case that $U_d(\mathbf{C}, t_i) < U_d(\mathbf{C}', t_i)$. By definition of attacker's SSE response g, we have,

$$U_d(\mathbf{C}', g(\mathbf{C}')) = \max_{t_i \in T_a} U_d(\mathbf{C}', t_i)$$

$$> \max_{t_i \in T_a} U_d(\mathbf{C}, t_i) = U_d(\mathbf{C}, g(\mathbf{C})).$$

It follows that the defender is better off using $\mathbf{C}'$, which contradicts the assumption $\mathbf{C}$ is an SSE strategy of the defender. ∎

Theorems 12.1 and 12.4 together imply the following corollary.

Corollary 12.1. *In security games with the* SSAS *property, any defender's SSE strategy is also an NE strategy.*

We can now answer the original question posed in this paper: when there is uncertainty over the type of game played, should the defender choose an SSE strategy or a mixed-strategy NE or some combination of the two? For domains that satisfy the *SSAS* property, we have proven that any of the defender's SSE strategies is also an NE strategy.

Among our motivating domains, the LAX domain satisfies the *SSAS* property since all schedules are of size 1. Other patrolling domains, such as patrolling a port, also satisfy the *SSAS* property. In such domains, the defender could thus commit to an SSE strategy, which is also now known to be an NE strategy. The defender retains the ability to commit, but is still playing a best-response to an attacker in a simultaneous-move setting (assuming that the attacker plays an equilibrium strategy – it does not matter which one, due to the interchange property shown above). However, the FAMS domain does not naturally satisfy the *SSAS* property because marshals must fly complete tours (though, in principle, they could fly as civilians on some legs of a tour). The question of selecting SSE versus NE strategies in this case is addressed experimentally in Section 12.6.

12.4.4 Uniqueness in Restricted Games

The previous sections show that SSE strategies are NE strategies in many cases. However, there may still be multiple equilibria to select from (though this difficulty is alleviated by the interchange property). Here we prove an even stronger uniqueness result for an important restricted class of security domains, which includes the LAX domain. In particular, we consider security games where the defender has homogeneous resources that can cover any single target. The *SSAS* property is trivially satisfied, since all schedules are of size 1. Any vector of coverage probabilities $\mathbf{c} = \langle c_i \rangle$ such that $\sum_i^n c_i \leq K$ is a feasible strategy for the defender, so we can represent the defender strategy by marginal coverage probabilities. With a minor restriction on the attacker's payoff matrix, the defender always has a unique minimax strategy that is also the unique SSE and NE strategy. Furthermore, the attacker also has a unique NE response to this strategy.

Theorem 12.5. *In a security game with homogeneous resources that can cover any single target, if for every target $t_i \in T$, $U_a^c(t_i) \neq E^*$, then the defender has a unique minimax, NE, and SSE strategy.*

Proof. We first show the defender has a unique minimax strategy. Let $T^* = \{t | U_a^u(t) \geq E^*\}$. Define $\mathbf{c}^* = \langle c_i^* \rangle$ as

$$
c_i^* = \begin{cases} \dfrac{U_a^u(t_i) - E^*}{U_a^u(t_i) - U_a^c(t_i)}, & t_i \in T^*, & (12.5a) \\[2ex] 0, & t_i \notin T^*. & (12.5b) \end{cases}
$$

Note that E^* cannot be less than any $U_a^c(t_i)$ – otherwise, regardless of the defender's strategy, the attacker could always get at least $U_a^c(t_i) > E^*$ by attacking t_i, which contradicts the fact that E^* is the attacker's best response utility to a defender's minimax strategy. Since $E^* \geq U_a^c(t_i)$ and we assume $E^* \neq U_a^c(t_i)$,

$$1 - c_i^* = \frac{E^* - U_a^c(t_i)}{U_a^u(t_i) - U_a^c(t_i)} > 0 \Rightarrow c_i^* < 1.$$

Next, we will prove $\sum_i^n c_i^* \geq K$. For the sake of contradiction, suppose $\sum_i^n c_i^* < K$. Let $\mathbf{c}' = \langle c_i' \rangle$, where $c_i' = c_i^* + \epsilon$. Since $c_i^* < 1$ and $\sum_i^n c_i^* < K$, we can find $\epsilon > 0$ such that $c_i' < 1$ and $\sum_i^n c_i' < K$. Then every target has strictly higher coverage in $\mathbf{c}'$ than in $\mathbf{c}^*$; hence, $E(\mathbf{c}') < E(\mathbf{c}^*) = E^*$, which contradicts the fact that E^* is the minimum of all $E(\mathbf{c})$.

Next, we show that if $\mathbf{c}$ is a minimax strategy, then $\mathbf{c} = \mathbf{c}^*$. By the definition of a minimax strategy, $E(\mathbf{c}) = E^*$. Hence, $U_a(\mathbf{c}, t_i) \leq E^* \Rightarrow c_i \geq c_i^*$. On the one hand, $\sum_i^n c_i \leq K$ and, on the other hand, $\sum_i^n c_i \geq \sum_i^n c_i^* \geq K$. Therefore, it must be the case that $c_i = c_i^*$ for any i. Hence, $\mathbf{c}^*$ is the unique minimax strategy of the defender.

Furthermore, by Theorem 12.1, we have that $\mathbf{c}^*$ is the unique defender's NE strategy. By Theorem 12.4 and the existence of SSE (Basar and Olsder, 1995), we have that $\mathbf{c}^*$ is the unique defender's SSE strategy. ∎

Theorem 12.6. *In a security game with homogeneous resources that can cover any one target, if for every target $t_i \in T$, $U_a^c(t_i) \neq E^*$ and $U_a^u(t_i) \neq E^*$, then the attacker has a unique NE strategy.*

Proof. $\mathbf{c}^*$ and T^* are the same as in the proof of Theorem 12.5. Given the defender's unique NE strategy $\mathbf{c}^*$, in any attacker's best response, only $t_i \in T^*$ can be attacked with positive probability, because,

$$U_a(\mathbf{c}^*, t_i) = \begin{cases} E^* & t_i \in T^* & (12.6a) \\ U_a^u(t_i) < E^* & t_i \notin T^* & (12.6b) \end{cases}$$

Suppose $\langle \mathbf{c}^*, \mathbf{a} \rangle$ forms an NE profile. We have

$$\sum_{t_i \in T^*} a_i = 1 \qquad (12.7)$$

For any $t_i \in T^*$, we know from the proof of Theorem 12.5 that $c_i^* < 1$. In addition, because $U_a^u(t) \neq E^*$, we have $c_i^* \neq 0$. Thus we have $0 < c_i^* < 1$ for any $t_i \in T^*$. For any $t_i, t_j \in T^*$, necessarily $a_i \Delta U_d(t_i) = a_j \Delta U_d(t_j)$. Otherwise, assume $a_i \Delta U_d(t_i) > a_j \Delta U_d(t_j)$. Consider another defender's strategy $\mathbf{c}'$ where $c_i' = c_i^* + \epsilon < 1$, $c_j' = c_j^* - \epsilon > 0$, and $c_k' = c_k^*$ for any $k \neq i, j$.

$$U_d(\mathbf{c}', \mathbf{a}) - U_d(\mathbf{c}^*, \mathbf{a}) = a_i \epsilon \Delta U_d(t_i) - a_j \epsilon \Delta U_d(t_j) > 0.$$

Hence, $\mathbf{c}^*$ is not a best response to $\mathbf{a}$, which contradicts the assumption that $\langle \mathbf{c}^*, \mathbf{a} \rangle$ is an NE profile. Therefore, there exists $\beta > 0$ such that, for any $t_i \in T^*$, $a_i \Delta U_d(t_i) = \beta$. Substituting a_i with $\beta / \Delta U_d(t_i)$ in Equation (12.7), we have

$$\beta = \frac{1}{\displaystyle\sum_{t_i \in T^*} \frac{1}{\Delta U_d(t_i)}}.$$

Then we can explicitly write down $\mathbf{a}$ as

$$a_i = \begin{cases} \dfrac{\beta}{\Delta U_d(t_i)}, & t_i \in T^*, & \text{(12.8a)} \\[2ex] 0, & t_i \notin T^*. & \text{(12.8b)} \end{cases}$$

As we can see, $\mathbf{a}$ defined by (12.8a) and (12.8b) is the unique attacker NE strategy. ∎

The implication of Theorem 12.5 and Theorem 12.6 is that in the simultaneous-move game, both the defender and the attacker have a unique NE strategy, which gives each player a unique expected utility as a result.

12.5 Multiple Attacker Resources

To this point we have assumed that the attacker will attack exactly one target. We now extend our security game definition to allow the attacker to use multiple resources to attack multiple targets simultaneously. To keep the model simple, we assume homogeneous resources (for both players) and schedules of size 1. The defender has $K < n$ resources that can be assigned to protect any target, and the attacker has $L < n$ resources that can be used to attack any target. Attacking the same target with multiple resources is equivalent to attacking with a single resource. The defender's pure strategy is a coverage vector $\mathbf{d} = \langle d_i \rangle \in \mathcal{D}$, where $d_i \in \{0, 1\}$ represents whether t_i is covered or not. Similarly, the attacker's pure strategy is an attack vector $\mathbf{q} = \langle q_i \rangle \in \mathcal{Q}$. We have $\sum_i^n d_i = K$ and $\sum_i^n q_i = L$. If pure strategies $\langle \mathbf{d}, \mathbf{q} \rangle$ are played, the attacker gets a utility of

$$U_a(\mathbf{d}, \mathbf{q}) = \sum_i^n q_i \left(d_i U_a^c(t_i) + (1 - d_i) U_a^u(t_i) \right),$$

while the defender's utility is given by

$$U_d(\mathbf{d}, \mathbf{q}) = \sum_i^n q_i \left(d_i U_d^c(t_i) + (1 - d_i) U_d^u(t_i) \right).$$

Table 12.5. *A security game with multiple attacker resources where the defender's SSE strategy is not an NE strategy.*

	t_1		t_2		t_3	
	C	U	C	U	C	U
Def	0	-1	-100	$-100 - \epsilon$	0	$0 - \epsilon$
Att	$100 - \epsilon$	100	0	10	$5 - \epsilon$	5

The defender's mixed strategy is a vector **C** that specifies the probability of playing each $\mathbf{d} \in \mathcal{D}$. Similarly, the attacker's mixed strategy **A** is a vector of probabilities corresponding to all $\mathbf{q} \in \mathcal{Q}$.

In security games with multiple attacker resources, the defender's SSE strategy may not be part of any NE profile, even if there are no scheduling constraints. Consider the game shown in Table 12.5.

There are three targets t_1, t_2, t_3. The defender has one resource, and the attacker has two resources. Therefore, the defender's pure strategy space is the set of targets to protect: $\{t_1, t_2, t_3\}$, whereas the attacker's pure strategy space consists of the pairs of targets: $\{\langle t_1, t_2 \rangle, \langle t_1, t_3 \rangle, \langle t_2, t_3 \rangle\}$. If the defender protects t_1 and the attacker attacks $\langle t_1, t_2 \rangle$, the defender's utility is $U_d^c(t_1) + U_d^u(t_2) = -100 - \epsilon$ and the attacker's utility is $U_a^c(t_1) + U_a^u(t_2) = 110 - \epsilon$. In this example, t_1 is very appealing to the attacker no matter whether or not it is covered, so t_1 is always attacked. If t_2 is attacked, the defender gets a very low utility, even if t_2 is defended. So in the SSE, the defender wants to make sure that t_2 is not attacked. The defender's SSE strategy places at least .5 probability on t_2, so that t_1 and t_3 are attacked instead of t_2 (recall that the attacker breaks ties in the defender's favor in an SSE). The attacker's SSE response is $\mathbf{A} = \langle 0, 1, 0 \rangle$, that is, to always attack t_1 and t_3. The other .5 defense probability will be placed on t_1 because $\Delta U_d(t_1) > \Delta U_d(t_3)$. So, the SSE profile is $\langle \mathbf{C}, \mathbf{A} \rangle$, where $\mathbf{C} = \langle .5, .5, 0 \rangle$.

Next, we show that there is no NE in which the defender plays **C**. Suppose there is an NE profile $\langle \mathbf{C}, \mathbf{A}' \rangle$. Given **C**, the attacker's utility for attacking t_1 is higher than the utility for attacking t_2, so it must be that t_1 is always attacked in this NE. Therefore, the attacker never plays $\langle t_2, t_3 \rangle$. However, this implies that t_1 is the most appealing target for the defender to cover, because $U_d(t_1, \mathbf{A}) > U_d(t_i, \mathbf{A}), i \in \{2, 3\}$. So, to be a best response, the coverage of t_1 would need to be 1 instead of 0.5, contradicting the assumption that **C** is an equilibrium strategy for the defender.

12.6 Experimental Results

While our theoretical results resolve the leader's dilemma for many interesting classes of security games, as we have seen, there are still some cases where SSE strategies are distinct from NE strategies for the defender. One such case is when security games do not satisfy the *SSAS* property, and another is when the attacker has multiple resources. We conduct experiments to further investigate these two cases, offering evidence about the frequency with which SSE strategies differ from all NE strategies across randomly generated games using thirty-six different parameter settings.

For a particular game instance we first compute an SSE strategy C using the DOBSS mixed-integer linear program (Pita et al., 2008). We then use the linear feasibility program below to determine whether or not this SSE strategy is part of some NE profile by attempting to find an appropriate attacker response strategy.

$$A_{\mathbf{q}} \in [0, 1], \text{ for all } \mathbf{q} \in \mathcal{Q} \tag{12.9}$$

$$\sum_{\mathbf{q} \in \mathcal{Q}} A_{\mathbf{q}} = 1 \tag{12.10}$$

$$A_{\mathbf{q}} = 0, \text{ for all } U_a(\mathbf{q}, \mathbf{C}) < E(\mathbf{C}) \tag{12.11}$$

$$\sum_{\mathbf{q} \in \mathcal{Q}} A_{\mathbf{q}} U_d(\mathbf{d}, \mathbf{q}) \leq Z, \text{ for all } \mathbf{d} \in \mathcal{D} \tag{12.12}$$

$$\sum_{\mathbf{q} \in \mathcal{Q}} A_{\mathbf{q}} U_d(\mathbf{d}, \mathbf{q}) = Z, \text{ for all } d \in D \text{ with } C_{\mathbf{d}} > 0 \tag{12.13}$$

Here, $\mathcal{Q}$ is the set of attacker pure strategies, which is just the set of targets when there is only one attacker resource. The probability that the attacker plays $\mathbf{q}$ is denoted by $A_{\mathbf{q}}$, which must be between 0 and 1 (Constraint 12.9). Constraint 12.10 forces the probabilities to sum to 1. Constraint 12.11 prevents the attacker from placing positive probabilities on pure strategies that give the attacker a utility less than the best-response utility $E(\mathbf{C})$. In Constraints 12.12 and 12.13, Z is a variable representing the maximum expected utility the defender can get among all pure strategies given the attacker's strategy $\mathbf{A}$, and $C_{\mathbf{d}}$ denotes the probability of playing $\mathbf{d}$ in $\mathbf{C}$. These two constraints require the defender's strategy $\mathbf{C}$ to be a best response to the attacker's mixed strategy. Therefore, a feasible solution $\mathbf{A}$ is an NE strategy for the attacker. Conversely, if $\langle \mathbf{C}, \mathbf{A} \rangle$ is an NE profile, $\mathbf{A}$ must satisfy all of the LP constraints.

We first test single-attacker games, fixing the number of targets at ten and the number of defender resources at three. We vary the number of schedules, the size of the schedules, and the number of resource types. Each test set consists of

Table 12.6. *Number of instances out of*
10000 single-attacker security games in
which SSE is not NE

	5	10	15	20
2S / 1R	316	103	27	3
2S / 2R	313	82	22	2
2S / 3R	297	101	18	3
3S / 1R	933	555	165	32
3S / 2R	858	494	172	35
3S / 3R	867	551	155	35
4S / 1R	990	912	515	183
4S / 2R	1029	950	492	190
4S / 3R	1005	927	483	173

10000 games, with payoffs drawn from $U[-100,0]$ for $U_d^u(t_i)$ and $U_a^c(t_i)$, and $U[0,100]$ for $U_d^c(t_i)$ and $U_a^u(t_i)$ Table 12.6 summarizes our results. A column represents a number of schedules, and a row represents a pair of schedule size and number of resource types. For example, looking at row 2 and column 2, we see that among 10000 games with five schedules of size 2 and one resource type, there are 316 cases in which the defender's SSE strategy is not an NE strategy. The number of cases in which the defender's SSE strategy is not an NE strategy is never more than 10.5% in any of the thirtysix settings we tested. This number decreases as we increase the number of schedules. With twenty available schedules, the number is less than 2%. The main implication of these results is that, in practice, committing to an SSE strategy is likely to be a good approach in almost all cases. This is particularly true in domains like FAMS, where schedule sizes are relatively small (2 in most cases), and the number of possible schedules is large relative to the number of targets.

Table 12.7 shows the results for varying numbers of attacker resources. Again, each set has 10000 games. As the number of attacker resources increases, the number of cases in which the defender's SSE strategy is not an NE strategy increases. With two, three, and four attacker resources, the numbers are 27%, 54%, and 69% respectively, which implies the defender cannot simply play an SSE strategy when there are multiple attacker resources. This result poses an interesting direction for future work, since it is unclear how a defender should play in these games if the attacker's ability to observe the mixed strategy is uncertain.

Table 12.7. *Number of
instances out of 10000
multiple-attacker security
games in which SSE is not NE*

	2	3	4
#SSE$\neq$NE	2692	5368	6873

12.7 Summary and Related Work

There has been significant interest in understanding the interaction of observability and commitment in general Stackelberg games. Bagwell's early work (Bagwell, 1995) questions the value of commitment to pure strategies given noisy observations by followers; but the ensuing and ongoing debate illustrated that the leader retains her advantage in case of commitment to mixed strategies (Huck and Müller, 2000; van Damme and Hurkens, 1997). The value of commitment for the leader when observations are costly is also studied in (Morgan and Vardy, 2007). In contrast with this research, our work focuses on real-world security games, illustrating subset, equivalence, interchangeability, and uniqueness properties that are nonexistent in general Stackelberg games studied previously.

Pita et al. (2009) provide experimental results on observability in Stackelberg games. They test a variety of defender strategies against human players (attackers) who choose their optimal attack when provided with limited observations of defender strategy. Results show the superiority of a defender's strategy that is computed assuming human "anchoring bias" in attributing probability distribution over the defender's actions. This research complements ours, which provides new mathematical foundations. Testing the insights of our research with the experimental paradigm of Pita et al. (2009), with expert players, is an interesting topic for future research.

Going back to the foundations of game theory, Von Neumman and Morgenstern (2004) provided a key result on interchangeability: for two-player zero-sum games, any combination of players' maximin strategies is in equilibrium. However, our security games are neither zero-sum nor strategically zero-sum (as seen earlier).

To summarize, this paper is focused on a general class of defender-attacker Stackelberg games that are directly inspired by real-world security applications. The paper confronts fundamental questions of how a defender should compute her mixed strategy. In this context, this paper provides four key contributions. First, exploiting the structure of these security games, the paper shows that the Nash equilibria in security games are interchangeable, thus alleviating the defender's equilibrium selection problem for simultaneous-move games. Second, resolving the defender's dilemma, it shows that under the *SSAS* restriction on security games, any Stackelberg strategy is also a Nash equilibrium strategy; furthermore, this strategy is unique in a class of real-world security games of which ARMOR is a key exemplar. Third, when faced with a follower that can attack multiple targets, many of these properties no longer hold, providing a key direction for future research. Fourth, our experimental results emphasize positive properties of security games that do not fit the *SSAS* property. In practical terms, these contributions imply that defenders in applications such as ARMOR (Pita et al., 2008) and IRIS (Tsai et al., 2009) can simply commit to SSE strategies, thus helping to resolve a major dilemma in real-world security applications.

Acknowledgments

This research was supported by the United States Department of Homeland Security through the Center for Risk and Economic Analysis of Terrorism Events (CREATE). Korzhyk and Conitzer are supported by NSF IIS-0812113, ARO 56698-CI, and an Alfred P. Sloan Research Fellowship. However, any opinions, conclusions or recommendations herein are solely those of the authors and do not necessarily reflect views of the funding agencies. We thank Ronald Parr for detailed comments and discussions.

13

Evaluating Deployed Decision-Support Systems for Security: Challenges, Analysis, and Approaches

Matthew E. Taylor, Christopher Kiekintveld, and Milind Tambe

13.1 Introduction

As discussed in other chapters of this book, an increasing number of technically sophisticated tools are available to support decisionmaking for security-resource allocation in many different domains. In this chapter we discuss the question of evaluating these deployed security systems, using examples from our own research to illustrate some of the key challenges in doing evaluation for security systems. Two of the primary difficulties are (1) that we cannot rely on adversaries to cooperate in evaluation, which makes it difficult to validate models, and (2) there is (thankfully) very little data available about real-world terrorist attacks.

Despite the difficulties of comprehensive evaluation in security domains, it is only by asking the question, how well does a system work? that policy makers can decide how to allocate finite resources to to different security measures. We discuss the goals of security systems, the elements that comprise these systems, and different approaches for evaluation. Every approach has drawbacks, so in lieu of an ideal test, we advocate a comprehensive style of evaluation that uses diverse metrics and data to perform cost-benefit analysis for the complete system. We also emphasize that the focus of the evaluation is not, is system X the perfect security system? which is an impossible standard. Rather, the relevant question is which of the available alternatives should be used? Providing strong evidence that one alternative is superior to other approaches is often feasible, even when providing exact quantitative measures of value is not. As a community, we must strive to perform the best possible evaluations using the tools and data available, but we cannot let the absence of an ideal evaluation prevent us from deploying effective technologies. However, we must also recognize weaknesses in the current evaluations, and view them as opportunities to develop new techniques and to gather new data to improve our understanding of the value of different approaches to security.

Section 13.2 provides a brief background of the security applications discussed in this chapter in the context of evaluation – more detailed descriptions of these systems are provided in other chapters of the book. Section 13.3 describes the three steps involved in formulating a decision-support system for security: abstracting the model, solving the model, and then accurately deploying the solution. Section 13.4 describes the different types of evaluations that have been conducted on two systems in our case study. Section 13.5 discusses the goals of a deployed security system and the inherent difficulties in measuring the performance of such a system. For instance, unlike many types of technical applications, a security system does not have binary behavior; no security system is able to provide 100% protection and it does not make sense to say that it "does" or "does not" work. Instead, systems must be evaluated on basis of *risk reduction*, often by indirect measures such as increasing adversary cost and uncertainty or reducing the effectiveness of an adversaries' attack.

Section 13.6 discusses the pros and cons of different evaluation techniques, tying together the discussion in Sections 13.3–13.5. Related work is discussed in Section 13.7. Finally, Section 13.8 ends the chapter with a discussion of future work, in terms of enhancing the evaluation of our specific applications and the challenge of security evaluation in general.

13.2 Background: ARMOR and IRIS

The importance of security games as a research topic is driven by the recent development and deployment of several applications that assist major security organizations with making resource allocation decisions using algorithmic analysis based on game theory. These include the ARMOR system deployed at the LAX International Airport (LAX) (Pita et al., 2008) to assist the Los Angeles World Airport policy (LAWA) and the IRIS system deployed by the Federal Air Marshals Service (FAMS) (Tsai et al., 2009). While these systems share a similar approach in that they apply game-theoretic modeling techniques and emphasize randomized, unpredictable scheduling of security resources and activities, each system poses unique challenges in system design, modeling and solution techniques, and evaluation. ARMOR was the first system developed using this methodology, and it has the longest deployment history – our discussion of evaluation focuses largely on ARMOR and includes additional discussion of more recent systems when appropriate.

The ARMOR system has been deployed since 2007 by the Los Angeles World Airports (LAWA) police at LAX, the fifth busiest airport in the United States (and largest destination), serving 70 to 80 million passengers a year. LAX is considered a primary terrorist target on the West Coast and many individuals have been arrested for plotting or attempting to attack LAX (Stevens et al., 2009). Police have designed multiple rings of protection for LAX, including vehicular checkpoints, police patrols of roads, and inside terminals (some with bomb-sniffing canine units, also known as K9 units), passenger screening, and baggage screening. Because of the high demands on LAX security, due in part to the large physical area and high density of passenger and cargo traffic, police do not have enough resources (e.g., officers and K9 units) to provide constant security for every area and event at the airport. This limitation leads to the question of how best to allocate the limited resources to improve security at the airport.

ARMOR addresses two specific security problems by increasing the unpredictability of security schedules and weighting defensive strategy based on the targets' importance. First, there are many roads that are entry points to LAX. When and where should vehicle checkpoints be set up on these roads? Pertinent information includes typical traffic patterns on inbound roads, the areas each road accesses within LAX, and areas of LAX which may have more or less importance as terrorist targets. Second, how and when should the K9 units patrol the eight terminals at LAX? Here it is important to consider the time-dependent passenger volumes per terminal, as well as the attractiveness of different terminals. In both cases, a predictable pattern can be exploited by an observant attacker.

The approach taken by ARMOR uses game-theoretic models to derive scheduling strategies for the police resources. This is modeled as a Bayesian Stackelberg game (Conitzer and Sandholm, 2006), in which the police (e.g., defenders) must commit to a (randomized) security policy. Each possible attacker type observes the security policy and then selects and optimal attack strategy based on their preferences (i.e., *utilities* or utility *payoff matrices*). The solution to this game is called a Strong Stackelberg Equilibrium, and yields an optimal randomized strategy for the policy. ARMOR uses an algorithm called DOBSS (Paruchuri et al., 2008) to solve these game instances and recommend schedules for checkpoints and canine patrols to the LAWA police. The schedules account for three key factors: (1) Attackers are able to observe the security policy using surveillance; (2) attackers change their behavior in response to the security policy; and (3) the risk/consequence of an attack varies depending on the target.

The IRIS system was designed to address scheduling problems faced by the Federal Air Marshals Service (FAMS). FAMS is charged with law enforcement and antiterrorism on commercial airline flights, which is accomplished primarily by placing armed marshals on individual flights. There are tens of thousands of flights operated by U.S. airlines each day, and the FAMS lack the resources to place marshals on every flight. This leads to a resource-allocation challenge that is similar to that addressed by ARMOR: how best to place the available marshals on the possible flights to maximize security. In addition to the overall constraint on the number of air marshals available, this problem is complicated by the presence of complex physical and temporal constraints on which flight tours the air marshals can feasibly fly, as well as other idiosyncratic constraints. Flights are also diverse in the potential risk and consequence of a terrorist attack against the flight, based on many factors including the source and destination airports, aircraft size, and flight path. The schedules produced by IRIS must optimize over all these constraints and variations in flight valuation, resulting in a significantly more complex problem space than for the ARMOR scheduler (Kiekintveld et al., 2009).

13.3 Formulating the Problem

Having introduced ARMOR and IRIS, we now describe the basic elements of these decision-support tools and the process that was used to design them. In each case, the complete system includes a domain model based on expert elicitation, a game-theoretic solution algorithm used to analyze the model, and a software application designed around the algorithm that allows data inputs, visualization of the solution, and so on. To fully evaluate the system we must evaluate each of these components, as well as the way the system is actually used in practice (e.g., how the recommended solutions are implemented by the security forces).

We focus first on the process of formulating a model of the domain, since this is the basis for all subsequent analysis. This model must have sufficient detail that it can provide useful decision support, it must accurately represent the domain, and it must not be so complex that it is intractable for analysis. The problem of computing a solution is discussed in the next section and is the problem that is most familiar to computer scientists. While other chapters have discussed the computational difficulties in solving complex security problems, our discussion considers more broadly the assumptions behind the solution methods. A system may be theoretically sound but badly flawed if it is implemented poorly. The third and final step we discuss is implementing (and verifying) the system in a real-world setting.

13.3.1 Abstracting the Real-World Problem

The first step in developing a defensive measure is to determine what particular attack vector should be addressed. For example, the ARMOR system was designed to counteract a perceived defensive shortcoming at LAX, as identified in a Rand study (Stevens et al., 2009). In order to construct a model that can be solved, the real problem must be formulated as a quantitative problem. In the case of ARMOR, this involved focusing on a fixed number of checkpoint positions that could be either covered or not covered. How many officers were at a checkpoint, or what the skills of the particular officers were, is abstracted away.

To decide how important the different checkpoints were, we assigned them values based on their proximity to and the road layout relative to the terminals. The terminals, in turn, were evaluated by experts who estimated the utilities to the defenders if an attacker successfully attacked or was caught attempting to attack a particular terminal. The experts also estimated the utilities to the attackers if they successfully attacked were caught attacking a particular terminal.

Formulating a real-world problem as a solvable quantitative model requires abstraction, which by definition causes a loss of information. However, the goal is to minimize the loss of precision so that the optimal solution to the model will be near-optimal on the physical problem. The formulation chosen will also constrain the policy space. In ARMOR, checkpoints are constrained to last at least a certain amount of time, due to the time of setting up a checkpoint. Thus ARMOR could not schedule checkpoint #1 to be set up at 9:00 AM and taken down at 9:05 AM. The selection of this constrained solution space may also impact the optimality of the solution in the real world.

Besides modeling the utilities for attacks, one often wishes to attempt to model deterrence. One method is to test an attacker's optimal option with and without defense. If the attacker changes actions to a lower-valued action, she or he can be considered to be deterred. Another option is to consider that the attacker may choose to not attack at all, or attack a target that is outside the scope of the security system in question. In a game-theoretic setting, one option is to add a "stay at home" action to the attacker's action space. A second option would be to add an "attack another target" option. In the case of ARMOR, this could include the action "attack another target in Los Angeles" or "attack another airport in the United States." Notice that to the LAWA, these three possible actions are equivalent as they are all instances of successful deterrence with respect to LAX. However, for the city of Los Angeles or for the U.S. federal government, the "stay at home" action is clearly superior.

13.3.2 Solution Concepts and Computational Considerations

The previous section focused on the challenge of generating an abstract model of a real-world problem that accurately represents the underlying situation.

Once this model is generated, the next stage is to analyze this model determine the best course of action (strategy) for the security forces. Given the complexity of the models, we need fast computational methods to perform this analysis and generate recommendations.

13.3.2.1 Potential Solution Concepts

Given a precise mathematical model of a strategic interaction, the game theory literature provides many powerful tools for analyzing the model and make predictions and strategy recommendations. Unfortunately, there are many different solution concepts that may be applied in different situations, and which is the "best" solution method to use is not obvious. The starting point is typically a form of Nash equilibrium that predicts how players should act given that they are perfectly rational, and all players have exact common knowledge of the game model (including the possible actions, sequence of moves, payoffs for different outcomes, etc.). In real-world situations, these assumptions are often too strong since players may be uncertain about different aspects of the game or may not make mathematically optimal choices because to limits on their reasoning capabilities or other factors. Different solution concepts can be applied based on different assumptions about knowledge and rationality, but it is an important open question how well the solution concept and underlying assumptions correspond to the real-world situation, and this must be evaluated empirically.

There are alternatives to game-theoretic equilibrium solutions methods that should also be evaluated as potential candidates. The simplest is the uniform random strategy: Given a set of possible security actions, take each of them with equal probability. This has the appeal of simplicity and of being completely unpredictable (by definition). It also makes absolutely no assumptions about the adversary, so there is no chance that these assumptions may be incorrect or exploitable. However, it does not take into account the value of different actions, and may waste limited resources by performing less valuable actions too often. A weighted randomization can potentially account for this by selecting more valuable actions more frequently. The key question here is how to determine the weights for the randomization; in effect, a game-theoretic solution is one way to find these weights that is principled, since a game-theoretic solution is an instance of weighted randomization. There may be simpler approaches to finding a weighted randomization in some cases that could also be candidate strategies. Our evaluations of ARMOR and similar systems, discussed in subsequent sections, have consistently shown that game-theoretic solutions are superior to both uniform randomization and simple weighted randomization strategies.

The final point to mention regarding solution concepts is whether or not the attackers are assumed to be fully rational. For instance, in classical game theory settings, human behavior can be fully predicted if the utilities of the actors are known. In practice, however, humans are often not true "homo-economous" actors but may make suboptimal decisions based on noninfinite reasoning abilities.

ARMOR's game-theoretic model uses strong assumptions about the attacker's rationality to predict how it will behave and optimizes accordingly. Humans often do not always conform to the predictions of strict equilibrium models (though some other models offer better predictions of behavior (Erev et al., 2002)). In addition, ARMOR assumes that an attacker can perfectly observe the security policy, which may not be possible in reality.

13.3.2.2 Algorithmic Goals

Computer science often focuses on developing highly efficient algorithms with low worst-case complexity (or on proving that such efficient algorithm are not possible for a particular problem). For instance, a computer scientist may ask, can a solution be found in time polynomial in the number of joint actions? or can a solution be found with an amount of memory polynomial in the number of joint actions? Different methods for solving games can be compared against each other by measuring their running time, memory usage, scalability, and so on. However, when discussing real-world problems, a more pertinent question is, can a solution be found given our constraints?

Optimality proofs (or approximation guarantees) are also highly valuable in real-world applications. Without such guarantees, it is difficult to build confidence in the system, and there is a legitimate concern that the occurrence of an adverse event could be attributed to a poor-quality solution. While such proofs are often necessary, they are not sufficient to prove that a security system works. First, those in nontechnical fields (which are necessarily part of the system's funding, implementation, and staffing) may not value the results of a proof as highly as a mathematician. Second, just because the model has been optimally solved does not mean that the correct problem was modeled (Section 13.3.1) or that the solution was correctly implemented (Section 13.3.3).

13.3.3 Implementing the Solution

The final element to consider is how the tool is actually used in practice. Any decision-support system requires inputs from human users, and and the recommendations it makes must be implemented by the users as well. Problems at the interface between humans and the computer system may cause the overall system to be ineffective, even if the computer system is theoretically perfect! Based on our personal experience with implemented systems, we believe that a tight loop between the modelers, system developers, and end users is critical to a successful system. For instance, if those building the model do not understand how the solution will be implemented, they may not account for key factors in the real-world problem. Likewise, if the assumptions made when solving the model are violated, any optimality guarantees are invalidated.

While the above guideline is true of all deployed systems, security presents two unique challenges. First, those who perform the modeling and solving steps may not be able to make site visits and fully understand the proposed deployment. For instance, a game theory expert who may be working on developing safe convoy routes for patrols in Iraq may be unlikely to want to travel to Baghdad given the security risks. Further, in some cases, the full details of the defensive operation may not be available to the modelers or model solvers for security reasons, and they must work under assumptions that those with appropriate security clearances independently verify.

Second, data related to the deployed configuration and performance of the system may be classified or sensitive, and not available to researches. For instance, when working with the FAMS, we have developed a solution method that takes the utility matrices as input and outputs a schedule. However, as academic computer scientists, we do not have clearance to see the true utility matrices used by the FAMS, nor are we able to view the schedules produced by the production system. This enforced disconnect means that it is impossible for all members of the designing team to understand the full operation, and thus implementation and verification details fall most heavily on those security clearance to see the full picture.

Other questions related to implementation can best be answered in interviews and surveys of users, for instance:

- Do the users understand the day to day use of the system?
- Do users consistently enter correct inputs?
- Do users follow the recommendations of the system?
- What happens if there are unanticipated events (e.g., flight cancellations/delays, emergency situations, or security personnel call in sick)? Does the decision-support system effectively handle such situations?

13.4 Evaluating Case Studies

Having introduced two examples of decision-support systems for security and discussed the components of these systems, we now explore some of the existing evaluations we have performed on these systems. Latter sections of this chapter will refer back to these examples, when we discuss the overall effectiveness of the systems and delve into the strengths and weaknesses of different types of evaluations and metrics.

13.4.1 Comparison with Previous Best Practices

The most straightforward type of evaluation is to assume that the model is correct, and evaluate different potential strategies using the model. In particular, we can test the solutions used in ARMOR and IRIS against simpler randomization approaches, such as uniform random or simple heuristic weighted randomization. We can also test against strategies designed to replicate the best practices used by security forces. For example, by comparing the schedules generated by ARMOR with the previous scheduling practices at LAX (Cruz, 2009), we can answer the question, does ARMOR improve security? with more confidence.

There are some clear differences in ARMOR schedules and the previous scheduling practices at LAX. First, in the previous scheduling system, all checkpoints remained in place for an entire day, whereas now checkpoints are moved throughout the day according to ARMOR's schedule (adding to the adversary's uncertainty). Second, a fixed sequence of checkpoints was defined (i.e., checkpoints 2, 3, 1, etc.) to create a static mapping from date to checkpoint. This sequence was not optimized according to the importance of different targets, and the sequence would repeat (allowing the attacker to anticipate which checkpoint would be manned on any given day).

The LAX officers informed us that they had previously generated checkpoint schedules based on a cyclic strategy with random perturbations. A study of past schedules showed that patterns remained evident despite these random perturbations – no checkpoint was repeated for two consecutive days. Therefore, we also compared the ARMOR strategy against two strategies: (1) a "cyclic" strategy wherein the checkpoints were scheduled in a cyclic order on all inbound roads; and (2) a "restricted uniform" strategy which was a uniformly random strategy with the additional restriction that no checkpoint was repeated on two consecutive days.

Our first experiments attempt to replicate as closely as possible the scheduling policies in use at LAX prior to ARMOR. Police officers place one checkpoint on any of the five inbound roads, and the rewards of the terminals were randomly chosen between 1 and 10. We vary the duration for which the adversary can make observations from 0 to 100 days, in increments of 25 days. We averaged our results over 100 trials. In these simulations, we assume that the adversary

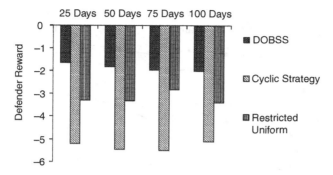

Figure 13.1. This figure compares ARMOR strategies (which use the DOBBS algorithm) and policies representative of previous methods where adversaries have the option to attack once every 25 days.

can use simple pattern recognition techniques to recognize patterns in the check-point schedules. The adversary maintains a history of observed checkpoints and generates confidence intervals over sequences of observations.

Figure 13.1 shows our experimental results. The x-axis represents the number of observations available to the adversary, and the y-axis represents the average defender reward. The ARMOR strategy has a higher average defender reward compared to the other two strategies. The reason is that the adversary can better predict the defender action in case of cyclic and restricted uniform strategies than with the ARMOR strategy. Therefore, simple pattern-recognition techniques are sufficient for the adversary to exploit the patterns in the cyclic and restricted uniform strategies. These patterns can be avoided by the use of uniformly random strategies, but a uniform random strategy does not take into account the different preferences over the defender's targets. ARMOR provides weights for the different targets such that the average defender reward is the highest when compared against both cyclic and restricted uniform strategies. Additionally, ARMOR strategies are not just weighted random strategies since they also account for the fact that the adversary observes the defender's strategy and then makes an informed rational choice.

Comparing schedules generated by ARMOR against a benchmark uniform random schedule shows that ARMOR's schedule is much more efficient. For example, Figure 13.2 shows the expected reward for the police using ARMOR's schedule (calculated using DOBSS) compared with a uniform random benchmark strategy in the canines domain. ARMOR is able to make such effective use of resources that using three canines scheduled with DOBSS yields higher utility than using six canines with uniform random scheduling!

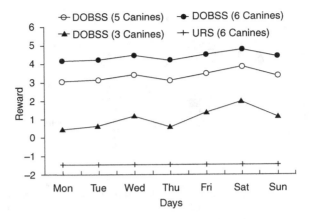

Figure 13.2. This figure shows that ARMOR (powered by the DOBBS algorithm) can outperform the baseline solution method, even using many fewer K9 units, which may achieve substantial cost savings. The x-axis shows the results from seven different days, and the y-axis shows the expected utility for the different scheduling methods.

Scheduling for the FAMS domain has undergone multiple mathematical tests using real-world schedules and withstood expert scrutiny, but the exact results of these tests are not released. Figure 13.3a shows the results of a mathematical evaluation done with hypothetical payoffs, to better measure the success of the system. Results show the expected payoff when a single air marshal is scheduled in the FAMS domain over 20, 100, and 200 schedules. In these experiments, this equated to 10, 50, and 100 flights, of which half were "departures" and half were "return" flights carrying the air marshals. The x-axis in these graphs shows the expected payoff for IRIS, six different methods of weighting the schedules, uniform random coverage, and no coverage (i.e., the single air marshal protects no planes).

In the full FAMS problem, there are too many schedules to enumerate, and it is difficult to decide how to weight the flights, even if they are enumerated. This weighting is a simple way of determining which schedules to cover, and may improve the performance of the defender relative to uniform random. In these simple tests, the problem space was small enough that all schedules could be easily enumerated. IRIS clearly outperforms its competitors.

Utilities are generated as random numbers drawn uniformly from the ranges of numbers as follows:

- Defender payoff for covering a flight that is attacked: [+5000, +10000]
- Defender payoff for not covering a flight that is attacked: [−10000, −5000]

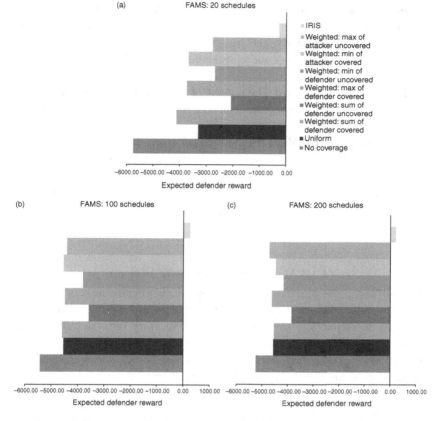

Figure 13.3. These graphs show the results of scheduling with the IRIS algorithm called ASPEN vs. other possible scheduling methods. In the case of (a) 20, (b) 100, and (c) 200 schedules, the IRIS scheduling method is superior. Results are averaged over 30 independent trials each.

- Attacker payoff for attacking a flight that is not covered: [+5000, +10000]
- Attacker payoff for attacking a flight that is covered: [−10000, −5000]

The six naive weighted random strategies are as follows. In all cases a mixed-probability distribution is obtained by normalizing these weights.

Max. of attacker reward The weight of a schedule is the maximum of the attacker rewards for a successful attack over all flights covered in the schedule.

Min. of attacker penalty The weight of a schedule is the minimum of the attacker penalty for a failed attack over all flights covered in the schedule.

Min. of defender penalty The weight of a schedule is the minimum of defender penalties for a successful attack over all flights covered in the schedule.

Max. of defender reward The weight of a schedule is the maximum of defender rewards for capturing an attacker over for all flights covered in the schedule.

Sum of defender penalties The weight of a schedule is the sum of the defender penalties for a successful attack over all flights covered in the schedule.

Sum of defender rewards The weight of a schedule is sum of defender rewards for capture over all flights covered in the schedule.

13.4.2 Mathematical Sensitivity Analysis

The analyses in the previous section compare the effectiveness of different scheduling policies, but they do so based on all of the assumptions in the model (e.g., that the actions and payoffs are correctly specified for both players, and that the attacker is perfectly rational). To build more confidence in the approach, we must also validate the model itself. A first step is to better understand the impact of the different assumptions using sensitivity analysis.

In this type of evaluation, important parameters of the model are varied to test how the output of the model changes to different inputs. One important input to the ARMOR model is the distribution of different types of attackers. For example, some attackers may be highly organized and motivated, whereas others are amateurish and more likely to surrender. Different types of attackers can be modeled as having different payoff matrices. Changing the percentages of each attacker can help show the system's sensitivity to assumptions regarding the composition of likely attackers, and (indirectly) the system's dependence on precise utility elicitation. In Figure 13.4(a)–13.4(c), there are two adversary types with different reward matrices. Figure 13.4(a) demonstrates that DOBSS has a higher expected utility than that of a uniform random strategy on a single checkpoint, regardless of the percentage of "type one" and "type two" adversaries. Figures 13.4(b) and (c) shows that DOBSS again dominates uniform random for two and three checkpoints, respectively.

Further sensitivity analysis can be applied to other parameters of the model. The payoffs that describe the preferences of the two players for different

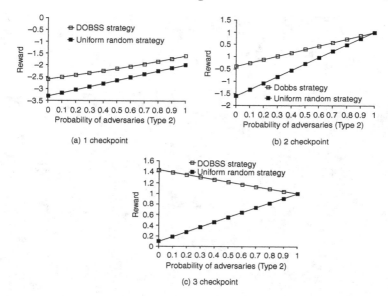

Figure 13.4. This figure compares ARMOR's schedules (generated by the algorithm named DOBBS) with a uniform random baseline schedule. Figures a–c show the utility of schedules for 1–3 vehicle checkpoints varying the relative probability of two different attacker types. The x-axes show the probability of the two attacker types (where 0 corresponds to 0% attack type 2, and 100% attack type 1) and y-axes show the expected utility of ARMOR and a uniform random defense strategy.

outcomes are a very important set of parameters. These parameters are estimates of the true utilities determined through elicitation sessions with experts. Unfortunately, it is known that game-theoretic models can be quite sensitive to payoff noise (Kiekintveld and Wellman, 2008), and arbitrary changes in payoffs can lead to arbitrary changes in the optimal schedule. There is some evidence that ARMOR is robust to certain types of variations. In one experiment, we multiplied all of the defender's negative payoffs for successful attacks by a factor of four, essentially increasing the impact of a successful attack. We found that in the one and three checkpoint case, the strategies were unchanged. In the two-checkpoint case the actions were slightly different, but the overall strategy and utility were unchanged. Unfortunately, there is also evidence that this does not generalize to all payoffs in security games. Kiekintveld et al. (2011) show that in general, adding small amounts of noise to the attacker's payoffs in security games can cause large deviations in the defender's payoffs (though the changes in the optimal strategy are less drastic).

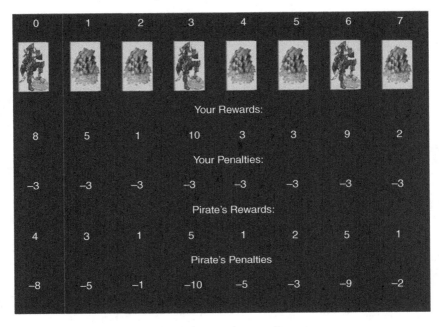

0	1	2	3	4	5	6	7

Your Rewards:

8	5	1	10	3	3	9	2

Your Penalties:

-3	-3	-3	-3	-3	-3	-3	-3

Pirate's Rewards:

4	3	1	5	1	2	5	1

Pirate's Penalties

-8	-5	-1	-10	-5	-3	-9	-2

Figure 13.5. Screenshot of the "pirates and treasure" game.

13.4.3 Human Trials

Another set of assumptions the game models use for ARMOR and IRIS is that the attackers are perfectly rational and will always choose the mathematically optimal attack strategy. To test the sensitivity of the solutions to variations in human behavior, we ran a series of controlled laboratory experiments with human subjects (Pita et al., 2009). In these experiments, subjects play a "pirates and treasure" game designed to simulate an adversary planning an attack on an LAX terminal, shown in Figure 13.5. Subjects are given information about the payoffs for different actions and the pirates' strategy for defending their gold (analogous to the security policy for defending airport terminals). Subjects receive cash payments at the conclusion of the experiment, based on their performance in the game.

These experiments have provided additional support for quality of ARMOR's schedules against human opponents. We have tested many conditions, varying both the payoff structure and the observation ability, ranging from no observation of the defense strategy to perfect observation. The results show that ARMOR's schedules achieve higher payoffs than the uniform random benchmark across all experimental conditions tested, often by a large margin.[1] These results demonstrate that ARMOR schedules outperform competing methods when playing against human adversaries. They also demonstrate that further improvements may potentially be feasible to ARMOUR's strategies when playing against human adversaries.

13.4.4 Arrest Data

Ideally, we would be able to use data from the operation of a deployed system to provide further validation of the modeling assumptions. For example, in the case of ARMOR we might be interested in the number of attacks prevented by the system. Unfortunately, such data is very limited in the case of ARMOR; there have been no major attacks on the airport, but it is impossible to say how many attacks would have occurred *without* ARMOR.

We were able to obtain some data on the arrest record at ARMOR checkpoints. Though the use of such data has multiple caveats (see Section 13.5 for more discussion), it can still provide some useful information. We received summarized and actual reports from the LAX police regarding the number of violations that they detected at checkpoints in 2007, 2008, and January 2009. For example, we received the following report for January 2009:

1. January 3, 2009: Loaded 9 mm pistol discovered
2. January 3, 2009: Loaded 9 mm handgun discovered (no arrest)
3. January 9, 2009: 16 handguns, 4 rifles, 1 pistol, and 1 assault rifle discovered – some fully loaded
4. January 10, 2009: 2 unloaded shotguns discovered (no arrest)
5. January 12, 2009: Loaded 22 cal rifle discovered
6. January 17, 2009: Loaded 9 mm pistol discovered
7. January 22, 2009: Unloaded 9 mm pistol discovered (no arrest)

Figure 13.6 tabulates the number of violations for the year prior to the deployment of ARMOR and during 2008 when ARMOR was in use. The x-axis breaks down the violations into different types and the y-axis represents the number of violations. The number of violations is substantially higher at LAX after ARMOR was deployed than in the preceding period. For example, only four drug related offenses were detected before the deployment of ARMOR while thirty such offenses were detected after the deployment. While we must be careful about drawing too many conclusion from this data due to the large number of uncontrolled variables (e.g., the number of checkpoints was not consistent

---

[1] New defense strategies developed in this work show even better performance against some (suboptimal) human adversaries by explicitly exploiting the attacker's weaknesses.

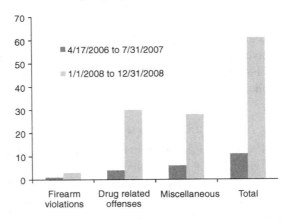

Figure 13.6. This figure shows how the number of arrests in three categories changed before and after the ARMOR deployment at LAX.

during this period), the ARMOR checkpoints do appear to provide some useful service to the airport.

13.4.5 Qualitative Expert Evaluations

Given the sparseness and limitations of the available data from the field, evaluations of the system by security experts become a very important source of information. Though they are typically qualitative in nature, they are one of the few ways to gather evidence on the quality of the modeling assumptions and the effectiveness of the holistic system, as it is actually deployed and used on a day-to-day basis. Security procedures at LAX are subject to numerous internal and external security reviews (not all of which are public). The available qualitative reviews indicate that ARMOR is both effective and highly visible.

Director James Butts of the LAWA police reported that ARMOR "makes travelers safer" and even gives them "a greater feeling of police presence" (Murr, 2007). Erroll Southers, Assistant Chief of LAWA police, told a Congressional hearing that "LAX is safer today than it was eighteen months ago," due in part to ARMOR. A recent external study by Israeli transportation security experts concluded that ARMOR was a key component of the LAX defensive setup. The ARMOR team has also been awarded Letters of Commendation from the city of Los Angeles in recognition of the efforts toward securing the Los Angeles International Airport. Thus, the domain experts have been highly supportive of ARMOR, and it would be very hard to deploy the system without their support. They are also likely to identify potential problems with the system quickly. While such studies are not very useful for quantifying ARMOR's benefit, they all suggest that the domain experts believe that ARMOR generates better schedules than their previous approaches did.

ARMOR was designed as a mixed-initiative system that would allow police to override the recommended policies. In practice, users have not chosen to modify the recommended schedules, which suggests that they are confident of the outputs. Although such studies are not very useful for directly quantifying ARMOR's benefit, it would be very hard to deploy the system without the support of such experts. Furthermore, if there were an obvious problem with the system, these experts would likely identify it quickly.

Expert opinions have emphasized that an important benefit of the system is its transparency and visibility, which contribute to deterrence. ARMOR assumes that adversaries are intelligent and have the ability to observe the security policy: Knowing about the system does not reduce its effectiveness. The deployment of ARMOR has been quite visible: ARMOR has been covered on local Los Angeles TV stations (including FOX and NBC), in newspapers (including the Los Angeles and the *International Herald Tribune*), and in a national magazine (*Newsweek*).

The IRIS system has been tested both qualitatively and quantitatively, showing that it performs better than human schedulers, but the results of these tests are not available in the public domain. However, James B. Curren, a special assistant in the office of Flight Operations at the Federal Air Marshals Service, has affirmed the effectiveness of IRIS:

> We have tested IRIS and found it to be applicable to our needs in creating uncertainty as to FAM presence on selected city pairs of flights. After extensive testing we have implemented IRIS on a trial run of flight selections and have continued to expand the number of flights scheduled using IRIS. Our exact use of IRIS is sensitive information and we can only state that we are satisfied with IRIS and confident in using this scheduling approach.

Furthermore, internal governmental studies have both recommended that random scheduling be implemented, which is precisely what IRIS accomplishes (GAO, 2009)[2]:

> Because the number of air marshals is less than the number of daily flights, FAMS's operational approach is to assign air marshals to selected flights it deems high risk – such as the nonstop, long-distance flights targeted on September 11, 2001. In assigning air marshals, FAMS seeks to maximize coverage of flights in 10 targeted high-risk categories, which are based on consideration of threats, vulnerabilities, and consequences. In July 2006, the Homeland Security Institute, a federally funded research and development center, independently assessed FAMS's

---

[2] This report is a public version of the restricted report GAO-09-53SU.

operational approach and found it to be reasonable. However, the institute noted that certain types of flights were covered less often than others. The institute recommended that FAMS increase randomness or unpredictability in selecting flights and otherwise diversify the coverage of flights within the various risk categories. As of October 2008, FAMS had taken actions (or had ongoing efforts) to implement the Homeland Security Institute's recommendations. GAO found the institute's evaluation methodology to be reasonable.

13.5 Goals for Security Decision-Support Systems

Any security system can be evaluated using a wide variety of metrics, including both costs and benefits. For the purposes of analysis, we divide benefits into two categories: *direct* and *indirect*. Direct benefits speak to benefits that may be measured, such as

- reduced security costs;
- attacks prevented or mitigated during execution;
- increased numbers of attackers caught; or
- reduced damage from successful attacks.

By contrast, indirect benefits include

- attacks prevented through deterrence;
- increased attacker planning time;
- increased requirements for a successful attack;
- improved public perceptions of security; or
- improved (qualitative) assessments of security by experts.

Regardless of how such benefits are partitioned, some are easier to directly measure than others. However, all of them speak to the idea of defender utility: Given finite resources, how can the defender maximize security per dollar spent? As discussed previously, no security system can be 100% effective – there is always a chance that, given enough resources and planning, any adversary may compromise a system. Compromising system may, however, require higher amounts of equipment, manpower, and/or planning relative to disabling the system. Thus, the question becomes not, is the system effective? but, is system A more effective than system B? or how much does the system improve defensive capabilities per dollar spent? We next elaborate upon two of these themes: utility and deterrence.

13.5.1 Security per Dollar

Evaluating security systems requires a full cost-benefit analysis that takes a comprehensive view of both the benefits and the costs of the system. There is always additional defensive capability that could be purchased — another guard could be hired, one more piece of technology could be installed or upgraded, and so on. Of course, additional security typically comes with diminishing returns, and there is a policy decision to be made about how many resources to devote to security. Improving the efficiency of security can be used to either (1) increase defensive abilities on a fixed budget; and/or (2) decrease expenditure for a fixed defensive capability. Such increases in efficiency are the primary goal of decision-support systems like ARMOR and IRIS.

Recall that Figure 13.6 showed how the defender's utility changed with different numbers of K9 units. This kind of graph of the trade-off between defensive capability and cost can allow policy makers to more easily see the trade-off between money and security when using the ARMOR system. More importantly one can easily see the extent to which ARMOR helps increase security relative to uniform random (or other randomization strategies), which is a critical factor when deciding whether or not to implement a given security technique. It directly follows that countermeasure investments with the highest cost-effectiveness ratio should be implemented first, assuming that there is no interdependence between proposed measures. Edmunds and Wheeler (2009) Determining exactly how much safer ARMOR makes the airport is a very difficult question, but as we will discuss in the following sections, arguing that ARMOR improves safety on a per-office basis (and thus safety per dollar spent) is not difficult.

13.5.2 Threat Deterrence

A key goal of many security systems is *deterrence*: An effective system will not only identify and prevent successful attacks, but will also dissuade potential attackers. Unfortunately, it is typically impossible to directly measure the deterrence effect. To measure deterrence directly, one needs to know how many attacks *did not occur* because of security, a generally unmeasurable counterfactual.

In all the cases relevant to this chapter, we assume that the attacker is adaptive and does not act blindly, but takes the defender's actions into account. It is only through this adaptability that defensive measures could deter an attacker. For instance, one could model the uncertainty due to chance or attacker choices via an *event tree model* or a *decision tree model* (Edmunds and Wheeler, 2009). We choose to focus on game-theoretic methods because they have strong mathematical underpinnings and are ideally suited to reasoning about adaptable, rational actors. Game models naturally factor in deterrence in that an intelligent attacker is assumed to switch to a different strategy if the defender uses security resources to make the original strategy undesirable.

How to best understand and accurately model deterrence is a topic of current research in the threat assessment community (Taquechel, 2010). For instance, for a defensive measure to be an effective deterrent, it must be *credible* in the eyes of the attacker (Berejikian, 2002), which may involve complex *signalling* effects between the parties (Gerson and Boyars, 2007). As mentioned above, ARMOR has been well-publicized in the popular press. Although there are many less public security measures employed at LAX, ARMOR may lead a potential attacker to decide not to attack LAX and to instead stay at home and not attack. Another possible outcome of ARMOR's publicity is that an attacker selects a more vulnerable target. This is a win from the standpoint of LAX, but it may or may not be an improvement for the city of Los Angeles, the state of California, or the United States, depending on the target selected. However, if LAX is not targeted due to deterrence measures, the eventual target is presumably less attractive to the attackers, resulting in a net increase in the defender's utility.

13.6 Types of Evaluation

This section of the chapter ties together the discussion of the previous sections, showing how the different evaluations performed on ARMOR and IRIS help to provide evidence that we are making progress in attaining the goals of the security system.

13.6.1 Model-based/algorithmic

The first type of evaluations (and the most natural for computer scientists) are based on analysis of the model and the underlying algorithms. Given assumptions about the attacker (e.g., the payoff matrix is known), game-theoretic tools can be used to determine the attacker's expected payoff. Additionally, deterrence can be measured by including a "stay home" action, returning neutral reward. These types of analyses speak to such concerns.

First, the sensitivity of the solution method can be examined. No model will be perfect, but a solution to that model would ideally be robust to small imperfections in the model. This type of analysis is able to speak to the potential impact of different kinds of abstraction and modeling error on the final solution.

Second, the utility of the solution method can be directly estimated from algorithmic evaluations. For instance, the attacker resources versus expected attacker utility and the defender resources versus expected defender utility can both be estimated. To the extent that the model is correct, these utilities can be determined exactly, providing both policy makers and security professionals with an important tool for deciding what defensive measures to implement.

Table 13.1. *This table summarizes the types of experiments we have conducted on our security systems and show how they help verify the problem formulation and/or that the system is accomplishing its goals.*

Summary of Evaluation Types

Evaluation	Problem formulation			Goal accomplishments	
	Abstraction	Solution	Implementation	Direct benefit	Indirect benefit
Algorithmic	✓	✓		✓	✓
Cost/Benefit				✓	
Relative Benefit	✓		✓	✓	
Human Experiments			✓	✓	
Operational Record	✓		✓	✓	
High Level Evaluations			✓	✓	✓

Finally, the underlying algorithms can be evaluated, both to prove correctness (or a close approximation), and to evaluated the computational effort required to compute a solution for problems with different sizes and properties.

13.6.2 Cost-benefit analysis

Another type of analysis, which can combine both algorithmic results and those from the implementation, is a full cost-benefit analysis of the deployed system. For instance, the cost of implementation and maintenance on the system can be directly measured. The benefit of the system can be measured both by changes in the defenders' utility (e.g., Figure 13.2) and in terms of less tangible factors (such as such as quantifying increases in travel time or a decrease in civil liberties).

A system-wide cost/benefit analysis can help security professionals decide where to allocate finite resources to best protect the entire area by changing staffing levels and/or implementing new security measures. Additionally, such studies can provide important information to other sites that may consider deploying a new security measure, such as ARMOR. The ultimate goal of this analysis is to answer the questions how useful is this defensive measure? and how does utility change for different levels of defender/attacker resources?

13.6.3 Relative benefit

Measuring the *relative* benefit of defensive measures is similar to measuring the absolute utility, as described in the previous section. However, an important difference is that such measurements may be less brittle to model inaccuracies. For instance, when deciding whether or not to implement ARMOR, a site may consider the absolute utility of ARMOR using a cost-benefit analysis, which depends on the assumptions about the attacker. A relatively simple analysis could instead look at how utility will be changed by a proposed security method.

For instance, Figure 13.1 shows how the utility of ARMOR compares to different scheduling strategies. A relative benefit analysis makes it easier to answer the question, should this measure be implemented? and may be particularly useful when discussing security with professionals who are leery of implementing decision-theoretic methods.

13.6.4 Human behavioral experiments

Human psychological studies can help to better simulate attackers in the real world (e.g., Figure 13.5). Evaluations on an abstract version of the game may test base assumptions, or a detailed rendition of the target in a virtual reality setting with physiological stress factors could test situated behavior. Human subjects may allow researchers to better simulate the actions of attackers, who may not be fully rational. Human tests suffer from the fact that participants are not drawn from the same population as the actual attackers (i.e., undergraduate college students).

In some situations, it may be possible to conduct realistic human studies in the true setting, that is, employ a "red team." Such tests can use qualified security personnel attempt to probe security defenses provides realistic information in lifelike situations using the true defenses (including those that are not visible). However, such a test is very difficult to conduct because some security must be alerted (so that the team is not endangered) while remaining realistic, the tests are often not repeatable, and a single test is likely unrepresentative. To the extent that such tests are feasible, they would speak to both the implementation of the system and how well it accomplishes its direct goals.

13.6.5 Operational record

Analysis of the operational record of a system provides confirmation that the system works, but is not as useful as one may initially think. Ideally, the system would be enabled and disabled for randomized periods of time, allowing for a careful study of the system. Unfortunately, this is typically infeasible.

Consider the ARMOR system: That there are arrests resulting from the system shows that the system does allow rule breakers to be caught. However, comparing the number of arrests before and after ARMOR may or may not be useful. For instance, an increase in the number of arrests could be an indication that ARMOR is more effective than the previous system. However, it could also mean that more people are violating the rules during this time period, so in fact a lower number of criminals are caught. Alternatively, a lower number of arrests could mean that deterrence from ARMOR is convincing more criminals to stay away. Or, a lower number of arrests could mean that more people are circumventing the system. Without knowing the number of criminals that are not caught, it is impossible to tell how well a particular piece of the security is performing.

An additional complication is that, thankfully, most security threats are very low-frequency events. This means that data is collected relatively infrequently, making analysis of the operational record more sparse than in other (non-security) deployed applications.

13.6.6 High-Level evaluations

While computer scientists traditionally prioritize precise, repeatable studies, this is not always possible in the security community; computer scientists are used to quantitative evaluations in controlled studies; whereas, security specialists are more accepting of qualitative metrics on deployed systems. For instance, Lazarick (1999) summarized a multiyear airport security initiative by the FAA where the highest ranked evaluation methodology (of seven) relied on averaging *qualitative* expert evaluations.

Assuming that the high-level evaluation is done appropriately, it may address the abstraction and implementation questions arising from problem formulation, as well both the direct and indirect goals. While these studies generally do not produce quantitative numbers that can be used to determine the utility of a security measure, they may uncover flaws in that measure, or in the security of the entire system as a whole. If no flaws are found, the study may support the hypothesis that the security measure in question does improve overall security. As with the other types of evaluation, the goal is not to prove that the system works, but to provide evidence toward this effect.

13.7 Related Work

Security is a complex research area, spanning many disciplines, and policy evaluation is a persistent challenge. Many security applications are evaluated primarily on the basis of theoretical results; situated evaluations and even laboratory experiments with human subjects are relatively rare. In addition, existing general methodologies for risk and security evaluation often rely heavily on expert opinions and qualitative evaluations.

Lazarick (1999) is a representative example that relies heavily on expert opinions. In the study, seven tools/approaches used to evaluate airport security were compared as part of a competitive bidding process. At the end of the multiyear security initiative, the highest ranked evaluation methodology relied on averaging qualitative expert evaluations.

A second example of a high-level methodology for per-facility and regional risk assessment, such as was described by Baker (2005). The methodology relies heavily on expert opinions and evaluations from local technical staff/experts, similar to Lazarick (1999). The three key questions in the methodology are: (1) Based on the vulnerabilities identified, what is the likelihood that the system will fail? (2) What are the consequences of such failure (e.g., cost or lives)? (3) Are these consequences acceptable? This approach enumerates all vulnerabilities and threats in an attempt to determine what should (or must) be improved. There is no quantitative framework for evaluating risk.

Many in the risk analysis community have recently argued for game theory as a paradigm for security evaluation, with the major advantage that it explicitly models the adaptive behavior of an intelligent adversary. Cox (2008) provides a detailed discussion of the common risk = threat × vulnerability × consequence model, including analysis of an example use of the model. He raises several arguments as weaknesses of the approach, including:

(1) The values are fundamentally subjective;
(2) rankings of risk are often used but are insufficient;
(3) there are mathematical difficulties with the equation, including dependencies between the multiplied terms; and
(4) the model does not account for adaptive, intelligent attackers.

One of the main recommendations of the paper is to adopt more intelligent models of attacker behavior, instead of simpler, static risk estimates.

Bier et al. (2009) provide a high-level discussion of game-theoretic analysis in security applications and their limitations. The main argument is that the *adaptive* nature of the terrorist threat leads to many problems with static models – such models may overstate the protective value of a policy by not anticipating an attacker's options to circumvent the policy. They explicitly propose using quantitative risk analysis to provide probability/consequence numbers for game-theoretic analysis.

Beir (2007) performs a theoretical analysis of the implications of a Bayesian Stackelberg security game that is very similar to the one solved by ARMOR, although most of the analysis assumes that the defender does *not* know the attacker's payoffs. The primary goal is to examine intuitive implications of the model, such as the need to leave targets uncovered in some cases so as not to drive attackers towards more valuable targets. There are no "real world" evaluation of the model. Other work (Bier et al., 2008) considers high-level budget allocation (e.g., to large metropolitan areas). While the study uses real data, its focus is not model evaluation but the implications resulting from the model.

Game theory does have much to offer in our view, but it should not be considered a panacea for security evaluation. One difficulty is that human behavior often does not correspond exactly to game-theoretic predictions in controlled studies. Weibull (2004) describes many of the complex issues associated with testing game-theoretic predictions in a laboratory setting, including discussing the ongoing argument over whether people typically play the Nash equilibrium or not (a point discussed at length in the literature, such as in Erev et al. (2002)). This is one reason we believe behavioral studies with humans are an important element for security system evaluation.

Many of the issues we describe in acquiring useful real-world data for evaluation purposes are mirrored in other types of domains. Blundell and Costa-Dias (2009) describe approaches to experimental design and the analysis of policy proposals in microeconomics, where data is limited in many of the same ways: It is often not possible to run controlled experiments, and many desired data cannot be observed. They describe several classes of statistical methods for these cases, some of which may be valuable in the security setting (though data sensitivity and sparse observations pose significant additional challenges). In truth, it is often hard to evaluate complex deployed systems in general — in our field a test of the prototype often suffices (c.f., Scerri et al. (2008)).

Jacobson et al. (2005) describe a deployed model for screening airline passenger baggage. The model includes detailed information regarding the estimated costs of many aspects of the screening process, including variables for attack probability and the costs of a failed detection, but they note that these are difficult to estimate and leave it to other security experts to determine. One particularly interesting aspect of the approach is that they perform sensitivity analysis on the model in order to assess the effect of different values on the overall decisions. Unfortunately, the authors have little to say about actually setting the input values to their model; in fact, there is no empirical data validating their screening approach.

Kearns and Ortiz (2003) introduce algorithms for a class of "interdependent" security games, where the security investment of one player has a positive externality and increases the security of other players. They run the algorithms on data from the airline domain but do not directly evaluate their approach, instead looking at properties of the equilibrium solution and considering the broad insight that this solution yields regarding the benefits of subsidizing security in such games.

Lastly, the field of *fraud detection* (Kou et al., 2004), encompassing credit card fraud, computer intrusion, and telecommunications fraud, is also related. Similar to the physical security problem, data is difficult to access, researchers often do not share techniques, and deterrence is difficult (or impossible) to measure. Significant differences include:

1. Humans can often classify (in retrospect) false positives and false negatives, allowing researchers to accurately evaluate strategies.
2. Companies have significant amounts of data regarding known attacks, even if they do not typically share the data outside the company. Some datasets do exist for common comparisons (c.f., the 1998 DARPA Intrusion Detection Evaluation data).[3]

---

[3] For data and program details, see http://www.ll.mit.edu/mission/communications/ist/index.html.

3. The frequency of such attacks is much higher than physical terrorist attacks, providing significant training/evaluation data.
4. Defenders can evaluate multiple strategies (e.g., classifiers) on real-time data; whereas, physical security may employ and evaluate, only, one strategy at a time.

13.8 Conclusions

This chapter has discussed existing evaluations of the deployed ARMOR and IRIS systems. These results show how such systems can be reasonably evaluated, and in particular show that ARMOR works well in theory, and that security experts agree it is beneficial. In many ways, this level of evaluation goes beyond what is typical of applications, even those deployed in real-world settings. Overall, we find strong evidence to support the use of ARMOR over previous methods.

Another point worth stressing is that ARMOR and IRIS are relatively easy to use. ARMOR in particular has been instrumental in aiding the police forces to efficiently and more conveniently generate schedules to deploy more and more units. For example, consider a situation when only two canines need to be scheduled for two hours each over any of the seven terminals. Each canine could be assigned to any of the seven terminals each hour, making the search space as large as $7^4 (= 2401)$ combinations. This search space grows exponentially with the number of canines and the number of hours for which the schedule needs to be generated, making it impractical for human schedulers. Thus, ARMOR has played a significant role in reducing, if not completely eliminating, the work of officers who manually constructed patrolling schedules. Additionally, the use of ARMOR has also made it possible for the security officers to update the generated schedules, in case more resources become available or new constraints need to be incorporated. Furthermore, even though ARMOR was designed as a mixed initiative system, users have chosen not to modify ARMOR schedules in practice, which suggests that the output schedules are indeed high-quality, and that domain experts have not chosen to tweak the system's decisions. These added benefits have been a contributing factor toward the continued use of schedules generated by ARMOR. Most importantly, when considering the cost of implementing a decision-support system, it is important to consider ways in which the system may actually reduce security costs.

While none of the evaluation tests presented can calculate a measure's utility with absolute accuracy, understanding what each test *can* provide will help evaluators better understand what tests *should* be run on deployed systems. The goal of such tests will always be to provide better understanding to the "customer," whether researchers, users, or policy makers. By running multiple types of tests, utility (the primary quantity) can be approximated with increasing reliability.

At a higher level, thorough cost-benefit analyses can provide information to policy makers at the interdomain level. For instance, consider the following example from Tengs and Graham (1996):

> To regulate the flammability of children's clothing we spend $1.5 million per year of life saved, while some 30% of those children live in homes without smoke alarms, an investment that costs about $200,000 per year of life saved.

This kind of comparative cost-benefit analysis is beyond the scope of the current study; however, these statistics show how such an analysis can be used to compare how effective measures are across very different domains, and could be used to compare different proposed security measures.

In the future we plan to use this framework to help decide which evaluation tests are most important to determining the utility of a deployed, security-focused decision-support system. Additionally, we intend to continue collaborating with security experts to determine if our evaluations are sufficiently general to cover all existing types of security tests.

Currently, the majority of our evaluations have been conducted on the ARMOR system. However, we intend to continue testing IRIS and other newly developed domains, to both better evaluate the domains and to attempt to discover or improve evaluation techniques in the context of deployed systems.

Finally, a new type of decision-support system is currently being developed at the Teamcore lab, which will focus on scheduling patrols on the Los Angeles subway system to look for ticketless travelers. While this application can still be framed as a security problem, we expect that there will be much more data available. In particular, we will have many events when "attackers" are caught using the subway system without a ticket, and we may be able to enable and disable the system on different days, allowing us to measure how the deterrence effect impacts the number of ticketless travelers over time.

Acknowledgments

The authors would like to thank Manish Jain, James Pita, and Vicki Bier for helpful comments and suggestions, Sergeant Jim Holcomb for supplying ARMOR-related arrest data, and First Sargent Cruz for discussing pre-ARMOR scheduling procedures. This research was supported in part by the United States

Department of Homeland Security through the National Center for Risk and Economic Analysis of Terrorism Events (CREATE) under grant number 2007-ST-061-000001. However, any opinions, findings, and conclusions or recommendations in this document are those of the authors and do not necessarily reflect views of the United States Department of Homeland Security.

PART V

Short Bios

Author Bios

Lieutenant Fred S. Bertsch IV graduated the U.S. Coast Guard Academy in 2001 with honors, earning a bachelor of science degree in operations research. During his Coast Guard career, he has served more than six years afloat on Coast Guard cutters. Following his first tour aboard the U.S. Coast Guard cutter (USCGC) *Tampa* (WMEC 902) in Porstmouth, Virginia, he was assigned as the commanding officer of USCGC *Cobia* (WPB 87311) in Mobile, Alabama. Fred Bertsch has also commanded two additional Coast Guard patrol boats, USCGC *Aquidneck* (WPB 1309) and USCGC *Nantucket* (WPB 1316). He commanded the USCGC *Aquidneck* for a year while forward deployed to Patrol Forces Southwest Asia in the Kingdom of Bahrain, supporting Operations Iraqi Freedom and Enduring Freedom. Fred Bertsch earned a masters' degree in industrial engineering from Purdue University. Implementing his experience and education, he served onboard the Atlantic Area Planning and Operations Analysis staff for two and a half years. During this period, he was an integral part of the efforts to develop mitigation strategies for the decommissioning of eight 123-foot patrol boats, implementing the standard operational planning process, and developing risk-based strategies for resource allocation.

Vincent Conitzer is the Sally Dalton Robinson Professor of Computer Science and Professor of Economics at Duke University. He received PhD (2006) and MS (2003) degrees in computer science from Carnegie Mellon University and an AB (2001) degree in applied mathematics from Harvard University. His research focuses on computational aspects of microeconomics, in particular, game theory, mechanism design, voting/social choice, and auctions. This work uses techniques from, and includes applications to, artificial intelligence and multi-agent systems. Conitzer has received the IJCAI (International Joint Conference on Artificial Intelligence) Computers and Thought Award, a National Science Foundation Career Award, a Sloan fellowship, the inaugural Victor

Lesser dissertation award, an honorable mention for the ACM (Association for Computing Machinery) dissertation award, and several awards for papers and service at the AAAI (National Conference on Artificial Intelligence) and AAMAS (International Conference on Autonomous Agents and Multiagent Systems) conferences.

Shane Cullen started his government career as a sniper in the United States Army. Upon graduation from George Mason University, he supported the implementation of a system that digitized medical records for the Army Medical Department as a contractor. By 2002, he was a United States Secret Service Uniformed Division Officer assigned to the Vice Presidential Protective Division. Mr. Cullen joined DHS S&T as a contractor in 2005 supporting forensic and law enforcement technology projects for local, state, and federal agencies. In November 2007, he joined DHS S&T as a federal employee and now serves as a Program Manager for Law Enforcement-Related Technologies with particular emphasis on traditional forensic analysis; small-scale device and computer forensics; and tagging, tracking, and locating technology.

Joe DiRenzo III is Coast Guard Atlantic Area's chief of operations analysis. He is a retired Coast Guard officer who spent nine years in the Navy, in both the submarine and surface warfare communities, before transiting to the Coast Guard. Following service on USCGC *Gallatin* and USCGC *Vashon*, Dr. DiRenzo was assigned to the Greater Antilles Section in San Juan, Puerto Rico, as a command center controller and then chief of intelligence. In 1997 he was detailed to USCGC *Jefferson Island*, homeported in Portland, Maine, as the inaugural Coast Guard liaison officer assigned to the Constellation battle group (CRUDESGRU ONE staff) and PELELIU ARG (PHIBRON ONE staff) deployed to the Arabian Gulf. In 2000 Dr. DiRenzo was detailed to the Atlantic Area staff in Portsmouth, Virginia, serving initially as the Operation's Division regional strategic assessment coordinator, then as anti-terrorism coordinator. Following his retirement from active duty in 2003, he has served in a number of roles as a Coast Guard civilian.

Dr. DiRenzo is one of the most published authors in the history of the Coast Guard. A five-time winner of the service's prestigious JOC Alex Haley Award, he has published more than 300 articles on various maritime terrorism and port security topics in publications such as *Marine News*, the *Maritime Reporter*, *Proceedings*, the *American Legion Magazine*, *National Defense*, and *Undersea Warfare*. He has lectured at numerous military, academic, and law enforcement educational institutions, including the Canadian Forces College, and was the keynote speaker at Dalhouise University's 2007 Maritime Security Conference.

Dr. DiRenzo is a 1982 graduate of the United States Naval Academy, holds a master's degree in business administration from California Coast University, and is a graduate of both the Naval War College and Marine Corps Command and Staff College. He completed his PhD in business administration (homeland security specialization) in 2007 at Northcentral University in Prescott, Arizona. He is currently an adjunct professor at the Joint Forces Staff College, in Norfolk, Virginia, and teaches at both American Military University and Northcentral University.

Manish Jain is currently a PhD candidate at the University of Southern California. He is a part of the Teamcore Research Group, led by Professor Milind Tambe. His work is on the applications of game-theoretic and large-scale optimization techniques, including the scheduling of flights and air marshals for the Federal Air Marshals Service and of checkpoints for the Los Angeles International Airport (LAX) police. He has coauthored papers on the subject of security games that have been presented a major artificial intelligence and operations research conferences. His work has been published in the journal *Interfaces*, and he was a finalist for the EURO Excellence in Practice Award. He has also received a Letter of Commendation from the city of Los Angeles for his contributions to the development of the security assistant deployed at LAX.

Lieutenant Commander Erik Jensen is a 1995 graduate of the State University of New York Maritime College at Fort Schuyler in the Bronx, New York, where he was awarded a BS degree in meteorology and oceanography, with a concentration in environmental science. He holds a Master of Aeronautical Science Degree, with specializations in aviation/aeronautical management and safety systems, awarded by Embry-Riddle Aeronautical University, where he was recognized in *Who's Who in American Colleges and Universities* in 2003. He is currently an adjunct instructor at Embry-Riddle Aeronautical University. Assignments include marine safety staff work in the Eighth Coast Guard District; Merchant Marine licensing supervisor at the Regional Exam Center in New Orleans, Louisiana; primary and intermediate flight training at Naval Air Station (NAS) Whiting Field, Florida; advanced flight training at NAS Corpus Christi, Texas, where he earned his Wings of Gold in 1999; a five-year tour at Coast Guard Air Station Corpus Christi, performing various collateral duties and qualifying as an aircraft commander in the HU-25 A/B/C Falcon; a four-year tour at Coast Guard Air Station Cape Cod, Massachusetts, where he served as the flight safety department head for three of the four years; and more than a year as the Aviation Forces Manager at Coast Guard Atlantic Area. He is currently serving as an aviation opperational analyst and expert within the LANT-7 Operational Analysis Division of Atlantic Area and was recently selected for promotion to commander.

LCDR Jensen's awards include three Achievement Medals, a Commandant's Letter of Commendation, a Military Outstanding Volunteer Service Medal, and Naval Aviator Wings. LCDR Jensen is designated Coast Guard Aviator #3439 and has more than 3200 hours of flight time.

Erim Kardeş

Christopher Kiekintveld is an assistant professor at the University of Texas at El Paso. His research focuses on computational decision making and tools for designing intelligent agents, particularly for complex multi-agent systems. His contributions span many areas, including computational game theory, distributed optimization, risk analysis, adversarial reasoning, agent-based modeling and simulation, auctions, and trading agents. He received his PhD in 2008 from the University of Michigan for his thesis work on trading agent design and strategic reasoning using simulation and empirical game-modeling techniques. During this time, he was a lead developer for Deep Maize, a champion agent designed for the Trading Agent Competition Supply Chain Management game. His most recent work applies game theory to real-world homeland security problems to generate unpredictable, risk-based resource-allocation strategies. He has contributed to algorithmic advances that dramatically increase the scalability of game theory solutions for security resource-allocation problems, as well as new modeling techniques that improve the robustness of solutions to many different kinds of uncertainty about the models and human behavior. The IRIS system based on this research is currently deployed by the Federal Air Marshals Service, and the GUARDS system developed for the Transportation Security Administration is currently under evaluation for nationwide deployment. The work was recently acknowledged with a best paper award at the top international conference on multi-agent systems and was a finalist for the EURO Excellence in Practice Award.

Dmytro Korzhyk is a PhD student in Duke University's Department of Computer Science. His main research interest is in computational aspects of game theory. Dmytro has published work on efficient algorithms for computing optimal strategies to commit to in security games, as well as on issues of observability in general-sum normal-form games. He has been a reviewer for the *Artificial Intelligence Journal* and AAMAS. Dmytro is a recipient of the J.B. Duke Fellowship at Duke. Dmytro received MS (2007) and BS (2006) degrees in computer science from National Technical University (NTU) of Ukraine, where he was also a recipient of the Scholarship of the President of

Ukraine. During his years at NTU of Ukraine, Dmytro was a finalist of Top-Coder Algorithm Competitions, Google Code Jam, and the ACM International Collegiate Programming Contest.

Sarit Kraus (PhD Computer Science, Hebrew University, 1989) is a professor of computer science at Bar-Ilan University and adjunct professor at the Institute for Advanced Computer Studies, University of Maryland. She has worked extensively in the following areas: development of intelligent systems, negotiation and cooperation in mixed open environments (including people), personalization, learning and clustering, optimization of complex systems, and security of physical systems. In 1995 Kraus was awarded the International Joint Conference on Artificial Intelligence (IJCAI) Computers and Thought Award (the premier award for a young AI scientist). In 2001 she was awarded the IBM Faculty Partnership Award, and in 2002 she was elected as AAAI Fellow (Association for the Advancement of Artificial Intelligence). In 2007 she was awarded the ACM SIGART Agents Research Award, and her paper with Professor Barbara Grosz was a winner of the IFAAMAS Influential Paper Award (joint winner). In 2008 she was elected as a European Coordinating Committee for Artificial Intelligence (ECCAI) Fellow, and in 2010 she was awarded the EMET prize. She has published more than 270 papers in leading journals and at major conferences and is an author of the book *Strategic Negotiation in Multiagent Environments* (2001) and a coauthor of a book on heterogeneous active agents (2000, both published by MIT Press). Kraus is an associate editor of the journal *Annals of Mathematics and Artificial Intelligence* and is on the editorial board of the journal *Autonomous Agents and Multi-Agent Systems, Journal of Applied Logic, Journal of Philosophical Logic*, and *ACM Transactions on Intelligent Systems and Technology*.

Reuma Magori-Cohen is a researcher in statistics and computational biology. Her fields of interest are various and include immunology,genetics, epidemiology, and psychology. She has been teaching probability, statistics, operations research, and optimization at Bar-Ilan University since 2005.

Janusz Marecki is a research staff member at the mathematical sciences department at IBM T.J. Watson Research Center. Janusz obtained his PhD in artificial intelligence from University of Southern California and Dr.Sc in mathematical modeling from State Scientific and Research Institute of Information Infrastructure in Ukraine. Prior to joining IBM Research, Janusz was a research assistant at the European Laboratory for Nuclear Research, a research associate at the Ukrainian Academy of Sciences, and a lecturer at the Academy of Computer Sciences in Poland. His research interests are in reasoning under uncertainty, with an emphasis on planning under uncertainty in cooperative and adversarial agent systems. An author of more than 80 refereed publications and four patents, Janusz is a recipient of a commendation from the Los Angeles Airport Police, a commendation from the Department of Homeland Security, and an Invention Award from the IBM CEO.

Lieutenant Commander Ben Maule is currently assigned to Operations Analysis Division at U.S. Coast Guard Atlantic Area, Portsmouth, Virginia. Originally from Denver, Colorado, LCDR Maule is a 1998 graduate of the United States Coast Guard Academy, where he earned a bachelor of science degree in mechanical engineering. Upon graduation, LCDR Maule served aboard the USCG cutter *Gallatin* as the auxiliary and electrical assistant, gaining qualification as an Engineer Officer in Training. In 2000, LCDR Maule was accepted to Naval Flight Training and began his aviation career in Pensacola, Florida. Earning his designation as a Naval Aviator in 2001, LCDR Maule transferred to Coast Guard Air Station Traverse City, Michigan, where he earned his qualification as an aircraft commander. He served as the communications officer, schedules officer, education services officer, and aviation materiel officer. In 2005, LCDR Maule transferred to the Alaska Patrol (ALPAT) division at Coast Guard Air Station Kodiak, Alaska. There he served as the awards officer, chief schedules officer, and HH65 assistant operations officer. LCDR Maule deployed aboard Coast Guard cutters in the Bering Sea six times and to the Eastern Pacific once during the three years he was assigned to Air Station Kodiak. In 2008, LCDR Maule attended Purdue University, earning a master's degree in industrial engineering, with emphasis in operations research. Upon completion of this program, LCDR Maule transferred to the Coast Guard Atlantic Area Command in Portsmouth, Virginia.

Fernando Ordóñez is an associate professor in the Industrial and Systems Engineering Department at the University of Southern California. He is also a faculty member in the Industrial Engineering Department at the University of Chile. His research focuses on convex optimization, optimization under uncertainty, complexity of algorithms, sensitivity analysis, and applications of optimization to engineering and management science. His work has been supported with grants from the National Science Foundation, PATH, Caltrans, and the Department of Homeland Security. He is an area editor of *Computers & Industrial Engineering*. Dr. Ordóñez received a BS and a mathematical engineering degree from the University of Chile in 1996 and 1997, respectively, and his PhD in operations research from the Massachusetts Institute of Technology in 2002.

Praveen Paruchuri is currently a postdoctoral Fellow at Carnegie Mellon University with Professor Katia Sycara. He obtained his PhD in 2007 in the area of security using multi-agent systems under the guidance of Professor Milind Tambe at the University of Southern California. Praveen's broad research interests are in the fields of applied artificial intelligence, agents/multi-agent systems, decision-game-theoretic reasoning, practical security systems, and automated negotiation. He was given the Best Paper Award at the SASEMAS International workshop '05 and was nominated (as a coauthor) for the Best Paper Award in AAMAS '08 for developing security algorithms. His game-theoretic algorithm named DOBSS initiated and became the heart of the ARMOR security scheduler that is currently deployed at the Los Angeles International Airport. This work has been described in various national and international news media such as *Newsweek*, *Los Angeles Times*, *Times of India*, and *Lenta.Ru*. He is the first author of a book and has published many papers, including two finalists for best paper awards and holds two provisional patents based on his work on improving security. He was officially nominated by USC in 2008 for the TR-35 Award and was profiled as an innovator of this work by the USC Stevens Institute for Innovation.

Jonathan P. Pearce is a quantitative strategist at Knight Capital Group, where he works on automated trading algorithms. He received his PhD in computer science from the University of Southern California in 2007, where he did research in artificial intelligence and multi-agent systems under Professor Milind Tambe. He received his M.Eng. and SB in computer science and his SB in finance from the Massachusetts Institute of Technology. Jonathan's research interests include markets, distributed optimization, computational game theory, and privacy in collaborative environments. His papers have been published in the *Journal of Autonomous Agents and Multiagent Systems* (JAAMAS) as well as in the proceedings of the AAAI, IJCAI, and AAMAS conferences.

James Pita is a doctoral student in computer science at the University of Southern California. He is a member of the Teamcore Research Group, led by Professor Milind Tambe. His research focuses on the application of game-theoretic techniques, including the randomized scheduling of resources for the Transportation Security Administration in a risk-based manner and the scheduling of checkpoints and canines for the Los Angeles International Airport (LAX) police. He has received a Letter of Commendation from the city of Los Angeles for his contributions to the development of the security assistant deployed at LAX. He was a finalist for the EURO Excellence in Practice Award for the published work he coauthored in *Interfaces*. In addition to the systems he has helped deploy, his research examines novel game-theoretic approaches within security settings for addressing human-response uncertainty due to cognitive limitations.

Christopher Portway received his BS in Computer Science at USC, where he performed research with Milind Tambe. He later earned his M.S.E. in Computer Science – Intelligent Systems from the University of Michigan. He is currently working at Siemens Corporate Research.

Shyamsunder Rathi has completed his MS in computer science from University of Southern California. He has worked with the ARMOR and IRIS teams as part of Teamcore Research Group, under the guidance of Professor Milind Tambe. At present, he works as a software engineer at Brocade Communications Systems in San Jose, California.

Erroll G. Southers, a former FBI special agent, was President Barack Obama's first nominee for assistant secretary of the Transportation Security Administration and Governor Arnold Schwarzenegger's deputy director for critical infrastructure of the California Office of Homeland Security. He is the associate director of the National Homeland Security Center for Risk and Economic Analysis of Terrorism Events (CREATE) at the University of Southern California (USC), where he developed the Executive Program in Counter-Terrorism and serves as an adjunct professor of homeland security and public policy. Mr. Southers is also the managing director of the Counter-Terrorism and Infrastructure Protection Division of the international security consulting firm TAL Global Corporation. Mr. Southers was the assistant chief of homeland security and intelligence at the Los Angeles World Airports Police Department, the nation's largest such force. He began his law enforcement career with the Santa Monica Police Department and was appointed to the faculty and tactical staff of the Rio Hondo Police Academy. In the FBI, he investigated foreign counterintelligence and terrorism matters and served as a member of SWAT. He has testified as a subject matter expert before the full Congressional Committee on Homeland Security and lectures at the Joint Chiefs of Staff antiterrorism seminars.

Southers earned his BA degree at Brown University and his MPA at USC, and he is a senior Fellow of the UCLA School of Public Affairs. He lectures widely on terrorism and international security and has appeared on CNN, MSNBC, National Public Radio (NPR), and a host of other media outlets.

Erin Steigerwald is the Program Manager for the Transportation Security Administration's (TSA) unpredictable security measures implementation program, TSA Security Playbook, a position she has held since December 2008 when the program rolled out nationally to 458 federalized airports. The Playbook concept is designed to create a transportation security system that increases unpredictability, thereby frustrating terrorist plans and potentially deterring attacks. Playbook also acts as a flexible and deployable system of counter-measures, coordinated at the local level, and intended to address emergency conditions or hostile acts. Since January 2011, Ms. Steigerwald has also been working on TSA Administrator Pistole's Risk-Based Security (RBS) project, for which she served as a Site Lead for the launch of TSA PreCheck at Detroit Metropolitan Wayne County Airport (DTW) on October 4, 2011.

Milind Tambe is a professor of computer science and industrial and systems engineering at the University of Southern California (USC). He leads the Teamcore Research Group at USC, with research focused on agent-based and multi-agent systems. He is a Fellow of AAAI (Association for Advancement of Artificial Intelligence) and recipient of the ACM (Association for Computing Machinery) Autonomous Agents Research Award. He is also the recipient of the Christopher Columbus Fellowship Foundation Homeland security award, U.S. First Coast Guard District's Operational Excellence Award, Certificate of Appreciation from the U.S. Federal Air Marshals Service, a special commendation given by the Los Angeles World Airports police from the city of Los Angeles; a USC Viterbi School of Engineering use-inspired research award; an Okawa Foundation faculty research award; the RoboCup Scientific Challenge Award; the USC Steven B. Sample Teaching and Mentoring Award; and the ACM recognition of service award. The papers of Professor Tambe and his research group have been selected as best papers or have been finalists for best papers at a dozen premier artificial intelligence and operations research conferences and workshops, and their algorithms have been deployed for real-world use by several agencies, including the LAX police, the Federal Air Marshals Service, and the Transportation Security Administration. He received his PhD from the School of Computer Science at Carnegie Mellon University.

Matthew E. Taylor is an assistant professor in the Computer Science Department at Lafayette College. He received his doctorate from the University of Texas at Austin in 2008, supervised by Peter Stone. After graduation, Dr. Taylor worked for two years as a postdoctoral research assistant at the University of Southern California with Milind Tambe. Current research interests include intelligent agents, multi-agent systems, reinforcement learning, and transfer learning.

Jason Tsai is a PhD student at the University of Southern California. He completed his undergraduate studies as an economics major at Harvard University and has worked at the management consulting firm Oliver Wyman. He is currently a member of the Teamcore Research Group, led by Professor Milind Tambe, which focuses on multi-agent systems research with a use-inspired motivation. His research interests are in interdisciplinary applications of multi-agent techniques, such as in security, transportation, finance, and social psychology. Past projects include game-theoretic resource allocation for the Federal Air Marshal Service as well as for urban network domains. His work for the Federal Air Marshal Service advanced the state of the art in solving massive Stackelberg games and was recognized with a first prize at the third annual Department of Homeland Security Research Summit in 2009 as well as the Best Industry Track Paper Award at the Autonomous Agents and Multi-Agent Systems (AAMAS) conference in 2009. His current work uses social psychology to inform the design of agents that possess realistic emotional as well as cognitive components.

Craig Western graduated from the University of Southern California in May 2011 with a degree in Mechanical Engineering. Honored as a USA Presidential Scholar in 2007, Craig has pursued engineering opportunities both working in robotics at NASA's Jet Propulsion Laboratory in Pasadena, California, and volunteering in international development as a project manager of USC's Engineers Without Borders program in Honduras. Craig's work with the TEAMCORE research group during his undergraduate career at USC focused on the ARMOR project and the application of game theory to security problems. Craig is currently spending a year in Taipei, Taiwan, as a Luce Fellow, undertaking Chinese language study and serving as a member of the Precision Systems Control Laboratory at National Taiwan University.

Zhengyu Yin is a PhD student in the Computer Science Department of University of Southern California. He is a member of the Teamcore Research Group at USC led by Professor Milind Tambe. His primary research interests focus on multi-agent systems, game theory, and optimization. Before joining USC, he received a bachelor's degree with honors from the Department of Computer Science and Technology, Tsinghua University, in 2008.

References

Chapter 1

N. Basilico, N. Gatti, and F. Amigoni. Leader-follower strategies for robotic patrolling in environments with arbitrary topologies. In *International Conference on Autonomous Agents and Multiagent Systems (AAMAS)*, 2009.

C. F. Camerer. *Behavioral Game Theory: Experiments in Strategic Interaction*, Princeton University Press, New Jersey, 2003.

V. Conitzer and T. Sandholm. Computing the optimal strategy to commit to. In *ACM Conference on Electronic Commerce*, 2006.

J. Dickerson, G. Simari, V. Subrahmanian, and S. Kraus. A graph-theoretic approach to protect static and moving targets from adversaries. In *International Conference on Autonomous Agents and Multiagent Systems (AAMAS)*, 2010.

D. Fudenberg and J. Tirole. *Game Theory*. MIT Press, 1991.

GAO United States Government Accountability Office Federal Air Marshal Service Has Taken Actions to Fulfill Its Core Mission and Address Workforce Issues, but Additional Actions Are Needed to Improve Workforce Survey, http://www.gao.gov/highlights/d09273high.pdf, 2009.

J. C. Harsanyi and R. Selten. A generalized Nash solution for two-person bargaining games with incomplete information. *Management Science*, 18(5):80–106, 1972.

M. Jain, E. Kardes, C. Kiekintveld, F. Ordonez, and M. Tambe. Security Games with Arbitrary Schedules: A Branch and Price Approach. In *Proceedings of Association for Advancement of Artificial Intelligence (AAAI)*, 2010.

M. Jain, D. Korzhyk, O. Vanek, V. Conitzer, M. Pechoucek, and M. Tambe. A Double Oracle Algorithm for Zero-Sum Security Games on Graphs. In *International Conference on Autonomous Agents and Multiagent Systems (AAMAS)*, 2011a.

M. Jain, C. Kiekintveld, and M. Tambe. Quality-bounded Solutions for Finite Bayesian Stackelberg Games: Scaling up. In *International Conference on Autonomous Agents and Multiagent Systems (AAMAS)*, 2011b.

C. Kiekintveld, M. Jain, J. Tsai, J. Pita, M. Tambe, and F. Ordonez. Computing Optimal Randomized Resource Allocations for Massive Security Games. In *International Conference on Autonomous Agents and Multiagent Systems (AAMAS)*, 2009.

C. Kiekintveld, J. Marecki, and M. Tambe. Approximation Methods for Infinite Bayesian Stackelberg Games: Modeling Distributional Uncertainty. In *Proceedings of the*

International Conference on Autonomous Agents and Multiagent Systems (AAMAS), 2011.

D. Korzhyk, V. Conitzer, and R. Parr. Complexity of computing optimal Stackelberg strategies in security resource allocation games. In *National Conference on Artificial Intelligence (AAAI)*, 2010.

A. Murr. The Element of Surprise. *Newsweek National News*, http://www.newsweek.com/2007/10/13/random-checks.html, 2007

J. Nash. Non-cooperative Games. *The Annals of Mathematics.* 54, 2: 286–295, 1951.

P. Paruchuri, J. P. Pearce, M. Tambe, F. Ordonez, and S. Kraus. An Efficient Heuristic Approach for Security Against Multiple Adversaries. In *International Conference on Autonomous Agents and Multiagent Systems (AAMAS)*, 2007.

P. Paruchuri, J. Pearce, J. Marecki, M. Tambe, F. Ordonez, and S. Kraus. Coordinating randomized policies for increasing security of agent systems. In *Journal of Information Technology and Management (ITM)*, 10:67–79, 2009.

J. Pita, M. Jain, C. Western, C. Portway, M. Tambe, F. Ordonez, S. Kraus, and P. Paruchuri. Deployed ARMOR protection: The application of game theoretic model for security at the Los Angeles International Airport. In *International Conference on Autonomous Agents and Multiagent Systems (AAMAS)*, Industry Track, 2008.

J. Pita, M. Jain, M. Tambe, F. Ordonez, S. Kraus, and R. Magori-Cohen. Efficient solutions for real-world Stackelberg games. In *International Conference on Autonomous Agents and Multiagent Systems (AAMAS)*, 2009.

J. Pita, C. Kiekintveld, M. Tambe, S. Cullen, and E. Steigerwald. GUARDS – Game Theoretic Security Allocation on a National Scale. In *International Conference on Autonomous Agents and Multiagent Systems (AAMAS)*, 2011.

R. Powell. Defending against terrorist attacks with limited resources. *American Political Science Review* 101(3): 527–541, 2007.

J. Tsai, S. Rathi, C. Kiekintveld, F. Ordonez, and M. Tambe. IRIS – a tool for strategic security application in transportation networks. In *International Conference on Autonomous Agents and Multiagent Systems (AAMAS)*, Industry Track, 2009.

J. Tsai, Z. Yin, J. Kwak, D. Kempe, C. Kiekintveld, and M. Tambe. Urban Security: Game-Theoretic Resource Allocation in Networked Physical Domains. In *Proceedings of Association for Advancement of Artificial Intelligence (AAAI)*, 2010.

O. Vanek, B. Bošanský, M. Jakob, and M. Pechoucek. Transiting areas patrolled by a mobile adversary. In *IEEE CIG*, 2010.

J. von Neumann and O. Morgenstern. *Theory of Games and Economic Behavior*, Princeton University Press, New Jersey, 1944.

H. von Stackelberg. *Marktform und Gleichgewicht*. Springer. 1934. (*translated: Market Structure and Equilibrium*. 1st Edition. 2010).

W.A. Wagenaar. Generation of Random Sequences by Human Subjects: A Critical Survey of Literature. *Psychological Bulletin* 77(1):65–72, 1972.

Z. Yin, D. Korzhyk, C. Kiekintveld, V. Conitzer, and M. Tambe. Stackelberg vs. Nash in Security Games: Interchangeability, Equivalence, and Uniqueness. In *Proceedings of the International Conference on Autonomous Agents and Multiagent Systems (AAMAS)*, 2010.

Chapter 3

J.J. Corbett & J. Winebrake, (2008, Nov 10). The Impacts of Globalisation on International Maritime Transport Activity: Past Trends and Future Perspectives, Paper presented at the Global Forum on Transportation and Environment in a Globalising World. Retrieved from http://www.oecd.org/dataoecd/10/61/41380820.pdf

R.A. Pape, (2003). The Strategic Logic of Suicide Terrorism. *American Political Science Review,* 97(3), 343–361. Retrieved ABI/GLOBAL Database.

Chapter 4

General Description: Just the Facts. http://www.lawa.org/lax/justTheFact.cfm, 2007.

N. Billante. The Beat Goes On: Policing for Crime Prevention. http://www.cis.org.au/IssueAnalysis/ia38/ia38.htm, 2003.

G. Brown, M. Carlyle, J. Salmeron, and K. Wood. Defending Critical Infrastructure. *Interfaces,* 36(6):530–544, 2006.

V. Conitzer and T. Sandholm. Computing the Optimal Strategy to Commit to. In *International Conference on Electronic Commerce (EC),* 2006.

D. Fudenberg and J. Tirole. *Game Theory.* MIT Press, 1991.

J. C. Harsanyi and R. Selten. A Generalized Nash Solution for Two-person Bargaining Games With Incomplete Information. *Management Science,* 18(5):80–106, 1972.

R. C. Larson. A Hypercube Queuing Model for Facility Location and Redistricting in Urban Emergency Services. *Computer and OR,* 1(1):67–95, 1974.

A. Murr. The Element of Surprise. *Newsweek National News,* http://www.msnbc.msn.com/id/21035785/site/newsweek/page/0/, September 28, 2007.

P. Paruchuri, J. P. Pearce, J. Marecki, M. Tambe, F. Ordóñez, and S. Kraus. Playing games for security: An efficient exact algorithm for solving bayesian stackelberg games. In *International Conference on Autonomous Agents and Multiagent Systems (AAMAS),* 2008.

P. Paruchuri, J. P. Pearce, M. Tambe, F. Ordóñez, and S. Kraus. An Efficient Heuristic Approach for Security Against Multiple Adversaries. In *International Conference on Autonomous Agents and Multiagent Systems (AAMAS),* 2007.

P. Paruchuri, M. Tambe, F. Ordóñez, and S. Kraus. Security in Multiagent Systems by Policy Randomization. In *International Conference on Autonomous Agents and Multiagent Systems (AAMAS),* 2006.

P. Paruchuri, M. Tabme, F. Ordóñez, and S. Kraus. Safety in Multiagent Systems by Policy Randomization. In *International Workshop on Safety and Security in Multiagent Systems (SASEMAS),* 2005.

S. Ruan, C. Meirina, F. Yu, K. R. Pattipati, and R. L. Popp. Patrolling in a Stochastic Environment. In *10th Intl. Command and Control Research and Tech. Symp.,* 2005.

D. Stevens and et al. Implementing Security Improvement Options at Los Angeles International Airport. http://www.rand.org/pubs/documented_briefings/2006/RAND_DB499-1.pdf, 2006.

W. A. Wagenaar. *Generation of Random Sequences by Human Subjects: A Critical Survey of Literature.* 1972.

Chapter 5

Federal Air Marshal Service. http://en.wikipedia.org/wiki/Federal_Air_Marshal_Service, 2008.

TSA: Federal Air Marshals. http://www.tsa.gov/lawenforcement/programs/fams.shtm, 2008.

R. Avenhaus, B. von Stengel, and S. Zamir. Inspection games. In R. J. Aumann and S. Hart, editors, *Handbook of Game Theory*, volume 3, chapter 51, pages 1947–1987. North-Holland, Amsterdam, 2002.

N. Billante. The Beat Goes On: Policing for Crime Prevention. http://www.cis.org.au/IssueAnalysis/ia38/ia38.htm, 2003.

M. Blanco, A. Valino, J. Heijs, T. Baumert, and J. G. Gomez. The Economic Cost of March 11: Measuring the direct economic cost of the terrorist attack on March 11, 2004 in Madrid. *Terrorism and Political Violence*, 19(4):489–509, 2007.

G. Brown, M. Carlyle, J. Salmeron, and K. Wood. Defending Critical Infrastructure. *Interfaces*, 36(6):530–544, 2006.

L. Chen and P. Pu. Survey of preference elicitation methods. Technical report, Ecole Politechnique Federale de Lausanne, 2004.

V. Conitzer and T. Sandholm. Computing the optimal strategy to commit to. In *ACM Conference on Electronic Commerce*, 2006.

D. Kenney. *Police and Policing: Contemporary Issues*. Praeger, 1989.

C. Kiekintveld, M. Jain, J. Tsai, J. Pita, M. Tambe, and F. Ordonez. Computing Optimal Randomized Resource Allocations for Massive Security Games. In *International Conference on Autonomous Agents and Multiagent Systems (AAMAS)*, 2009.

R. Looney. Economic Costs to the United States Stemming From the 9/11 Attacks. *Strategic Insights*, 1(6), August 2002.

P. Paruchuri, J. P. Pearce, J. Marecki, M. Tambe, F. Ordonez, and S. Kraus. Playing games with security: An efficient exact algorithm for Bayesian Stackelberg games. In *International Conference on Autonomous Agents and Multiagent Systems (AAMAS)*, 2008.

P. Paruchuri, J. P. Pearce, M. Tambe, F. Ordonez, and S. Kraus. An Efficient Heuristic Approach for Security Against Multiple Adversaries. In *International Conference on Autonomous Agents and Multiagent Systems (AAMAS)*, 2007.

J. Pita, M. Jain, C. Western, C. Portway, M. Tambe, F. Ordonez, S. Kraus, and P. Parachuri. Depoloyed ARMOR protection: The application of a game-theoretic model for security at the Los Angeles International Airport. In *International Conference on Autonomous Agents and Multiagent Systems (AAMAS) (Industry Track)*, 2008.

S. Ruan, C. Meirina, F. Yu, K. R. Pattipati, and R. L. Popp. Patrolling in a Stochastic Environment. In *10th Intl. Command and Control Research and Tech. Symp.*, 2005.

T. Sandholm, A. Gilpin, and V. Conitzer. Mixed-integer programming methods for finding Nash equilibria. In *National Conference on Artificial Intelligence (AAAI)*, 2005.

P. Thornton. London Bombings: Economic cost of attacks estimated at 2bn, July 2005.

H. von Stackelberg. *Marktform und Gleichgewicht*. Springer, Vienna, 1934.

B. von Stengel and S. Zamir. Leadership with commitment to mixed strategies. Technical Report London School of Economics-Centre for Discrete and Applicable Mathematics (LSE-CDAM)-2004-01, CDAM Research Report, 2004.

W. A. Wagenaar. *Generation of Random Sequences by Human Subjects: A Critical Survey of Literature.* 1972.

H. Willis, A. Morral, T. Kelly, and J. Medby. *Estimating Terrorism Risk.* RAND Corporation, 2005.

Chapter 6

Air traffic control: By the numbers. In http://www.natca.org/mediacenter/ bythenumbers.msp#1.

TSA I Transportation Security Administration I U.S. Department of Homeland Security. In http://www.tsa.gov/.

N. Agmon. On events in multi-robot patrol in adversarial environments. In *International Conference on Autonomous Agents and Multiagent Systems (AAMAS)*, 2010.

N. Agmon, S. Kraus, G. Kaminka, and V. Sadov. Adversarial uncertainty in multi-robot patrol. In *International Joint Conference on Artificial Intelligence (IJCAI)*, 2009.

N. Basilico, N. Gatti, T. Rossi, S. Ceppi, and F. Amigoni. Extending algorithms for mobile robot patrolling in the presence of adversaries to more realistic settings. In *IAT*, 2009.

V. Conitzer and T. Sandholm. Computing the optimal strategy to commit to. In *International conference on Electronic Commerce (EC)*, 2006.

D. Fudenberg and J. Tirole. *Game Theory.* MIT Press, 1991.

M. Jain, E. Kardes, C. Kiekintveld, M. Tambe, and F. Ordóñez. Security games with arbitrary schedules: A branch and price approach. In *National Conference on Artificial Intelligence (AAAI)*, 2010.

C. Kiekintveld, M. Jain, J. Tsai, J. Pita, M. Tambe, and F. Ordóñez. Computing optimal randomized resource allocations for massive security games. In *International Conference on Autonomous Agents and Multiagent Systems (AAMAS)*, 2009.

D. Korzhyk, V. Conitzer, and R. Parr. Complexity of computing optimal Stackelberg strategies in security resource allocation games. In *National Conference on Artificial Intelligence (AAAI)*, 2010.

R. C. Larson. A hypercube queueing model for facility location and redistricting in urban emergency services. *Computers and OR*, 1(1):67–95, 1974.

P. Paruchuri, J. Marecki, J. Pearce, M. Tambe, F. Ordóñez, and S. Kraus. Playing games for security: An efficient exact algorithm for solving Bayesian Stackelberg games. In *International Conference on Autonomous Agents and Multiagent Systems (AAMAS)*, 2008.

P. Paruchuri, M. Tambe, F. Ordonez, and S. Kraus. Security in multiagent systems by policy randomization. In *International Conference on Autonomous Agents and Multiagent Systems (AAMAS)*, 2006.

J. Pita, M. Jain, J. Marecki, F. Ordóñez, C. Portway, M. Tambe, C. Western, P. Paruchuri, and S. Kraus. Deployed ARMOR protection: The application of a game theoretic model for security at the Los Angeles International Airport. In *International Conference on Autonomous Agents and Multiagent Systems (AAMAS)*, 2008.

J. Tsai, S. Rathi, C. Kiekintveld, F. Ordóñez, and M. Tambe. IRIS - a tool for strategic security allocation in transportation networks. In *International Conference on Autonomous Agents and Multiagent Systems (AAMAS)*, 2009.

W. A. Wagenaar. Generation of Random Sequences by Human Subjects: A Critical Survey of Literature. 1972.

Z. Yin, D. Korzhyk, C. Kiekintveld, V. Conitzer, and M. Tambe. Stackelberg vs. Nash in security games: Interchangeability, equivalence, and uniqueness. In *International Conference on Autonomous Agents and Multiagent Systems (AAMAS)*, 2010.

Chapter 7

R. Beard and T. McLain. Multiple uav cooperative search under collision avoidance and limited range communication constraints. In *IEEE Conference on Decision and Control (CDC)*, 2003.

N. Borisov and J. Waddle. Anonymity in structured peer-to-peer networks. In *University of California, Berkeley, Technical Report No. UCB/CSD-05-1390*, 2005.

G. Brown, M. Carlyle, J. Salmeron, and K. Wood. Defending critical infrastructures. *Interfaces*, 36(6):530–544, 2006.

J. Brynielsson and S. Arnborg. Bayesian games for threat prediction and situation analysis. In *International Conference on Information Fusion (FUSION)*, 2004.

D. M. Carroll, C. Nguyen, H. Everett, and B. Frederick. Development and testing for physical security robots. http://www.nosc.mil/robots/pubs/spie5804-63.pdf, 2005.

V. Conitzer and T. Sandholm. Choosing the optimal strategy to commit to. In *ACM Conference on Electronic Commerce*, 2006.

D. Dolgov and E. Durfee. Approximating optimal policies for agents with limited execution resources. In *Proceedings of International Joint Conference on Artificial Intelligence (IJCAI)*, 2003.

D. Dolgov and E. Durfee. Constructing optimal policies for agents with constrained architectures. Technical report, Univ of Michigan, 2003.

D. Fudenberg and J. Tirole. *Game Theory*. MIT Press, 1991.

J. C. Harsanyi and R. Selten. A generalized Nash solution for two-person bargaining games with incomplete information. *Management Science*, 18(5):80–106, 1972.

A. Murr. Random checks. In *Newsweek National News*, http://www.newsweek.com/id/43401, Sept., 28, 2007.

C. Ozturk, Y. Zhang, and W. Trappe. Source-location privacy in energy-constrained sensor network routing. 2004.

P. Paruchuri, J. P. Pearce, J. Marecki, M. Tambe, F. Ordonez, and S. Kraus. Playing games for security: An efficient exact algorithm for solving bayesian stackelberg. In *International Conference on Autonomous Agents and Multiagent Systems (AAMAS)*, 2008.

P. Paruchuri, J. P. Pearce, M. Tambe, F. Ordonez, and S. Kraus. An efficient heuristic approach for security against multiple adversaries. In *International Conference on Autonomous Agents and Multiagent Systems (AAMAS)*, 2007.

P. Paruchuri, M. Tambe, F. Ordonez, and S. Kraus. Towards a formalization of teamwork with resource constraints. In *International Conference on Autonomous Agents and Multiagent Systems (AAMAS)*, 2004.

P. Paruchuri, M. Tambe, F. Ordonez, and S. Kraus. Security in multiagent systems by policy randomization. In *International Conference on Autonomous Agents and Multiagent Systems (AAMAS)*, 2006.

J. Pita, M. Jain, J. Marecki, F. Ordonez, C. Portway, M. Tambe, C. Western, P. Paruchuri, and S. Kraus. Deployed armor protection: The application of a game theoretic model for security at the los angeles international airport. In *International Conference on Autonomous Agents and Multiagent Systems (AAMAS) (Industry Track)*, 2008.

R. Poole and G. Passantino. A risk based airport security policy. 2003.

M. Puterman. *Markov Decision Processes: Discrete Stochastic Dynamic Programming*. John Wiley and Sons, 1994.

T. Roughgarden. Stackelberg scheduling strategies. In *TOC: ACM Symposium on Theory of Computing*, 2001.

T. Sandholm, A. Gilpin, and V. Conitzer. Mixed-integer programming methods for finding nash equilibria. In *National Conference on Artificial Intelligence (AAAI)*, 2005.

C. Shannon. A mathematical theory of communication. *The Bell Labs Technical Journal*, pages 379–457,623,656, 1948.

H. V. Stackelberg. Marktform and gleichgewicht. In *Springer*, 1934.

Chapter 8

R. Avenhaus, B. von Stengel, and S. Zamir. Inspection games. In R. J. Aumann and S. Hart, editors, *Handbook of Game Theory*, volume 3, chapter 51, pages 1947–1987. North-Holland, Amsterdam, 2002.

T. Basar and G. J. Olsder. *Dynamic Noncooperative Game Theory*. Academic Press, San Diego, CA, 2nd edition, 1995.

M. Breton, A. Alg, and A. Haurie. Sequential Stackelberg equilibria in two-person games. *Optimization Theory and Applications*, 59(1):71–97, 1988.

V. Conitzer and T. Sandholm. Computing the optimal strategy to commit to. In *ACM Conference on Electronic Commerce*, 2006.

N. Gatti. Game theoretical insights in strategic patrolling: Model and algorithm in normal-form. In *European Conference on AI (CAI)*, 2008.

A. Jiang and K. Leyton-Brown. A polynomial-time algorithm for action-graph games. In *Artificial Intelligence*, 679–684, 2006.

D. Koller and B. Milch. Multi-agent influence diagrams for representing and solving games. *Games and Economic Behavior*, 45(1):181–221, 2003.

G. Leitmann. On generalized Stackelberg strategies. *Optimization Theory and Applications*, 26(4):637–643, 1978.

R. D. Luce and H. Raiffa. *Games and Decisions*. John Wiley and Sons, New York, 1957. Dover republication 1989.

M. J. Osbourne and A. Rubinstein. *A Course in Game Theory*. MIT Press, 1994.

P. Paruchuri, J. P. Pearce, J. Marecki, M. Tambe, F. Ordonez, and S. Kraus. Playing games with security: An efficient exact algorithm for Bayesian Stackelberg games. In *International Conference on Autonomous Agents and Multiagent Systems (AAMAS)*, 2008.

J. Pita, M. Jain, C. Western, C. Portway, M. Tambe, F. Ordonez, S. Kraus, and P. Parachuri. Depoloyed ARMOR protection: The application of a game-theoretic model for security at the Los Angeles International Airport. In *International Conference on Autonomous Agents and Multiagent Systems (AAMAS) (Industry Track)*, 2008.

T. Roughgarden. Stackelberg scheduling strategies. *SIAM Journal on Computing*, 33(2):332–350, 2004.

T. Sandler and D. G. A. M. Terrorism and game theory. *Simulation and Gaming*, 34(3):319–337, 2003.

V. Srivastava, J. Neel, A. B. MacKenzie, R. Menon, L. A. Dasilva, J. E. Hicks, J. H. Reed, and R. P. Gilles. Using game theory to analyze wireless ad hoc networks. *IEEE Communications Surveys and Tutuorials*, 7(4), 2005.

H. von Stackelberg. *Marktform und Gleichgewicht*. Springer, Vienna, 1934.

B. von Stengel and S. Zamir. Leadership with commitment to mixed strategies. Technical Report London School of Economics-Centre for Discrete and Applicable Mathematics (LSE-CDAM)-2004-01, CDAM Research Report, 2004.

K. wei Lye and J. M. Wing. Game strategies in network security. *International Journal of Information Security*, 4(1–2):71–86, 2005.

Chapter 9

C. Barnhart, E. Johnson, G. Nemhauser, M. Savelsbergh, and P. Vance. Branch and price: Column generation for solving huge integer programs. In *Operations Research*, volume 46, 316–329, 1994.

N. Basilico, N. Gatti, and F. Amigoni. Leader-follower strategies for robotic patrolling in environments with arbitrary topologies. In *International Conference on Autonomous Agents and Multiagent Systems (AAMAS)*, 2009.

D. Bertsimas, and J. N. Tsitsiklis. *Introduction to Linear Optimization*. Athena Scientific, 1994.

M. Breton, A. Alg, and A. Haurie. Sequential Stackelberg equilibria in two-person games. *Optimization Theory and Applications* 59(1):71–97, 1988.

V. Conitzer, and T. Sandholm. Computing the optimal strategy to commit to. In *ACM Conference on Electronic Commerce*, 2006.

E. Halvorson, V. Conitzer, and R. Parr. Multi-step multi-sensor hider-seeker games. In *International Joint Conference on Artificial Intelligence (IJCAI)*, 336–341, 2009.

C. Kiekintveld, M. Jain, J. Tsai, J. Pita, M. Tambe, and F. Ordóñez. Computing optimal randomized resource allocations for massive security games. In *International Conference on Autonomous Agents and Multiagent Systems (AAMAS)*, 2009.

D. Korzhyk, V. Conitzer, and R. Parr. Complexity of computing optimal stackelberg strategies in security resource allocation games. In *National Conference on Artificial Intelligence (AAAI)*, 2010.

G. Leitmann. On generalized Stackelberg strategies. *Optimization Theory and Applications* 26(4):637–643, 1978.

P. Parachuri, J. P. Pearce, J. Marecki, M. Tambe, F. Ordonez, and S. Kraus. Playing games with security: An efficient exact algorithm for Bayesian Stackelberg games. In *International Conference on Autonomous Agents and Multiagent Systems (AAMAS)*, 2008.

J. Pita, H. Bellamane, M. Jain, C. Kiekintveld, J. Tsai, F. Ordóñez, and M. Tambe. Security applications: Lessons of real-world deployment. In *ACM Special Interest Group on Electronic Commerce (SIGECOM) Issue 8.2*, 2009.

J. Tsai, S. Rathi, C. Kiekintveld, F. Ordóñez, and M. Tambe. IRIS: a tool for strategic security allocation in transportation networks. In *International Conference on Autonomous Agents and Multiagent Systems (AAMAS) (Industry Track)*, 2009.

B. von Stengel, and S. Zamir. Leadership with commitment to mixed strategies. Technical Report London School of Economics-Centre for Discrete and Applicable Mathematics (LSE-CDAM)-2004-01, CDAM Research Report, 2004.

Chapter 10

M. Aghassi and D. Bertsimas. Robust game theory. *Math. Program.*, 107(1–2):231–273, 2006.

N. Agmon, V. Sadov, S. Kraus, and G. Kaminka. The impact of adversarial knowledge on adversarial planning in perimeter patrol. In *International Conference on Autonomous Agents and Multiagent Systems (AAMAS)*, 2008.

G. Brown, M. Carlyle, J. Salmerón, and K. Wood. *Defending Critical Infrastructure*. Interfaces, 2006.

J. Cardinal, M. Labbé, S. Langerman, and B. Palop. Pricing of geometric transportation networks. In *17th Canadian Conference on Computational Geometry*, 2005.

V. Conitzer and T. Sandholm. Computing the optimal strategy to commit to. In *International Conference on Electronic Commerce (EC)*, 2006.

M. Friedman. The use of ranks to avoid the assumption of normality implicit in the analysis of variance. *Journal of the American Statistical Association*, 32 No. 100:675–701, 1937.

D. Fudenberg and J. Tirole. *Game Theory*. MIT Press, 1991.

J. C. Harsanyi and R. Selten. A generalized Nash solution for two-person bargaining games with incomplete information. *Management Science*, 18(5):80–106, 1972.

C. Kiekintveld, M. Jain, J. Tsai, J. Pita, M. Tambe, and F. Ordóñez. Computing Optimal Randomized Resource Allocations for Massive Security Games. In *International Conference on Autonomous Agents and Multiagent Systems (AAMAS)*, 2009.

Y. A. Korilis, A. A. Lazar, and A. Orda. Achieving network optima using stackelberg routing strategies. In *IEEE/ACM Transactions on Networking*, 1997.

A. Nilim and L. E. Ghaoui. Robustness in markov decision problems with uncertain transition matrices. In *Conference on Neural Information Processing Systems (NIPS)*, 2004.

F. Ordóñez and N. E. Stier-Moses. Robust wardrop equilibrium. In *Workshop on Network Control and Optimization (NET-COOP)*, 2007.

P. Paruchuri, J. Marecki, J. Pearce, M. Tambe, F. Ordóñez, and S. Kraus. Playing games for security: An efficient exact algorithm for solving bayesian stackelberg games. In *International Conference on Autonomous Agents and Multiagent Systems (AAMAS)*, 2008.

P. Paruchuri, M. Tambe, F. Ordonez, and S. Kraus. Security in multiagent systems by policy randomization. In *International Conference on Autonomous Agents and Multiagent Systems (AAMAS)*, 2006.

J. Pita, M. Jain, J. Marecki, F. Ordóñez, C. Portway, M. Tambe, C. Western, P. Paruchuri, and S. Kraus. Deployed armor protection: The application of a game theoretic model for security at the los angeles international airport. In *International Conference on Autonomous Agents and Multiagent Systems (AAMAS)*, 2008.

A. Rubinstein. *Modeling Bounded Rationality*. MIT Press, 1998.

K. E. See, C. R. Fox, and Y. S. Rottenstreich. Between ignorance and truth: Partition dependence and learning in judgment under uncertainty. *Journal of Experimental Psychology: Learning, Memory, and Cognition*, 32:1385–1402, 2006.

H. Simon. Rational choice and the structure of the environment. *Psychological Review*, 63:129–138, 1956.

A. Tversky and D. J. Koehler. Support thoery: A nonextensional representation of subjective probability. *Psychological Review*, 101:547–567, 1994.

B. von Stengel and S. Zamir. Leadership with commitment to mixed strategies. Technical Report London School of Economics-Centre for Discrete and Applicable Mathematics (LSE-CDAM)-2004-01, CDAM Research Report, 2004.

K. K. Yuen. The two-sample trimmed t for unequal population variances. *Biometrika*, 61:165–170, 1974.

Chapter 11

M. Aghassi and D. Bertsimas. Robust game theory. *Mathematical Programming: Series A and B*, 107(1):231–273, 2006.

N. Agmon, S. Kraus, G. A. Kaminka, and V. Sadov. Adversarial uncertainty in multi-robot patrol. In *IJCAI*, 2009.

T. Alpcan and T. Basar. A game theoretic approach to decision and analysis in network intrusion detection. In *Proc. of the 42nd IEEE Conference on Decision and Control*, 2003.

O. Armantier, J.-P. Florens, and J.-F. Richard. Approximation of Bayesian Nash equilibrium. *Journal of Applied Econometrics*, 23(7):965–981, December 2008.

N. Basiloco, N. Gatti, and F. Amigoni. Leader-follower strategies for robotic patrolling in environments with arbitrary topologies. In *International Conference on Autonomous Agents and Multiagent Systems (AAMAS)*, 2009.

V. M. Bier. Choosing what to protect. *Risk Analysis*, 27(3):607–620, 2007.

G. Cai and P. R. Wurman. Monte Carlo approximation in incomplete information, sequential auction games. *Decision Support Systems*, 39(2):153–168, 2005.

S. Ceppi, N. Gatti, and N. Basilico. Computing Bayes-Nash equilibria through support enumeration methods in Bayesian two-player strategic-form games. In *Proceedings of the ACM/IEEE International Conference on Intelligent Agent Technology (IAT)*, Milan, Italy, September 15–18, 2009.

V. Conitzer and T. Sandholm. Computing the optimal strategy to commit to. In *ACM Conference on Electronic Commerce*, 2006.

N. Gatti. Game theoretical insights in strategic patrolling: Model and algorithm in normal-form. In *European Conference on AI (ECAI)*, 2008.

J. C. Harsanyi. Games with incomplete information played by Bayesian players (parts i–iii). *Management Science*, 14, 1967–8.

M. Jain, C. Kiekintveld, and M. Tambe. Quality-bounded solutions for finite Bayesian Stackelberg games: Scaling up. In *International Conference on Autonomous Agents and Multiagent Systems (AAMAS)*, 2011.

C. Kiekintveld, M. Jain, J. Tsai, J. Pita, F. Ordóñez, and M. Tambe. Computing optimal randomized resource allocations for massive security games. In *International Conference on Autonomous Agents and Multiagent Systems (AAMAS)*, 2009.

V. Krishna. *Auction Theory*. Academic Press, 2002.

R. D. Luce and H. Raiffa. *Games and Decisions*. John Wiley and Sons, New York, 1957. Dover republication 1989.

D. McFadden. Quantal choice analysis: A survey. *Annals of Economic and Social Measurement*, 5(4):363–390, 1976.

K. C. Nguyen and T. A. T. Basar. Security games with incomplete information. In *Proc. of IEEE Intl. Conf. on Communications (ICC 2009)*, 2009.

P. Paruchuri, J. P. Pearce, J. Marecki, M. Tambe, F. Ordonez, and S. Kraus. Playing games with security: An efficient exact algorithm for Bayesian Stackelberg games. In *International Conference on Autonomous Agents and Multiagent Systems (AAMAS)*, 2008.

J. Pita, M. Jain, F. Ordóñez, M. Tambe, S. Kraus, and R. Magori-Cohen. Effective solutions for real-world Stackelberg games: When agents must deal with human uncertainties. In *International Conference on Autonomous Agents and Multiagent Systems (AAMAS)*, 2009.

J. Pita, M. Jain, C. Western, C. Portway, M. Tambe, F. Ordonez, S. Kraus, and P. Paruchuri. Depoloyed ARMOR protection: The application of a game-theoretic model for security at the Los Angeles International Airport. In *International Conference on Autonomous Agents and Multiagent Systems (AAMAS) (Industry Track)*, 2008.

D. M. Reeves and M. P. Wellman. Computing best-response strategies in infinite games of incomplete information. In *International Conference on Uncertainty in AI (UAI)*, 2004.

T. Sandler and D. G. A. M. Terrorism and game theory. *Simulation and Gaming*, 34(3):319–337, 2003.

P. Taylor and L. Jonker. Evolutionary stable strategies and game dynamics. *Mathematical Biosciences*, 16:76–83, 1978.

J. Tsai, S. Rathi, C. Kiekintveld, F. Ordóñez, and M. Tambe. IRIS - A tools for strategic security allocation in transportation networks. In *International Conference on Autonomous Agents and Multiagent Systems (AAMAS) (Industry Track)*, 2009.

H. von Stackelberg. *Marktform und Gleichgewicht*. Springer, Vienna, 1934.

K. wei Lye and J. M. Wing. Game strategies in network security. *International Journal of Information Security*, 4(1–2):71–86, 2005.

Chapter 12

K. Bagwell. Commitment and observability in games. *Games and Economic Behavior*, 8:271–280, 1995.

T. Basar and G. J. Olsder. *Dynamic Noncooperative Game Theory*. Academic Press, San Diego, CA, 2nd edition, 1995.

N. Basilico, N. Gatti, and F. Amigoni. Leader-follower strategies for robotic patrolling in environments with arbitrary topologies. In *International Conference on Autonomous Agents and Multiagent Systems (AAMAS)*, 2009.

V. Conitzer and T. Sandholm. Computing the optimal strategy to commit to. In *ACM Conference on Electronic Commerce*, 2006.

D. Fudenberg and J. Tirole. *Game Theory*. MIT Press, October 1991.

S. Huck and W. Müller. Perfect versus imperfect observability – an experimental test of Bagwell's result. *Games and Economic Behavior*, 31(2):174–190, 2000.

C. Kiekintveld, M. Jain, J. Tsai, J. Pita, M. Tambe, and F. Ordonez. Computing optimal randomized resource allocations for massive security games. In *International Conference on Autonomous Agents and Multiagent Systems (AAMAS)*, 2009.

G. Leitmann. On generalized Stackelberg strategies. *Optimization Theory and Applications*, 26(4):637–643, 1978.

J. Morgan and F. Vardy. The value of commitment in contests and tournaments when observation is costly. *Games and Economic Behavior*, 60(2):326–338, August 2007.

H. Moulin and J. P. Vial. Strategically zero-sum games: The class of games whose completely mixed equilibria cannot be improved upon. *International Journal of Game Theory*, 7(3-4):201–221, September 1978.

J. Pita, M. Jain, F. Ordóñez, M. Tambe, S. Kraus, and R. Magori-Cohen. Effective solutions for real-world Stackelberg games: When agents must deal with human uncertainties. In *International Conference on Autonomous Agents and Multiagent Systems (AAMAS)*, 2009.

J. Pita, M. Jain, C. Western, C. Portway, M. Tambe, F. Ordonez, S. Kraus, and P. Parachuri. Deployed ARMOR protection: The application of a game-theoretic model for security at the Los Angeles International Airport. In *International Conference on Autonomous Agents and Multiagent Systems (AAMAS) (Industry Track)*, 2008.

J. Tsai, S. Rathi, C. Kiekintveld, F. Ordóñez, and M. Tambe. IRIS a tool for strategic security allocation in transportation networks. In *International Conference on Autonomous Agents and Multiagent Systems (AAMAS) (Industry Track)*, 2009.

E. van Damme and S. Hurkens. Games with imperfectly observable commitment. *Games and Economic Behavior*, 21(1–2):282–308, 1997.

J. von Neumann and O. Morgenstern. *Theory of Games and Economic Behavior*. Princeton University Press, May 2004.

B. von Stengel and S. Zamir. Leadership with commitment to mixed strategies. Technical Report London School of Economics-Centre for Discrete and Applicable Mathematics (LSE-CDAM)-2004-01, CDAM Research Report, 2004.

Chapter 13

G. H. Baker. A vulnerability assessment methodology for critical infrastructure sites. In *DHS Symposium: R and D Partnerships in Homeland Security*, 2005.

J. Berejikian. A cognitive theory of deterrence. *Journal of Peace Research*, (39):165–183, 2002.

V. M. Bier. Choosing what to protect. *Risk Analysis*, 27(3):607–620, 2007.

V. M. Bier, N. Haphuriwat, J. Menoyo, R. Zimmerman, and A. M. Culpen. Optimal resource allocation for defense of targets based on differing measures of attractiveness. *Risk Analysis*, 28(3):763–770, 2008.

V. M. Bier, Jr. L. A. Cox, and M. N. Azaiez. Why both game theory and reliability theory are important in defending infrastructure against intelligent attacks. In *Game Theoretic Risk Analysis and Security Theats*, volume 128. Springer US, 2009.

R. Blundell and M. Costa-Dias. Alternative approaches to evaluation in empirical microeconomics. *Journal of Human Resources*, 2009.

V. Conitzer and T. Sandholm. Computing the optimal strategy to commit to. In *Proc. of Conference on Electronic Commerce*, 2006.

First Sargent Cruz. Personal communication, August 20 2009.

T. Edmunds and R. Wheeler. Setting priorities. In Stephen M. Maurer, editor, *WMD Terrorism*, chapter 7, pages 191–209. MIT Press, Cambridge, MA, 2009.

I. Erev, A. E. Roth, R. L. Slonim, and G. Barron. Predictive value and usefulness of game theoretic models. *International Journal of Forecasting*, 18(3):359–368, 2002.

The United States Government Accountability Office: GAO. Aviation security: Federal air marshal service has taken actions to fulfill its core mission and address workforce issues, but additional actions are needed to improve workforce survey, January 2009. GAO-09-273.

M. Gerson and J. Boyars. The future of U.S. deterrence; constructing effective strategies to deter states and non-state actors, 2007. www.cna.org/documents/D0017171.A2.pdf.

S. H. Jacobson, T. Karnai, and J. E. Kobza. Assessing the impact of deterrence on aviation checked baggage screening strategies. *International J. of Risk Assessment and Management*, 5(1):1–15, 2005.

M. Kearns and L. E. Ortiz. Algorithms for interdependent security games. In *Neural Information Processing Systems (NIPS)*, 2003.

C. Kiekintveld and M. Wellman. Selecting strategies using empirical game models: An experimental analysis of meta-strategies. In *International Conference on Autonomous Agents and Multiagent Systems (AAMAS)*, 2008.

C. Kiekintveld, M. Jain, J. Tsai, J. Pita, F. Ordónez, and M. Tambe. Computing optimal randomized resource allocations for massive security games. In *International Conference on Autonomous Agents and Multiagent Systems (AAMAS)*, 2009.

C. Kiekintveld, J. Marecki, and M. Tambe. Approximation methods for infinite Bayesian Stackelberg games: Modeling distributional payoff uncertainty. In *International Conference on Autonomous Agents and Multiagent Systems (AAMAS)*, 2011.

Y. Kou, C. Lu, S. Sinvongwattana, and Y.P. Huang. Survey of fraud detection techniques. In *Proc. of IEEE Networking*, 2004.

Jr. L. A. Cox. Some limitations of "risk = threat x vulnerability x consequence" for risk analysis of terrorist attacks. *Risk Analysis*, 28(6):1749–1761, 2008.

R. Lazarick. Airport vulnerability assessment – a methodology evaluation. In *Proc. of 33rd IEEE International Carnahan Conference on Security Technology*, 1999.

A. Murr. Random checks. In *Newsweek National News*. September 2007. http://www.newsweek.com/id/43401.

P. Paruchuri, J. P. Pearce, J. Marecki, M. Tambe, F. Ordonez, and S. Kraus. Playing games with security: An efficient exact algorithm for Bayesian Stackelberg games. In *International Conference on Autonomous Agents and Multiagent Systems (AAMAS)*, 2008.

J. Pita, M. Jain, C. Western, C. Portway, M. Tambe, F. Ordonez, S. Kraus, and P. Paruchuri. Deployed ARMOR protection: The application of a game theoretic model for security at the Los Angeles International Airport. In *Proc. of International Conference on Autonomous Agents and Multiagent Systems (AAMAS)*, 2008.

J. Pita, M. Jain, M. Tambe, F. Ordonez, S. Kraus, and R. Magori-Cohen. Effective solutions for real-world stackelberg games: When agents must deal with human uncertainties. In *Proc. of International Conference on Autonomous Agents and Multiagent Systems (AAMAS)*, 2009.

P. Scerri, T. Von Goten, J. Fudge, S. Owens, and K. Sycara. Transitioning multiagent technology to UAV applications. In *Proc. of International Conference on Autonomous Agents and Multiagent Systems (AAMAS) Industry Track*, 2008.

D. Stevens, T. Hamilton, M. Schaffer, D. Dunham-Scott, J. J. Medby, E. W. Chan, J. Gibson, M. Eisman, R. Mesic, C. T. Kelly, J. Kim, T. LaTourrette, and K. J. Riley. Implementing security improvement options at Los Angeles international airport, 2009. www.rand.org/pubs/documented_briefings/2006/RAND_DB499-1.pdf.

E. F. Taquechel. Validation of rational deterrence theory: Analysis of U.S. government and adversary risk propensity and relative emphasis on gain or loss. Master's thesis, Naval Postgraduate School, March 2010.

T. O. Tengs and J. D. Graham. Risks, costs, and lives saved: Getting better results from regulation. In *The opportunity costs of haphazard social investments in lifesaving*. American Enterprise Institute, Washington, 1996.

J. Tsai, S. Rathi, C. Kiekintveld, F. Ordóñez, and M. Tambe. IRIS - A tools for strategic security allocation in transportation networks. In *International Conference on Autonomous Agents and Multiagent Systems (AAMAS) (Industry Track)*, 2009.

J. Weibull. Testing game theory. In Steffen Huck, editor, *Advances in Understanding Strategic Behavior: Game Theory, Experiments and Bounded Rationality.*, pages 85–104. Palgrave MacMillan, 2004.

Index

AAMAS (International Conference on Autonomous Agents and Multiagent Systems), 68
Abu Zubaydah, 39
active shooter tactics, 27–8
adversaries
  bounded rationality, 194, 198, 199, 212
  pure strategy reaction, 6
  surveillance behaviors of, 6
  uncertainty of surveillance capability, 19–20, 194
agent systems. *See* multiagent security games; policy randomization for agent systems
Air India flight 182 attack (1985), 28
airport protection
  airline baggage screening, 280
  economic impact and, 35
  shoe removal, 28–9
  uninspected cargo bomb threats, 40
  see also specific airports
Airports Council International (ACI), 35
Airport Security Advisory Committee (ASAC), 44
Alfred P. Sloan Research Fellowship, 253
Allouni, Tayseer, 34
al-Qaeda
  Jamiyyatt Ul Islam Saheeh, 39
  operational planning cycle, 44–5
  simultaneous attacks, 30
  Yemen based activities, 31–3
  see also bin Laden, Osama
al-Qaeda in the Arabian Peninsula (AQAP), 31–3
anchoring theories, 194–5, 199, 211
approximation algorithms, 227–31

see also infinite Bayesian Stackelberg games
approximation guarantees, defined, 260
arbitrary schedules. *See* branch-and-price approach
Armenian Secret Army for the Liberation of Armenia, 38
ARMOR (Assistant for Randomized Monitoring Over Routes)
  comparison of algorithms, 13, 90–2
  cost-benefit analysis, 272–3
  DOBSS algorithm, 16, 77, 79–80, 263–4, 266–7
  expert evaluations, 22
  overview, 1, 9, 47–8, 50, 93
  software features, 67–70
  system architecture, 76–80
    interface, 77–9
    matrix generation, 79
    mixed strategy and schedule generation, 80
  see also evaluating deployed decision-support systems; Los Angeles World Airports (LAWA) Police Division
ASAP (Agent Security via Approximate Policies) algorithm, 13, 68, 69, 133, 147, 150–4
ASPEN (Accelerated SPARS Engine) algorithm, 10, 13–4, 17, 178–80, 184–9, 265
attacker, use of term, 6
attacker-defender games. *See* Bayesian Stackelberg games
attacker payoff distributions, 215–9

311